The True Meaning
of the
Constitution

The True Meaning of the Constitution

of the

Constitution

Ratifier Understanding

Charles F. Patterson

Bentham Press
1767 Stewart Rd. ◆ Xenia, OH 45385

First printing 2002

ISBN 0-9709163-4-5

LCCN 2001131239

ATTENTION CORPORATIONS, UNIVERSITIES, COLLEGES, AND PROFESSIONAL ORGANIZATIONS: Quantity discounts are available on bulk purchases of this book for educational, gift purposes, or as premiums for increasing magazine subscriptions or renewals. Special books or book excerpts can also be created to fit specific needs. For information, please contact Bentham Press, 1767 Stewart Rd., Xenia, OH 45385; 937-372-5307.

TABLE OF CONTENTS

This book is dedicated to the interlibrary-loan librarians who work hard to supply the missing links.

ACKNOWLEDGMENTS

I am indebted to the historians who are referenced in this book. Cathy Bowman of About Books, Inc., did an outstanding job of designing this book, and I greatly appreciate her professionalism and cooperative attitude.

Congress and the U.S. Supreme Court have assumed powers far beyond the powers granted to them by the Constitution. Unconstitutional actions by Congress and the Court are the most widely visible signs of the breakdown of the rule of law in the United States.

In *The Federalist*, No. 16, Alexander Hamilton said that the people (electorate) were the "natural guardians of the Constitution." That statement showed remarkable foresight, given that the Constitution requires all federal and state officials to be "bound by Oath or Affirmation, to support this Constitution." Hamilton indicated that the electorate would be "enlightened enough to distinguish between a legal exercise and an illegal usurpation of authority." Unfortunately, the vast majority of twenty-first century Americans are not as enlightened as Hamilton anticipated. One reason for the lack of enlightenment is that it has been impossible for twenty-first century Americans to learn the true (original) meaning of the Constitution in a reasonable amount of time. This book makes it possible.

If for no other reason, the original meaning of the Constitution will remain important from an historical standpoint.

Introduction

On February 27, 1860, Abraham Lincoln made an extremely important speech at the Cooper Union Institute in New York City. Lincoln took great care to write the speech. Printed in whole or in part in many American newspapers, Lincoln's Cooper Union speech boosted Lincoln's political stock to the point that he was able to win the Republican presidential nomination on the third ballot on May 18, 1860.[1] On November 6, 1860, Lincoln was elected president. He defeated Senator Stephen A. Douglas, the Democratic party candidate. Douglas had defeated Lincoln in Illinois in 1858 in a famous contest for a U.S. Senate seat.

In his Cooper Union speech, Lincoln went to great length to show that, based on the *original meaning* of the Constitution, Congress had the power to prohibit slavery in the territories.[2] Lincoln presented voting records of the framers of the unamended Constitution to refute an 1857 Supreme Court ruling, in *Dred Scott v. Sandford*, which said that Congress did not have the power to prohibit slavery in the territories. That erroneous Court ruling was supported by Senator Douglas. Douglas, however, used a different rationale than the Court did. Lincoln, in his Cooper Union speech, refuted both the Court's and Douglas' rationales.

The words of the Constitution are not definitive relevant to the power of Congress to prohibit slavery in the territories. Lincoln determined the original meaning of the Constitution by examining the actions of the framers. That method is perfectly valid unless most of the ratifiers understood the Constitution to have a different meaning. In his Pulitzer Prize winning 1996 book, *Original Meanings*, historian Jack Rakove stated: "the authority of the Constitution as supreme law rests on its ratification. . . . the understanding of the ratifiers is the preeminent and arguably sole source for reconstructing original meaning. . . ."[3]

Most of the ratifiers of the unamended Constitution must have understood that Congress, under the Constitution, would have the power to prohibit slavery in the territories because:

- The famous and popular Northwest Ordinance of 1787 prohibited slavery in the Northwest Territories. (Only one member of the 1787 Congress voted against the Northwest Ordinance of 1787.[4] One of the three congressmen from New York voted against the Ordinance. All three congressmen from Virginia, both congressmen from North Carolina, both congressmen from South Carolina, and both congressmen from Georgia voted for the Ordinance.[5])

- Article IV of the Constitution authorizes Congress to "make all needful Rules and Regulations respecting the Territory or other Property belonging to the United States." The Articles of Confederation granted no such power to Congress.

- In *The Federalist*, No. 38, James Madison indicated that the Northwest Ordinance of 1787 was in the public interest and necessary—but clearly unconstitutional; however, under the Constitution, Congress would have the power to make the Northwest Ordinance constitutional.[6]

- When the Northwest Ordinance was reenacted in 1789 by the First Congress (the first Congress under the Constitution), it was reenacted "without a word of opposition."[7] Many framers and ratifiers were in that Congress. I am aware of no evidence that any framer or ratifier, inside or outside of Congress, claimed during the eighteenth century that the 1789 reenactment of the Northwest Ordinance was unconstitutional.

Abraham Lincoln made his first inaugural address on March 4, 1861, at a time of *severe crisis*. Seven states had seceded from the

Union during the three months prior to Lincoln's inauguration. Several more states were on the brink of secession. In an attempt to preserve the Union and avert the impending Civil War, Lincoln made several conciliatory statements to voters in slave states. However, it was difficult to satisfy them; their appetites had been whetted by the Court's ruling in *Dred Scott*. Many voters in slave states thought that Lincoln should at least offer federal protection to slavery in the territories.[8] However, Lincoln indicated that the policy of the federal government would not be influenced by the Court's erroneous ruling in *Dred Scott*.

Lincoln talked about the "evil effect" of "erroneous" Supreme Court decisions. He then declared to his first inaugural audience: "if the policy of the Government is to be . . . [determined by] decisions of the Supreme Court, . . . the people will have ceased to be their own rulers, having to that extent practically resigned their government into the hands of that eminent tribunal. . . ."[9] Lincoln reiterated a key principle of law when he said: "the intention of the lawgiver is the law."[10] That principle is true for all laws except provisions of constitutions where ratifier understanding differs from framer intent.

In effect, Lincoln said that presidents should abide by constitutional laws and make, or continue in force, proper policies (law enforcement, etc.) even after the Court rules those laws and policies unconstitutional. Lincoln knew that the Constitution *requires* presidents to "preserve, protect and defend the Constitution of the United States," and "take Care that the [constitutional federal] Laws be faithfully executed."

During the Civil War, Supreme Court Chief Justice Roger Taney, in preparation for a case that never materialized, sketched a ruling that would have declared a federal military draft law unconstitutional.[11] If the Court had made such a ruling, President Lincoln would have continued to administer the military draft law until such time as Congress either repealed it or superseded it. After all, Lincoln defied Taney during the Civil War on a habeas corpus ruling.[12] Taney had a much stronger constitutional argument with respect to the habeas corpus matter than he had with respect to the military draft law.

In his first inaugural address, Lincoln said: "the maintenance inviolate of the rights of the States, and especially the right of each State to order and control its own domestic institutions according to its own judgment exclusively, is essential . . ."[13] Governors have a *duty* to enforce clearly constitutional state laws, whatever the Court rules, because: (1) governors are required to take an oath or affirmation to support the U.S. Constitution (not the Court); and (2) governors are required to take care that constitutional state laws are faithfully enforced (except against people who are either pardoned by a governor or acquitted in a court of law—even when a jury acquits by nullifying a law for the purposes of the case it tries).

Lincoln's predecessor, James Buchanan, took an unconstitutionally subservient approach to Supreme Court decisions. In his inaugural address in 1857, Buchanan stated: "[Relevant to] the question of domestic slavery in the Territories! . . . To . . . [the Court's soon-to-be-delivered decision in the Dred Scott case], . . . I shall cheerfully submit, whatever this may be, . . ."[14] Buchanan made that statement despite the fact he was about to put his hand on a Bible and say: "I do solemnly swear that I will . . . preserve, protect and defend the Constitution of the United States." The Constitution requires only the president to take such a strong oath.

Thomas Jefferson's position on judicial authority was much closer to Lincoln's position than to Buchanan's position. In 1804, President Jefferson wrote a letter to Abigail Adams (a great letter writer, wife of President John Adams, and mother of President John Quincy Adams) in which Jefferson stated: "You think it devolved on the judges to decide on the validity of the sedition law. But nothing in the Constitution has given them a right to decide for the Executive, any more than to the Executive to decide for them. . . ."[15] Although Jefferson expected judges to rule unconstitutional laws unconstitutional and void *for the purposes of individual cases*, he wrote to Abigail Adams that the judiciary would be "a despotic branch" if the judges were to "decide what laws are constitutional . . . for the Legislature and Executive . . ."[16]

Noted historian Clinton Rossiter wrote about framer James Wilson: "No man had a higher reputation for legal and political learning in 1787, . . ."[17] Wilson is regarded by most constitutional historians as the most useful delegate at the Constitutional Convention other than James Madison. Justice James Wilson declared, in his highly regarded 1791 law lectures: "whoever would be obliged to obey a constitutional law, is justified in refusing to obey an unconstitutional act of the legislature. . . . when a question, even of this delicate nature, occurs, every one who is called to act, has a right to judge. . . ."[18] In *The Federalist,* No. 51, James Madison said: "In republican government, the legislative authority necessarily predominates. . . ." The Constitution says: "All legislative Powers herein granted shall be vested in a Congress of the United States, . . ." It follows that: (1) no American is obligated to obey Court legislation ("Miranda" rights, etc.); and (2) every American is obligated to obey constitutional laws (federal laws and the state laws of the state they are in) even though the Court has ruled those laws unconstitutional.

If Court legislation were binding on the federal government, the United States would not have a republican form of government. If Court legislation were binding on the states, no state would have a republican form of government. The Constitution provides a republican form of government for the United States, and the Constitution guarantees "to every State in this Union a Republican Form of Government."

In *Dred Scott,* the Court stated: "The words of the Constitution should be given the meaning they were intended to bear, when that instrument was framed and adopted."[19] The Court has made statements of this kind in many cases. Such statements have often been made in an attempt to deceive people into believing that Court rulings were dictated by the original meaning of the Constitution.

When Court members support rulings which are contrary to the original meaning of the Constitution, they do not acknowledge that their rulings are incompatible with the original meaning of the Constitution. However, some legal scholars who support Court amendments acknowledge that the Court often amends the Constitution under the guise of interpretation. For example, a very useful college textbook written by three law professors acknowledges that many amendments have been made by the Court.[20] Under a paragraph heading "Amendment by Judicial Interpretation," the text-book states: "The greatest change to the written Constitution has been made by the Supreme Court in 'interpreting' the Constitution. . . ."[21] Under a paragraph titled "The Living Constitution," the textbook states: "The Constitution . . . is radically different from the Constitution that was written on paper. . . ."[22]

Article V of the Constitution provides four alternative processes for amending the Constitution. No court is involved in any of those processes. The amending of the Constitution by any court is absolutely unconstitutional.

The Constitution requires that all federal officials "be bound by Oath or Affirmation to support this Constitution." That oath would be meaningless if people who take it are authorized to take official actions incompatible with the Constitution. Sane members of the federal judiciary are aware of the fact that their rulings do not support the Constitution when their rulings are *clearly* contrary to the original meaning of the Constitution, as lawfully amended. A willful (knowing) violation of either an oath or an affirmation is perjury. Perjury in an official act is an impeachable offense. It is a high crime.

In *Marbury v. Madison*, Chief Justice Marshall said for a unanimous Court:

> "Why does a judge swear to discharge his duties agreeably to the constitution of the United States, if that constitution forms no rule for his government? . . . If such be the state of things, this is worse than solemn mockery. . . . to take this oath [insincerely], becomes . . . a crime."[23]

During the seventeenth century, some judges were impeached and removed from office by Parliament for rendering unconstitutional opinions.[24] Rendering unconstitutional opinions was a "high crime and misdemeanor." Justice Joseph Story, a member of the Supreme Court from 1811 to 1844, stated: "what are and what are not high crimes and misdemeanors is to be ascertained by a recurrence" to English law.[25] Although that statement is questionable in some respects, there can be no doubt the ratifiers of the unamended Constitution understood that the term "high Crimes and Misdemeanors" included things which Parliament identified as high crimes and misdemeanors when they removed officials from office prior to 1787 via the impeachment process. Members of the federal judiciary who have rendered an official opinion clearly contrary to the original meaning of the Constitution or a constitutional statute have: (1) committed a high crime and misdemeanor; or (2) become mentally incompetent (for which they can be removed from office under the "good Behaviour" provision).

Congress has failed to specify a process to fully implement the "good Behaviour" provision. Article III says: "The Judges, both of the supreme and inferior Courts, shall hold their Offices during good Behaviour, . . ." Use of revised meaning of the Constitution is not "good Behaviour." In the Constitutional Convention on July 21, 1787, George Mason said: "They could declare an unconstitutional law void. But with regard to every law however unjust, oppressive or pernicious, which did not come plainly under this description, they would be under the necessity as Judges to give it free course. . . ."[26] Members of the federal judiciary who fail to comply with the "good Behaviour" provision can be removed from office. (The "good Behaviour" provision is discussed at length in Chapter 5 of this book in the discussion of Article III, Section 1.) George Mason made the statement quoted in this paragraph in an unsuccessful attempt to get some "Judges" involved in the veto process. The Constitutional Convention rejected the intense efforts of George Mason, James Madison, and James Wilson to involve "Judges" in the lawmaking process.

Fear of judicial activism in the colonies is perhaps best exemplified by a statement made by Massachusetts Chief Justice Thomas Hutchinson in 1767. Hutchinson said: "the *Judge* should never be the *Legislator*: Because then the Will of the Judge would be the Law: and this tends to a State of Slavery."[27] Hutchinson's statement is consistent with the Constitution, quite thought-provoking, and *greatly* appreciated by people familiar with it who have been grossly abused by biased judges.

Most framers were familiar with an anti-judicial-activism statement made by Sir William Blackstone. From 1775 until well into the nineteenth century, Blackstone's *Commentaries on the Laws of England* were the "staple of legal education" in the United States.[28] According to Thomas Jefferson, the prevalent view among lawyers was: "Blackstone is to us what the Alcoran is to the Mahometans, that everything which is necessary is in him, and what is not in him is not necessary. . . ."[29] From 1770 until at least 1800, Blackstone's *Commentaries* were by far the best books on law in the United States and England. Most framers were lawyers and several others were quite knowledgeable in the law. (Although George Mason was not a lawyer, he was a judge.) In his famous *Commentaries*, Blackstone stated: "to set the judicial power above that of the legislative . . . would be subversive of all government."[30] That principle applies perfectly to England where Parliament, by itself, has the power to amend the "English constitution."[31] The absolute legislative supremacy supported by Blackstone, attractive to many framers, needed to be modified to apply it to the United States under its Constitution. Why? Because (1) Congress, by itself, or with the approval of all federal officials, would not have the power to amend the Constitution, and (2) all federal judges and all state judges in America would have the power and the duty to declare laws to be unconstitutional and void *for the purposes of cases before them* if the laws clearly violated the Constitution.

Blackstone's anti-judicial-activism statement was Americanized by the concept, expressed by George Mason at the Constitutional Convention, that judges could declare laws unconstitutional and void *only* if the laws were "plainly" unconstitutional. Legislative supremacy would defer to, and *only* to, constitutional supremacy in America. The concept of constitutional supremacy was proclaimed as follows in the famous "Massachusetts Circular Letter" of 1768: "as the supreme Legislative derives its Power & Authority from the Constitution, it cannot overleap the Bounds of it, without destroying its own foundation; . . ."[32] That circular letter stimulated the "united action of all colonies."[33]

A large majority of the ratifiers of the unamended Constitution understood that it would be unacceptable for judges and justices in the U.S. to leap the "Bounds" of the Constitution or the latest applicable constitutional statutes. Nevertheless, many Americans who opposed ratification of the Constitution expressed concern about possible usurpation of legislative power by members of the judiciary.

In *The Federalist*, No. 81, Alexander Hamilton addressed the issue of possible usurpation of legislative power by the judiciary. Hamilton wrote:

> "the supposed danger of judiciary encroachments on the legislative authority which has been upon many occasions reiterated is in reality a phantom. . . . This may be inferred with certainty from the general nature of the judicial power, . . . from its comparative weakness, and from its total incapacity to support its usurpations by force. And the inference is greatly fortified by the consideration of the important constitutional check which the power of instituting impeachments in one part of the legislative body, and of determining upon them in the other, would give to that body upon the members of the judicial department. This is alone a complete security . . . "[34]

Removing judges who usurped legislative power has proven to be a key part of a "complete security" against judicial usurpation in England. During the seventeenth century, Parliament took several actions that made it crystal clear to English judges that legislative power must not be usurped by members of the judiciary. The three most important such actions Parliament took were:

- Impeachment and removal of judges for the "high crimes and misdemeanors" of rendering unconstitutional opinions[35]
- Abolishment of the Court of Star Chamber (The 1641 act which dissolved the Star Chamber stated: "the said judges have not kept themselves to the points limited by the said statute, but have undertaken to punish where no law doth warrant, to make decrees for things having no such authority, . . ."[36])
- Enactment of the English Bill of Rights in 1689 which reinforced, in the minds of English judges, the fact that judicial rulings were illegal if they were in conflict with the latest applicable laws passed

by Parliament, even when those rulings were consistent with decrees made by the king or queen (The English Bill of Rights stated: "King James the Second, by the assistance of . . . evil counsellors, judges, and ministers employed by him, did endeavor to subvert . . . the laws and liberties of this kingdom. . . . By assuming and exercising a power of dispensing with and suspending of laws, and the execution of laws, without consent of parliament. . . ."[37])

It was quite reasonable for Alexander Hamilton to predict that the impeachment process would be "a complete security" against "judiciary encroachment on legislative authority." Hamilton knew that Parliament's impeachment power had been instrumental in eliminating judicial encroachments on legislative authority in England after 1689. There was reason to believe that Congress would remove members of the federal judiciary who encroached on state or federal legislative authority. Removal of members of the federal judiciary who encroached on legislative authority promised to greatly deter such behavior.

Instead of being "a complete security"—what one might expect from a group of capable watchdogs—the congressional authority to impeach and remove members of the federal judiciary who usurp legislative powers has proven to be almost a complete insecurity— what one might expect from a group of toothless toads. Congress could almost certainly put an end to usurpation of legislative power by federal judges and justices by removing a few members of the federal judiciary.

If most members of the Senate wanted Court members to rule in a constitutional manner, the Senate would refuse to confirm people nominated to the Court who failed to promise, during confirmation hearings, to abide by the original meaning of the Constitution. If a nominee to the Court in 2002 were to testify that they would abide by the true meaning of the Constitution, that nominee would be rejected even if they had total knowledge of the law, a record of total compliance with the law, and the integrity of Mother Theresa.

The 1987 rejection of Robert Bork by the Senate occurred primarily because Bork said that he would interpret the Constitution based on "how the words used in the Constitution would have been understood at that time."[38] Such judicial philosophy was attacked by Justice William Brennan who said, in a 1985 speech titled "The Constitution of the United States: Contemporary Ratification," that jurisprudence of original intent was "little more than arrogance cloaked as humility" because original intent could not be discovered.[39]

The true meaning of most clauses of the Constitution is known. For other clauses, the bounds of true meaning are known. Most judges do not want to be constrained by those bounds. The dictionary definition of "arrogance" includes presumption of power. The jurisprudence of "Contemporary Ratification"—rule by judges as opposed to rule by law—is a jurisprudence of assumption of power. That *is* arrogance.

Former Supreme Court law clerk Edward Lazarus, a liberal himself, wrote that during Robert Bork's confirmation hearings: "the case against original intent was made to the point of exhaustion by panels of mainly liberal legal scholars, . . ."[40] Lazarus pointed out that Bork, in his testimony before the Senate Judiciary Committee, was not consistent with original intent when he supported the Court's ruling to the effect that segregation in public schools violated the Fourteenth Amendment.[41] Bork was not rejected by the Senate because he was not completely honest. *He was rejected because he was not dishonest enough.*

Relevant to the defeat of Bork in the Senate, Lazarus stated: "Liberals deluded themselves into thinking that, a bit of mendacity aside, they had found a true mission in upholding 'the rule of law' against the forces of darkness."[42] The mendacity of the liberals helped to keep the obviously unconstitutional *Roe v. Wade* ruling from being reversed during the twentieth century. (It was considered a "very strong possibility" that Bork would provide the crucial fifth vote to reverse *Roe*.[43])

During the Senate confirmation hearings of attorney general-designate John Ashcroft in 2001, Ashcroft was subjected to such inflammatory questions that major national newscasts pointed out how well he kept his cool. Although Ashcroft kept his cool, I had the feeling that he lost some of his self-respect when he climbed aboard the bandwagon flying the liberal banner: "*Roe v. Wade* is the law of the land." Ashcroft testified that he considered *Roe* (the "right" to abortion) settled law and would enforce it. Furthermore, Ashcroft, an opponent of *Roe*, vowed that he would not, as attorney general, seek ways to overturn it. President George Washington, in his famous farewell address, said that the Constitution:

> "containing within itself a provision for its own amendment, has a just claim for your confidence and support. . . . The basis of our political system is the right of the people to make and alter their constitution of government. But the constitution which at any time exists till changed by an explicit and authentic act of the whole people is sacredly obligatory on all."[44]

An example of the Court going outside the bounds of original meaning to rule many constitutional state statutes unconstitutional occurred in 1972 when the Court, in *Furman v. Georgia*,[45] ruled: "The imposition and carrying out of the death penalty [for persons convicted of murder or rape] constitutes cruel and unusual punishment, in violation of the Eighth and Fourteenth Amendments, . . ." The discussion of the Eighth Amendment in this book makes it clear that the imposition of the death penalty on persons convicted of murder or rape did *not* constitute cruel and unusual punishment in the United States in the eighteenth century.

Roe v. Wade was decided in 1973 by the same justices who had decided *Furman* in 1972. For the Court to rule, in effect, that states can neither terminate the lives of properly convicted adult murderers nor enact laws to protect the lives of totally innocent unborn children struck many Americans as being illogical and immoral. Morality aside, *Roe* and *Furman* were *gross* usurpations of power. The Court and Congress seem to have an unwritten understanding that Congress gives the Court freedom to invalidate constitutional state laws and impose laws on states. In return, the Court upholds unconstitutional acts of Congress.

Former Supreme Court law clerk Edward Lazarus, in his 1998 book *Closed Chambers*, stated that the Court is "so intent on law-making . . . [that it often rewrites] whole swaths of constitutional law . . ."[46] Lazarus also observed that justices "in many important cases resort to transparently deceitful and hypocritical arguments and factual distortions . . ."[47]

If you would like to hear a debate between an honest and knowledgeable advocate of a Supreme Court that always rules in a constitutional manner and an honest and knowledgeable advocate of a Supreme Court which can rule in an unconstitutional manner, you will probably find Appendix A to be interesting.

Appendix B discusses the fascinating 1803 case of *Marbury v. Madison*. Many Americans learned, while taking a course in American history, that *Marbury* was the first case in which the Supreme Court ruled an act of Congress unconstitutional. *Hayburn's Case*,[48] which occurred in 1792, was the first case in which a federal court ruled an act of Congress unconstitutional.[49]

Hayburn's Case was presided over by three judges; two of the three were framers and members of the Court (Justice James Wilson and Justice John Blair).[50][51] At least three other members of the Court (Chief Justice John Jay, Justice William Cushing, and Justice James Iredell) refused to fully comply with the act because it was unconstitutional.[52] Because at least five of the six members of the Court (The Court had only six members from 1790 to 1806.) were on record that the act of Congress relevant to *Hayburn's Case* was unconstitutional, it is obvious that the Court would have declared the act to be unconstitutional if it had had an opportunity to do so. Justice William Paterson (an influential framer), in his instructions to a federal circuit court jury in Pennsylvania in 1795, made the following statement about the Constitution:

> "What is a Constitution? . . . it is paramount to the power of the Legislature, and can be revoked or altered only by the authority that made it. . . . What are Legislatures? Creatures of the Constitution; they owe their existence to the Constitution; they derive their powers from the Constitution; it is

their commission; and, therefore, all their acts must be conformable to it, or else they will be void. . . . In short,
gentlemen, the Constitution is the sun of the political system, around which all Legislative, Executive, and Judicial
bodies must revolve. Whatever may be the case in other countries, yet in this, there can be no doubt, that every act of the
Legislature, repugnant to the Constitution, is absolutely
void."[53]

In *Marbury*, the Court ruled that a small portion of the Judiciary
Act of 1789 was unconstitutional. The fact that the Court ruled an
act of Congress to be unconstitutional in *Marbury* is far from being
the most important aspect of *Marbury*. The Court already had the
implicit constitutional power to rule laws to be unconstitutional if
(1) the laws were clearly unconstitutional, and (2) the laws were
involved in a case properly before the Court. How so? Court members are on oath or affirmation to support the Constitution, and the
Court has the constitutional duty to rule on all cases brought to it
for which it has jurisdiction. Between 1776 and 1786, judges in many
states—including Massachusetts, Pennsylvania, and Virginia (the
states with the largest populations in 1787)—declared statutes to be
unconstitutional even though those judges had no explicit authority to do so.[54]

The framers were *well aware* that judges had ruled state statutes
to be unconstitutional for the purposes of cases before the judges.
Yet the Constitution does not prohibit judges from ruling federal
statutes to be unconstitutional. Most framers and ratifiers of the
Constitution must have understood that judges could rule statutes
unconstitutional for the purposes of cases before them. In *The Federalist*, No. 78, Alexander Hamilton said:

"courts of justice, whose duty it must be to declare all acts
contrary to the . . . [clear meaning] of the Constitution void.
Without this, all the reservations of particular rights or privileges would amount to nothing. . . . A constitution is, in fact,
and must be regarded by the judges as, a fundamental law. . . .

where the will of the legislature, declared in its statutes, stands in opposition to that of the people, declared in the Constitution, the judges ought to be governed by the latter rather than the former. They ought to regulate their decisions by the fundamental laws rather than those which are not fundamental."[55]

Most twenty-first century Americans are unaware of the fact that the part of the Judiciary Act of 1789 ruled unconstitutional by the Court in *Marbury* was constitutional. The Court did not use the original meaning of the Constitution in *Marbury*, thereby setting the precedent for the Court to usurp the power to amend the Constitution. That is *by far* the most important aspect of *Marbury*. Other intriguing aspects of *Marbury* known by only a tiny fraction of living Americans are included in Appendix B.

Between *Marbury* in 1803 and *Dred Scott* in 1857, the Court ruled no act of Congress unconstitutional. In *Dred Scott*, the Court ruled the "Missouri compromise unconstitutional and void" because it prohibited slavery "in the territory of the United States north of the line . . . thirty-six degrees thirty minutes north latitude . . ."[56] The Missouri Compromise was an important law passed by Congress in 1820. The approach used by Abraham Lincoln to prove the constitutionality of the Missouri Compromise can be used to prove the constitutionality of the part of the Judiciary Act of 1789 ruled unconstitutional in *Marbury*.

In *The Federalist*, No. 78, Alexander Hamilton stated:

"The judiciary, . . . have neither FORCE nor WILL . . . and must ultimately depend upon the aid of the executive arm even for the efficacy of its judgments. . . . the judiciary is beyond comparison the weakest of the three departments of power; that it can never attack with success either of the other two; . . ."[57]

When the Court rules that a federal or state statute is unconstitutional, despite the fact that the statute is constitutional, the Court is illegally amending the Constitution, exerting its "WILL" in capital letters, assuming the power of two-thirds of the House, two-thirds of the Senate, and three-fourths of the state legislatures. This is extreme usurpation of power.

Appendix C presents the twelve articles of amendment to the Constitution agreed to by Congress on September 25, 1789. Ten of those proposed amendments became the Bill of Rights on December 15, 1791. Appendix C is included herein because it must be considered when determining the original meaning of most provisions of the Bill of Rights. This point is developed in the discussion of the Second Amendment in Chapter 10 of this book.

The original meaning of the U.S. Constitution, from the Preamble to the Twenty-seventh Amendment, is presented herein. If the rule of law is to prevail in the United States, it is necessary that court rulings be consistent with the Constitution and the latest applicable constitutional statutes. At least until such time as foolproof lie detectors are developed and used regularly on members of the judiciary, we need better laws to augment the Constitution. Characteristics of good laws include definitiveness, clarity, and little or no discretion for judges.

Aristotle wisely said: "The best laws should be constructed as to leave as little as possible to the decision of the judge."[58] James Madison agreed. Madison observed that laws were bad to the extent they failed "to mark with precision the duties of those who are to obey them, and to take from those who are to administer them a discretion, which might be abused, . . ."[59] Despite the wise counsel of Aristotle and Madison, many American laws give wide discretion to judges.

Why do we have so many laws which give wide discretion to judges? The main reason is that such laws are very beneficial to lawyers. Lawyers have enormous influence in the lawmaking process by virtue of lobbies and the disproportionate number of lawyers in legislatures. The famous English legal reformer Jeremy Bentham wrote in 1808: "The power of the lawyer is in the uncertainty of the law."[60]

Unnecessary uncertainty in the meaning of the Constitution and other laws has been created by erroneous Court rulings. These rulings have encouraged lower courts to make more and more erroneous rulings. Such rulings and laws which give unnecessary discretion to judges have increased the uncertainty of the law and have led to more cases reaching all courts, more lawyers, more judges, and more corruption. Almost everything is up for grabs in the courts in America. In most court cases, judges have enormous power. Enormous judicial power facilitates widespread corruption. An indication of the judicial corruption problem in the United States is presented in the eye-opening book GREYLORD Justice, Chicago Style.

In A Fragment on Government, published in 1776, Jeremy Bentham advocated a major expansion of nonpunishable political speech and writings.[61] As a young man, Bentham revered the law and the judgments he heard Chief Justice Lord Mansfield deliver.[62] However, Bentham turned away from the practice of law because of the "lies, hypocrisies, greed, venality, corruption, and fraud" he observed in England in the courts and the offices of lawyers.[63] Bentham would find much improvement in the area of nonpunishable political speech and writing in twenty-first century England and America. However, it would be interesting to see whether Bentham would find the courts and law offices of twenty-first-century America to be better or worse than the courts and law offices of late-eighteenth-century England relevant to "lies, hypocrisies, greed, venality, corruption, and fraud."

Bentham would probably find twenty-first-century American judges and lawyers to be no more ethical than late-eighteenth-century English judges and lawyers. Witness (1) the 1989 book GREYLORD Justice, Chicago Style, (2) the May 1989 Reader's Digest article "Justice for Sale," (3) the 1991 book The Litigation Explosion, (4) the 1999 Frontline television program "Justice for Sale" hosted by Bill Moyers, and (5) the January 2000 Reader's Digest article "Trial Lawyers on Trial."

The November 1, 1999, issue of People had an article about the small, financially-strapped Laura Ingalls Wilder Library in Mansfield, Missouri. Laura Ingalls Wilder wrote a popular series of books which led to the television program Little House on the Prairie. She helped found the library named after her, and she specified in her will that the library receive all royalties from her books after her daughter died. However, when her daughter died in 1968, the royalties went to a lawyer who was the executor of the daughter's estate. In 1972, the library received a $28,011 check from Wilder's publisher. That was all they received. In 1999, the library filed a lawsuit in a federal court in an attempt to recover the royalties due it—millions of dollars. *People* quoted two law professors. One law professor indicated that the royalties clearly should have reverted to the library when the daughter died; the other law professor predicted a hard-fought, close battle in the federal lawsuit.[64] Given the uncertainty relevant to who would win the high-profile Laura Ingalls Wilder Library case in a federal court, it would not be surprising if massive injustice often occurs in low-profile cases in state courts.

The extreme unfairness of some judges, district attorneys, and prosecutors was shown in the riveting *Frontline* television program "The Case for Innocence," which first aired on January 11, 2000. Men who had been convicted of murder in conjunction with rape had *desperately* sought to prove their innocence through DNA testing. Several courts refused for years to grant requests for DNA tests. At least two men were kept in prison after DNA tests proved their innocence. Another man was denied a retrial after DNA testing showed that he was innocent. One man was executed, and the state destroyed evidence which people tried hard to have tested to determine whether or not the man executed had committed the crime for which he was executed. "The Case for Innocence" showed that the appellate criminal justice system in America is broken.

It would have been ideal to follow up "The Case for Innocence" with a program that showed some of the many people who have committed crimes and been freed because of law enforcement officer "violations" of Court-made "law." It is atrocious to (1) free people who are obviously guilty, and (2) fail to free people who are obviously innocent.

If you are an innocent defendant in a criminal case or a party in a civil case in which you are lawfully in the right, and you are fortunate enough to have an unbiased judge presiding, you should still be *very concerned* about the relative abilities of the lawyers involved. A major flaw in the legal system in America was addressed by Harvard

Law School Dean Roscoe Pound in a speech that he delivered to the American Bar Association in 1906. Pound spoke out against the "sporting theory of justice" when he said:

> "In America, we take it as a matter of course that a judge should be a mere umpire, to pass upon objections and hold counsel to the rules of the game . . . It leads the most conscientious judge to feel that he is merely to decide the contest, as counsel presents it, according to the rules of the game, not to search independently for truth and justice."[65]

Pound's criticism of the legal system in the United States "galvanized a spirit of reform"; however, the "sporting theory of justice" remains the heart of the legal system in America.[66] It is to the advantage of the legal establishment to promote the myth that truth and justice will emerge from what amount to games between lawyers. The public relations efforts of the legal establishment in America have worked. With less than five percent of the world's population, the United States has about seventy percent of the world's lawyers, a legal system that is expensive and unjust, and a citizenry largely unaware of the extent of the problems with the legal system in America.

In his 1983 book *Why Courts Don't Work*, West Virginia Supreme Court Justice Richard Neely said: "An old country lawyer summarized it all: 'When I was young I lost a lot of cases I should have won. Now I win a lot of cases I should lose. So overall justice is done.'"[67] This may have been justice for the old lawyer in terms of the number of games he won in court. However, it was anything but justice for the many people who lost cases they should have won.

Justice Neely also acknowledged that judges often failed to "perform competently or even honestly."[68] Injustice occurs in an enormous number of cases because of the large disparity in lawyer ability, corrupt judges, incompetent judges, lazy judges, large uncertainty in the law, and unethical lawyers.

Although federal judges are probably, on the whole, more ethical than state judges, many federal judges are unethical. During the late 1990s, investigative reporters from Kansas City, Minneapolis, and New York revealed that federal judges issued court orders in hundreds of cases in which they had a financial interest.[69] Those judges clearly violated a 1974 ethics law in which Congress prohibited federal judges from handling cases (setting hearings, granting motions, conducting trials, throwing out legal claims, etc.) involving matters in which the judges have a financial interest.

The fact that many federal judges break the law by hearing cases in which they have a financial interest should be considered the tip of the iceberg. As it is relatively easy to see the tip of an iceberg, it is relatively easy to employ the Freedom of Information Act to obtain information on the financial holdings of judges. It is far more difficult to discover cash bribes and bribes via special deals on such things as automobiles and vacations.

Biased judicial rulings are made in many trial courts and appeal courts, especially in ordinary cases which receive no media attention. Most biased rulings are made in return for bribes or personal favors. Personal favors include (1) help in securing appointments to office, (2) help in being put on a ballot to run for office, and (3) financial support in elections. Judicial corruption is facilitated by the propensity of legislative bodies to make laws which give wide discretion to judges, failure to remove judges who do not abide by what little definitiveness there is in the laws, and almost total lack of vigilance by law enforcement officials and citizens. American citizens were much more vigilant during the time the Constitution was created and ratified. Historian Jack Rakove stated that in the mid-1780s: "emerging American notions of popular government implied that all branches of government, even those directly representative of the people, required continuous and close supervision from a vigilant citizenry. . . ."[70]

America will never again have the kind of continuous and close supervision of courts that existed in the eighteenth century. However, this could be more than compensated for *if* a practical, foolproof lie detector is developed and given to all judges, jurors, prosecutors, lawyers, and witnesses involved in legal cases in America. If future Americans use such a system, they will probably view the twentieth-century justice system in America much like we view trial by fire, trial by water, and trial by battle. In those ordeals, which were jointly administered by judges and clergymen prior to 1215, it was thought that divine intervention would rescue innocent people. (A papal decree in 1215 withdrew clergymen from participation in trials by ordeal.[71])

Until foolproof lie detectors are developed, lie detectors such as are now used on employees of the Central Intelligence Agency should be used on all judges and justices. Members of the judiciary should be removed from office if such tests indicate they knowingly made one or more biased rulings. That would greatly reduce judicial bias.

With modern medical and computer technology, a foolproof lie detector system may be near. The tools needed may well exist for a practical, foolproof lie detector. In that event, the primary work to be done includes putting the right tools together and proving reliability. If foolproof lie detectors become available, their use in the legal system will be fought tooth and nail by the legal establishment. Why? The power of lawyers and wrongdoers is the uncertainty of the law *and* the facts. The ready availability of the truth—and the assurance that judges and jurors would be unbiased to the extent practicable—would greatly reduce the number of trials and the number of lawyers. Furthermore, lawyering would not be nearly as lucrative as it now is. It would be well worth taking on the legal establishment. The benefits would be enormous in terms of *greatly reducing crime, solving crimes, eliminating the punishment of innocent people, reducing civil disputes, and just resolution of civil disputes.*

It should always be illegal for governments to use lie detectors to determine political and religious *opinions*. (Violence in conjunction with those opinions is another matter.) The right against self-incrimination was developed to prevent people from incriminating themselves because of their political or religious *opinions*. Once those things are precluded, *in the interest of justice*, the right against self-incrimination can be safely dispensed with by constitutional amendment.

James Madison was in great writing form when he wrote, in *The Federalist*, No. 51: "If men were angels, no government would be necessary. If angels were to govern men, neither external nor internal controls on government would be necessary."[72] Yet, within two centuries, judges in America obtained enormous power because the external and internal controls which Madison deemed necessary had virtually disappeared. Americans are, as they plunge into the twenty-first century, effectively assuming that judges are angels.

The Preamble

> *We the People of the United States, in Order to form a more perfect Union, establish Justice, insure domestic Tranquility, provide for the common defence, promote the general Welfare, and secure the Blessings of Liberty to ourselves and our Posterity, do ordain and establish this Constitution for the United States of America.*

Original Meaning in 21st Century Plain English

We the electorate of the United States, for ourselves and all of our succeeding generations, establish this Constitution for the United States of America in order to:

- Restructure Congress from one chamber to two chambers, one of which shall be composed of legislators elected directly by the electorate, so that Congress can be safely entrusted with major lawmaking power

- Provide the United States Congress with sufficient power to solve the severe financial and trade problems which have developed under, and proved unsolvable under, the Articles of Confederation

- Create an executive branch to manage the United States in a manner consistent with this Constitution, constitutional statutes, and constitutional treaties

- Create a Supreme Court and authorize Congress to establish auxiliary courts (All courts in the United States shall rule in a manner consistent with this Constitution, the latest applicable constitutional statutes, and constitutional treaties which have not been overridden by constitutional statutes or amendments to this Constitution.)

This Constitution is intended to facilitate orderly federal government finance, free trade within the United States, fair trade with other nations, and more justice in order to:

- Raise the standard of living of citizens of the United States

- Reduce discord between citizens of the United States

- Greatly increase respect for the United States throughout the world

- Greatly increase the ability of the United States to raise the funds necessary to defend the United States and preserve the freedom of its citizens

Discussion of the Preamble

George Washington lamented the weakness of the Articles of Confederation in a letter to John Jay on August 1, 1786. Washington wrote: "What a triumph for our enemies to verify their predictions! What a triumph for the advocates of despotism to find that we are incapable of governing ourselves. . . ."[73]

Under the Articles of Confederation, the United States government had no power to tax. Congress could request the states to provide funds to the United States, but the states almost always provided less funds than Congress requested. In 1786, the total income of the United States government was less than one-third of the interest on the national debt.[74] Millions of dollars issued by Congress were worth only one or two cents per dollar.[75] A dollar bill was commonly referred to as a "Continental." The most powerful expression of contempt was "the popular saying: 'not worth a Continental.'"[76] Most of the good money in circulation was foreign coins.

Seven states issued paper money. In three other states, there were bitter controversies between proponents and opponents of state paper money.[77] Most of the money issued by states depreciated significantly. Some state legislatures passed laws which forced creditors to accept state paper money at face value even though the paper money was worth much less than its face value. James Madison later said: "In the internal administration of the States a violation of Contracts had become familiar in the form of depreciated paper made a legal tender, . . ."[78]

Discriminatory British trade practices were a serious problem which Congress, under the Articles of Confederation, had insufficient power to solve. Congress had a poor bargaining position in commercial treaty negotiations because (1) Congress could not enact statutes which set duties on imported goods, and (2) Congress had no power to enforce commercial treaties.

A "source of dissatisfaction & discord" in the mid-1780s, in the words of James Madison, was that "some of the States, which having no convenient ports for foreign commerce, were subject to be taxed by their neighbors, thro whose ports, their commerce was carried on. New Jersey, placed between Philadelphia & N. York, was likened to a cask tapped at both ends; and N. Carolina, between Virginia & S. Carolina to a patient bleeding at both arms. The Articles of Confederation provided no remedy for the complaint: . . ."[79] Connecticut charged higher duties on goods from Massachusetts than on goods from England.[80]

Shays' Rebellion in Massachusetts—and uprisings in other states—deeply concerned many Americans. On December 26, 1786, during the time that Shays' Rebellion was taking place, George Washington wrote a letter in which he expressed his concern about "the combustibles in every state."[81] Washington went on to write: "I feel . . . infinitely more than I can express . . . for the disorders which have arisen, . . . Good God! Who besides a tory could have foreseen, or a Briton have predicted them!"[82] Congress had no authority, under the Articles of Confederation, to help states check rebellions.

It was very difficult to amend the Articles of Confederation because the legislatures of all thirteen states had to ratify amendment proposals made by Congress. (It took more than three years to get the Articles ratified by all states.) Congress proposed some modest amendments to the Articles. None of the proposed amendments were ratified by all thirteen states.

The most important new powers granted to Congress by the Constitution were:

- The power to tax everything but exports (However, the unamended Constitution required direct taxes to be apportioned among the states.)

- The power to set duties on all imported goods in order to effectively deal with trade discrimination by foreign countries (Quite apart from the vital revenue which the federal government was to receive from import taxes, it was very important that Congress was given the sole power to set import tax levels so as to reduce trade discrimination.)

- The power to prohibit states from interfering with free trade except by imposing nondiscriminatory sales taxes and total bans on products

- Wide power relevant to creating and regulating federal courts

- The power to admit new states

- The power to regulate areas of the United States which were not part of any state

- The power and means to help states put down insurrections

- The sole power to coin money

Members of Congress prior to 1789 characterized it quite differently. John Adams asserted that Congress was "not a legislative but a diplomatic assembly."[83] Thomas Burke characterized Congress as a "deliberating executive assembly."[84] Thomas Jefferson characterized Congress as "both legislative and executive." Relevant to governmental functions assigned by the Constitution, Congress, under the Articles of Confederation:

- Had executive functions (It served as commander-in-chief. It directed diplomatic efforts with foreign countries. It made treaties. It requested funds to carry on the Revolutionary War and Congress' overseas diplomatic operations.)
- Had legislative functions (It borrowed money from foreign countries on the credit of the United States. It raised and supported military forces. It approved treaties. It made laws dealing with captured ships. It established a court. It made interstate postal laws.)

Furthermore, various congressional committees of the Continental Congress served as an appellate court from 1776 until the establishment of the first federal judicial court in 1780. The "legislative court" of the Continental Congress determined whether state court decisions were correct relevant to whether captured ships were captured legally and how the proceeds of legally captured ships and cargoes were to be distributed.[85]

In *The Federalist*, No. 57, James Madison wrote about the House of Representatives and the close relationship its members would have with their constituents if the proposed Constitution were ratified. Madison called that relationship "the genuine and characteristic means by which republican government provides for the liberty and happiness of the people."[86] The major statute-making power of Congress under the Constitution, relative to the minor statute-making power of Congress under the Articles of Confederation, was justified in large part by the creation of a legislative chamber composed of representatives elected directly by the electorate. Congress would obtain the structural characteristics of Parliament which were popular in the United States. The House of Representatives might have been called the House of Commons had it not mildly implied that (1) the other chamber was the House of Lords, and (2) the House of Representatives would have grossly disproportionate representation as was known to exist in the British House of Commons as a result of the so-called "rotten boroughs."

Perpetuity

Under the Articles of Confederation, the Union was to be perpetual. The word "perpetual" was used six times in the Articles (twice as "perpetual Union," twice as "perpetual union," and twice as "the union shall be perpetual"). The framers of the Constitution wanted all states in the Union under the Articles to become members of the Union under the Constitution. However, the first priority of the framers of the Constitution was that the Constitution be strong enough. They knew that some states, particularly Rhode Island, would be very reluctant to ratify the Constitution. If the only way to obtain a United States government with sufficient authority was to form a Union with nine states, the framers of the Constitution were prepared to do so.

Was the Union established by ratification of the Constitution by nine or more states understood by the ratifiers to be perpetual? In his first inaugural address, Abraham Lincoln used an implicit argument in his attempt to prove that the Union under the Constitution was perpetual. Lincoln said:

> "I hold that in contemplation of universal law and of the Constitution, the Union of these States is perpetual. Perpetuity is implied, if not expressed, in the fundamental law of all national governments. It is safe to assert that no government proper ever had a provision in its organic law for its own termination. . . . the faith of all the then thirteen States expressly plighted and engaged that it [the Union] should be perpetual, by the Articles of Confederation . . . one of the declared objects for ordaining and establishing the Constitution was '*to form a more perfect Union.*' But if destruction of the Union by one or by a part only of the States be lawfully possible, the Union is *less* perfect than before the Constitution, having lost the vital element of perpetuity. It follows from these views that no State upon its own mere motion can lawfully get out of the Union; . . ."[87]

Unfortunately, the word "perpetual" does not appear in the Constitution. The framers of the Constitution were aware of the fact that the Constitution itself was a possible vehicle for the termination of the Union which was to have been perpetual. Critics of the proposed Constitution would have had a golden opportunity to poke fun at a "perpetual Union" under the Constitution which did not include some of the members of the "perpetual Union" under the Articles of Confederation.

The Preamble provides the only explicit evidence in the Constitution that the Union under the Constitution was intended to be perpetual. The key word is "Posterity." "We the People of the United States, in Order to . . . secure the Blessings of Liberty to ourselves and our Posterity . . . establish this Constitution . . ." Posterity means "all succeeding generations." It is puzzling that Lincoln, in his first inaugural address, neglected the Preamble word "Posterity" and discussed the Preamble phrase "to form a more perfect Union." Perhaps he wanted to present fresh rationale in a constitutional debate which may have grown stale during the prior decade.

In *The Federalist*, No. 2, John Jay said that members of the Constitutional Convention "joined the people in thinking that the prosperity of America depended on its Union. To preserve and perpetuate it was the great object of . . . that convention. . . ."[88] In the Convention on July 14, delegate Roger Sherman presented rationale in support of those delegates who wanted new states admitted on an equal footing with the original states. Sherman said: "We are providing for our posterity, for our children and our grand Children, who would be as likely to be citizens of new Western States, as of the old States."[89]

Another strong indication that the Union under the Constitution was understood by most ratifiers to be perpetual comes from two letters. The first letter was written by Alexander Hamilton to inform James Madison that New York might ratify the Constitution on the condition that if certain amendments were "not adopted within a limited time, the state (New York) shall be at liberty to *withdraw* from the Union, . . ."[90] Hamilton was opposed to conditional ratification. He indicated that his support for amendments would be limited to "rational recommendations." (In the letter, Hamilton mentioned "a disturbance in the City of Albany on the

4th of July which has occasioned bloodshed. The antifoederalists were the aggressors & the Federalists were the Victors. . . ."[91] The disturbance occurred when a parade of Constitution supporters met a parade of Constitution opponents. One person was killed and eighteen people suffered serious injuries.[92]

Madison replied to Hamilton in a letter which stated: "a *conditional ratification*, . . . does not make N. York a member of the New Union, and consequently that she could not be received on that plan. . . . The Constitution requires an adoption *in toto*, and *for ever*. It has been so adopted by the other States. . . ."[93] Those two letters are especially noteworthy given the intense desire of both men for New York to join the "New Union." Hamilton read Madison's letter to the New York Ratifying Convention in Poughkeepsie, and, on July 26, 1788, there finally emerged a 30-27 majority for unconditional ratification.[94] Madison's letter tells us—in no uncertain terms—that the father of the Constitution:

- Understood that the Union under the Constitution was to be perpetual

- Believed that the other ratifiers had the same understanding (Madison was a ratifier as well as a framer.)

On September 5, 1787, six days prior to the end of the four-month Constitutional Convention, the draft preamble read: "We the people of the States of New Hampshire, Massachusetts, Rhode-Island and the Providence Plantations, . . . and Georgia establish the following Constitution for the Government of Ourselves and our Posterity."[95] That draft preamble was unanimously approved by the Convention on August 7.[96] It includes the most important part of the Preamble.

The Committee of Style modified the draft preamble and presented the Preamble, in its final form, to the Convention on September 7. The Committee substituted "United States" for "States of New Hampshire, . . . and Georgia." That change was good for three reasons. First, all thirteen of the original states might not have ratified. Second, it would have been awkward for the United States to begin operating under a constitution which named member states that were not members. Third, citizens of new states might have felt slighted because some states were named in the Constitution and their states were not named.

The Committee of Style added the flowery purpose statement: "in Order to form a more perfect Union, establish Justice, insure domestic Tranquility, provide for the common defence, promote the general Welfare, and secure the Blessings of Liberty." The purpose of the Articles of Confederation was stated therein rather plainly: "common defence, the security of their Liberties, and their mutual and general welfare." The word "welfare" meant "prosperity."

In Defense of the Articles of Confederation

A negative context is almost always used relevant to the Articles of Confederation. That is *very unfair* to the framers of the Articles who were contending with pressing problems related to the Revolutionary War during the framing of the Articles in 1777. Had the framers of the Articles proposed articles of confederation which authorized Congress to levy taxes, such articles "would never have been ratified."[97] The Articles, a necessary stepping stone to the Constitution, proved that the United States needed much more power than granted by the Articles. In the Articles, thirteen states entered "into a firm league of friendship with each other, for their common defence, . . ." The Articles began with the words:

> "To all to whom these Presents shall come, we the under signed Delegates of the States affixed to our Names send greeting. Whereas the Delegates of the United States of America in Congress assembled did on the fifteenth day of November in the Year of our Lord One Thousand Seven Hundred and Seventy seven, and in the Second Year of the Independence of America agree to certain articles of Confederation and perpetual Union between the States of Newhampshire, Massachusetts-bay, Rhodeisland and Providence Plantations, . . ."[98]

Given the realistic constraints on their work, the framers of the Articles did *at least* as good a job in 1777 as the framers of the Constitution did a decade later. The unamended Constitution is deficient in both clarity and anticipating the concerns of the electorate. The concerns of the electorate would have been greatly reduced had the unamended Constitution included those things which are included in the first eleven amendments. More Americans probably opposed ratification of the Constitution in 1787–88 than supported ratification of the Constitution.[99]

Article I

CHAPTER 3

Article I, Section 1

All legislative Powers herein granted shall be vested in a Congress of the United States, which shall consist of a Senate and a House of Representatives.

Original Meaning in 21st Century Plain English

All laws made by the federal government must be statutes or treaties which are approved within Congress as specified herein. Congress is composed of two chambers, the Senate and the House of Representatives.

Discussion of Article I, Section 1

The first words of the body of the Constitution were used to state that no law could be made by the federal government without being approved within Congress. In *The Federalist,* No. 33, Alexander Hamilton said: "What is a LEGISLATIVE power but a power of making LAWS?"[100] The requirement that laws made by the federal government be approved within Congress is related to the first provision of the English Bill of Rights which says that the "suspending of laws, or the execution of laws, . . . without consent of parliament, is illegal." The English Bill of Rights, frequently reprinted in America between 1763 and 1776, was called "the second Magna Carta."[101]

Magna Carta is the foundation of all English and American laws which limit the discretion of government officials.[102]

The supremacy of the legislative branch was a concept supported by the framers, as indicated in *The Federalist*.[103] James Madison stated: "In republican government, the legislative authority necessarily predominates."[104] In the Constitutional Convention, John Dickinson expressed his concern about the possibility of lawmaking by federal judges. Dickinson observed that the judiciary of Aragon "became by degrees, the lawgiver."[105]

Federal judges have never had the constitutional authority to make law, although they have always had the authority to make *minor* court rules. Eighteenth-century federal statutes even required federal judges to use the state court rules of the state they were in if that was practicable. Although it is constitutional for federal courts to hear common-law cases, both civil and criminal, federal judges have never been authorized to make common law. It was understood that federal judges would use the eighteenth-century common law used in the states unless superseded by the Constitution, a constitutional statute, or a constitutional treaty. In the eighteenth century, each state employed most of the English common law. However, the common law varied slightly from state to state.

Federal statutes of 1789 directed federal courts in state A to use state A's juror qualifications, forms (for judgments, etc.), modes of process, court fees, and, to the extent practicable, the mode of forming juries.[106] Section 29 of the Judiciary Act of 1789 stated:

> "And jurors in all cases to serve in the courts of the United States shall be designated by lot or otherwise in each State respectively according to the mode of forming juries therein now practised, so far as the laws of the same shall render such designation practicable by the courts or marshals of the United States; and the jurors shall have the same qualifications as are requisite for jurors by the laws of the State of which they are citizens, to serve in the highest courts of law of such state."[107]

The federal Process Act of September 29, 1789, stated that "the forms of writs . . . and modes of process and rates of fees . . . in the circuit and district courts, in suits at common law, shall be the same in each state respectively as are now used or allowed in the supreme courts of the same."[108] Relevant to a draft bill for the Judiciary Act of 1789, Justice Edward Shippen, of the Philadelphia Court of Common Sessions, said in a July 13, 1789, letter to U.S. Senator Robert Morris:

> "There are some loose Expressions in the Bill concerning the Common Law, but is no where said the Judges should decide according to it. The American states have generally adopted it, either in their Constitutions or by Act of Assembly. The United States should likewise adopt it; and it should not be left to the Judges to make the Law, but only to declare it. . . ."[109]

The United States had a one-chambered Congress from July 4, 1776, until March 3, 1789. In 1787, only Pennsylvania had a one-chambered legislature; the other twelve states had two-chambered legislatures.[110] The prospect of replacing the one-chambered Congress with a two-chambered Congress was one of the major reasons that the Constitution was ratified.[111] James Madison said, in *The Federalist*, No. 62, that the Senate "must be in all cases a salutary check on the government. It doubles the security of the people by requiring the concurrence of two distinct bodies in schemes of usurpation or perfidy, where the ambition or corruption of one would otherwise be sufficient. . . ."[112]

The prospect of a two-chambered Congress enabled the framers to make the "Great Compromise," in which representation in the House of Representatives would be based on population—very important to most framers from states with relatively large populations—and representation in the Senate would be equal for all states—very important to most framers from states with relatively small populations.

Although the Constitution vests "All [federal] legislative Powers" in Congress, the president has (1) the power to veto bills passed by Congress, and (2) the "Power, by and with the Advice and Consent of the Senate, to make Treaties." All federal statutes must be approved by at least half of the senators who vote and a majority of the representatives who vote. All treaties must be approved by at least two-thirds of the senators present. For all votes on proposed statutes and proposed treaties, a majority of the members of the chamber which is voting must be present. All laws made by the federal government must, to be constitutional, be in the form of a statute or a treaty.

Contrary to the Constitution, Congress has often delegated lawmaking power to the executive branch. Most details of modern federal laws, including tax laws and environmental cleanup laws, are devised by federal agencies.[113] Congress often provides only general guidance using terms like "just and reasonable" and "excessive profits."[114] Congress has occasionally delegated lawmaking authority to private groups, federal judges, and agencies of Congress. Because of its unconstitutional nature, delegation of lawmaking power by Congress resulted in bitter political controversies during the first 40 years under the Constitution.[115]

If the Court consistently ruled that Congress could not delegate lawmaking power without an amendment to authorize it, Congress would have a greater tendency to abide by the Constitution. That would put much more pressure on the Court to abide by the Constitution. Because the Court has almost always approved delegation of lawmaking power by Congress: (1) members of Congress have much more time to spend on their reelection efforts, and (2) members of Congress can blame federal agencies for many unpopular "federal laws."

John Locke, English author of *Two Treatises on Government*, observed that the location of legitimate legislative authority can be determined only by "the sovereign people."[116] Most ratifiers must have understood that Congress could not delegate its lawmaking power because of the combination of (1) Locke's philosophy on legislative authority, (2) the common-law prohibition of redelegation of delegated authority, and (3) Section 1 of Article I of the Constitution.[117]

Proposed laws to organize the Post Office were defeated in both the first and second Congresses under the Constitution. Those proposed laws would have empowered the postmaster general, an official in the executive branch, to establish post offices and post roads.[118] Some members of Congress, including James Madison, objected to the proposed post office/post road laws because they would have unconstitutionally delegated legislative authority to the executive branch.[119] The Constitution grants the power to "establish Post Offices and post Roads" only to Congress.

The Court has always *said* that delegation of lawmaking power by Congress is unconstitutional, but the Court has almost always *ruled* that such delegation of power is constitutional.[120] Even with the help of more than three thousand congressional committee staffers and about ten thousand unconstitutional personal staffers (Each senator was allowed forty, and each representative was allowed twenty-two.), Congress delegated much lawmaking power to executive branch agencies during the 1990s. Members of Congress during the 1990s spent less than half the time per work week legislating than did members of Congress during the 1790s. The public pays members of Congress to legislate in the public interest, not to solicit campaign funds and give preferential treatment to those who make large political "contributions." A CBS News/New York Times poll conducted in 1990 found that 71 percent of those surveyed thought that "most members of Congress are more interested in serving special interest groups than the people they represent."[121] The American people have (1) an explicit constitutional right to have all laws made by the federal government approved within Congress, and (2) an implicit constitutional right to have all members of Congress legislate in the interest of the people they represent.

Article I, Section 2, Paragraph 1

The House of Representatives shall be composed of Members chosen every second Year by the People of the several States, and the Electors in each State shall have the Qualifications requisite for Electors of the most numerous Branch of the State Legislature.

Original meaning in 21st Century Plain English

Members of the U.S. House of Representatives shall be elected every other year. People shall be eligible to vote for their representative in the U.S. House of Representatives if they are eligible to vote for their representative in the chamber of their state legislature which has the most legislators.

Discussion of Article I, Section 2, Paragraph 1

Two-year terms for members of the U.S. House of Representatives were chosen as a compromise between those framers who favored one-year terms and those framers who favored three-year terms. Under the Articles of Confederation, members of Congress served one-year terms. They sometimes served three years in a row, and then, because of term limits, returned to state government for three years before they were eligible to again become members of Congress.

Prior to 1776, only adult white male freeholders (owners of real estate) voted in elections of members of the British House of Commons and elections of members of colonial legislatures in America.[122] By 1787, most states extended the right of suffrage beyond freeholders. In some states, merchants, mechanics, and freeholders were allowed to vote. Free black men were allowed to vote in some states. Women were precluded from voting in all states except New Jersey. Women who were citizens of New Jersey could vote in that state prior to 1807. An amendment to the New Jersey constitution was made in 1807 to prevent women in New Jersey from voting.[123]

At the Constitutional Convention, Gouverneur Morris led a group of framers who tried to "restrain the right of suffrage to free-holders" in elections of members of the U.S. House of Representatives.[124] Oliver Ellsworth said: "The right of suffrage was a tender point, and strongly guarded by most of the State Constitutions. The people will not readily subscribe to the National Constitution if it should subject them to be disfranchised. . . ."[125] George Mason said: "Eight or nine States have extended the right of suffrage beyond the freeholders, what will the people there say, if they should be disfranchised. . . ."[126] Benjamin Franklin said: "It is of great consequence that we should not depress the virtue & public spirit of our common people; of which they displayed a great deal during the war, and which contributed principally to the favorable issue of it. . . . The sons of a substantial farmer, not being themselves freeholders, would not be pleased at being disfranchised, and there are a great many persons of that description."[127] Ellsworth, Mason, and Franklin prevailed.

Major constitutional restrictions on the power of the states to determine voter qualifications appear in the Fifteenth, Nineteenth, Twenty-fourth, and Twenty-sixth Amendments. The Fifteenth Amendment makes it unconstitutional to deny people the right to vote because of their "race, color, or previous condition of servitude." The Nineteenth Amendment makes it unconstitutional to deny people the right to vote because of their sex. The Twenty-fourth Amendment makes it unconstitutional to deny people the right to vote in federal elections because of "failure to pay any poll tax or other tax." The Twenty-sixth Amendment makes it unconstitutional to deny people who are eighteen years of age or older the right to vote "on account of age."

On several occasions, the Court and Congress have usurped the right of states to determine voter qualifications. The Court ruled that laws were unconstitutional if they allowed only property owners to vote in municipal bond elections.[128] In the Voting Rights Act of 1965, Congress suspended literacy tests and educational requirements.[129] Despite the fact that literacy tests and educational requirements are constitutional, the Court has refused to rule the Voting Rights Act of 1965 unconstitutional.[130]

Unfair tests, administered unfairly, were used in the twentieth century to prevent many blacks and Hispanics from voting in some Southern states. The problem, as serious as it was, should have been solved by amending the Constitution to prevent literacy tests and educational requirements from being used to prevent people from voting. In 1964, the Twenty-fourth Amendment was ratified. It prohibited poll taxes. Poll taxes had been used to unfairly reduce minority voting in some Southern states. Considering that the Twenty-fourth Amendment was ratified in 1964, it would seem that an amendment which eliminated literacy tests and educational requirements could have been ratified during the 1960s. Problem solving by unconstitutional actions encourages more unconstitutional actions.

In 1970, Congress passed an obviously unconstitutional law which prohibited states from preventing U.S. citizens who were at least 18 years old from voting because of their age. Several states quickly appealed to the U.S. Supreme Court. In 1970, the Court ruled that:

- Congress could impose voter-age requirements on states for federal elections.[131] (This part of the Court's ruling was unconstitutional.)

- Congress could not impose voter-age requirements on states for nonfederal elections. (This part of the Court's ruling was constitutional.)

Congress then proposed a constitutional amendment to the states which would—if ratified by at least 38 states—prevent all states from prohibiting U.S. citizens who are at least 18 years old from voting in any election because of their age. It took only 107 days for 38 states to ratify that proposed amendment. On July 1, 1971, it became the Twenty-sixth Amendment.

Article I, Section 2, Paragraph 2

No Person shall be a Representative who shall not have attained to the Age of twenty five Years, and been seven Years a Citizen of the United States, and who shall not, when elected, be an Inhabitant of that State in which he shall be chosen.

Original Meaning in 21st Century Plain English

All members of the United States House of Representatives must (1) be at least 25 years old, (2) have been a citizen of the United States for at least seven years, and (3) have been a resident of the state in which they were elected at the time they were elected.

Discussion of Article I, Section 2, Paragraph 2

The U.S. Constitution includes the following five qualifications for members of the U.S. House of Representatives: (1) they must be at least 25 years old; (2) they must have been a citizen of the United States for at least seven years; (3) they must have been a resident of the state in which they were elected when they were elected; (4) they must not simultaneously hold any other office in the federal government (Article I, Section 6, Paragraph 3); and (5) they must be bound by oath or affirmation to support the U.S. Constitution (Article VI, Paragraph 3).

The Constitution does not prohibit the states from imposing additional qualifications—except for the Article VI ban on religious tests for federal offices ("no religious Test shall ever be required as a Qualification to any Office . . . under the United States"). Any state can pass a constitutional law which requires that, in future elections to the U.S. House of Representatives, candidates from that state must be at least 30 years old. It would be unconstitutional for a state to pass a law which said that members of the U.S. House of Representatives from that state could be as young as 21 years of age, or any other age less than 25 years.

The Articles of Confederation—agreed to by all thirteen original states—included a form of congressional term limits. The Articles stated: "no person shall be capable of being a delegate for more than three years in any term of six years; . . ."[132] Noted historian Jack Rakove stated that the term-limit provision of the Articles of Confederation "clearly reflected the Americans' early commitment to the republican principle of rotation in office, . . ."[133] Concerns about "the dangers of entrenched power" outweighed "the merits of experience."[134]

The famous Virginia Plan included a form of term limits for one chamber of Congress. Paragraph 4 of the Virginia Plan stated: "Resolved that members of the first branch of the National Legislature ought to be elected by the people of the several States every [blank] for a term of [blank]; to be of the age of [blank] years at least, to receive liberal stipends by which they may be compensated for the devotion of their time to public service; to be ineligible to any office established by a particular State, or under the authority of the United States, except those peculiarly belonging to the functions of the first branch, during the term of service, and for the space of [blank] after its expiration; to be incapable of reelection for the space of [blank] after the expiration of their term of service, . . ."[135]

Since the framers seriously considered *mandating* term limits *and* severe restrictions on state officeholding for *all* members of the U.S. House of Representatives, the framers certainly did not intend to deny state X the right to limit terms or state officeholding of members of the U.S. House of Representatives from state X. A ban on state-imposed term limits for representatives in Congress would have unduly jeopardized ratification of the Constitution. Many Americans in 1787-88 strongly supported the republican principle of rotation in office. The Constitution:

- Does not ban any members of Congress from serving consecutive terms

- Does not prohibit any members of Congress from holding state offices while they are members of Congress

The fact that the framers omitted these Virginia Plan suggestions does not preclude state X from adopting them for representatives in Congress from state X. If state X were to enact a law which prohibited the governor of state X from simultaneously being a member of Congress, that law would be constitutional. This was more obvious during the eighteenth century in those states threatened with rebellions. Relevant to Shays' Rebellion in 1786–87: "Only by the most vigorous action was Governor Bowdoin able to quell the uprising; . . ."[136] It would have been unacceptable for state judges to draw state salaries while serving in Congress and neglecting their state jobs.

The Constitution does not grant the federal government the power to set term limits for members of the U.S. House of Representatives. The Constitution does not prohibit state X from establishing term limits for representatives in Congress from state X. The intent of the framers with respect to all areas not covered by the Constitution is stated in the Tenth Amendment: *"The powers not delegated to the United States by the Constitution, nor prohibited by it to the States, are reserved to the States respectively, or to the people."* In 1995, the Court unconstitutionally ruled that state constitutional provisions which limited the number of terms which members of the U.S. House of Representatives from those states could serve were unconstitutional because of Article I, Section 2, Paragraph 2.[137]

Article I, Section 2, Paragraph 3

Representatives and direct Taxes shall be apportioned among the several States which may be included within this Union, according to their respective Numbers, which shall be determined by adding to the whole Number of free Persons, including those bound to Service for a Term of Years, and excluding Indians not taxed, three fifths of all other Persons. The actual Enumeration shall be made within three Years after the first Meeting of the Congress of the United States, and within every subsequent Term of ten Years, in such Manner as they shall by Law direct. The Number of Representatives shall not exceed one for every thirty Thousand, but each State shall have at Least one Representative; and until such enumeration shall be made, the State of New Hampshire shall be entitled to chuse three, Massachusetts eight, Rhode-Island and the Providence Plantations one, Connecticut five, New-York six, New Jersey four, Pennsylvania eight, Delaware one, Maryland six, Virginia ten, North Carolina five, South Carolina five, and Georgia three.

Original Meaning in 21st Century Plain English

The number of representatives in the House of Representatives from each state and the total amount of direct taxes which may be imposed on the people of each state by Congress shall be in proportion to an apportionment number for each state which shall be determined by adding:

- The number of free persons (excluding Indians who are not taxed)

- The number of persons who are indentured servants (white immigrants from Great Britain, Germany, and other parts of Europe, who work as servant-laborers for a period of years—usually from five to seven years—in the United States in return for their transportation to the United States plus, oftentimes, the resources to start their own farms or small businesses when they complete their terms as servant-laborers)

- Three-fifths of the number of persons who are slaves (black persons who have not been freed)

An apportionment number for each state shall be determined (1) within three years of the first meeting of Congress under the Constitution, (2) within every subsequent period of ten years, and (3) in a manner which Congress shall direct by law. The number of representatives in the U.S. House of Representatives shall not exceed one for every apportionment number of thirty thousand, but each state which ratifies this Constitution shall have at least one representative. Until an apportionment number is determined, the number of representatives in the House of Representatives from each state which ratifies this Constitution shall be as follows; one from Delaware, one from Rhode Island, three from Georgia, three from New Hampshire, four from New Jersey, five from Connecticut, five from North Carolina, five from South Carolina, six from Maryland, six from New York, eight from Massachusetts, eight from Pennsylvania, and ten from Virginia.

Discussion of Article I, Section 2, Paragraph 3

The phrase "those bound to Service for a Term of Years" means indentured servants. The phrase "all other Persons" means black persons who are slaves. The "three fifths" provision became inoperative when the Thirteenth Amendment was ratified.

Voting Districts

The Constitution does not specify how states should determine their voting districts for members of the U.S. House of Representatives. However, most ratifiers almost certainly understood that voting districts within a state would be of approximately equal population. In *The Federalist*, No. 57, James Madison stated: "The city of Philadelphia is supposed to contain between fifty and sixty thousand souls. It will therefore form nearly two districts for the choice of federal representatives. . . ."[138] In *The Federalist*, No. 56, Madison discussed the unrepresentative nature of the House of Commons, where half of the representatives were elected by a total of 5,723 persons (about one-tenth of one percent of the population).[139] In the Constitutional Convention, James Wilson said that the "boroughs in England [used as voting districts for members of the House of Commons] which has been allowed on all hands to be the rotten part of the [English] Constitution, . . ."[140] It is obvious that the framers did not consider the House of Commons to be consistent with a republican form of government because of the "rotten boroughs."

The federal government structured by the Constitution is an example of what Article IV, Section 4 of the Constitution means by the phrase "a Republican Form of Government." The U.S. Supreme Court erroneously ruled in 1964 that it was unconstitutional for Colorado to model its upper legislative chamber on the U.S. Senate despite the fact that a majority of voters in every county in Colorado had approved the voting districts in a referendum.[141]

Before 1962, the Court never ruled on a voting district case. Since 1962, the Court has ruled that state legislator voting districts in several states were unconstitutional because each state legislator did not represent approximately the same number of people. The Court based its rulings on the Fourteenth Amendment despite the fact that the Fourteenth Amendment, even if it is assumed to be constitutional, does not prohibit unequal voting districts. Some of the voting districts for state representatives could have been legitimately ruled unconstitutional because they were so far out of balance, from a population standpoint, that they would not have been consistent with the ratifiers understanding of a republican form of government.

Direct Taxes

What are direct taxes? In the Constitutional Convention on August 20, Rufus King (an influential framer who was considered to be enthusiastic, sharp-witted, and persuasive by historian Clinton Rossiter[142]) "asked what was the precise meaning of *direct* taxation."[143] To that question, James Madison noted: "No one answered."[144] It is a bit puzzling that Gouverneur Morris, who never seemed bashful, did not offer a precise definition of direct taxation. At the Constitutional Convention, on July 17, Gouverneur Morris indicated that he understood direct taxes to be all taxes other than taxes on consumption. Morris said: "for the deficiencies of taxes on consumption, it must have been the meaning of Mr. Sherman [who had just read an enumeration of powers which included the power of levying taxes on trade, but did not include the power of direct taxation], that the General Government should recur to quotas & requisitions, . . ."[145] The framers intended for direct taxes to include (1) any real estate taxes which might be imposed by the federal government, and (2) any per capita taxes which might be imposed by the federal government. Direct taxes were not intended to include duties paid by importers or excises paid by producers in the United States. Duties paid by importers and excises paid by producers were considered to be indirect taxes because consumers paid them indirectly in the form of higher prices.

Excise taxes paid directly by consumers were probably intended to be indirect taxes. However, a significant *minority* of the members of the Third Congress maintained that any excise taxes imposed directly on consumers were direct taxes.[146] Despite the objections of many of its members, the Third Congress imposed excise taxes directly on consumers of carriages without apportioning those taxes. During debates in the Third Congress over the proposed carriage tax, the distinctions between direct taxes and indirect taxes which had been presented by Alexander Hamilton in *The Federalist* were used to help justify the carriage tax.[147]

In *The Federalist*, No. 21, Hamilton stated:

"Imposts, excises, and, in general, all duties upon articles of consumption, . . . The amount to be contributed by each citizen will in a degree be at his own option, . . . Impositions of this type usually fall under the denomination of indirect taxes, and must for a long time constitute the chief part of the revenue raised in this country. Those [taxes] of the direct kind, which principally relate to land and buildings, may admit to a rule of apportionment. Either the value of the land, or the number of people, may serve as a standard. . . ."[148]

In *The Federalist*, No. 36, Hamilton stated:

"The taxes . . . may be subdivided into those of the *direct* and those of the *indirect* kind. Though the objection be made to both, yet the reasoning upon it seems to be confined to the former . . . And indeed, as to the latter, by which must be understood duties and excises on articles of consumption, one is at a loss to conceive what can be the nature of the difficulties apprehended. . . ."[149]

The framers may have considered taxes on wages, salaries, interest, dividends, and capital gains to be direct taxes because such taxes have no resemblance to taxes on articles of consumption. On the other hand, the framers may have considered such taxes to be indirect taxes, because they have little or no resemblance to real estate taxes or per capita taxes.

A federal income tax law enacted by Congress in 1894 included taxes on income from real estate which was rented. This was effectively a select real estate tax. In 1895, in *Pollock v. Farmers' Loan & Trust Co.*,[150] the Court ruled that the federal income tax law enacted in 1894 was unconstitutional, in part because it did not apportion the tax resulting from real estate among the states as required by Article I. *Pollock* led to the Sixteenth Amendment which stated that Congress has the "power to lay and collect taxes on incomes, from whatever source derived, without apportionment among the several States, . . ." The discussion of the Sixteenth Amendment in this book addresses *Pollock* in some depth. *Pollock* is one of the most important and controversial cases in the history of the Court.

Article I, Section 2, Paragraph 4

> *When vacancies happen in the Representation from any State, the Executive Authority thereof shall issue Writs of Election to fill such Vacancies.*

Original Meaning in 21st Century Plain English

When a vacancy occurs in the U.S. House of Representatives for whatever reason (death, resignation, etc.), an election shall be held to determine who will fill the vacancy.

Discussion of Article I, Section 2, Paragraph 4

Members of the House of Representatives were the only members of the federal government which were required, by the unamended Constitution, to be elected directly by the electorate. To insure that the House would remain purely republican, the Constitution requires that all vacancies in the House be filled by persons elected directly by the electorate.

At the Constitutional Convention, James Wilson, George Mason, and James Madison led the effort to obtain direct election of one branch of Congress. Wilson said: "No government could long subsist without the confidence of the people. In republican Government this confidence was peculiarly essential. . . ."[151] Madison said that he "considered the popular election of one branch of the National Legislature as essential to every plan of free government. . . ."[152] After a debate, six states voted for the proposition: "that members of the first branch of the National Legislature ought to be elected by the people of the several States."[153] Two states voted against the proposition, and two states were divided.

Article I, Section 2, Paragraph 5

The House of Representatives shall chuse their Speaker and other Officers; and shall have the sole Power of Impeachment.

Original Meaning in 21st Century Plain English

The members of the U.S. House of Representatives shall choose all of their officers from their members. One such officer shall be called speaker. The speaker of the U.S. House of Representatives shall preside over the U.S. House of Representatives.

The U.S. House of Representatives has the sole power to impeach federal officials. If, *and only if*, the U.S. House of Representatives impeaches a federal official, the U.S. Senate shall determine, by a trial held in the Senate, whether or not to remove that federal official from office via the impeachment process.

Article I, Section 3, Paragraph 1

The Senate of the United States shall be composed of two Senators from each State, chosen by the Legislature thereof, for six Years; and each Senator shall have one Vote.

Original Meaning in 21st Century Plain English

The Senate of the United States shall be composed of two senators from each state. The state legislature of state A shall choose U.S. senators from state A. The term of each U.S. senator chosen for a full term shall be six years, except as provided by Article I, Section 3, Paragraph 2. Each U.S. senator shall have one vote in the U.S. Senate.

Discussion of Article I, Section 3, Paragraph 1

The fiercest struggle during the Constitutional Convention concerned the relative strength of each state in Congress.[154] That struggle led to the "Great Compromise," the major feature of which was that each state would have equal representation in the Senate, and representation in the House of Representatives would be based on population. The "Great Compromise" was a compromise between the Articles of Confederation, which gave equal power in Congress to each state, and the Virginia Plan, which proposed that representation in both chambers of Congress be based on population. The "Great Compromise" was not entirely great. It resulted in significantly more federal power per resident in states with relatively small populations (such as Delaware and North Dakota) than enjoyed by residents of states with relatively large populations (such as California and New York).

The Seventeenth Amendment, ratified in 1913, provided for election of U.S. senators by the electorate. Even before the Seventeenth Amendment was ratified, popular election of U.S. senators had become common. By 1912, 29 of the 48 states held elections for U.S. senators, the results of which were binding on state legislators.[155]

The Constitution specifies one vote in the Senate for each senator. There is no explicit constitutional provision concerning the relative voting strength of each representative in the House. Framers from the less-populated states obviously wanted to make sure that senators from the more-populated states did not obtain voting strength proportionate to the populations they represented.

Article I, Section 3, Paragraph 2

Immediately after they (the U.S. senators in the first U.S. Senate) shall be assembled in Consequence of the first Election, they shall be divided as equally as may be into three Classes. The Seats of the Senators of the first Class shall be vacated at the Expiration of the second Year, of the second Class at the Expiration of the fourth Year, and of the third Class at the Expiration of the sixth Year, so that one third may be chosen every second Year; and if Vacancies happen by Resignation, or otherwise, during the Recess of the Legislature of any State, the Executive thereof may make temporary Appointments until the next Meeting of the Legislature, which shall then fill such Vacancies.

Original Meaning in 21st Century Plain English

The first order of business for the first U.S. Senate shall be to divide the senators into three groups. Each group shall have an equal number of senators if the number of U.S. senators is eighteen or twenty-four. Otherwise, no group shall have more than one member more than any other group. The senators in the first group shall have two-year terms. The senators in the second group shall have four-year terms. The senators in the third group shall have six-year terms. It is desirable that one-third of the senators be chosen every second year. When vacancies occur in the U.S. Senate, the state legislatures of the states with less than two U.S. senators shall determine who shall fill those vacancies. When vacancies occur in the U.S. Senate from states whose legislatures are not in session, the governors of those states may make temporary appointments to the U.S. Senate. Temporary appointments to the U.S. Senate shall remain in effect until such time as the appropriate state legislatures fill the vacancies.

Discussion of Article I, Section 3, Paragraph 2

Part of this paragraph was superseded by the second paragraph of the Seventeenth Amendment which states: "When vacancies happen in the representation of any State in the Senate, the executive authority of such State shall issue writs of election to fill such vacancies: *Provided,* That the legislature of any State may empower the executive thereof to make temporary appointments until the people fill the vacancies by election as the legislature may direct."

Article I, Section 3, Paragraph 3

No Person shall be a Senator who shall not have attained to the Age of thirty Years, and been nine Years a Citizen of the United States, and who shall not, when elected, be an Inhabitant of that State for which he shall be chosen.

Original Meaning in 21st Century Plain English

All U.S. senators shall (1) be at least thirty years old, (2) have been a United States citizen for at least nine years, and (3) have been a resident of the state they represent at the time they were chosen.

Discussion of Article I, Section 3, Paragraph 3

The Constitution includes five qualifications for U.S. senators. Members of the U.S. Senate must: (1) be at least thirty years old; (2) have been a citizen of the U.S. for at least nine years; (3) have been a resident of the state from which they were chosen at the time they were chosen to be U.S. senators; (4) not hold any other office in the federal government during the time they are a U.S. senator (by virtue of Article I, Section 6, Paragraph 2); and (5) be bound by oath or affirmation to support the Constitution (by virtue of Article VI, Paragraph 3).

The Constitution does not forbid state A from imposing additional qualifications on members of the U.S. Senate from state A—except for the Article VI ban on religious tests. It would be constitutional for state A to:

- Forbid people from serving successive terms as a U.S. senator from state A

- Forbid people from serving more than two terms as a U.S. senator from state A

- Forbid people from serving as a U.S. senator from state A while holding office in state A or any other state

- Forbid people who have been convicted of a felony from serving as a U.S. senator from state A

- Forbid people from running for, or being appointed to, the U.S. Senate from state A unless they are between 35 and 80 years of age

State legislatures could have used whatever qualifications they wanted to use in their selection of U.S. senators, as long as those qualifications were not banned by the Constitution. Even though the states could not impose religious tests on candidates for Congress, almost all states imposed religious tests on state officials.[156] It was virtually impossible for a non-Christian to become a member of Congress in the eighteenth century, and, in most states, it was virtually impossible for a non-Protestant to be elected to Congress.[157] It would be amazing if all state legislatures in the eighteenth century did not utilize some qualification (religious, moral, gender, racial, age, term limit, residence, wealth, no simultaneous state office while a U.S. senator, etc.) not mandated by the Constitution. Most state legislatures probably used several unmandated qualifications.

In 1995, the U.S. Supreme Court ruled that states could not impose term limits on U.S. senators representing those states because of Article I, Section 3, Paragraph 3.[158] In making that ruling, the Court defied (1) the understanding of the ratifiers of the Constitution, (2) the Tenth Amendment, and (3) the will of a large majority of the American voters who voted on term limits. Term-limit proposals were on ballots in fourteen states in 1992. Voters approved those term-limit proposals in all fourteen states. Almost two voters voted for term limits for every voter who voted against term limits. In many states, laws or politicians prevented term-limit referendums.

Did the Court make its unconstitutional 1995 term-limit ruling to insure favorable treatment from Congress? The Court is dependent on Congress for much of its funding, all funding increases, and continued freedom for the Court to legislate. The Court's 5-4 term-limit ruling and the strong dissent make it obvious that the Court could easily reverse itself.

Article I, Section 3, Paragraph 4

The Vice President of the United States shall be President of the Senate, but shall have no Vote, unless they be equally divided.

Original Meaning in 21st Century Plain English

The vice-president of the United States shall (1) preside over the U.S. Senate, and (2) have the additional title of president of the Senate. The vice-president of the U.S. shall have no vote in the Senate unless there is a tie vote among the senators. In the event of a tie vote among the senators, the vice-president of the U.S. may cast the tie-breaking vote.

Article I, Section 3, Paragraph 5

The Senate shall chuse their other Officers, and also a President pro tempore, in the Absence of the Vice President, or when he shall exercise the Office of President of the United States.

Original Meaning in 21st Century Plain English

The Senate shall choose all of its officers except its president. The Senate shall choose one of its members to be the provisional president of the Senate. The provisional president of the Senate shall (1) have the title of president pro tempore, and (2) preside over the Senate in the absence of the vice-president of the U.S., including those times that the vice-president is serving as president of the United States.

Article I, Section 3, Paragraph 6

The Senate shall have the sole Power to try all Impeachments. When sitting for that Purpose, they shall be on Oath or Affirmation. When the President of the United States is tried, the Chief Justice shall preside: And no Person shall be convicted without the Concurrence of two thirds of the Members present.

Original Meaning in 21st Century Plain English

If, and only if, the U.S. House of Representatives impeaches a federal official, a trial shall be held in the U.S. Senate to determine whether or not to remove the impeached official from office. When the Senate serves as a jury in a trial of an impeached official, all senators who serve as jurors shall be on oath or affirmation. No official shall be convicted of an impeachment charge by the Senate unless at least two-thirds of the senators present vote that the official is guilty of the same impeachment charge. A majority of the senators must be present for all such votes. When the president of the United States is tried by the Senate, the chief justice of the U.S. Supreme Court shall preside.

Article I, Section 3, Paragraph 7

Judgment in Cases of Impeachment shall not extend further than to removal from Office, and disqualification to hold and enjoy any Office of honor, Trust or Profit under the United States: but the Party convicted shall nevertheless be liable and subject to Indictment, Trial, Judgment and Punishment, according to Law.

Original Meaning in 21st Century Plain English

Officials who are impeached by the House of Representatives and convicted by the Senate shall be removed from office and disqualified from holding any federal office in the future. No further punishment may be imposed by Congress on people it removes from office. However, people who have been removed from office by Congress via the impeachment process shall be liable to indictment, trial in a court of law, judgment, and punishment, according to law.

Comments on Article I, Section 3, Paragraph 7

Federal officials may be legitimately removed from office via the impeachment process only for conduct related to their office. Examples of criminal conduct for which a federal official may be properly removed from office via the impeachment process are: (1) bribery; (2) treason (as defined by the Constitution); and (3) perjury in an official action. All officials are bound by oath or affirmation to support the Constitution, and a knowing violation of that oath or affirmation is perjury.

Noncriminal conduct for which an official may be properly impeached by the House and convicted by the Senate includes: (1) failure to do something which the official had a duty to do; and (2) doing something which the official had no authority to do (such as authorizing federal money to be spent for a purpose other than the purpose for which it was appropriated).

Officials of Great Britain who were removed from office via the impeachment process during the seventeenth century were often condemned to death by Parliament as traitors.[159] It was not until the nineteenth century that Parliament adopted a policy of removing ministers from office humanely by a simple vote of no confidence.[160]

Article I, Section 4, Paragraph 1

The Times, Places and Manner of holding Elections for Senators and Representatives, shall be prescribed in each State by the Legislature thereof; but the Congress may at any time by Law make or alter such Regulations, except as to the Places of chusing Senators.

Original Meaning in 21st Century Plain English

The times, places, and manner of holding elections to determine who will serve in Congress shall be prescribed in each state by its legislature. Congress may pass laws to supersede such state laws, except that Congress has no authority to prescribe the places for choosing senators.

Discussion of Article I, Section 4, Paragraph 1

Prior to 1842, Congress did not pass any law under their "Times, Places and Manner" authority.[161] Acting on their "Manner" authority, Congress passed a law in 1842 which required each state to establish single-member, compact, near-equally-populated districts for members of the U.S. House of Representatives.[162] That law was constitutional, at least with respect to single-member districts and near-equally-populated districts. The criteria established by the 1842 "Manner" law remained in effect until 1911.[163] The lapse of federal "Manner" legislation in 1911 was probably due to the refusal of Congress to put teeth into the law and the refusal of courts to get involved.[164]

Given the fact that no act of Congress has been in effect since 1911 to mandate near-equally-populated congressional districts (not to mention the historic lack of court concern about congressional districts), it was surprising when: (1) in 1969, the Court invalidated Missouri's 1967 Redistricting Act because some districts deviated from the average Missouri congressional district by three percent, and (2) in 1983, the Court invalidated congressional districts in New Jersey even though the deviation in population from district to district was less than one percent.[165] There is no evidence that the framers or ratifiers considered such minor deviations in congressional district population to be unconstitutional.

Article I, Section 4, Paragraph 2

The Congress shall assemble at least once in every Year, and such Meeting shall be on the first Monday in December, unless they shall by Law appoint a different Day.

Original Meaning in 21st Century Plain English

Congress shall convene at least once every year. Congress shall convene on the first Monday in December, unless Congress enacts a law to specify a different day for the mandatory convening of Congress.

Discussion of Article I, Section 4, Paragraph 2

On September 13, 1788, the one-chambered Congress under the Articles of Confederation selected the first Wednesday in March as the day that the first two-chambered Congress under the Constitution would assemble.[166] Therefore, the first Congress under the Constitution officially began on March 4, 1789, and ended two years later with the expiration of the first terms of the members of the first U.S. House of Representatives. (The first U.S. House of Representatives did not have a quorum until April 1, 1789, and the first U.S.

Senate did not have a quorum until April 7, 1789.[167]) In odd-numbered years from 1791 to 1933, Congress did not meet between March 4 and first Monday in December, unless the president of the United States, "on extraordinary Occasions," convened a special session of the new Congress.

From 1790 to 1930, most first-term members of Congress were not seated in Congress until about thirteen months after they had been elected. The Twentieth Amendment, which became law in 1933, established that new Congresses would convene at "noon on the 3d day of January," about two months after first-term members had been elected, unless Congress "shall by law appoint a different day."

Prior to the Twentieth Amendment, every Congress under the Constitution held one "lame-duck" session which normally lasted about three months—from the first Monday in December of even-numbered years to the early part of March of the following years. Members of Congress during "lame-duck" sessions included some members who had been defeated and other members who did not seek to be re-elected.

"Lame-duck" sessions of Congress were controversial for several reasons.[168] "Lame-duck" representatives sometimes got to determine who the next president of the United States would be. Presidents Thomas Jefferson and John Quincy Adams were both selected by "lame-duck" Houses, and there was much controversy on each occasion. In 1801, the "lame-duck" House, still under Federalist control, almost chose Aaron Burr over Thomas Jefferson for president of the U.S. even though it was well known that Burr was only a candidate for vice-president on a ticket headed by Jefferson. On the day before Jefferson was inaugurated, the "lame-duck" Senate approved 42 Federalist justices of the peace for the District of Columbia. That was a factor in *Marbury v. Madison*. A "lame-duck" House chose John Quincy Adams to be president despite the fact that Adams had less votes than Andrew Jackson. Even though Adams "conducted his administration with great dignity and in a fine spirit of public service, he was unable to overcome the opposition which he encountered on his election to office . . ."[169]

The Twentieth Amendment was proposed to the state legislatures by Congress in March of 1932. Within one year, all 48 states ratified.[170]

Article I, Section 5, Paragraph 1

Each House shall be the Judge of the Elections, Returns and Qualifications of its own Members, and a Majority of each shall constitute a Quorum to do Business; but a smaller Number may adjourn from day to day, and may be authorized to compel the Attendance of absent Members, in such Manner, and under such Penalties as each House may provide.

Original Meaning in 21st Century Plain English

The U.S. House of Representatives shall have the power to resolve controversies relevant to (1) who has been elected to the U.S. House of Representatives, and (2) who is constitutionally unqualified to be a member of the U.S. House of Representatives. A majority of the members of the U.S. House of Representatives shall be present for all U.S. House of Representatives' votes except when (1) the House selects a president of the United States, (2) the House votes to adjourn for the day in a manner consistent with House rules, and (3) the House votes to compel the attendance of absent members—with or without imposing penalties on absent members—in a manner consistent with House rules.

The U.S. Senate shall have the power to resolve controversies relevant to (1) who has been elected to the U.S. Senate, and (2) who is constitutionally unqualified to be a member of the U.S. Senate. A majority of the members of the U.S. Senate must be present for all U.S. Senate votes except when (1) the Senate votes to adjourn for the day in a manner authorized by Senate rules, and (2) the Senate votes to compel the attendance of absent members—with or without imposing penalties on absent members—in a manner authorized by Senate rules.

Article I, Section 5, Paragraph 2

Each House may determine the Rules of its Proceedings, punish its Members for disorderly Behaviour, and, with the Concurrence of two thirds, expel a Member.

Original Meaning in 21st Century Plain English

The U.S. Senate has the power to determine its rules of procedure, punish senators for disorderly behavior, and expel senators if two-thirds or more of the senators vote to expel. The U.S. House of Representatives has the power to determine its rules of procedure, punish representatives for disorderly behavior, and expel representatives if two-thirds or more of the representatives vote to expel.

Article I, Section 5, Paragraph 3

Each House shall keep a Journal of its Proceedings, and from time to time publish the same, excepting such Parts as may in their Judgment require Secrecy; and the Yeas and Nays of the Members of either House on any question shall, at the Desire of one fifth of those Present, be entered on the Journal.

Original Meaning in 21st Century Plain English

The U.S. Senate shall keep and publish a record of its proceedings. The U.S. House of Representatives shall keep and publish a record of its proceedings. The Senate may exclude from its published records those proceedings which the senators vote to be keep secret. The House of Representatives may exclude from its published records those proceedings which the representatives vote to keep secret. The votes of every senator present in the Senate shall be individually recorded on any question if one-fifth or more of the senators present request it. The votes of every representative present in the House of

Representatives shall be individually recorded on any question if one-fifth or more of the representatives present request it. All votes cast on whether or not to override vetoes shall be individually recorded.

Article I, Section 5, Paragraph 4

Neither House, during the Session of Congress, shall, without the Consent of the other, adjourn for more than three days, nor to any other Place than that in which the two Houses shall be sitting.

Original Meaning in 21st Century Plain English

Neither the U.S. Senate nor the U.S. House of Representatives shall, without the consent of the other, (1) adjourn for more than three days, or (2) adjourn to a place other than the place in which they are sitting.

Article I, Section 6, Paragraph 1

The Senators and Representatives shall receive a Compensation for their Services, to be ascertained by Law, and paid out of the Treasury of the United States. They shall in all Cases, except Treason, Felony and Breach of the Peace, be Privileged from Arrest during their Attendance at the Session of their respective Houses, and in going to and returning from the same; and for any Speech or Debate in either House, they shall not be questioned in any other Place.

Original Meaning in 21st Century Plain English

The federal government shall pay members of Congress an amount to be determined by an act of Congress. Members of Congress shall forever be immune from lawsuits and criminal charges for anything they say in debates or speeches in Congress. Members of Congress shall be immune from arrest for debt (1) during all sessions of Congress that they attend, (2) during the time they are traveling from their permanent residence to a session of Congress, and (3) during the time they are traveling to their permanent residence from a session of Congress. However, members of Congress may be arrested at any time for treason, felony, or breach of the peace.

Discussion of Article I, Section 6, Paragraph 1

Under the Articles of Confederation, members of Congress were paid by their respective state governments. With about one month left in the Constitutional Convention, the draft constitution included the clause: "The members of each House shall receive a compensation for their services, to be ascertained and paid by the State, in which they shall be chosen."[171]

On August 14, Oliver Ellsworth made a motion to pay members of Congress "out of the Treasury of the U. S. an allowance not exceeding (blank) dollars per day or the present value thereof."[172] After a debate, the Convention voted nine states to two to pay members of Congress out of the national treasury. The main reason for making the change was that most framers thought that Congress would be too dependent on state legislatures if members of Congress were not paid by the United States.

The congressional immunity provisions were not new. They had counterparts in both the Articles of Confederation and the English Bill of Rights. The most important immunity deals with things that members of Congress say in Congress. By "any other place," the framers meant to include all courts and state legislatures. State legislatures sometimes tried cases in the eighteenth century. The only immunity which members of Congress have, other than from things they say in Congress, is a limited freedom from arrest for debt—valuable in the eighteenth century and the early portion of the nineteenth century when debtors were subject to imprisonment.[173]

Article I, Section 6, Paragraph 2

No Senator or Representative shall, during the Time for which he was elected, be appointed to any civil Office under the Authority of the United States, which shall have been created, or the Emoluments whereof shall have been encreased during such time; and no Person holding any Office under the United States, shall be a Member of either House during his Continuance in Office.

Original Meaning in 21st Century Plain English

No member of Congress shall, during the time for which they were elected to Congress, be appointed to any civil office in the federal government (1) which was created during the time for which they were elected to Congress, or (2) for which the compensation for serving was increased during the time for which they were elected to Congress. No member of Congress shall hold any other office in the federal government.

Discussion of Article I, Section 6, Paragraph 2

Despite this constitutional provision, the Court ruled in 1937 that Senator Hugo L. Black's 1937 appointment to the Court could not be challenged in the Court despite the fact that Black had recently participated in the passage of legislation for the benefit of Supreme Court justices.[174]

In *Ex parte Albert Levitt,* lawyer Albert Levitt contended "that the appointment of Mr. Justice Black by the President and confirmation by the Senate of the United States were null and void by reason of his ineligibility under Article I, Section 6, clause 2, of the Constitution of the United States, . . ."[175] The Court ruled: "One having no interest other than as a citizen and a member of the bar of the Supreme Court of the United States may not question the validity of the appointment of a Justice of such court. . . . To entitle a private individual to invoke the judicial power to determine the validity of executive or legislative action he must show that he has sustained or is in immediate danger of sustaining a direct injury as a result of that action, and it is not sufficient that he has merely a general interest common to all members of the public."[176]

In *effect*, the Court said: "We don't like Article I, Section 6, Paragraph 2, and we will *not* enforce it. It might discourage some members of Congress from increasing the salaries or other benefits enjoyed by Court members." The Court's refusal to uphold the Constitution in *Ex Parte Albert Levitt* is even more shameful in view of the fact that there had been vigorous opposition to Black's nomination to the Court in Senate confirmation hearings. Black's confirmation was difficult because he was a former member of the Ku Klux Klan.[177]

Article I, Section 7, Paragraph 1

All Bills for raising Revenue shall originate in the House of Representatives; but the Senate may propose or concur with Amendments as on other Bills.

Original Meaning in 21st Century Plain English

All bills (proposed laws) concerned with federal taxes and other ways of obtaining income (sales, leases, etc.) for the federal government shall originate in the U.S. House of Representatives. However, the U.S. Senate may propose changes to revenue bills originating in the House of Representatives. The Senate must concur with all revenue bills before they can become law.

Discussion of Article I, Section 7, Paragraph 1

This is a useless provision from a legislative standpoint. It makes no difference whether the Senate or the House of Representatives originates a bill as long as both chambers must approve all bills before they become law. This provision was involved in the so-called "Great Compromise" made at the Constitutional Convention.

Even after the "Great Compromise," the "money bill" provision was painfully contested. Some delegates, including James Madison,

Oliver Ellsworth, and Charles Pinkney, realized that the clause was worthless from a legislative standpoint. Among those three delegates, Ellsworth was the only one who did not contest it. Several delegates, including George Mason, Nathaniel Gorham, Edmund Randolph, and Caleb Strong, fought passionately to give the exclusive power of originating money bills to the House of Representatives. On August 8, the Convention voted seven states to four to strike out a provision of the draft constitution which gave the House of Representatives sole power to originate money bills. On August 13, the Convention voted seven states to four not to reinsert the provision.

The reason that the money bill provision was eventually reinserted may best be understood by the statement made by Hugh Williamson on August 15: "some think this restriction on the Senate [to forbid them from originating money bills] essential to liberty, others think it of no importance. Why should not the former be indulged?"[178] Williamson was right. Whatever was in the air in Philadelphia to make such a large minority of the delegates feel so strongly about this curious provision would probably be in the air at the ratifying conventions.

On September 8, the Convention approved, nine states to two, the provision: "All bills for raising revenue shall originate in the House of Representatives."

Despite the constitutional requirement that all revenue lawmaking begin in the House, Congress has delegated some revenue lawmaking to the executive branch, including the power to determine income tax details[179] and the power to change tariffs on imported goods.[180]

Article I, Section 7, Paragraph 2

Every Bill which shall have passed the House of Representatives and the Senate, shall, before it become a Law, be presented to the President of the United States; If he approve he shall sign it, but if not he shall return it, with his Objections to that House in which it shall have originated, who shall enter the Objections at large on their

Journal, and proceed to reconsider it. If after such Reconsideration two thirds of that House shall agree to pass the Bill, it shall be sent, together with the Objections, to the other House, by which it shall likewise be reconsidered, and if approved by two thirds of that House, it shall become a Law. But in all such Cases the Votes of both Houses shall be determined by yeas and Nays, and the Names of the Persons voting for and against the Bill shall be entered on the Journal of each House respectively. If any Bill shall not be returned by the President within ten Days (Sundays excepted) after it shall have been presented to him, the Same shall be a Law, in like Manner as if he had signed it, unless the Congress by their Adjournment prevent its Return, in which Case it shall not be a Law.

Original Meaning in 21st Century Plain English

All bills which are passed by Congress shall be reviewed by the president before becoming a law unless the president previously reviewed the bill, vetoed the bill, and both the Senate and the House of Representatives have repassed the bill by at least a two-thirds majority. If the president approves a bill passed by Congress, he shall sign it. If the president disapproves of a bill passed by Congress, he shall veto it by returning it, with his objections, to the chamber (House of Representatives or Senate) where the bill originated, within ten days—not including Sundays—after the bill was presented to him. That chamber shall enter the president's objections on its official record, reconsider the bill, and, if they repass the bill by a two-thirds majority, it shall be sent with the president's objections to the other chamber. If the president vetoes a bill and Congress either overrides the veto or attempts to override the veto, the names of all members of Congress voting for and against the override shall be published in the congressional record. If the president fails to sign a bill or veto a bill within ten days—not including Sundays—the bill shall become law unless Congress adjourns before the ten days have expired.

Discussion of Article I, Section 7, Paragraph 2

The Virginia Plan contained a provision—based on the New York Constitution—which gave the veto power to a Council of Revision made up of the "Executive" and "a convenient number of the National Judiciary."[181] Congress would have been able to override vetoes made by such a council by a simple majority vote of both chambers.[182] When the Council of Revision clause was first discussed in the Convention, Elbridge Gerry said: "It was quite foreign from the nature of [judicial] office to make them judges of the policy of public measures."[183] Gerry moved "to postpone the clause in order to propose 'that the National Executive shall have a right to negative any Legislative act which shall not be afterwards passed by [blank] parts of each branch of the national Legislature.'"[184] Gerry's motion passed.

Several attempts by James Madison to obtain judicial participation in the federal veto process failed. On August 15, 1787, Madison made his final attempt to involve "the judges of the supreme court" in the federal veto process.[185] Madison's motion was rejected, eight states to three. It is extremely ironic that the Court, with no amendment to justify it, has become a body that judges the "the policy of public measures" under the pretext of interpreting law.

Article I, Section 7, Paragraph 3

Every Order, Resolution, or Vote to which the Concurrence of the Senate and the House of Representatives may be necessary (except on a question of Adjournment) shall be presented to the President of the United States; and before the Same shall take Effect, shall be approved by him, or being disapproved by him, shall be repassed by two thirds of the Senate and House of Representatives, according to the Rules and Limitations prescribed in the Case of a Bill.

Original Meaning in 21st Century Plain English

Except for adjournment, amendment proposals, and removal from office via impeachment, every congressional action which requires the concurrence of the U.S. Senate and the U.S. House of Representatives shall be presented to the president of the U.S. before taking effect. If disapproved by the president, such actions must be repassed by at least a two-thirds majority in both the Senate and the House of Representatives. The same rules as prescribed in this Constitution for bills are applicable to actions which require the concurrence of the Senate and the House of Representatives, such as declarations of war.

Discussion of Article I, Section 7, Paragraph 3

The amendment process of Article V does not give any authority to the president. When the Senate and House of Representatives approved what became the Bill of Rights, Congress did not present the proposed amendments to President George Washington to approve or disapprove. Congress merely requested President Washington to transmit copies of the proposed amendments "to the Executives of the several states which have ratified the Constitution. . . . and like Copies to the Executives of Rhode Island and North Carolina."[186] Framer error is responsible for the fact that Article I, Section 7, Paragraph 3, *by itself*, indicates that the president can exercise veto power on (1) amendments to the Constitution proposed by Congress and (2) removal of officials from office by Congress via the impeachment process.

Article I, Section 8, Paragraph 1

The Congress shall have Power To lay and collect Taxes, Duties, Imposts and Excises, to pay the Debts and provide for the common Defence and general Welfare of the United States; but all Duties, Imposts and Excises shall be uniform throughout the United States;

Original Meaning in 21st Century Plain English

Congress shall have the power to impose and collect:

- Taxes (However, direct taxes must be apportioned among the states as specified in Article I, Section 2, Paragraph 3.)

- Duties (Duties are taxes on goods brought into the United States after having been produced elsewhere. Duties may be based on the value of the goods, weight of the goods, point of origin, vessel carried in, or any other basis that Congress specifies. Duties are paid directly by importers. Most duties are paid indirectly by consumers who are not importers.)

- Imposts ("Imposts" were *probably* a synonym for duties. The term "Imposts" may have been more commonly used in some states, and the term "Duties" may have been more commonly used in other states.)

- Excises (Excises are taxes on goods manufactured or produced in the United States; excises did not include license fees in 1787–88.[187])

Congress shall have the power to use tax receipts to: (1) pay debts incurred by the states as a result of the Revolutionary War; (2) pay debts of the United States; (3) provide for the defense of the United States; and (4) provide for the general welfare (coin money, pay federal officials, etc.) of the United States as indicated in this Constitution. All taxes imposed on goods entering the United States shall be uniform throughout the United States for a given type of goods. All taxes imposed on goods manufactured or produced in the United States shall be uniform throughout the United States for a given type of goods.

Discussion of Article I, Section 8, Paragraph 1

Under the Articles of Confederation, Congress had no power to tax. In 1786, the total amount of money provided to the United States government by the states was less than a third of the interest on the national debt.[188] James Madison wrote, in his preface to *Notes of Debates in the Federal Convention of 1787*:

> "the radical infirmity of the 'articles of Confederation' was the dependence of Congress on the voluntary and simultaneous compliance with its Requisitions, by so many independant Communities, each consulting more or less its particular interests & convenience and distrusting the compliance of the others. . . . It was seen that the public debt rendered so sacred by the cause in which it had been incurred remained without any provision for its payment. The reiterated and elaborate efforts of Congress to procure from the States a more adequate power to raise the means of payment had failed. The effect of the ordinary requisitions of Congress had only displayed the inefficiency of the authority making them; none of the States having duly complied with them, some having failed altogether or nearly so; . . ."[189]

The inability of the United States to pay the interest on the national debt: (1) created major financial problems (notes issued by Congress were worth one or two cents on the dollar[190]); (2) made it unlikely that the United States, under the Articles, would be able to raise the amount of money needed for national defense in the future; and (3) was considered disgraceful by many Americans who believed that the debt needed to be repaid to make the United States a fully respectable nation.

Article I, Section 8, Paragraph 1 was probably considered by most framers and ratifiers to be the most important paragraph in the Constitution because it provided the United States government with (1) the power to tax, (2) the excellent prospect of paying its debts, and (3) greatly improved credit which could be used to finance future national defense needs.

The phrase "provide for the common Defence and general Welfare of the United States" was, in essence, taken from the Articles of Confederation which stated: "All charges of war, and all other expences that shall be incurred for the common defence or general welfare, and allowed by the united states in congress assembled, shall be defrayed out of a common treasury, which shall be supplied by the several states, . . ."[191] Some opponents of the Constitution complained that the phrase "provide for the common Defence and general Welfare of the United States" amounted to an unlimited power. In *The Federalist*, No. 41, James Madison made a powerful argument that the phrase "provide for the common Defence and general Welfare of the United States" only conferred a power to spend for purposes enumerated in the Constitution. Madison said:

> "Some who have not denied the necessity of the power of taxation have grounded a very fierce attack against the Constitution, . . . It has been urged and echoed that the power to 'to lay and collect taxes, duties, imposts, and excises, to pay the debts, and provide for the common defense and general welfare of the United States,' amounts to an unlimited commission to exercise every power which may be alleged to be necessary for the common defense or general welfare. No stronger proof could be given of the distress under which these writers labor for objections, than their stooping to such a misconstruction. Had no other enumeration or definition of the powers of Congress been found in the Constitution, than the general expressions just cited, the authors of the objection might have had some color for it; . . . But what color can the objection have, when a specification of the objects alluded to by these general terms immediately follows and is not even separated by a longer pause than a semicolon? . . . For what purpose could the enumeration of particular powers be inserted, if these and all others were meant to be included in the preceding general power? Nothing is more natural nor common than first to use a general phrase, and then to explain and qualify it by a recital of particulars. But the idea of an enumeration of particulars which neither explain nor qualify the general meaning, and can have no other effect than to confound and mislead, is an absurdity, . . . The

objection here is the more extraordinary, as it appears that the language used by the convention is a copy from the Articles of Confederation. The objects of the Union among the States, as described in article third, are 'their common defense, security of their liberties, and mutual and general welfare.' The terms of article the eighth are still more identical: . . . A similar language again occurs in article ninth. Construe either of these articles by the rules which would justify the construction put on the new Constitution, and they vest in the existing Congress a power to legislate in all cases whatsoever. But what would have been thought of that assembly, if, attaching themselves to these general expressions and disregarding the specifications which ascertain and limit their import, they had exercised an unlimited power of providing the common defense and general welfare? . . ."[192]

The Constitution was ratified on the basis of assurances by signers of the Constitution that the federal government's powers would be limited to those enumerated in the Constitution. The general acceptance of the established practice, under the Articles, of modest support for religion and education (a power not written in the Articles of Confederation) was taken for granted as an unwritten part of the Constitution. It *may* also have been assumed that Congress would retain its unwritten power to charter banks.

Congress has drastically expanded its spending power, and the Court has approved. The predictions of many opponents of the Constitution, relevant to the unlimited spending power which Congress would assume under the Constitution, have largely come true, thanks to much "stooping" to "confound and mislead" by Congress and the Court.

Article I, Section 8, Paragraph 2

(Congress shall have the power) *To borrow Money on the credit of the United States;*

Original Meaning in 21st Century Plain English

Congress shall have the power to borrow money on the credit of the United States.

Article I, Section 8, Paragraph 3

(Congress shall have the power) *To regulate Commerce with foreign Nations, and among the several States, and with the Indian Tribes;*

Original Meaning in 21st Century Plain English

In order to effectively combat discriminatory trade laws of foreign nations, Congress shall have the power to impose restrictions on goods brought into the United States from foreign nations. In order to insure that there is free trade within the United States, Congress shall have the power to regulate the commerce from state to state. States may prohibit products from being bought and sold therein for health or moral reasons. Products which states allow to be bought and sold therein shall not be taxed based upon the state or country in which the products were produced. In order to minimize conflicts between Indians and non-Indians, Congress shall have the power to regulate commerce between Indian tribes and non-Indians.

Discussion of Article I, Section 8, Paragraph 3

To combat discriminatory trade laws of foreign nations, the primary tool in the hands of Congress is the power to set duties on imported goods. The Constitution forbids Congress from imposing duties or other taxes on exported goods. It is not clear that Congress has the constitutional power to prohibit exports.

The meaning of the phrase "To regulate Commerce . . . among the several States" has been dramatically expanded by Congress and the Court during the nineteenth and twentieth centuries. According to constitutional historian Robert J. Steamer, that phrase was involved in more litigation prior to 1950 than any other phrase in the Constitution, and, over time, "became the single most important source of national power."[193]

Problems with commerce in the United States under the Articles of Confederation were vividly recalled by James Madison in the 1830s when he wrote:

"some of the States, which having no convenient ports for foreign commerce, were subject to be taxed by their neighbors, through whose ports, their commerce was carried on. New Jersey, placed between Philadelphia & New York, was likened to a cask tapped at both ends; and North Carolina, between Virginia & South Carolina, to a patient bleeding at both arms. The Articles of Confederation provided no remedy for the complaint: . . . The want of authority in Congress to regulate Commerce had produced in Foreign nations, particularly Great Britain, a monopolizing policy injurious to the trade of the U. S. and destructive to their navigation [By "navigation," Madison meant "shipping industry."]; . . . The want of a general power over Commerce, led to an exercise of the power separately, by the States, which not only proved abortive, but engendered rival, conflicting and angry regulations. . . . the States having ports for foreign commerce, taxed & irritated the adjoining States, trading through them, as New York, Pennsylvania, Virginia & South Carolina. Some of the States, as Connecticut, taxed imports as from Massachusetts higher than imports even from Great Britain of which Massachusetts complained to Virginia and doubtless to other States. . . . In sundry instances as of New York, New Jersey, Pennsylvania & Maryland, the navigation laws treated the Citizens of other States as aliens."[194]

In *The Federalist*, No. 22, Alexander Hamilton stated that one of the things which rendered the Articles of Confederation "altogether unfit for the administration of the affairs of the Union" was the lack of "power to regulate commerce."[195] Hamilton indicated that the main problem with commerce was that states were competing among themselves for foreign trade. Hamilton said:

"No nation acquainted with the nature of our political association would be unwise enough to enter into stipulations with the United States, conceding on their part privileges of importance, while they were apprised that the engagements on the part of the Union might at any moment be violated by its members, and while they found from experience that they might enjoy every advantage they desired in our markets without granting us any in return but such as their momentary convenience might suggest. . . ."[196]

Hamilton went on to quote an encyclopedia about problems with commerce in Germany due to the fact there was no national power to regulate commerce in Germany. The encyclopedia words quoted were:

"The commerce of the German empire is in continual trammels from the multiplicity of the duties which the several princes and states exact upon the merchandises passing through their territories, by means of which the fine streams and navigable rivers with which Germany is so happily watered are rendered almost useless."[197]

In the same paragraph that Hamilton presented the severe problems with German commerce, he warned that commerce in the United States, under the Articles of Confederation, was drifting towards the same problems as existed with commerce in Germany. Hamilton stated:

"The interfering and unneighborly regulations of some States, contrary to the true spirit of the Union, have, in different instances, given just cause of umbrage and complaint to others, and it is to be feared that examples of this nature, if not restrained by a national control, would be multiplied and extended till they became . . . injurious impediments to the . . . [commerce] between the different parts of the . . .

[United States]. . . . the people of this country might never permit . . . [the German experience] to be strictly applicable to us, yet we may reasonably expect from the gradual conflicts of State regulations that the citizens of each would at length come to be considered and treated by the others in no better light than that of foreigners and aliens."[198]

The fact that the proposed Constitution gave the federal government the power to regulate commerce was not opposed by many Americans during 1787–88. James Madison stated, in *The Federalist*, No. 45:

"The powers delegated by the proposed Constitution to the federal government are few and defined. Those which are to remain in the State governments are numerous and indefinite. The former will be exercised principally on external objects, as war, peace, negotiation, and foreign commerce; with which last the power of taxation will, for the most part, be connected. . . . The regulation of commerce, it is true, is a new power; but that seems to be an addition which few oppose and from which no apprehensions are entertained. . . . The change relating to taxation may be regarded as the most important; . . ."[199]

In 1787–88, the need for federal regulation of commerce was obvious. However, neither the framers nor the ratifiers thought that the proposed federal power to regulate commerce included the power to:

- Inhibit, much less prohibit, interstate commerce (The entire rationale for Congress' power "To regulate Commerce . . . among the several States" was to remove undue state restrictions on commerce. Roger Sherman said at the Constitutional Convention: "The power of the U. States to regulate trade . . . can controul interferences of the State regulations when such interferences happen; . . ."[200])

- Limit the amount of crops raised on a farm

- Impose wage restrictions and working conditions on manufacturers

- Impose health and safety standards on states

- Restrict *intrastate* commerce

- Prohibit a state from taxing waste deposited therein from other states at a higher rate than charged for waste generated within the state

If Americans in 1787–88 thought that the power to regulate commerce included the things just mentioned, the Constitution would not have been ratified by a sufficient number of states. It was ratified based on the assurances provided by James Madison, Alexander Hamilton, and other framers that the power to regulate interstate commerce was given to the federal government in order to insure *unrestrained* trade among the states. In *The Federalist*, No. 11, Hamilton stated:

> "An unrestrained intercourse between the States themselves will advance the trade of each by an interchange of their respective productions, not only for the supply of reciprocal wants at home, but for exportation to foreign markets."[201]

Prior to 1903, the Court took the view that Congress, under their power to regulate commerce "among the several States," could only protect free trade within the United States by keeping commerce channels free from obstruction by states.[202] That view was correct. However, the Court, relying on the commerce clause, ruled in 1903 that Congress could prohibit lottery tickets from being transported across state lines.[203] The 1903 lottery case[204] was a traumatic experience for some members of the Court; it was decided by a 5-4 margin after the case was argued three times before the Court.[205] The dissenters, including Chief Justice Melville W. Fuller, correctly pointed out that (1) allowing Congress to suppress lotteries gave Congress a sweeping police power which the Tenth Amendment reserved to the states, (2) Congress' power to regulate commerce among the states does not include the power of prohibition, and (3)

Congress' motive for the lottery law was to suppress gambling—not to regulate commerce.

During the remainder of the twentieth century, a myriad of unconstitutional federal laws (in areas such as morals, welfare, health, and safety) were made by Congress under its assumed, and Court-approved, national police power.

In addition to prohibiting and otherwise restricting much interstate commerce, the federal government has limited some *intrastate* commerce. Furthermore, federal officials gather data on intrastate commerce by requiring citizens to fill out forms which the government has no authority to require. To illustrate, assume that you own a small farm in the middle of state X. You can't earn a living off the farm, so you get a job. To supplement your income, you raise hay and sell it to people in your county to feed to their horses. You clear about two thousand dollars a year. You duly report your gross income, expenses, and net income from your hay operation to the Internal Revenue Service. You pay all of your taxes. You get no federal payment of any kind. You get a form in the mail from the federal government which you must either fill out or face criminal penalties. The form has many questions such as how many goats you have and how many acres of sunflowers you planted. The federal government claims that it gets its authority for this form from its regulation of interstate commerce. There is no interstate commerce involved. The word "interstate" has been revised by the federal government to mean "interstate and intrastate."

In addition to revising the meaning the word "interstate," the Court has revised the meaning of the word "commerce." In 1992, in the case of *Chemical Waste Management v. Hunt*, the Court ruled that "the disposal of hazardous waste constitutes an article of commerce, . . ."[206] Paying to dump garbage in a landfill does not constitute commerce—especially when that garbage is hazardous waste. All definitions of "commerce" involve exchanging something of value for something of value. Nobody gives something of value in return for hazardous waste. In fact, people with hazardous waste have to pay to get anybody to accept it.

In *Chemical Waste Management v. Hunt,* the Court ruled that the commerce clause was violated by an Alabama law which: (1) imposed on the operator of each Alabama hazardous waste disposal site a fee of $26.50 per ton for all hazardous waste disposed of at the site, and (2) imposed an additional fee of $72.50 per ton for hazardous waste generated outside of Alabama and disposed of at Alabama hazardous waste disposal sites.

In *Chemical Waste Management,* the lone Court dissenter was Chief Justice William Rehnquist. In his dissent, Rehnquist said:

> "the Court continues to err by its failure to recognize that waste—in this case admittedly *hazardous* waste—presents risks to the public health and environment . . . Under force of this Court's precedent, though, it increasingly appears that the only avenue by which a State may avoid the importation of hazardous wastes is to ban such waste disposal altogether, regardless of the waste's source . . . the Court today gets it exactly backward when it suggests that Alabama is attempting to 'isolate itself from a problem common to several States,' . . . To the contrary, it is the 34 States that have no hazardous waste facility whatsoever, . . . that have isolated themselves [from dealing with the problem of hazardous waste disposal] . . . In sum, the only sure byproduct of today's decision is additional litigation. . . ."[207]

Article I, Section 8, Paragraph 4

> (Congress shall have the power) *To establish an uniform Rule of Naturalization, and uniform Laws on the subject of Bankruptcies throughout the United States;*

Original Meaning in 21st Century Plain English

Congress shall have the power to enact naturalization and bankruptcy laws if, and only if, such laws are uniform throughout the United States.

Discussion of Article I, Section 8, Paragraph 4

There is nothing to link naturalization and bankruptcies except that the framers wanted to emphasize that statutes on naturalization and statutes on bankruptcies were to be *uniform* throughout the United States.

Under the Articles of Confederation, Congress had no power to enact naturalization or bankruptcy laws. The Constitution gives Congress the power to enact federal naturalization and bankruptcy laws if, and only if, such laws *are uniform throughout the United States*.

Naturalization Law and the Louisiana Purchase Treaty

The uniformity of naturalization laws became one of the constitutional problems in 1803 when the Louisiana Purchase Treaty was proposed. Article III of the Louisiana Purchase Treaty made the inhabitants of the vast former French province of Louisiana (about seventeen times larger than the state of Louisiana) citizens of the United States.[208] The naturalization of people under the Louisiana Purchase Treaty was not consistent with the naturalization laws established by Congress; therefore, the U.S. naturalization laws were not uniform. President Thomas Jefferson drafted a 375-word amendment for Congress to propose to the states. It would have removed all doubts about the constitutionality of the Louisiana Purchase Treaty. Historian Jack Rakove wrote that Secretary of State James Madison "helped to still . . . [Jefferson's] overly scrupulous objection by arguing that the treaty clause of the Constitution provided all the authority needed . . ."[209] Madison was right. Jefferson finally recommended to the Senate that it ratify the treaty without an amendment to make it crystal clear to everyone that the treaty was constitutional. There were fears that Napoleon would withdraw the offer, and there were fears that three-fourths of the states would not ratify an amendment such as Jefferson desired. Most senators probably believed that the treaty was vital *and* constitutional. The Senate ratified the treaty on October 20, 1803.

Was the Louisiana Purchase Treaty constitutional or unconstitutional? The Constitution does not explicitly provide for acquiring territory because it was taken for granted by the framers. The framers and ratifiers were quite aware that the United States had acquired land as a result of the Treaty of Paris which officially ended the Revolutionary War. It was fairly obvious that the United States would acquire more land by future treaties. At the Constitutional Convention, George Mason argued that the Senate's power should be reduced; in his argument, Mason stated: "the Senate . . . could already sell the whole Country by means of Treaties."[210] Treaty power included selling and buying land.

Historian Stephen Ambrose stated that on January 12, 1803, President Jefferson requested "an open-ended (up to $9,375,000) appropriation for the purchase of New Orleans."[211] Although the Federalists protested for various reasons, Congress promptly approved the appropriation requested by Jefferson. Jefferson must have thought that it was constitutional for Congress to appropriate money to buy New Orleans. (On January, 18, 1803, Jefferson sent a secret message to Congress in which he requested an appropriation of $2,500 for what became known as the Lewis and Clark Expedition.[212] Congress complied in secret, and that appropriation *was* constitutionally questionable.)

After Congress appropriated money to purchase New Orleans, President Jefferson sent James Monroe to France with instructions to purchase New Orleans. Prior to sending Monroe to France, Jefferson had instructed Robert Livingston, the United States minister in Paris, to "negotiate for a tract of land on the lower Mississippi for use as a port . . ."[213] Monroe and Livingston were "dazed" when Napoleon offered to sell to the United States the entire "Louisiana country."[214] Although "staggered" by Napoleon's proposal, Monroe and Livingston "decided to accept."[215] On April 30, 1803, Monroe and Livingston signed the proposed treaty. Several weeks later, Jefferson was astonished when he first heard about the proposed treaty. On July 4, 1803, the *National Intelligencer,* a Washington D.C. newspaper, reported that Napoleon had sold Louisiana to the United States.[216] It was "stunning news," but the "logical outcome" of the "adoption of the Constitution."[217]

Relevant to the Louisiana Purchase Treaty naturalization issue, the most constitutionally questionable aspect of the treaty, treaties are approved by the Senate, and the Constitution does not require that treaties be consistent with acts of Congress as a whole. Treaties which do not violate the Constitution itself are constitutional. Constitutional treaties supersede prior statutes, and constitutional statutes supersede prior treaties.

One of the amendments to the U.S. Constitution proposed by the minority at the Pennsylvania Ratifying Convention included the provision: "That no treaties which shall be directly opposed to the existing laws of the United States in Congress assembled, shall be valid until such laws shall be repealed or made conformable to such treaty, . . ."[218] That proposed amendment shows that some Americans were alert to the possible by-passing of the House of Representatives, the people's House, to make laws. It is puzzling that the other large states, especially Virginia, did not recommend an amendment at least as strong as the treaty amendment proposed by the minority at the Pennsylvania Ratifying Convention. The North Carolina Ratifying Convention, on August 1, 1788, recommended a treaty amendment which included the words quoted in this paragraph that were first proposed by the minority at the Pennsylvania Ratifying Convention on December 12, 1787. No other state ratifying convention recommended such an amendment.

Bankruptcy Law

Although all federal naturalization laws have probably been constitutional, modern federal bankruptcy laws are definitely unconstitutional because:

- During the eighteenth century, proceedings under bankruptcy statutes could be initiated only by creditors.[219] Prior to 1800: (1) bankruptcy statutes existed in England, but not in the United States or the American colonies; (2) bankruptcy statutes were both civil and criminal in nature; (3) bankruptcy statutes applied only to traders (merchants); and (4) judges could not forgive debts of a debtor without the consent of a majority of the debtor's creditors. Most framers and ratifiers of the unamended Constitution must have associated the word "Bankruptcies" with English bankruptcy statutes and bankruptcy proceedings in England.

• Modern federal bankruptcy law is, in effect, not uniform throughout the United States because it permits state laws to determine how much property bankrupt people are entitled to keep after their debts are discharged in federal bankruptcy courts. (State laws vary widely with respect to the value of property that bankrupt people are allowed to retain. In 1902, the Court made the illogical ruling: "The constitutional requirement that bankruptcy laws be uniform throughout the United States is not violated by the [federal] bankruptcy act . . . because . . . bankrupts are allowed the exemptions prescribed by the state law in force at the time of the filing of the petition in bankruptcy."[220])

• Modern federal bankruptcy statutes violate the right of creditors to trial by jury which is "secured" by the Seventh Amendment and its counterparts in state constitutions. Congress has enacted bankruptcy statutes and created bankruptcy courts with no right to trial by jury despite the fact that almost all claims against persons and corporations that file for bankruptcy are of a kind that could have resulted in suits at common law from 1789 to 1791.

One of the main reasons that the Constitutional Convention was convened was to prevent states from forgiving private debts, postponing private debts, or otherwise making it difficult for creditors to recover the true amount of money owed to them.[221] That is why the Constitution states: "No State shall . . . pass any . . . Law impairing the Obligation of Contracts, . . ." The refusal of many state courts to enforce debt contracts during the 1780s led James Madison and other Americans to demand a federal court system.[222] Framer James Wilson said that the whole Constitution could be justified by two provisions, the provision which prohibited states from impairing the obligation of contracts and the provision which prohibited states from emitting bills of credit.[223]

At the Constitutional Convention, the subject of bankruptcies did not come up until there were less than three weeks remaining. Roger Sherman opposed granting the federal government the power to make bankruptcy laws. Sherman said: "Bankruptcies were in some cases punishable with death by the laws of England, . . ."[224] Despite the opposition of Sherman, the Convention approved a clause which granted Congress the power to establish uniform bankruptcy laws throughout the United States.

In 1787, insolvency laws in some states allowed debtors to get out of jail by turning over all of their property. (However, debts were not discharged in insolvency proceedings unless the value of the property given up by the debtor covered the debt.) The first state in the United States to abolish imprisonment for debt was Kentucky, which did so in 1821. No other state did so until the 1830s. All states did so by 1857, when Massachusetts became the last state to abolish imprisonment for debt.[225]

If the framers meant for Congress to have the power to make national insolvency laws, they would have said so. Just three paragraphs before the paragraph giving Congress the power to make uniform bankruptcy laws, the Constitution gives Congress the "Power To lay and collect Taxes, Duties, Imposts and Excises, . . ." The word "Imposts" in the Constitution is far more redundant than the word "Insolvencies" would have been. The framers obviously intended for states to have the power to enact insolvency laws as long as those laws did not violate the obligation of contracts. Bankruptcy laws, because they can be used to discharge debt contracts without the unanimous consent of creditors, are an example of the type of laws which the Constitution forbids states from making.

The first United States bankruptcy law, enacted in 1800, "applied to 'any merchant, or other person, residing within the United States, actually using the trade of merchandise, by buying or selling in gross, or by retail, or dealing in exchange, or as a banker, broker, factor, underwriter, or marine insurer,' and to involuntary bankruptcy."[226] The 1800 federal bankruptcy statute was "quasi-criminal in nature" and limited to actions by creditors against debtors.[227] The Bankruptcy Act of 1800 allowed unpaid portions of debt to be nullified if two-thirds or more of the debtor's creditors, *in number and value*, agreed.[228] It was repealed by Congress in 1803. The second national bankruptcy act was enacted by Congress in 1841 and repealed in 1843.

When national bankruptcy laws were not in place, state laws were used. Some state laws provided for the discharge of debt contracts with the consent of only two-thirds or three-quarters of the creditors. Those laws were sometimes challenged in court because they violated the Constitution's prohibition on state laws which impaired the obligation of contracts. One such case was M'Millan v. M'Neill [229], in which the Court correctly ruled in 1819: "A state bankrupt or insolvent law which not only liberates the person of the debtor, but discharges him from all liability for the debt, so far as it attempts to discharge the contract, is repugnant to the constitution of the United States, and it makes no difference in the application of this principle whether the law was passed before or after the debt was contracted." The Court unconstitutionally overruled M'Millan in 1827 in when it ruled: "A bankrupt or insolvent law of any state, which discharges both the person and the debtor, and his future acquisitions of property, is not 'a law impairing the obligation of contracts,' so far as respects debts contracted subsequent to the passage of such law."[230] When the framers used the word "contracts," they meant agreements between two or more people which obligate the people to do something or to refrain from doing something. This is the fundamental nature of a contract. The state law ruled constitutional in 1827 clearly impaired the obligation of contracts.

Hard times have a tendency to facilitate unconstitutional laws. The "Panic of 1819" was followed by a severe depression.[231] James Buchanan later said in the Senate: "The years 1819, 1820, and 1821 were the most disastrous which the country had ever experienced since the adoption of the Federal Constitution. Not only merchants and speculators were then involved, but the rage for speculation had extended to the farmers and mechanics throughout the country and had rendered vast numbers of them insolvent."[232]

In 1820, according to noted historian Charles Warren, "for the first time in the history of the world, [bankruptcy] legislation was proposed [in Congress] to benefit debtors at large, instead of merely to enable creditors to reach the property of merchants and traders. The contest was initiated by . . . a motion to amend . . . [a bankruptcy] bill by providing that any person imprisoned for debt might voluntarily file a petition to be adjudged bankrupt. This was an entirely unheard of and novel proposal; . . ."[233]

Despite the fact that the economy in the United States was in a severe depression during the early 1820s, no bankruptcy bill was passed by Congress for the following reasons:

- Many members of Congress correctly maintained that it was unconstitutional for Congress to enact a general insolvency law for the United States. (The "bankruptcy" bills introduced in Congress in the 1820s would have allowed either all imprisoned debtors or all debtors to petition for bankruptcy. Those bills were, in reality, insolvency bills.)

- Some members of Congress believed that it was immoral to impair the obligation of contracts.

- The proposed "bankruptcy" laws would have required all debtors who petitioned for bankruptcy to turn over their real estate. Freeholds and homesteads were protected from creditors by a few state insolvency laws. Therefore, some members of Congress wanted an exemption for some real estate.

Congress was able to get a second national bankruptcy law passed in 1841 by resorting to a great deal of political bargaining. After Congress passed the Bankruptcy Act of 1841, many states enacted laws which exempted various amounts of homesteads and other property from being taken from debtors in bankruptcy proceedings.[234] Those laws were unconstitutional because they impaired the obligation of contracts.

The third national bankruptcy law was passed in 1867. In order to "appease the debtors," the advocates of this law accepted, "with grave misgivings as to its constitutionality," all state exemptions of debtor property in bankruptcy proceedings.[235] Later national bankruptcy acts also allowed state laws to define exemptions. Therefore, bankruptcy laws enacted for individuals since 1867 have not been uniform "throughout the United States." The amount exempted from bankruptcy proceedings in some states became more than ten times the amount exempted in other states.[236]

In 1902, the Court ruled that, *despite the uniformity requirement* in the Constitution for bankruptcy legislation, it was constitutional for a federal bankruptcy law to allow each state to determine how much property people who reside therein are entitled to retain after their debts are eliminated by a federal bankruptcy court judge.[237] [238] As a result, the value of property that debtors could keep in bankruptcy proceedings varied enormously during the twentieth century in the United States. In some states, debtors could pay their bankruptcy lawyers handsome fees, have their debts erased by judges, and leave bankruptcy court as millionaires, even though they entered bankruptcy court with more debts than assets. People with large assets who could see bankruptcy looming on the horizon could move to a state where they would be able to retain more property after a bankruptcy judge distributed their nonexempt property.

Thomas Jefferson, in his book *Notes on the State of Virginia*, first published in 1785, included a section on the laws of Virginia. Jefferson discussed only those laws which were different from the laws of England. The first Virginia law Jefferson discussed was its insolvency law, about which he wrote: "Debtors unable to pay their debts, and making faithful delivery of their whole effects, are released from confinement, and their persons are for ever discharged from restraint for such previous debts: but any property they may afterwards acquire will be subject to their creditors."[239] In England and in some states in the United States, debtors remained in prison even after they surrendered all of their property to their creditors. Jefferson was rightly proud of Virginia's insolvency law. It was a step towards the elimination of debtors' prisons, and creditors retained some hope of eventually being paid.

The harshness of debtor law in the United States during the eighteenth century is perhaps best illustrated by the fact that two framers, James Wilson and Robert Morris, were jailed for debt during the 1790s. Wilson was one of the principal framers. According to noted historian Clinton Rossiter, Wilson was second in importance only to James Madison at the Constitutional Convention.[240] Wilson was jailed for debt in North Carolina while he was a United States Supreme Court justice, and it was with great difficulty that Justice Wilson gained his release from jail.[241] Wilson had gone to North Carolina to avoid imprisonment for debt in Pennsylvania.[242]

Robert Morris was a merchant and land speculator who served effectively in the very important position of Superintendent of Continental Finance during the Revolutionary War. Historian Jack Rakove wrote that demands of the hectic early days of the Revolutionary War "placed a severe strain on members [of Congress] who enjoyed their colleagues' confidence and found themselves elected to numerous committees. Men like Silas Deane, John Adams, and Robert Morris would attend committee meetings in the early morning, sit in Congress much of the day, and return to committee sessions in the evening, sometimes working there until midnight."[243] Robert Morris served as a U.S. senator from Pennsylvania from 1789 to 1795 and was one of two men who signed the Declaration of Independence, the Articles of Confederation, and the U.S. Constitution. Morris spent three and one-half years in debtors' prison in Pennsylvania and was fortunate to be released from prison because at least one of his creditors employed the Bankruptcy Act of 1800.[244] [245] Morris was imprisoned from February 16, 1798, to August 31, 1801.[246] Although Morris' debts were not discharged, he was released from jail by a federal judge when he turned over all of his property, except the clothes on his back, to the court/bankruptcy commission. Morris was, in his own words, "a free Citizen . . . without one cent."[247] Morris, once a very rich man, spent his last few years in a small house in Philadelphia. The house was paid for by one of Morris' former business associates, framer Gouverneur Morris (no relation), and put in the name of Robert Morris' wife to shield it from creditors. Morris was three million dollars in debt when he died in 1806.

Robert Morris was highly thought of by leaders of both political parties—even after he was jailed for debt. George Washington, a Federalist party leader, visited and dined with Morris in debtors' prison on November 27, 1798.[248] Washington was deeply appreciative of

Morris' strong efforts in support of the Revolutionary War. Morris and Washington were in agreement that it was necessary and proper for the United States to have federally-chartered banks which emitted bank notes which were readily convertible to gold and silver.

President Thomas Jefferson, leader of the Democratic-Republican party, would have liked Robert Morris to be secretary of the navy if Morris could regain the public's confidence. On March 12, 1801, President Jefferson wrote a note to Secretary of State James Madison which said: "What a misfortune to the public that R. Morris has fallen from his height of character. If he could get from confinement, and the public give him confidence, he would be a most valuable officer in that station [secretary of the navy] and in our council. But these are two impossibilities in the way."[249] One impossibility was eliminated when Morris was fortunate to be released from prison less than five months later, but Morris could not regain the confidence of the commercial community or the public. Morris probably would have made an excellent secretary of the navy with his privateering experience, his knowledge of commerce, and his desire to regain at least a portion of his good name. It is a credit to Jefferson that he saw through his rhetoric against banks and bank notes to even think about Morris for a prominent position in his administration.

Given the severe eighteenth-century debtor law, the eighteenth-century meaning of bankruptcy, and the prohibition of state interference with the obligation of contracts, the ratifiers certainly did not understand that Congress would have the power to make laws which: (1) allowed debtors to voluntarily declare themselves bankrupt; (2) allowed federal judges (or federal trustees or whatever) to nullify or postpone debts without the concurrence of most creditors (in number and in value); or (3) allowed each state to determine how much property its residents are entitled to retain after debts are nullified in bankruptcy proceedings.

During the eighteenth century in Britain, creditors of debtor merchants had their choice of (1) filing suits at common law against debtor merchants, or (2) initiating bankruptcy proceedings against debtor merchants. Debtor merchants could not, by themselves, deny creditors their right to sue at common law. In the United States, the right to a jury trial in suits at common law is "guaranteed" by the Seventh Amendment and its counterparts in state constitutions. Nevertheless, the U.S. Supreme Court has, in effect, ruled that modern federal bankruptcy law prevents creditors from exercising their constitutional right to trial by jury after a debtor files for bankruptcy.[250]

The book *America: What Went Wrong?* documents the "explosion" of corporate bankruptcies as a result of the revision of U.S. Bankruptcy Code in 1978. That law made it easier for companies to stay in business while they attempted to solve their problems. It resulted in an enormous amount of money ending up in the pockets of lawyers instead of being returned to creditors. Bankruptcies are quite lucrative for lawyers.

In 1992, *Time* magazine discussed a *Yale Law Journal* article which suggested that Chapter 11 type bankruptcies should be abolished. Of the 326 companies studied which filed Chapter 11 bankruptcy petitions between 1964 and 1989, only 20 percent managed to emerge successfully, and bondholders *lost an average of 67 percent more of their investments* when companies failed under Chapter 11 than when companies failed under prior law.[251] The Court ruled in 1987 that secured creditors are not even entitled to interest payments on their loans from the time that companies have asked for protection from creditors under Chapter 11 of the U.S. Bankruptcy Code to the time that bankruptcy judges approve reorganization plans. When creditors (banks, insurance companies, etc.) suffer losses, many Americans receive less interest and dividends. Hence, Chapter 11 bankruptcy lawyers are effectively paid, in large part, by the general public.

In addition to making a great deal of money in corporate bankruptcies, lawyers make a great deal of money in individual bankruptcies. And they do not want paralegals to have any bankruptcy business. Some paralegals handle individual bankruptcy cases, and they charge much lower fees than lawyers charge. In an article titled "Paralegals Behind Bars," *The Legal Reformer* reported that a paralegal in Tennessee named Clarence Graham was in jail for doing bankruptcy and other simple legal services.[252]

During the eighteenth century, many Americans were put in jail because they owed money to creditors. No American was put in jail for taking business away from lawyers. During the twentieth century no Americans were put in jail because they owed money to creditors. However, some Americans were put in jail because they took business away from lawyers.

Article I, Section 8, Paragraph 5

(Congress shall have the power) *To coin Money, regulate the Value thereof, and of foreign Coin, and fix the Standard of Weights and Measures;*

Original Meaning in 21st Century Plain English

Congress shall have the power to (1) authorize gold and silver coins to be minted and used as money, (2) regulate the value of coins issued by Congress, (3) regulate the value, in the United States, of coins issued by foreign governments, and (4) fix standards of weights and measures.

Discussion of Article I, Section 8, Paragraph 5

The only explicit monetary power granted to Congress by the Constitution is that of issuing coins and regulating the value of coins in the United States. Nevertheless, Congress, under the Constitution, has:

- Chartered banks
- Issued bills of credit (Bills of credit can be defined as paper money that is *not* readily convertible at face value into gold or silver coins. The terms "paper money" and "bills of credit" were used interchangeably by the framers and ratifiers.)
  - Made bills of credit legal tender (Creditors are required to accept bills of credit in payment of debts.)

Was it constitutional for Congress to charter banks, issue bills of credit, and make bills of credit legal tender? From George Washington's administration to Franklin D. Roosevelt's administration, few things were debated more intensely than Congress' power over currency.[253]

Federal Bank Charters

During the Constitutional Convention, James Madison made a motion that Congress be given the power "to grant charters of incorporation where the interest of the U. S. might require & the legislative provisions of individual States may be incompetent."[254] Such charters were understood by the framers to include one or more bank charters. Rufus King "thought the power unnecessary."[255] James Wilson replied: "It is necessary to prevent a *State* from obstructing the *general* welfare."[256] Wilson knew from experience that one or more federal bank charters would be necessary for the prosperity of the United States. King replied: "In Philadelphia & New York, it [the power to grant charters of incorporation] will be . . . [identified with] the establishment of a Bank, which has been a subject of contention in those Cities. In other places it will be . . . [identified with] mercantile monopolies." In *Banks and Politics in America from the Revolution to the Civil War*, Bray Hammond maintained that:

- A majority of the delegates to the Constitutional Convention would have voted to grant Congress the power to grant bank charters if bank charters were not controversial. Many of those delegates did not want to jeopardize getting the Constitution ratified by explicitly authorizing federal charters of incorporation.

- Some delegates who would have voted to give Congress the power to grant bank charters did not want to take the chance of having *a vote on the record against such charters*. With no vote on the record, it would be at least plausible to later declare that Congress had the power to charter banks.[257]

George Mason moved to modify Madison's motion to grant federal charters of incorporation "to the single case of Canals." In this form, the motion was defeated eight states to three. The Convention did *not* vote on the power of granting bank charters or general charters.

Based only on the notes taken at the Convention by Madison, most people would probably conclude that the federal government has no power to charter banks. However, many people would come to the opposite conclusion based upon:

- The fact that Congress, under the Articles of Confederation, established the Bank of North America despite the fact that the Confederation Congress had no explicit power to establish a corporation or a bank (The states made no attempt to have the federal bank charter revoked.)

- The fact that some constitutional amendments suggested by state ratifying conventions proposed to restrain Congress from establishing commercial corporations (Those amendment recommendations imply that some ratifiers thought that Congress under the Constitution would continue to have the unwritten power to charter commercial corporations.[258])

- The fact that the Constitution does not explicitly prohibit Congress from granting charters

- The fact that the Convention did not vote on general charters or bank charters

- James Wilson's statement at the Convention to the effect that a congressional power to grant charters "is necessary to prevent *a State* from obstructing the *general* welfare" (when combined with the "necessary and proper" clause and the "general Welfare" clause)

The Bank of North America, considered by historian Bray Hammond to be "the first real bank, in the modern sense, on the North American continent"[259]:

- Was proposed by Superintendent of Finance Robert Morris and approved by Congress as "a national bank" on May 26, 1781 (Congress resolved to promote and support the bank.)[260]

- Was incorporated by an ordinance of Congress on December 31, 1781[261]

- Began operating as a bank during the first half of January 1782, with the United States owning more than sixty percent of the shares (The government sold its shares as it needed money; 100 percent of the bank was privately owned in a short time.)[262]

- Was quickly supported by some states and other states did not oppose the bank (Before the end of January 1782, Connecticut made the bank's notes acceptable in payment of state taxes, Rhode Island made it a crime to counterfeit the bank's notes, and both Massachusetts and New York granted charters of incorporation under which the bank had a monopoly in those two states for the duration of the Revolutionary War.[263])

- Was granted a charter of incorporation by Pennsylvania (identical to the one granted by Congress) on April 1, 1782 (Some members of Congress, including James Madison, considered the charter of incorporation granted by Congress in 1781 to be unconstitutional. The New York and the Massachusetts state legislatures agreed with Madison.)[264]

- Was an outstanding institution which quickly operated more like a commercial bank than a national bank (The bank was chartered until 1929 when it was absorbed in a merger.)[265]

- Was well known to all framers, and most ratifiers were quite aware of it[266]

Despite the fact that the Bank of North America was useful to the United States government and the business community, some representatives of the farming community tried to put the bank out of business in 1785. They almost succeeded when the Pennsylvania legislature repealed the bank's Pennsylvania charter.[267] (That is almost certainly what Wilson had in mind at the Convention when he said that federal bank charters were "necessary to prevent a *State* from obstructing the *general* welfare.") A war of words over the Pennsylvania charter took place. It was "the gentlemen from the city" (including strong support from Robert Morris and James Wilson) versus "the gentlemen from the country."[268] The most effective participant in the bitter controversy was Thomas Paine, the common man with an uncommon ability to write and influence people. Paine had written two influential pamphlets in 1776 (*Commonsense*, a famous plea for American independence, and *The Crisis*, written during the darkest days of the Revolution, which includes the words: "These are the times that try men's souls, . . . The summer soldier and the sunshine patriot will, in this crisis, shrink from the service of his country; . . ."). In *Dissertations*, Paine declared that the Bank of North America was produced:

> "by the distresses of the times and the enterprising spirit of patriotic individuals, . . . Those individuals furnished and risked the money [by this time, all money at risk was private], and the aid which the government contributed was that of incorporating them [thus protecting the stockholders from additional liability and debtors' prison if the bank failed] . . . The war being now ended and the bank having rendered the service expected, or rather hoped for from it, the principal public use of it at this time is for the promotion and extension of commerce. The whole community derives benefit from the operation of the bank. It facilitates the commerce of the country. It quickens the means of purchasing and paying for country produce and hastens the exportation of it. The emolument, therefore, being to the community, it is the office and duty of government to give protection to the bank. . . . [In their condemnation of foreign investment in the bank's stock, enemies of the bank] must have forgotten which side of the Atlantic they were on, . . . The farmer will not take . . .

[paper money which is not readily converted to its face value in gold and silver] for produce, and he is right in refusing it. . . . [In contrast to inconvertible paper money,] bank notes . . . are promissory notes payable on demand and may be taken to the bank and exchanged for gold or silver without the least ceremony or difficulty."[269]

Most ratifiers *probably* assumed that Congress under the Constitution would have the power to establish a bank, considering that:

- Congress, under the Articles of Confederation, had established a bank (the Bank of North America) without the explicit authority to do so.
- Congress, under the Constitution, would have the key additional power to "lay and collect Taxes, Duties, Imposts and Excises." The Bank of the United States, established by Congress in 1791, was an important aid in collecting federal taxes.[270]
- Congress, under the Constitution, would have the "necessary and proper" clause to help justify establishing a bank.
- In 1791, Congress established the Bank of the United States. The Senate, in an unrecorded vote, passed a bill incorporating the bank on January 20, 1791, and the House passed the bill by a wide margin, 39 to 20, on February 8, 1791, after heated debates in which James Madison led the fight against the bill.[271]

I am aware of no evidence that any framer discussed national bank charters with ratifiers. During ratification, the framers seemed to go out of their way to avoid the subject of federal bank charters. Putting all of this together, it was *probably* constitutional for the United States to charter a national bank because a majority of the ratifiers *probably* assumed that the United States would have the power to charter a national bank. However, there is enough uncertainty that the Court could legitimately rule that the United States has no authority to charter a bank.

Bills of Credit

Was it constitutional for Congress to issue bills of credit? During the Constitutional Convention, the draft constitution put together by the Committee of Detail included the provision: "The Legislature of the United States shall have the power to . . . borrow money, and emit bills on the credit of the United States."[272] That provision was similar to a provision in the Articles of Confederation. At the Constitutional Convention on August 16, Gouverneur Morris made a motion to strike out "and emit bills on the credit of the U. States."[273] After a most interesting debate, the Convention voted nine states to two to strike the phrase. In so doing, did the Convention mean to prohibit Congress from emitting bills of credit? To answer this question, the statements of the delegates must be examined.

In support of his motion, Gouverneur Morris said:

- Bills of credit (paper money which is *not* readily convertible to its face value in gold or silver coins) would be (1) unnecessary if the credit of the United States was good, and (2) unjust if the credit of the United States was not good.

- "Striking out the words ['and emit bills of credit on the U. States'] will leave room still for notes of a *responsible* minister which will do all the good without the mischief." (Morris' phrase "notes of a *responsible* minister" probably referred to (1) interest-bearing treasury notes, and (2) convertible notes such as those which had been emitted by the Bank of North America under the authority of Congress and the guidance of Superintendent of Finance Robert Morris.)

- Wealthy Americans would oppose ratification of the Constitution "if paper emissions be not prohibited." (By "paper emissions," Morris meant "bills of credit.")

Morris intended for his motion to prohibit federal bills of credit. James Madison, the first delegate to discuss Morris' motion, clearly understood that Morris' motion, if adopted, would preclude Congress from emitting bills of credit. (Madison's remarks are included in the discussion of "legal tender" which follows this discussion of "bills of credit.")

Nathaniel Gorham "was for striking out ['and emit bills of credit on the U. States'], without inserting any prohibition. If the words stand they may suggest and lead to the measure."[274] After George Mason indicated that he understood that Morris' motion for striking out was equivalent to a prohibition—and dangerous in wartime—Gorham showed that he belatedly grasped the intent of Morris' motion by saying: "The power [of the Congress to obtain money for military expenditures] as far as it will be necessary or safe, is involved in that of borrowing."[275] Gorham's "without inserting any prohibition" remark suggests that he initially understood that Morris' motion would not prohibit Congress from emitting bills of credit. However, Gorham's later "borrowing" statement indicates that he understood that Morris' motion would prohibit Congress from emitting bills of credit.

George Mason said that he thought that Congress "would not have the power [to emit bills of credit] unless it were expressed." Mason, in arguing against Morris' motion, "observed that the late war could not have been carried on, had such a prohibition existed."[276]

John Mercer said that he "was a friend to paper money, though in the present state & temper of America," he would neither propose nor approve of it. However, he maintained that Morris' motion "will stamp suspicion on the Government to deny it discretion on this point. . . . The people of property would be sure to be on the side of the . . . [proposed Constitution], and it was impolitic to purchase their further attachment with the loss of the opposite class of Citizens."[277] Mercer clearly believed that Morris' motion would prohibit Congress from emitting bills of credit.

Oliver Ellsworth "thought this a favorable moment to shut and bar the door against paper money. . . . By withholding the power from the new Government, more friends of influence would be gained to it than by almost any thing else. Paper money can in no case be necessary. . . ."[278] Ellsworth clearly understood that Morris' motion would prohibit Congress from emitting bills of credit.

Edmund Randolph, despite his "antipathy to paper money, could not agree to strike out the words, as he could not foresee all the occasions which might arise." Obviously, Randolph understood that the motion, if adopted, would preclude Congress from emitting bills of credit.

Pierce Butler, who had seconded Morris' motion, "remarked that paper was a legal tender in no Country in Europe. He was urgent for disarming the Government of such a power." Butler wanted to prohibit paper money to preclude it from being made legal tender. John Langdon said that he would "rather reject the whole plan than retain the three words 'and emit bills.'"[279]

The framers that did not understand the ramifications of Morris' motion at the beginning of the debate understood the consequences of the motion by the time the vote was taken. The fact that Congress, under the Constitution, did not even consider issuing bills of credit until the War of 1812 is a further indication that the framers intended for bills of credit to be prohibited. Congress did not emit bills of credit until 1815, and Congress retired those bills soon after the War of 1812 ended.[280]

Although the framers intended for the Constitution to prohibit bills of credit, it is not certain that most ratifiers had the same understanding. There is nothing explicit in *The Federalist* that says Congress could not emit bills of credit. James Madison and Alexander Hamilton probably agreed with John Mercer that it would be "impolitic" to explicitly state it. Furthermore, the Constitution (1) explicitly prohibits the states from issuing bills of credit, and (2) does not explicitly prohibit the federal government from issuing bills of credit.

Legal Tender

Now we come to the question of whether the United States has the power to make bills of credit legal tender. During the debate in the Convention over whether the federal government should have the authority to emit bills of credit, James Madison said: "will it not be sufficient to prohibit the making them (federal bills of credit) a *tender*? This will remove the temptation to emit them with unjust views. And promissory notes in that shape may in some emergencies be best."[281]

Although initially opposed to Morris' motion to prohibit Congress from emitting bills of credit, Madison ended up voting for Morris' motion. Madison made a note in his journal to explain his switch. Madison said that he "acquiesced" to Morris' motion when he "became satisfied that striking out the words would not disable the Government from the use of public notes as far as they could be safe and proper; and would only cut off the pretext for a paper currency and particularly for making the bills a tender either for public or private debts."[282]

Although the vote of the Convention to prohibit bills of credit necessarily prevented bills of credit being declared legal tender, it is interesting that Madison and Butler were much more against making bills of credit a legal tender than they were against bills of credit.

The Court ruled in 1870, in *Hepburn v. Griswold*, that, although Congress had the "undisputed power" to emit bills of credit, in the interests of the "letter and spirit" of the Constitution, Congress could not make bills of credit legal tender if it impaired the value of private debts which existed prior to the law.[283] With respect to Congress' power to emit bills of credit, *Hepburn* was within the bounds of *ratifier* understanding. With respect to Congress' power to make bills of credit legal tender, the Court in *Hepburn* should have ruled that Congress had no authority to make bills of credit legal tender in any private contracts.

The Court went farther down the unconstitutional road in 1871 when it ruled that Congress could make bills of credit legal tender.[284] However, the Court ruled in 1872 that agreements requiring payment in silver and/or gold coin could not be satisfied by bills of credit.[285] For many years thereafter, almost all long-term private debt contracts specified repayment in gold coin made of high quality gold.[286] That practice ended in 1935 when the Court, in a 5-4 vote, sustained a 1933 joint resolution of Congress to the effect that it "was against public policy" to have gold clauses in private contracts and such clauses were void.[287]

Article I, Section 8, Paragraph 6

(Congress shall have the power) *To provide for the Punishment of counterfeiting the Securities and current Coin of the United States;*

Original Meaning in 21st Century Plain English

Congress shall have the power to make laws which specify the punishment (capital punishment, jail time, corporal punishment, fine, etc.) to be imposed on people who are convicted of counterfeiting United States securities (bonds, notes, etc.) or coins.

Article I, Section 8, Paragraph 7

(Congress shall have the power) *To establish Post Offices and post Roads;*

Original Meaning in 21st Century Plain English

Congress shall have the power to establish post offices and roads to be used to transport mail between post offices.

Discussion of Article I, Section 8, Paragraph 7

Does this clause: (1) merely empower Congress to designate existing buildings as post offices and existing roads as post roads (and pay for the use/maintenance of these buildings and roads); or (2) empower Congress to build new post offices and post roads (in addition to the power to designate existing buildings and roads as post offices and post roads)? This question was debated in and out of Congress for many years after the Constitution was ratified.[288]

In 1792, Congress worked on a bill to organize the post office. Under the bill, proprietors of stage coaches were to be paid to carry mail. A provision of the bill would have authorized proprietors of mail-carrying stage coaches to also carry passengers. That provision was attacked as unconstitutional and defeated.[289] The early Congresses were far more concerned about constitutionality than are modern Congresses.

Article I, Section 8, Paragraph 8

(Congress shall have the power) *To promote the Progress of Science and useful Arts, by securing for limited Times to Authors and Inventors the exclusive Right to their respective Writings and Discoveries;*

Original Meaning in 21st Century Plain English

Congress shall have the power to encourage the progress of science and useful arts by passing copyright and patent laws.

Article I, Section 8, Paragraph 9

(Congress shall have the power) *To constitute Tribunals inferior to the supreme Court;*

Original Meaning in 21st Century Plain English

Congress shall have the power to create federal courts and authorize state courts to try federal cases. The rulings of courts constituted by Congress shall be appealable to the United States Supreme Court unless Congress reduces the appellate jurisdiction of the Supreme Court.

Discussion of Article I, Section 8, Paragraph 9

The word "inferior" in this provision implies that the Supreme Court would have appellate jurisdiction over all rulings made by "inferior" courts. That is not the case, as is clear from reading Article III of the Constitution and the Judiciary Act of 1789. Relevant to Congress' power to constitute "inferior" courts, Alexander Hamilton said in *The Federalist*, No. 81:

> "The power of constituting inferior courts is evidently calculated to obviate the necessity of having recourse to the Supreme Court in every case of federal cognizance. It is intended to enable the national government to institute or *authorize*, in each State or district of the United States, a tribunal competent to the determination of matters of national jurisdiction within its limits. . . . the Supreme Court would have nothing more than an appellate jurisdiction 'with such *exceptions* and under such *regulations* as the Congress shall make.'"[290]

There have been many cases heard in "inferior" federal courts for which the Supreme Court has had no appellate jurisdiction. The Judiciary Act of 1789 made no provision for defendants in criminal cases to appeal verdicts to the Supreme Court. The dollar-in-controversy threshold of the Judiciary Act of 1789 prevented many civil cases from being appealed to the Court. In many civil and criminal cases, "inferior" federal courts have not been inferior to the Supreme Court. There are still many federal cases which cannot be appealed to the Court because: (1) the amount of money in controversy does not meet thresholds set by statute; or (2) the matter is heard in a special court (such as a bankruptcy court or a military court).

In 1788, a majority of the American electorate probably thought that Congress, under the Constitution, would authorize state supreme courts to try most federal cases.[291] In 1789, Senator Richard Henry Lee led an effort to authorize state supreme courts to hear most federal cases. The only federal courts would have been the Supreme Court and a few admiralty courts to hear maritime cases.[292] The Judiciary Act of 1789 created many courts which heard only federal cases. However, Lee did not lose completely. The trial of cases "arising under this Constitution, the Laws of the United States, and Treaties" was given to state courts.[293]

Article I, Section 8, Paragraph 10

> (Congress shall have the power) *To define and punish Piracies and Felonies committed on the high Seas, and Offences against the Law of Nations;*

Original Meaning in 21st Century Plain English

Congress shall have the power to enact laws which define (1) piracies, (2) felonies committed on the high seas, and (3) offenses against the law of nations. Congress shall also have the power to enact laws which specify the punishments for persons convicted of (1) piracies, (2) felonies committed on the high seas, and (3) offenses against the law of nations.

Article I, Section 8, Paragraph 11

> (Congress shall have the power) *To declare War, grant Letters of Marque and Reprisal, and make Rules concerning Captures on Land and Water;*

Original Meaning in 21st Century Plain English

Congress shall have the power to declare war. In time of war, Congress shall have the power to issue letters of marque to commission the owners of specified vessels to use those vessels to attack and capture enemy vessels and goods on the high seas. In time of peace, Congress shall have the power to issue letters of marque and reprisal to commission the owners of specified vessels to use those vessels to capture the ships and goods of nations which have wronged the United States or its citizens. Congress shall have the power to make laws concerning the capture of goods on land and the capture of vessels and goods on water.

Discussion of Article I, Section 8, Paragraph 11

Privateers are armed private vessels commissioned by a government to search for and capture vessels—usually commercial vessels—of specified nations. If you are a crew member of a privateer, and the privateer you are on is captured, you cannot be legally executed as a pirate if you or one of your fellow crew members can produce the appropriate letter of marque or a letter of marque and reprisal. An admiralty court cannot award a captured ship or cargo to the owners and crewmen of the vessel which made the capture unless the vessel which made the capture was properly commissioned as a privateer.

The United States used privateers extensively during the Revolutionary War and the War of 1812. Privateers were also commissioned by the U.S. when the U.S. was not at war—if a nation had wronged an American vessel, its crew, or cargo, and justice could not be obtained in any manner other than capturing the goods of offending nations. The U.S. could not wage a war over every incident. On the other hand, to sit idly by was to invite more wrongdoing by the offending nations. Letters of marque and reprisal were used to (1) retaliate for wrongs done to U.S. commercial vessels during peacetime, and (2) deter future wrongs. The "Law of Nations" allowed letters of marque and reprisal to be granted whenever citizens of one nation were oppressed and injured by another nation—and justice was denied.[294]

Privateering was abolished by the 1856 Declaration of Paris, but the United States, Mexico, Spain, and Venezuela did not concur.[295] The United States cannot constitutionally ratify a treaty abolishing privateering until the Constitution is amended to authorize Congress to give up the power to grant letters of marque and reprisal. A treaty *cannot* override the Constitution.

Article I, Section 8, Paragraph 12

(Congress shall have the power) *To raise and support Armies, but no Appropriation of Money to that Use shall be for a longer Term than two Years;*

Original Meaning in 21st Century Plain English

Congress shall have the power to raise and support armies, but no money shall be authorized by Congress to be used to raise and support armies more than two years in advance of when the money is to be spent.

Discussion of Article I, Section 8, Paragraph 12

At the Constitutional Convention, James Madison said: "as armies in time of peace are allowed on all hands to be an evil, it is well to discountenance them in the Constitution, . . ."[296] The Convention indirectly disapproves of armies in time of peace by the appropriation restriction under discussion. There is no other time limit on appropriations in the Constitution.

Most U.S. citizens from 1784 to 1800 were in favor of maintaining small garrisons of federal troops near the frontier to deter and deal with Indian attacks. However, there was not widespread support for the "provisional army" authorized by Congress in 1798. President Adams formed a "provisional army," although not as large as authorized by Congress. During the 1800 presidential campaign, Thomas Jefferson pledged to disband the U.S. "provisional army" and oppose an army until the United States was invaded.[297]

Many U.S. citizens from 1784 to 1800 were opposed to standing armies because:

• British soldiers restricted the liberties of American colonists during the decade prior to the Revolutionary War. Colonists complained bitterly about standing armies from the standpoints of (1) restriction of liberties, and (2) taxes imposed on colonists to house and feed British troops. The Declaration of Independence states: "[King George III] has kept among us, in times of peace, Standing Armies without the Consent of our legislature."

• Taxes promised to be high to support a U.S. standing army.

• Most American voters in the 1780s gave too much credit to the militia for the victory in the Revolutionary War.

• Many Englishmen had hated Oliver Cromwell's standing army during the 1650s.[298]

- The English Bill of Rights includes the provision: "That the raising or keeping a Standing Army within the Kingdom in Time of Peace unless it be with the Consent of Parliament is against Law."[299]

- The English militia had held their own against the standing armies of the King of Spain—leading Englishmen to believe that the militia was the best security for their liberties and their country.[300]

The United States may have any number of "Armies," but only one "Navy." The framers probably thought that only one navy would be needed because privateers would always augment the U.S. Navy. The modern U.S. Navy gets around the one-navy limit by having "fleets" and "task forces."

Article I, Section 8, Paragraph 13

(Congress shall have the power) *To provide and maintain a Navy;*

Original Meaning in 21st Century Plain English

Congress shall have the power to raise and maintain a navy and provide them with ships of war.

Article I, Section 8, Paragraph 14

(Congress shall have the power) *To make Rules for the Government and Regulation of the land and naval Forces;*

Original Meaning in 21st Century Plain English

Congress shall have the power to make rules for civilian federal employees and regulations for members of the U.S. military forces.

Where conflict exists between rules and regulations made by Congress and rules and regulations made by the executive branch for civilian and military personnel, the rules and regulations made by Congress shall prevail.

Article I, Section 8, Paragraph 15

(Congress shall have the power) *To provide for calling forth the Militia to execute the Laws of the Union, suppress Insurrections and repel Invasions;*

Original Meaning in 21st Century Plain English

Congress shall have the power to activate the militia to (1) enforce federal laws, (2) suppress insurrections, and (3) repel invasions.

Discussion of Article I, Section 8, Paragraph 15

George Washington did not have a merry Christmas in 1786. In a letter he wrote on December 26, 1786, Washington said: "I feel . . . infinitely more than I can express . . . for the disorders which have arisen, . . . Good God! Who besides a tory could have foreseen, or a Briton have predicted them!"[301]

On December 26, 1786, Shays' Rebellion was ongoing. More than anything else, it was Shays' Rebellion which persuaded Washington to attend the Constitutional Convention.[302] Noted historian Clinton Rossiter stated that Shays' Rebellion was "so frightening that it provided all the push that was still needed to get the right men to Philadelphia in the right frame of mind."[303]

Although Shays' Rebellion was the major disorder during the three-year period from 1785 to 1787, debt-based rural disorders had also occurred in Maryland, New Hampshire, New Jersey, Pennsylvania, South Carolina, and Virginia.[304] On February 21, 1787, with Shays' Rebellion still going on, Congress called for the Constitutional Convention. On October 24, 1787, James Madison wrote a letter to Thomas Jefferson (who represented the U.S. in France from 1784 to 1789), in which Madison said: "the evils issuing from . . . [debtor pressure] contributed more to the uneasiness which produced the convention" than Congress' lack of power to tax and regulate trade.[305]

The Constitutional Convention's solution for dealing with insurrections of poor farmers, and possible slave uprisings, was to give Congress the power to utilize the militia. This was a good solution because the militia was popular at that time, and there were no funds to keep a standing army. Furthermore, a standing army would have been unpopular in 1787. In *The Federalist*, No. 29, Alexander Hamilton wrote: "In times of insurrection, . . . it would be natural and proper that the militia of a neighboring State should be marched into another . . . to guard against the violence of faction or sedition. . . ."[306]

It also made sense to empower Congress to activate the militia to enforce laws, particularly tax laws relevant to imported goods.

Article I, Section 8, Paragraph 16

(Congress shall have the power) *To provide for organizing, arming, and disciplining, the Militia, and for governing such Part of them as may be employed in the Service of the United States, reserving to the States respectively, the Appointment of the Officers, and the Authority of training the Militia according to the discipline prescribed by Congress;*

Original Meaning in 21st Century Plain English

Congress shall have the power to specify how the militia will be organized, armed, and disciplined. Congress shall have the power to govern that part of the militia that Congress activates to serve the United States. Each state shall have (1) the power to appoint officers of militia units from their state, and (2) the authority of training the militia according to the discipline prescribed by Congress.

Discussion of Article I, Section 8, Paragraph 16

On August 23, 1787, the Constitutional Convention debated a provision suggested by the "Committee of Eleven" to give Congress the power "To make laws for organizing, arming & disciplining the Militia, and for governing such part of them as may be employed in the service of the U. S. reserving to the States respectively, the appointment of the officers, and authority of training the militia according to the discipline prescribed—"[307] Rufus King, "by way of explanation, said that by *organizing*, the Committee meant, proportioning the officers & men—by *arming*, specifying the kind size & caliber of arms—& by *disciplining* prescribing the manual exercise evolutions & c."[308]

James Madison "observed that '*arming*' as explained did not extend to furnishing arms; nor the term 'disciplining' to penalties & Courts Martial for enforcing them."[309]

Rufus King "added, to his former explanation that *arming* meant not only to provide for uniformity of arms, but included authority to regulate the modes of furnishing, either by the Militia themselves, the State Governments, or the National Treasury: that *laws* for disciplining, must involve penalties and every thing necessary for enforcing penalties."[310]

Article I, Section 8, Paragraph 17

(Congress shall have the power) *To exercise exclusive Legislation in all Cases whatsoever, over such District (not exceeding ten Miles square) as may, by Cession of particular States, and the Acceptance of Congress, become the Seat of the Government of the United States, and to exercise like Authority over all Places purchased by the Consent of the Legislature of the State in which the Same shall be, for the Erection of Forts, Magazines, Arsenals, dock-Yards, and other needful Buildings; —And*

Original Meaning in 21st Century Plain English

Congress shall have the exclusive power to: (1) make laws for a district not exceeding ten miles square (100 square miles) which may be given to the United States by one or more states and accepted by Congress as the capital of the United States; and (2) make laws for all other places acquired by the United States. The consent of the legislature of state A must be obtained before the U.S. can acquire land withing state A. Places within state borders that are acquired by the U.S. shall be used for the erection of (1) forts, (2) facilities for building and repairing ships, (3) warehouses to store military supplies, and (4) other necessary buildings.

Discussion of Article I, Section 8, Paragraph 17

Before the federal government acquires land within any state, the state legislature must consent. Before the "Consent" provision was added at the Constitutional Convention, Elbridge Gerry said that a provision to empower Congress to exercise legislative authority over all places purchased by the federal government for forts and other purposes "might be made use of to enslave any particular State by buying up its territory, and that the strongholds proposed would be a means of awing the State into an undue obedience to the General Government."[311]

Despite the obvious understanding of the ratifiers that the legislature of state A must agree before any land in state A becomes federal property, the Court has ruled that the federal government can take property within state A without the consent of state A if the federal government condemns the land.[312]

Article I, Section 8, Paragraph 18

(Congress shall have the power) *To make all Laws which shall be necessary and proper for carrying into Execution the foregoing Powers, and all other Powers vested by this Constitution in the Government of the United States, or in any Department or Officer thereof.*

Original Meaning in 21st Century Plain English

Congress shall have the power to make all laws which shall be necessary and proper for implementing the powers vested by this Constitution in the United States government.

Discussion of Article I, Section 8, Paragraph 18

In *The Federalist*, No. 33, Alexander Hamilton said that the necessary and proper clause had "been the source of much virulent invective and petulant declamation against the proposed Constitution. . . ."[313] Hamilton went on to say:

"What is a LEGISLATIVE power but a power of making LAWS? . . . a power to lay and collect taxes must be a power to pass all laws *necessary* and *proper* for the execution of that power; and what does the unfortunate and calumniated provision in question do more than declare the same truth, to wit, that the national legislature to whom the power of laying and collecting taxes had been previously given might, in the execution of that power, pass all laws *necessary* and *proper* to carry it into effect? I have applied these observations thus particularly to the power of taxation, because it is the immediate subject under consideration and because it is the most important of the authorities proposed to be conferred upon the Union. But the same process will lead to the same result in relation to all other powers declared in the Constitution. And it is *expressly* to execute these powers that the sweeping clause, as it has been affectedly called, authorizes the national legislature to pass all *necessary* and *proper* laws. . . . The [necessary and proper] declaration itself, though it may be chargeable with tautology or redundancy, is at least perfectly harmless. . . ."[314]

Hamilton may have regarded the necessary and proper clause as redundant. In any event, he made an excellent case for its redundancy. Most of the framers had struggled to enact effective and constitutional legislation in Congress under the Articles of Confederation. As a result of those struggles, most framers either believed that the clause was necessary or that it would result in substantially fewer headaches and heartburn in Congress under the Constitution. James Madison, in his discussion of the necessary and proper clause in *The Federalist*, No. 44, stated: "Without the *substance* of this power, the whole Constitution would be a dead letter. . . ."[315] To understand Madison's concern, we can think about the power of Congress to collect taxes. How would it be done? The Constitution does not specify the method that Congress would employ to collect taxes. Whichever method Congress selected, somebody or some state could claim was unconstitutional because the Constitution does not expressly grant this power to Congress. Such an argument would have been reasonable under the Articles, which specified that Congress only had the powers "expressly delegated to the United States." However, since the Constitution omitted the dreaded word "expressly," such an argument would be very weak under the Constitution.

Article I, Section 9, Paragraph 1

> *The Migration or Importation of such Persons as any of the States now existing shall think proper to admit, shall not be prohibited by the Congress prior to the Year one thousand eight hundred and eight, but a Tax or duty may be imposed on such Importation, not exceeding ten dollars for each Person.*

Original Meaning in 21st Century Plain English

Prior to 1808, each of the thirteen original states shall have the sole power to permit or forbid entrance into their state of voluntary immigrants and involuntary immigrants (slaves). However, Congress may impose a tax of up to ten dollars on each slave imported into the United States. Congress shall have the sole power to limit all immigration into the United States after December 31, 1807. Congress may prohibit the importation of slaves into the United States after December 31, 1807.

Article I, Section 9, Paragraph 2

The Privilege of the Writ of Habeas Corpus shall not be suspended, unless when in Cases of Rebellion or Invasion the public Safety may require it.

Original Meaning in 21st Century Plain English

People who are detained against their will by officials of the federal government shall have the privilege to employ the writ of habeas corpus unless it has been suspended by Congress. A writ of habeas corpus presented to a federal judge on behalf of a detainee shall cause the judge to order the federal official who is detaining the detainee to bring the detainee before the judge for the purpose of determining whether the detainee is being lawfully detained. Detainees who are brought before a judge on a writ of habeas corpus must be released if the judge determines that they are not being detained in a lawful manner. Congress is the only entity of the federal government that can suspend the privilege of habeas corpus. Congress may suspend it only during rebellions or invasions.

Discussion of Article I, Section 9, Paragraph 2

During the Civil War, President Lincoln suspended the privilege of the writ of habeas corpus. Congress did not pass a law to authorize Lincoln to suspend "the privilege of the writ of habeas corpus" until some time after Lincoln denied the privilege to people detained by the federal government. Lincoln's suspension of the privilege of the writ of habeas corpus before authorized to do so by Congress was unconstitutional because:

- Article I provisions apply to Congress unless specified otherwise. Chief Justice John Marshall correctly ruled in 1807 that Congress has the only federal authority to suspend the writ of habeas corpus.[316]

- Article II does not grant any such power to the president.

- The English Bill of Rights, very popular with framers and ratifiers, declared that it was illegal to suspend laws without the consent of Parliament. Only Parliament could suspend the writ of habeas corpus during the eighteenth century.

- In 1787 and 1788, only state legislatures were authorized to suspend the privilege of the writ of habeas corpus in states.

Article I, Section 9, Paragraph 3

No Bill of Attainder or ex post facto Law shall be passed.

Original Meaning in 21st Century Plain English

Congress shall pass no:

- Bill of attainder (A bill of attainder is a legislative act which (1) declares that a specific person has committed a crime, (2) imposes the death penalty on the person, and (3) imposes forfeiture of all of the attainted person's property to the government.)

- Ex post facto law (An ex post facto law makes it illegal to do X *and* prescribes punishment for people who did X before it was illegal to do X.)

Discussion of Article I, Section 9, Paragraph 3

Parliament probably issued its first bill of attainder in 1322 and its last bill of attainder in 1798.[317] People named by Parliament in bills of attainder were executed (if they survived their capture) unless pardoned by the king or queen. As an incentive for the king or queen to allow executions, all property of those attainted went to the king or queen unless pardons were granted.

Few full-blown bills of attainder were enacted in America. One was enacted in Virginia in 1778, and one was enacted in Pennsylvania in 1784.[318] Those two may have been the only full-blown bills of attainder enacted in the United States. States enacted many non-lethal "bills of attainder" during the Revolutionary War to confiscate the property of Tories (people who advocated submitting to British laws). Many bills of pains and penalties were also enacted by state legislatures during the Revolutionary War. Bills of pains and penalties were often used to banish Tories—sometimes under threat of death if they returned. Tories were banished by name in eight states. Pennsylvania expelled 490 individuals by name in 1776. New York convicted more than one thousand Tories by means of bills of attainder and bills of pains and penalties.[319]

During the Revolutionary War, every state passed laws which confiscated some Tory property.[320] The outstanding historian Wythe Holt stated: "Confiscation [of Tory property] proved lucrative to [state] governments that were desperately short of money."[321] North Carolina obtained six hundred thousand pounds from the sale of Tory property by the end of 1782.[322] From the end of 1782 to the end of 1790, North Carolina obtained about three hundred thousand pounds from the sale of Tory property. New York raised a total of four million dollars by selling property confiscated from Tories. With respect to ex post facto laws, Blackstone said in his *Commentaries on the Laws of England:*

> "laws *ex post facto:* when after an action is committed, the legislator then for the first time declares it to have been a crime, and inflicts a punishment upon the person who has committed it. Here it is impossible that the party could foresee that an action, innocent when it was done, should be afterwards converted to guilt by a subsequent law; he had therefore no cause to abstain from it; . . . All laws should be therefore made to commence *in futuro,* . . ."[323]

At the Constitutional Convention, John Dickinson said the term "ex post facto" in Blackstone's *Commentaries* "related to criminal cases only." Dickinson went on to say that further provisions "would be requisite" to "restrain the States from retrospective laws in civil cases." To a large extent, the Constitution's prohibition on state laws "impairing the Obligation of Contracts" restrains states from making retrospective laws in civil cases.

Although all ratifiers probably knew that the term "ex post facto Laws" applied to criminal laws, many ratifiers thought the term also applied to civil laws.[324] The Court ruled in 1798 that the term "ex post facto" applied only to criminal laws.[325]That ruling was within the bounds of ratifier understanding.

The Court has upheld unconstitutional retroactive laws which:

- Authorized deportation of aliens for doing things that were legal at the time they were done[326] (The Court has ruled that the only right that aliens have is the right to procedural due process.[327] That "right" benefits lawyers.)

- Terminated Social Security benefits of aliens deported for doing things that were legal at the time they were done[328]

- Rescinded the licenses to practice medicine of doctors who had previously been convicted of a felony[329] (Rescinding the license of a doctor to practice medicine was not considered by the Court to be a penalty!)

In 1867, the Court invalidated a federal statute which barred lawyers who had been involved in the war against the Union from practicing in federal courts.[330] The reason the Court gave was that the statute was retroactive. Although that ruling was constitutional, the Court has applied the term "ex post facto Law" in an inconsistent manner to the benefit lawyers.

Article I, Section 9, Paragraph 4

No Capitation, or other direct, Tax shall be laid, unless in Proportion to the Census or Enumeration herein before directed to be taken.

Original Meaning in 21st Century Plain English

Congress shall not impose any per capita tax or other direct tax unless such tax is apportioned among all states in the United States as specified in Article I, Section 2, Paragraph 3.

Discussion of Article I, Section 9, Paragraph 4

The impact of this paragraph was limited by the Sixteenth Amendment which says that "Congress shall have the power to lay and collect taxes on incomes, from whatever source derived, without apportionment among the several States, without regard for any census or enumeration."

Article I, Section 9, Paragraph 5

No Tax or Duty shall be laid on Articles exported from any State.

Original Meaning in 21st Century Plain English

Congress shall not impose a tax of any kind on manufactured or agricultural products leaving any state.

Article I, Section 9, Paragraph 6

No Preference shall be given by any Regulation of Commerce or Revenue to the Ports of one State over those of another; nor shall Vessels bound to, or from, one State, be obliged to enter, clear, or pay Duties in another.

Original Meaning in 21st Century Plain English

Congress shall give no preference to the ports of any state. Ships traveling to or from a state shall not be required by Congress to (1) enter any other state, (2) unload their cargo in any other state, or (3) pay any taxes in any other state.

Article I, Section 9, Paragraph 7

No Money shall be drawn from the Treasury, but in Consequence of Appropriations made by Law; and a regular Statement and Account of the Receipts and Expenditures of all public Money shall be published from time to time.

Original Meaning in 21st Century Plain English

No money shall be withdrawn from the United States Treasury unless it has been appropriated by Congress. A standard financial statement which accounts for all income received by the federal government and all expenditures made by the federal government shall be published from time to time by the Treasury Department.

Article I, Section 9, Paragraph 8

No Title of Nobility shall be granted by the United States: And no Person holding any Office of Profit or Trust under them, shall, without the Consent of the Congress, accept of any present, Emolument, Office, or Title, of any kind whatever, from any King, Prince, or foreign State.

Original Meaning in 21st Century Plain English

The federal government shall not grant any title of nobility (duke, marquis, earl, viscount, baron, etc.). No official of the federal government shall, without the consent of Congress, accept any gift, salary, office, or title of any kind from any king, prince, or foreign government.

Article I, Section 10, Paragraph 1

No State shall enter into any Treaty, Alliance, or Confederation; grant Letters of Marque and Reprisal; coin Money; emit Bills of Credit; make any Thing but gold and silver Coin a Tender in Payment of Debts; pass any Bill of Attainder, ex post facto Law, or Law impairing the Obligation of Contracts, or grant any Title of Nobility.

Original Meaning in 21st Century Plain English

No state of the United States under this Constitution shall:

- Enter into a treaty, alliance, or confederation with a foreign country or other state of the United States

- Authorize private shipowners to capture or attack ships

- Make coins or authorize coins to be made

- Emit paper money

- Require creditors to accept anything but gold or silver coins as payment of debt

- Emit bills of attainder

- Pass any law which prescribes punishment for doing things which were not crimes at the times they were done

- Pass any law which impairs the obligation of contracts (Any law that makes it more difficult for creditors to collect, in a timely manner, the full amount of money owed to them is a law which impairs the obligation of contracts.)

- Grant titles of nobility

Discussion of Article I, Section 10, Paragraph 1

The Articles of Confederation stated:

"No state [of the United States] without the Consent of the united states in congress assembled, shall . . . enter into any . . .

agreement, alliance, or treaty with any . . . king, prince or foreign state; . . . No two or more states [of the United States] shall enter into any treaty, confederation, or alliance what-ever between them, without the consent of the united states in congress assembled, . . ."[331]

The Articles of Confederation effectively said to state legisla-tors: "You can think about making treaties, alliances, and confederations outside of the Union, but it is very unlikely that Congress will approve your plans in that regard." The Constitution says to state legislators: "Do not even think about making treaties, alliances, or confederations outside of the Union."

Article I, Section 10, Paragraph 2

No State shall, without the Consent of the Congress, lay any Imposts or Duties on Imports or Exports, except what may be absolutely necessary for executing it's inspec-tion Laws: and the net Produce of all Duties and Imposts, laid by any State on Imports or Exports, shall be for the Use of the Treasury of the United States; and all such Laws shall be subject to the Revision and Controul of the Congress.

Original Meaning in 21st Century Plain English

No state shall, without the consent of Congress, impose any taxes or other fees on imports or exports—except what is essential to com-ply with its inspection laws. The net income (gross income minus inspection costs) from all state-imposed inspection fees shall be paid to the federal government by the states. All state laws which impose fees on imports or exports shall be subject to revision by Congress.

Article I, Section 10, Paragraph 3

No State shall, without the Consent of Congress, lay any Duty of Tonnage, keep Troops, or Ships of War in time of Peace, enter into any Agreement or Compact with another State, or with a foreign Power, or engage in War, unless actually invaded, or in such imminent Danger as will not admit of delay.

Original Meaning in 21st Century Plain English

No state shall, without the consent of Congress:

- Impose any taxes on any ships for entering a port, lying in a port, or leaving a port

- Maintain full-time military personnel or armed ships during peace-time

- Enter into any agreement with another state or foreign country (Paragraph 1 of Section 10 prohibits states from entering into treaties, alliances, and confederations. Hence, "Agreement or Compact" must refer to minor agreements. An agreement between state A and state B to construct a road or a bridge between a town in state A and a town in state B is an example of a minor agreement.)

- Engage in war unless invaded or in such imminent danger that common sense compels state forces to fire the first shot

Article II

CHAPTER 4

Article II, Section 1

The executive Power shall be vested in a President of the United States of America. He shall hold his Office during the Term of four Years, and, together with the Vice President, chosen for the same Term, be elected, as follows:

Each State shall appoint, in such Manner as the Legislature thereof may direct, a Number of Electors, equal to the whole Number of Senators and Representatives to which the State may be entitled in the Congress: but no Senator or Representative, or Person holding an Office of Trust or Profit under the United States, shall be appointed an Elector.

The Electors shall meet in their respective States, and vote by Ballot for two Persons, of whom one at least shall not be an Inhabitant of the of the same State with themselves. And they shall make a List of all the Persons voted for, and of the Number of Votes for each; which List they shall sign and certify, and transmit sealed to the Seat of the Government of the United States, directed to the President of the Senate. The President of the Senate shall, in the Presence of the Senate and House of Representatives, open all the

Certificates, and the Votes shall then be counted. The Person having the greatest Number of Votes shall be the President, if such Number be a Majority of the whole Number of Electors appointed; and if there be more than one who have such Majority, and have an equal Number of Votes, then the House of Representatives shall immediately chuse by Ballot one of them for President; and if no Person have a Majority, then from the five highest on the list the said House shall in like Manner chuse the President. But in chusing the President, the Votes shall be taken by States, the Representation from each State having one Vote; A quorum for this Purpose shall consist of a Member of Members from two thirds of the States, and a Majority of all the States shall be necessary to a Choice. In every Case, after the Choice of the President, the Person having the greatest Number of Votes of the Electors shall be the Vice President. But if there should remain two or more who have equal Votes, the Senate shall chuse from them by Ballot the Vice President.

Original Meaning in 21st Century Plain English

The executive power of the United States shall be held by the president of the United States who shall be elected for a term of four years. The vice-president of the United States shall be elected for the same four-year term as the president of the United States. The president and vice-president of the United States shall be elected as follows:

- Each state shall appoint, in a manner directed by its legislature, a number of presidential electors equal to the number of senators plus the number of representatives to which the state is entitled in Congress. However, no person who currently holds any federal office shall be appointed a presidential elector.

- Presidential electors shall meet in their respective states, and each presidential elector shall vote by secret ballot for two persons to be president of the United States. (Each such vote can be called an electoral vote.) No presidential elector shall cast more than one of their two electoral votes for a person who resides in the state in which the presidential elector resides.

- The presidential electors in each state shall make a list showing all who receive electoral votes in their state and the number of electoral votes received by each. Each presidential elector shall sign and certify the electoral vote list of their state, and the list shall then be sealed and transmitted to the president of the U.S. Senate.

- In an assembly in which all members of Congress are encouraged to attend, the president of the Senate shall open all certificates from the presidential electors, and the electoral votes shall then be counted.

- If one person has the most electoral votes and more than half of the presidential electors have voted for that person, that person shall be president of the United States.

- If two people are tied for the most electoral votes and they were both voted for by more than half of the presidential electors, the House of Representatives shall select one of the two to be president of the United States. In such cases the first priority of the House of Representatives shall be to select a president of the United States, and the person who is not selected to be president of the U.S. by the House shall be vice-president of the United States.

- If no person is voted for by a majority of the presidential electors (1) the five people with the most electoral votes shall be eligible to be selected president of the United States by the House of Representatives, and (2) the first priority of the House shall be to select a president of the United States.

- When the House of Representatives selects a president of the United States (1) the House shall vote by states, (2) each state shall have one vote, (3) at least two-thirds of the states must be represented by at least one representative, and (4) no person shall be selected president unless a majority of all states vote for that person.

- After a president of the United States is selected, the person who has the most electoral votes, excluding the president-elect, shall be vice-president of the U.S. unless there is a tie. In the event of a tie, the members of the U.S. Senate shall select a vice-president from among those tied with the most electoral votes, excluding the president-elect. In so doing, the senators shall vote by secret ballot.

Discussion of Article II, Section 1, Paragraphs 1, 2, and 3

The first major constitutional debate in Congress took place in the first session of the first Congress under the Constitution. Congress was working on a bill to establish a Department of Foreign Affairs and the office of secretary of foreign affairs. A *highly controversial provision* of the bill would have empowered the president to remove the secretary of foreign affairs without the consent of the Senate.[332] That highly controversial—and very important—provision was supported by President George Washington and influential Representatives James Madison, Fisher Ames, and Egbert Benson. A strong argument can be made that most ratifiers understood that the president could remove high level members of the executive department without the consent of the Senate. However, an even stronger argument can be made that most ratifiers understood that the president could not remove high level members of the executive department without the consent of the Senate.

The argument that most ratifiers understood that the president could remove all executive branch officials without the consent of the Senate is as follows:

- Article II of the Constitution begins with the sentence: "The executive Power shall be vested in a President of the United States of America." How can a president exercise "The executive Power" if he cannot dismiss executive branch officials who act contrary to presidential orders? Hence, the president has the implied power to remove all executive branch officials without the consent of Congress. Chief executives (kings, queens, emperors, tsars, etc.) of European governments had such power. (However, European chief executives had the power to dismiss "under the monarchical principle of divine right."[333])

- Article II also says that the president "shall take Care that the Laws be faithfully executed." Fisher Ames maintained, during a very interesting debate in the House of Representatives, that the president would not be able to control his officers and make sure that the laws were faithfully executed if he did not have the power to discharge executive branch officials.[334] If the president were not to have such power, Ames said: "You virtually strip him of his authority; you virtually destroy his responsibility."[335]

- If Madison and other members of Congress had supported something clearly contrary to understandings they had endorsed at their state ratifying conventions, they would have been excoriated. They were not criticized on that score. Hence, removal of executive branch officials was probably not an issue at many state ratifying conventions.

- If Washington or Madison had supported something clearly contrary to the intent of the framers at the Constitutional Convention, they would have been excoriated. They were not so criticized. Obviously, all framers did not have the same understanding with regard to the ways executive branch officials could be dismissed.

The argument that most ratifiers understood that the president could not remove high level executive branch officials without the consent of the Senate is as follows:

- In *The Federalist*, No. 77, Alexander Hamilton said:

"It has been mentioned as one of the advantages to be expected from the co-operation of the Senate, in the business of appointments, that it would contribute to the stability of the administration. The consent of that body would be necessary to displace as well as to appoint. A change of the Chief Magistrate, therefore, would not occasion so violent or so general a revolution in the officers of the government as might be expected if he were the sole disposer of offices. Where a man in any station had given satisfactory evidence of his fitness for it, a new President would be restrained from attempting a change in favor of a person more agreeable to him by the apprehension that a discountenance of the Senate might frustrate the attempt and bring some degree of discredit upon himself. . . ."[336]

- In the House of Representatives, Elbridge Gerry, in response to Madison's claim that the powers of appointment and removal were inherently executive, replied that such a premise could not have been deduced from any American precedent.[337] Evidently, the chief executives of states (called governors or presidents in 1787) could not, by themselves, appoint or remove executive branch officials. The principle of divine right was *not* accepted in the United States.

- Two members of the House of Representatives suggested that executive branch officials could be forced out of office only via the impeachment process.[338]

Several opponents of the highly controversial provision in the bill to establish a Department of Foreign Affairs thought that presidents had the implied power to remove executive branch officials, but that Congress did not have the authority to directly declare that constitutional power. Supporters of the bill were able to obtain the essence of the highly controversial provision by substituting a slightly less controversial provision which required the office of secretary of foreign affairs to be administered by the chief clerk in the department until a new secretary was appointed after a secretary was removed by the president.[339]

The substitution, engineered by Egbert Benson, was approved by a vote of thirty to eighteen in the House of Representatives. After the senators were equally divided, Vice-President John Adams cast the deciding vote in favor of the substitution.[340]

The major constitutional controversy in Congress in 1789 provides evidence that the Constitution does not *necessarily* mean that the Senate must consent to dismissals of executive branch personnel who were appointed with the consent of the Senate. *The Federalist,*

No. 77, combined with the major constitutional controversy in Congress in 1789, provides evidence that there is more than enough uncertainty for the Court to legitimately rule that the Senate must consent to dismissals of executive branch personnel who were appointed with the consent of the Senate.

Election of the President and the Vice-President

Although the framers knew that George Washington would, barring sickness or injury, be the first president of the U.S. if the Constitution was ratified, the framers' crystal ball was opaque beyond Washington. The method of selecting a president was debated at length at the Convention and had the delegates "running around in circles."[341] The delegates were torn between: (1) *election by Congress* of an "executive to consist of a single person," serve a seven-year term, and be "ineligible a second time" (That arrangement was approved by a vote of eight states to three on June 2 and approved a second time by a vote of seven states to three on July 26.); and (2) election of a single executive by "State Executives" (governors or presidents of states) or presidential electors chosen by state legislatures or state executives.

The framers created the presidential elector system (what has come to be called the "electoral college") as something of a "search committee" to nominate outstanding individuals from which the House of Representatives was expected, in most presidential elections, to select the president.[342] The framers anticipated that each presidential elector would usually cast one vote for a person who resided in their state and one vote for a person who resided in another state within their region.[343] The framers did not anticipate national political parties.

In 1796, John Adams, a Federalist, was elected president, and Thomas Jefferson, a Democratic-Republican, was elected vice-president. Straight party voting in 1800 resulted in an electoral college tie between Thomas Jefferson and his vice-presidential running mate, Aaron Burr. Although it was well known that Burr was not even a candidate for president, many Federalists plotted with Burr's friends to try to cheat Jefferson out of the presidency by voting for Burr to be president.[344] Had it not been for Alexander Hamilton's vigorous action, the plot might have succeeded.[345] As it was, it took seven days and thirty-six ballots in the House of Representatives before it was determined that Thomas Jefferson would become the third president of the United States.

The 1801 presidential selection experience in the House of Representatives led Congress to propose the Twelfth Amendment in 1803. It was ratified by the requisite thirteen states in 1804. The Twelfth Amendment (1) requires all presidential electors to vote for president on a presidential ballot, (2) requires all presidential electors to vote for vice-president on a vice-presidential ballot, and (3) specifies that when one person does not receive a majority of electoral votes for president, the House of Representatives must select a president from the three people receiving the most electoral votes for president.

Although the framers anticipated that presidential electors would be independent, by the 1830s all but one state made presidential electors totally dependent on the electorate by requiring that all presidential electors in a given state vote for the presidential candidate who received the most popular votes in that state.[346]

Article II, Section 1, Paragraph 4

The Congress may determine the Time of chusing the Electors, and the Day on which they shall give their Votes; which Day shall be the same throughout the United States.

Original Meaning in 21st Century Plain English

Congress may determine the time for choosing members of the electoral college and the day on which members of the electoral college shall vote. If Congress specifies a day for members of the electoral college to vote, that day shall be the same throughout the United States.

Article II, Section 1, Paragraph 5

No Person except a natural born Citizen, or a Citizen of the United States, at the time of the Adoption of this Constitution, shall be eligible to the Office of President; neither shall any Person be eligible to that Office who shall not have attained to the Age of thirty five Years, and been fourteen Years a Resident within the United States.

Original Meaning in 21st Century Plain English

Every president of the United States must (1) be at least thirty-five years old, (2) have resided in the United States for at least fourteen years, and (3) have been born a citizen of the United States or have been a citizen of the United States at the time the unamended Constitution was ratified by nine states. To be born a citizen of the United States, a person must either be born within the territorial limits of the United States or be, at the time of their birth, the child of a United States citizen.

Article II, Section 1, Paragraph 6

In case of the Removal of the President from Office, or of his Death, Resignation, or Inability to discharge the Powers and Duties of the said Office, the Same shall devolve on the Vice President, and the Congress may by Law provide for the Case of Removal, Death, Resignation or Inability, both of the President and the Vice President, declaring what Officer shall then act as President, and such Officer shall act accordingly, until the Disability be removed, or a President shall be elected.

Original Meaning in 21st Century Plain English

The vice-president shall act as president of the U.S. if the president of the United States (1) is removed from office via the impeachment process, (2) dies, (3) resigns, or (4) becomes unable to function as president because of sickness or injury. If the president of the U.S. is unable to perform the duties of president because of a temporary disability, the vice-president shall act as president until the president recovers or a new president is elected. Congress shall have the power to enact a law which specifies which officer of the federal government shall act as president of the U.S. in the event that both the president and vice-president are removed, die, resign, or become, through illness or injury, unable to perform the duties of president of the United States.

Article II, Section 1, Paragraph 7

The President shall, at stated Times, receive for his Services, a Compensation, which shall neither be encreased nor diminished during the Period for which he shall have been elected, and he shall not receive within that Period any other Emolument from the United States, or any of them.

Original Meaning in 21st Century Plain English

The president of the U.S. shall be paid by the federal government. Congress shall determine the president's salary and when the president shall be paid. However, the president's salary shall remain constant during any given term. Other than a salary from the federal government, the president shall not receive any payment or gift from the federal government or any state government during any term for which he was selected to be president of the United States.

Article II, Section 1, Paragraph 8

Before he enter on the Execution of his Office, he shall take the following Oath or Affirmation:—"I do solemnly swear (or affirm) that I will faithfully execute the Office of

President of the United States, and will to the best of my Ability, preserve, protect and defend the Constitution of the United States."

Original Meaning in 21st Century Plain English

Every person who is selected to be president of the United States shall, before becoming president, take the following oath or affirmation: "I do solemnly swear (or affirm) that I will faithfully execute the office of president of the United States, and will to the best of my ability, preserve, protect, and defend the Constitution of the United States."

Article II, Section 2, Paragraph 1

The President shall be Commander in Chief of the Army and Navy of the United States, and of the Militia of the several States, when called into the actual Service of the United States; he may require the Opinion, in writing, of the principle Officer in each of the executive Departments, upon any Subject relating to the Duties of their respective Offices, and he shall have Power to grant Reprieves and Pardons for Offences against the United States, except in Cases of Impeachment.

Original Meaning in 21st Century Plain English

The president of the United States:

- Shall be commander-in-chief of the United States Army, the United States Navy, and that portion of the militia which Congress calls up to serve the United States

- May require the principal officer in every executive department to provide written opinions upon any subject relating to their official duties

- Shall have the power to grant reprieves and pardons for all offenses against the United States except in cases of impeachment (If a federal official is removed from office by Congress via the impeachment process, the president cannot interfere with the judgment of Congress, but in all federal criminal cases tried in courts, the president can grant reprieves and pardons.)

Discussion of Article II, Section 2, Paragraph 1

On January 20, 2001, President Clinton, in his last few hours in office, pardoned billionaire fugitive Marc Rich. The Justice Department's ten-most-wanted list in January of 2001 included Rich—a man who had fled the United States to avoid trial in the biggest tax fraud case in the history of the United States. It is likely that political contributions and gifts played a part in Clinton's pardon of Rich. It is certain that a lawyer with close ties to Clinton and Rich was involved. No president in his right mind would have pardoned Rich on the merits of the case. Clinton had not lost his mind. Nevertheless, it was clearly constitutional for Clinton to pardon Rich.

The Constitution should be amended to preclude outrageous pardons in the future. It would probably make sense to include the following features in such an amendment: (1) no pardons during the final four months of a presidential term; and (2) all pardons approved by the president of the U.S. *and* the Judiciary Committee of the House of Representatives.

Article II, Section 2, Paragraph 2

He shall have Power, by and with the Advice and Consent of the Senate, to make Treaties, provided two thirds of the Senators present concur; and he shall nominate, and by and with the Advice and Consent of the Senate, shall appoint Ambassadors, other public Ministers and Consuls, Judges of the supreme Court, and all other Officers of the United States, whose Appointments are not herein otherwise provided for, and which shall be estab-

lished by Law: but the Congress may by Law vest the Appointment of such inferior Officers, as they think proper, in the President alone, in the Courts of Law, or in the Heads of Departments.

Original Meaning in 21st Century Plain English

The president of the U.S. shall have the power to make treaties with Indians and foreign governments if at least two-thirds of the senators present vote for the treaties. A majority of the senators must be present for all Senate votes on proposed treaties. Treaty proposals may be made by the president, the Senate, foreign countries, or Indians.

Congress may make laws which allow low-level federal officials to be appointed (installed in office) without the approval of the Senate. Such officials may be appointed by the president of the U.S. alone, members of the federal judiciary, or department heads (secretary of state, etc.). However, before any person is appointed to an office which requires the consent of the Senate, the president of the U.S. shall nominate that person for that office, and the nominee must be approved by a majority of the senators present in the Senate. A majority of the senators must be present for all votes to accept or reject nominations. The president of the U.S. shall nominate ambassadors, consuls, department heads, justices of the Supreme Court, and other federal officials which Congress has not authorized high-level federal officials to appoint without the approval of the Senate.

Discussion of Article II, Section 2, Paragraph 2

The phrase "Advice and Consent" was used in British state documents for more than one thousand years prior to 1787.[347] The framers made it clear as to how the Senate would provide "Consent." However, the framers did not make it clear as to how the Senate would provide "Advice." The framers were not all on the same wavelength with respect to how the Senate would provide advice.

In August of 1789, President George Washington, seeking to honor the letter of the Constitution, appeared in person before the Senate to obtain its advice as part of his preparation to negotiate an Indian treaty.[348] When the Senate referred the matter to a committee, Washington became so upset that he walked out of the Senate.[349] In August of 1789, 11 out of the 22 U.S. Senators were framers.[350] Most framers probably intended that the Senate would provide treaty "Advice": (1) when the Senate decided to do so; and (2) in a manner that the Senate thought best (entire Senate, Senate committee, designated senators, etc.). The Senate's response to President Washington's request for advice on an Indian treaty is probably the best clue we have as to what most framers intended relevant to Senate advice on treaties.

Treaties can (1) be superseded by federal statutes, and (2) bypass the House of Representatives to make laws which could not otherwise be made. To illustrate how treaties can bypass the House of Representatives, let us assume that the president and two-thirds of the members of the Senate want to do X. Furthermore, let us assume that more than half of the members of the House of Representatives are opposed to X. A treaty can be made to do X, and that treaty cannot be superseded by statute unless at least half of the members of the Senate vote to supersede the treaty.

Treaties can be used to supersede statutes which could not be repealed because a majority of the members of the House of Representatives were opposed to repeal. This characteristic of the Constitution was objected to in the form of suggested amendments to the Constitution by the minority at the Pennsylvania Ratifying Convention and the majority at the North Carolina Ratifying Convention.

Can Treaties Override the Constitution?

I would not have asked this question had I not heard the host of a radio talk show inform his audience in hushed tones in 1999 that treaties can supersede the Constitution. How, I wondered, could anybody get that idea?

Such an idea can be traced back to the 1920 Supreme Court case of *Missouri v. Holland* which challenged the validity of a federal law which restricted the hunting of migratory birds.[351] If the Tenth Amendment does anything, it prohibits the federal government from imposing hunting restrictions on people in states. Congress would not have even considered enacting the law under attack in *Missouri v. Holland* if it had not been for a treaty between the United States and Canada. The Court "validated" the federal statute which restricted the hunting of migratory birds in states. How did the Court "validate" the statute? In an opinion written by Justice Oliver Wendell Holmes, the Court ruled that the treaty power was not constrained by the Tenth Amendment.[352] Furthermore, the Court said: "There may be matters of the sharpest exigency for the national well being that an act of Congress could not deal with [for want of constitutional authority] but that a treaty followed by such an act could."[353]

The 1920 case of *Missouri v. Holland* was one of the things which drove Congress, in the early 1950s, to consider what is known as the Bricker Amendment.[354] The Bricker Amendment, which came within one vote of getting the two-thirds majority required in the Senate, would have made ineffective any treaty which conflicted with the Constitution.[355]

Although it is unlawful for a treaty to supersede the Constitution, the talk-show host did have something to be concerned about.

Article II, Section 2, Paragraph 3

The President shall have Power to fill up all Vacancies that may happen during the Recess of the Senate, by granting Commissions which shall expire at the End of their next Session.

Original Meaning in 21st Century Plain English

The president of the U.S. shall have the power to fill all vacancies in the federal government which occur during a Senate recess by making temporary appointments, but such temporary appointments shall expire at the end of the next session of the Senate.

Article II, Section 3

Section 3. He shall from time to time give to the Congress Information of the State of the Union, and recommend to their Consideration such Measures as he shall judge necessary and expedient; he may, on extraordinary Occasions, convene both Houses, or either of them, and in Case of Disagreement between them, with Respect to the Time of Adjournment, he may adjourn them to such Time as he shall think proper; he shall receive Ambassadors and other public Ministers; he shall take Care that the Laws be faithfully executed, and shall Commission all the Officers of the United States.

Original Meaning in 21st Century Plain English

Whenever the president of the U.S. sees fit, he shall: (1) give Congress information on the condition of the United States; and (2) recommend that Congress consider taking actions (making laws, declaring war, etc.) which he considers to be necessary and advantageous to the United States. On *extraordinary* occasions, the president of the U.S. may convene both Houses (the Senate and the House of Representatives) or either House. When there is a disagreement between the Senate and the House of Representatives with respect to the time of adjournment, the president of the U.S. may determine the time of adjournment. The president of the U.S. shall (1) receive ambassadors and other high officials of foreign governments, (2) take care that the laws of the United States are faithfully executed, and (3) commission all officers of the federal government. To commission a federal officer, the president shall (1) sign a formal written document which authorizes that officer to perform certain official duties, and (2) take care that the commission is issued to the officer.

Article II, Section 4

The President, Vice President and all civil Officers of the United States, shall be removed from Office on Impeachment for, and Conviction of, Treason, Bribery, or other high Crimes and Misdemeanors.

Original Meaning in 21st Century Plain English

The president, vice-president, and all civil officers of the United States shall be removed from office if the U.S. House of Representatives impeaches for, and the U.S. Senate convicts of: (1) treason; (2) bribery; or (3) gross maladministration (performing an official act in a manner clearly inconsistent with law, abuse of power, performing an official act which the official clearly had no authority to perform, or neglecting to do something which the official clearly had a duty to do).

Discussion of Article II, Section 4

The meaning of the phrase "high Crimes and Misdemeanors" has been the subject of much controversy. Constitutional historian Raoul Berger correctly stated that the term "high crimes and misdemeanors" was "lifted bodily from English law."[356] The framers modified the essence of English impeachment law only to the extent that:

- The Constitution makes the chief executive (president) impeachable whereas in England, the chief executive (king or queen) was not impeachable. (Blackstone said: "For as a king cannot misuse his power, without the advice of evil counsellors, and the assistance of wicked ministers, these men may be examined and punished."[357])

- The Constitution contains a narrow definition of treason in Article III, Section 3, Paragraph 1. This is far more important for treason prosecutions in federal courts than it is for impeachment prosecutions in Congress. Why? Much conduct which would be treason in England but not treason in the United States—such as attempting to subvert the Constitution—was a high crime and misdemeanor in England and, therefore, a high crime and misdemeanor in the United States.

• The Constitution restricts judgment in cases of impeachment to removal from office and disqualification to hold any office in the federal government after being removed from office. People removed from office by Parliament could be sentenced to death or jail by Parliament, and Parliament could also impose heavy fines.

• The Constitution prohibits the president from pardoning people "in Cases of Impeachment." The king could pardon people who had been impeached and removed from office by Parliament.[358] This difference is not as important as it seems at first glance because Parliament had potent tools (bills of attainder and bills of banishment) to deal with pardoned officials.[359]

The framers did not modify the phrase "high crimes and misdemeanors." Thus, "high crimes and misdemeanors" must have been understood by ratifiers to include acts deemed high crimes and misdemeanors by Parliament when it removed officials from office via the impeachment process. The phrase "high crimes and misdemeanors" was first used in the impeachment of the Earl of Suffolk in 1386.[360] In 1386, there was no such crime as a "misdemeanor."[361] It was not until the sixteenth century that the word "misdemeanors" supplanted the word "trespasses" to denote lessor crimes.[362] Although some "high crimes and misdemeanors" involved indictable crimes, "high crimes and misdemeanors" usually involved only maladministration of a kind that was not indictable.[363]

Officials were impeached in Parliament for the following nonindictable "high crimes and misdemeanors":

• Applying appropriated funds to purposes not specified in the appropriation (Earl of Suffolk in 1386)[364]

• Delaying justice by halting writs of appeal (Duke of Suffolk in 1450)[365]

- Ordering people to be put in jail for refusing to enter into bonds before he had the authority to require bonds (Attorney General Yelverton in 1621)[366]
- Allowing the Ordnance office to go unrepaired even though funds were appropriated for that purpose; and allowing contracts for powder to terminate because of failure to make payment (Lord Treasurer Middlesex in 1624)[367]
- Negligent preparation for an invasion; and loss of a ship through neglect (Commissioner of the Navy Peter Pett in 1668)[368]
- Helping to draw up a proclamation to suppress petitions to the King to call a Parliament (Chief Justice North in 1680)[369]
- Discharging a grand jury before they made their presentment; and arbitrarily granting blank general warrants (Chief Justice Scroggs in 1680)[370]
- Applying appropriated money to public purposes not specified in the appropriation (Sir Edward Seymour in 1680)[371]

In 1637, Justice Berkley was impeached along with other justices for uttering unconstitutional opinions.[372] Berkley was also impeached for verbally abusing and threatening a grand jury for making a presentment.[373] English legal expert Richard Wooddeson's summary on impeachment was paraphrased by Supreme Court Justice Joseph Story. Story agreed with Wooddeson that: "lord chancellors and judges and other magistrates have not only been impeached for bribery, and acting grossly contrary to the duties of their office, but for misleading their sovereign by unconstitutional opinions and for attempts to subvert the fundamental laws, and introduce arbitrary power...."[374] (Wooddeson succeeded William Blackstone as Vinerian lecturer, and Wooddeson was often cited in the United States.[375])

Some authorities have claimed that impeachment must involve a violation of a criminal law because Blackstone stated that an impeachment "is a prosecution of the already known and established law."[376] Blackstone did not mean that impeachments could only take place when a violation of criminal law was charged. He knew that impeachments also took place when officials were charged with either performing official duties in an improper manner or not performing their official duties. Blackstone said: "the first and principal [high misdemeanor] is the *mal-administration* of such high officers, as are in the public trust and employment. This is usually punished by the method of parliamentary impeachment."[377]

All officials removed from office by Parliament via the impeachment process were removed for matters concerning office. However, there was one impeachment charge for conduct outside office. In 1680, Chief Justice William Scroggs was impeached by the House of Commons. One of the charges against Scroggs was: "frequent and notorious excesses and debaucheries." Several other charges against Scroggs were for matters concerning office. They included granting oppressive warrants, arbitrarily discharging a grand jury before it made presentments, and making an illegal order to prevent publication of a book. The House of Lords was less concerned about Scroggs' behavior than the House of Commons, as indicated by the fact that the House of Lords refused the House of Commons' request to imprison Scroggs while he awaited trial in the House of Lords. Scroggs was not tried in the House of Lords because the session of Parliament was terminated by King Charles II, and the king dismissed Scroggs—probably much to the relief of Scroggs—before the next session of Parliament. If Scroggs would have been tried in the House of Lords, it is doubtful that they would have convicted him on the debauchery charge, and inconceivable that they would have convicted him on only the debauchery charge.

Impeachment of Members of Congress

It is likely that most ratifiers understood that Congress could impeach and remove senators via the impeachment process. Senators have a constitutional advisory role with respect to treaties and the appointment of high level executive branch personnel. In his *Commentaries on the Laws of England*, Blackstone said: "For as a king cannot misuse his power, without the advice of evil counsellors, and the assistance of wicked ministers, these men may be examined and punished."[378]

In 1797, the House of Representatives impeached Senator William Blount (a framer of the Constitution). The most serious impeachment charge against Blount was that he was involved in a conspiracy to launch a military expedition to take Florida and Louisiana from Spain and hand them over to England.[379] Soon after the House impeached Blount, the Senate expelled Blount—by a vote of twenty-five to one—as "guilty of a high misdemeanor, entirely inconsistent with his public trust and duty as a Senator."[380] Despite the fact that he had already been expelled from the Senate, Blount fought being impeached. He wanted to remain eligible for future federal office. The Senate voted fourteen to eleven that it "ought not to hold jurisdiction" as it dismissed impeachment charges against Blount.[381] The fourteen senators *probably* had one or more of the following thoughts:

- The Senate has no authority to try *former* officials on impeachment charges. Chief Justice Scroggs was not tried because he was dismissed after he was impeached and before he was to have been tried.

- Congress has no authority to remove members of Congress via the impeachment process.

- We have already expelled Blount. It is now more important for the Senate to legislate than to try Blount.

In *The Federalist*, No. 66, Alexander Hamilton discussed the impeachment process relevant to members of Congress. He said:

"A *fourth* objection to the Senate, in the capacity of a court of impeachments, is derived from its union with the executive in the power of making treaties. This, it has been said, would constitute the senators their own judges in every case of a corrupt or perfidious execution of that trust. After having combined with the Executive in betraying the interests of the nation in a ruinous treaty, what prospect, it is asked, would there be of their being made to suffer the punishment they would deserve when they were themselves to decide upon the accusation brought against them for the treachery of which they had been guilty? This objection has been circu-lated with more earnestness and with greater show of reason than any other which has appeared against this part of the plan; . . . The convention might . . . have had in view the punishment of a few leading individuals in the Senate . . . but they could not, . . . have contemplated the impeachment and punishment of two thirds of the Senate, consenting to an improper treaty, than of a majority of that or of the other branch of the national legislature, . . . How, in fact, could a majority in the House of Representatives impeach them-selves?. . ."[382]

The Virginia Ratifying Convention proposed the following amendment to the Constitution: "That some Tribunal other than the Senate be provided for trying impeachments of Senators."[383]

There is no record of anyone at the Constitutional Convention indicating that senators or representatives were immune from im-peachment. There are two instances of delegates at the Constitutional Convention speaking of impeachment of senators.[384]

Article III

CHAPTER 5

Article III, Section 1

The judicial Power of the United States, shall be vested in one supreme Court, and in such inferior Courts as the Congress may from time to time ordain and establish. The Judges, both of supreme and inferior Courts, shall hold their Offices during good Behaviour, and shall, at stated Times, receive for their Services, a Compensation, which shall not be diminished during their Continuance in Office.

Original Meaning in 21st Century Plain English

Except for impeachments and trials in military courts, all power to make rulings in federal cases shall be vested in (1) one Supreme Court, (2) lower federal courts which Congress creates, and (3) state courts which Congress authorizes to try federal cases. The judges of the Supreme Court and other courts which hear nonmilitary federal cases:

- Shall not be forced to vacate their offices as long as they perform their judicial duties properly (unbiased, lawfully, etc.) and are not convicted of a felony of any kind

147

- Shall be paid salaries and receive travel expenses from the federal government in amounts indicated by an act of Congress

- Shall not have their federal salaries or travel allowances reduced or delayed as long as they remain judges of federal cases

Discussion of Article III, Section 1

The phrase "one supreme Court" may seem like an oxymoron to some twenty-first century Americans. In Great Britain in 1787, there were several supreme courts. The famous Virginia Plan included the phrase "one or more supreme tribunals." The Virginia delegates *may* have envisioned one supreme court for maritime cases and one supreme court for other cases.

The "good Behaviour" Provision

The term "good Behaviour" has been controversial for at least two hundred years. Can federal judges be removed from office other than by impeachment? What constitutes misbehavior? Is all misbehavior impeachable? Can federal judges be removed from office for being convicted of felonies unrelated to their office? Before answering these questions, let us consider some key facts relevant to good behavior. (Key facts relevant to impeachable offenses are included in the discussion of Article II, Section 4.)

In 1701, Parliament enacted the Act of Settlement which established the tenure of all English judges as good behavior. Prior to 1701, most English judges could be removed from office by the king or queen even if the judges had behaved perfectly. Some English judges, in an effort to retain their offices, misapplied the law to please the king or queen. *Misapplication of the law by judges was the main thing that Parliament tried to prevent with the Act of Settlement's good behavior provision.* The Act of Settlement: (1) granted all English judges tenure for as long as they conducted themselves well (That prevented the king or queen from acting unilaterally to remove an English judge from office.); and (2) *allowed* the king or queen to terminate the tenure of an English judge *only* if formally requested to do so by both houses of Parliament.[385] If the king or queen did not comply with Parliament's request to remove a judge, Parliament could use the impeachment process to remove judges who had misapplied the law. The Act of Settlement did not eliminate (1) the parliamentary procedure of impeachment, or (2) a judicial proceeding in which a judge was convicted of acting "contrary to what belongs to his office."[386]

The good behavior provision of the Act of Settlement applied only to English judges. After 1701, some colonial assemblies tried to get the tenure of colonial judges changed to good behavior; however, English authorities (royal governors or the Privy Council) usually vetoed such efforts.[387] The tenure of some colonial judges was set at good behavior. However, English authorities worked to change the tenure of those judges to "at the King's pleasure."[388] The Declaration of Independence asserted, as one of its proofs of King George III's "absolute Tyranny over these States": "He has made [colonial] Judges dependent on his Will alone, for the tenure of their offices, and the amount and payment of their salaries."

Some state constitutions set judicial tenure at good behavior. The 1776 Maryland Constitution stated: "That the independency and uprightness of Judges are essential to the impartial administration of justice, . . . Judges ought to hold commissions during good behaviour; . . . Judges shall be removed for misbehaviour, on conviction in a court of law, and may be removed by the Governor, upon the address of the General Assembly; *Provided,* That two-thirds of all the members of each House concur in such address. . . ."[389] That statement emphasized that good behavior included impartiality and the rule of law.

The 1784 New Hampshire Constitution stated: "It is essential to the preservation of the rights of every individual, . . . that there be an impartial interpretation of the laws, . . . It is the right of every citizen to be tried by judges as impartial as the lot of humanity will admit. . . . the judges of the supreme . . . court should hold their offices so long as they behave well; . . ."[390] That statement reinforces the Maryland Constitution's inclusion of impartiality and the rule of law as necessary elements of good behavior. Judges in New Hampshire were removed by address of the state legislature.[391]

Only six states provided for impeachment, and four of those provided an alternative of either maladministration or misbehavior.[392]

Most ratifiers of the unamended Constitution must have understood that federal judges who misbehaved (were clearly partial, ruled clearly contrary to law because of mental incompetence or any other reason, etc.) could be removed from office. The ratifiers certainly did not understand that judges whose misbehavior fell short of an impeachable offense could not be removed from office. However, the framers did not specify a procedure for removing judges whose misbehavior fell short of an impeachable offense. Congress, under the "necessary and proper" clause, has the authority to spell out a procedure to remove judges for *all* types of misbehavior.[393] (The framers of the Constitution did not spell out a process for collecting import taxes. The Constitution does not explicitly authorize Congress to do so. However, nobody would claim that Congress does not have the authority to enact laws which specify a process for collecting import taxes.)

Congress has never spelled out a comprehensive process for removing judges for misbehavior. However, the Act of 1790 provided that upon conviction for bribery, a judge shall be "forever disqualified to hold any office."[394] The Act of 1790 is the only statute that Congress has enacted under the "good Behaviour" provision.

The framers considered specifying a removal process based on the Act of Settlement. John Dickinson "moved . . . [that] after the words 'good behaviour' [add] the words 'provided that they may be removed by the Executive on the application by the Senate and House of Representatives.'"[395] Gouverneur Morris objected to removal of judges "without a trial."[396] Since the Constitution does not specify a removal process for judicial misbehavior, Congress has complete freedom to do so. If the only words in the Constitution relevant to impeachment were the words of Article II, Section 4, Congress would have freedom to specify: (1) the body to impeach (House, House Committee, Congress, grand jury, etc.); (2) the body to try (Senate, twelve randomly selected senators, Supreme Court, twelve randomly selected citizens, etc.); (3) what percent of the impeachment body was needed to impeach; and (4) what percent of the trial body was needed to convict.

During a debate in Congress on January 13, 1802, Congressman David Stone said that members of the federal judiciary:

"shall . . . be removed from office by impeachment and conviction; but it does not follow that they may not be removed by other means. They shall hold their offices during good behavior, and they shall be removed from office upon impeachment and conviction of treason, bribery, and other high crimes and misdemeanors. If the words impeachment . . . [, misbehavior, and] high crimes and misdemeanors, be understood according to any construction of them hitherto received as established, it will be found, that although a judge guilty of high crimes and misdemeanors, is always guilty of misbehavior in office, yet that of the various species of misbehavior in office, which may render it exceedingly improper that a judge should continue in office, many of them are neither treason nor bribery; nor can they be properly dignified by the appellation of high crimes and misdemeanors; and for the impeachment of which no precedent can be found; nor would the words of the Constitution justify such impeachment. . . . Their misbehavior certainly is not an impeachable offence; still it is the ground by which the judges are to be removed from office. The process of impeachment, therefore, cannot be the only one by which the judges may be removed from office, under, and according to the Constitution. I take it, therefore, to be a thing undeniable, that there resides somewhere in the government a power to declare what amounts to misbehavior in office by the judges, and to remove them from office for the same without impeachment. . . . the Constitution does not prohibit their removal by the legislature."[397]

Although Congressman Stone was correct, he probably knew he was fighting an uphill battle. All Federalists and a significant number of Republicans were opposed to enacting a statute to authorize an Act of Settlement type procedure to remove federal judges. The reasons for the opposition to Congressman Stone were quite different.

The Federalists were unalterably opposed to a judicial removal process based on the Act of Settlement primarily because Federalists held all of the federal judgeships. The Judiciary Act of 1801, which became law on February 13, 1801, promised to keep Federalists in control of the federal judiciary for many years thereafter. Relevant to the Judiciary Act of 1801, Federalist U.S. Senator Gouverneur Morris (one of the principal framers of the Constitution) wrote on February 20, 1801, that the Federalists "are about to experience a heavy gale of adverse wind; can they be blamed for casting many anchors to hold their ship through the storm?"[398]

The Federalists were also unalterably opposed to the repeal of the Judiciary Act of 1801. However, it was repealed in March of 1802 because the Republicans were in control and no Republican thought that it was unconstitutional to repeal it. (Any statute enacted by Congress can be repealed by Congress.)

The Federalist party had been severely stung by Republican charges that the Sedition Act of 1798 was unconstitutional. The Federalists retaliated by claiming that the Republicans needed explicit authority to enact federal laws. It was an inconsistent position for the Federalists to take. Unfortunately for Congressman Stone and other people who wanted federal judges to be removed even though their misbehavior fell short of an impeachable offense, some Republicans in Congress—mainly former Anti-Federalists—wanted federal government powers to be explicitly stated in the Constitution.[399] President Jefferson tried hard to have a good relationship with all members of his party, even though his party was "composed of groups with irreconcilable ideas, . . ."[400] In 1805, Jefferson wrote: "The only cordial I wish to carry into retirement is the undivided good will of all with whom I have acted."[401]

Jefferson sided with the members of his party who wanted a constitutional amendment to authorize a removal process based on the Act of Settlement. Had Jefferson totally supported Congressman Stone, Jefferson would have been excoriated in the Federalist newspapers. There would have also been criticism from some Republican members of Congress. Jefferson did *not* want a Federalist resurgence.

Furthermore, Jefferson detested criticism. Criticism of Jefferson promised to be greatly reduced by constitutional amendments to explicitly cover the most constitutionally sensitive laws he favored.

Jefferson wanted an amendment relevant to the Louisiana Purchase Treaty when none was needed—as shown in this book in the discussion of Article I, Section 8, Paragraph 4. The Federalists and a few Republicans challenged the constitutionality of the Louisiana Purchase Treaty.

The frustration experienced by Congressman Stone must have become much more widespread as the result of the impeachment trial of Justice Samuel Chase in 1805. Chase was not removed from office despite his clear judicial misbehavior.

Congress has several options for putting teeth into the "good Behaviour" provision other than by resorting to the impeachment process. Using the impeachment process for all types of misbehavior would be unconstitutional and impractical. After participating in the impeachment trial of a federal judge in 1936, for misbehavior of a kind which does not meet the standards of an impeachable offense, Senator William McAdoo correctly stated that it was a "practical certainty that in a large majority of cases misconduct will never be visited with impeachment, . . . [the impeachment process is essentially] a standing invitation for judges to abuse their authority with impunity."[402]

A constitutional law could be passed by Congress to set up federal grand juries to investigate citizen complaints of judicial misbehavior by federal judges. In judicial misbehavior trials (1) juries should decide whether or not to remove judges, (2) nonlawyer members of grand juries which make presentments should prosecute, and (3) "expert witnesses" must not be required.

It would be constitutional, practical, and effective for Congress to (1) require lie detector tests to be given to all federal judges annually, and (2) require federal judges to be removed from office if lie detector tests indicate that the judges knowingly made one or more rulings which were not impartial. If Congress passes such a law, state legislatures might pass similar laws in order to sharply reduce partiality by state judges.

In 1790, Congress passed the "Act of 1790" which provided that federal judges would be "forever disqualified to hold any office" if they were convicted of bribery in a court of law.[403] Even in 1790, Congress wanted to reduce the amount of time it spent impeaching and convicting judges. The Act of 1790 serves as proof—the type of proof used by Abraham Lincoln to prove that Congress could constitutionally prohibit slavery in the territories—that a majority of the framers of the unamended Constitution intended that federal judges could be constitutionally removed from office without resorting to the impeachment process. I am aware of no constitutional controversy relevant to the judicial removal provision of the Act of 1790. Debates in Congress over proposed laws during the first few years under the Constitution often involved controversies about constitutionality.[404] President Washington made his first presidential veto on April 5, 1792, when he vetoed a bill because it was unconstitutional.[405]

The First Congress got its authority to enact the Act of 1790 from three places in the Constitution. The "good Behaviour" provision combined with the "necessary and proper" provision give Congress its authority to enact statutes to specify how misbehavior is to be determined. Bribery is misbehavior even though it is also an impeachable offense. However, the "good Behaviour" provision does not give Congress the authority to prevent judges removed for misbehavior from becoming judges of federal cases in the future. The members of the First Congress probably realized that they had the power, under their authority to establish and regulate federal courts, to prevent anyone convicted of a felony from being made a federal judge.

Some lawyers try to create confusion by saying something like: "The words 'during good behavior' are the common law equivalent of the words 'life tenure.'" While that is true, life tenure at common law was conditioned on good behavior and terminated by misbehavior.[406] At the Pennsylvania Ratifying Convention, Chief Justice McKean stated: "the judges may continue for life, if they shall so long behave themselves well."[407]

Federal district Judge John Pickering was removed from office via the impeachment process when the Senate, in 1804, found him guilty of (1) providing opinions clearly contrary to a federal statute, and (2) presiding while drunk.[408] Providing unconstitutional opinions was a high crime or misdemeanor in England. Providing opinions which are clearly contrary to a constitutional statute or the Constitution constitutes: (1) a high crime and misdemeanor (unless the judge is insane); *and* (2) misbehavior (even if the judge is insane). Pickering was widely considered to be insane; hence, it is questionable that he was guilty of a high crime. Presiding while drunk constitutes misbehavior. It is questionable that presiding while drunk constitutes an impeachable offense—even where public drunkenness is a misdemeanor.

In 1804, the House of Representatives impeached Supreme Court Justice Samuel Chase by a vote of 73 to 32.[409] The Senate tried Chase in 1805, but failed to get a two-thirds vote to convict Chase on any of the eight articles of impeachment. Before their vote on each article, the senators were asked: "Is Samuel Chase guilty or not guilty of a high crime or misdemeanor as charged in the article just read?"[410] On one article, there were no votes to convict; on four other articles, less than half of the senators voted to convict.[411] On the article for which the most senators voted to convict Chase, the vote was 19 to 15 (23 votes were needed to convict).[412]

A higher percentage of representatives, relative to senators, probably made use of the good behavior standard. It was obvious that Chase was guilty of misbehavior. In Chase's impeachment trial in the Senate, Congressman Caesar Rodney, lead prosecutor for the House managers and later attorney general of the U.S., said he relied on impeachment to enforce the good behavior requirement.[413] Although Rodney correctly maintained that an indictable offense was not required for impeachment and removal from office, he maintained that Chase had committed an indictable offense.[414]

One of the impeachment articles against Chase involved instructions he gave to a federal grand jury in Baltimore, Maryland, in 1803. In his instructions to the Baltimore grand jury, Chase was reported to have:

- Attacked the act of Congress which abolished the Judiciary Act of 1801, saying: "the independence of the National Judiciary is shaken to its foundation."

- Attacked the Maryland Constitution and universal suffrage, which Chase said would "certainly and rapidly destroy all protection to property and all security to personal liberty . . ."

- Declared: "The modern doctrine by our late reformers, that all men in a state of society are entitled to enjoy equal liberty and equal rights, have brought this mighty mischief among us, and I fear it will rapidly destroy progress, until peace and order, freedom and property shall be destroyed."[415] [416] (Chase obviously included President Thomas Jefferson as one of the "late reformers." The "modern doctrine" was included in the Declaration of Independence.)

President Jefferson wrote, in a letter to a congressman: "You must have heard of the extraordinary charge [instructions] of Chase to the Grand Jury at Baltimore. Ought this seditious and official attack on the principles of our Constitution, and on the proceedings of a State, to go unpunished?"[417] Based on a strict interpretation of the common-law crime of sedition, Chase's instructions to the federal grand jury were seditious. (Sedition and federal common-law crimes are discussed under the First Amendment in this book.) The impeachment article dealing with Chase's grand jury instructions was the count on which 19 of 34 senators voted guilty. Some senators who voted that Chase was guilty of a high crime or misdemeanor must have done so because they agreed with Thomas Jefferson and Caesar Rodney that Chase had committed an indictable crime. None of the other articles of impeachment involved a possible indictable crime, and most of the other articles involved far worse judicial behavior.

It was clear that Chase was extremely partial in *United States v. Callender*, a case prosecuted in 1800 under the Sedition Act of 1798. James Callender was "the most effective political writer in American politics" from 1795 to 1800.[418] In doing research for an anti-Federalist book he was writing, Callender corresponded with Thomas Jefferson. Jefferson and some of his political "lieutenants" supplied Callender with documents and encouraged Callender to complete *The Prospect Before Us*, the first volume of which was scheduled to be published at about the same time that Jefferson planned to begin his presidential campaign in 1800.[419] I will mention only some of Chase's actions which showed his partiality in *Callender*.

Chase made the erroneous ruling: "No evidence is admissible that does not go to justify the whole charge."[420] That ruling prevented at least one defense witness from testifying. At the impeachment trial of Chase, Chief Justice John Marshall was called as a defense witness for Chase. Upon being cross-examined, Marshall was forced to acknowledge that he had never heard of a witness in any other criminal case being deemed inadmissible because he could only prove part of a charge.[421] (If Marshall had said something which could have been easily disproved (1) it would not have helped Chase, and (2) it would have greatly increased the probability that Marshall would have been impeached.) In the sixth edition of his textbook *Criminal Law*, published in 1868, Francis Wharton correctly characterized the ruling made by Chase which is quoted in this paragraph as a "palpable and unprecedented violation of the law of evidence . . . a witness was rejected, who proved to be a material part of the defendant's case, simply because the particular witness was not able to prove the whole of it."[422]

Chase acted like he had no conception of what the Sixth Amendment term "impartial jury" means. Chase unreasonably ruled: "The only proper question [to determine whether a juror is biased] is, 'Have you ever formed and delivered an opinion upon the charge.' He must have delivered as well as formed an opinion."[423] Chase slammed the door on bias inquires by refusing to let the indictment be read to the jurors.[424] A juror named John Bassett was sworn in despite the fact that he told Chase that he had read extracts of the book in question and formed an "unequivocal opinion" that the book was seditious.[425] Chase conceded that he had refused to excuse Basset on his plea that "he had made up his mind, or formed an opinion, that the publication, called 'The Prospect before Us,' from which the words charged in the indictment as libellous were said to be extracted, but which he had never seen, was, according to the representation of it, which he had received, within the Sedition Law."[426]

William Wirt defended Callender. (Wirt later served as U.S. attorney general for a record 12 years, from 1817 to 1829, and became the presidential candidate of the Anti-Masonic party in 1832. The Anti-Masonic party was the first third party in the United States. Wirt was nominated to be president in 1831 in the first national nominating convention in the United States.[427] Wirt carried only Vermont, but he made a decent showing in some other states which helped Democrat Andrew Jackson defeat National Republican Henry Clay.) In *Callender*, the following exchange took place between Chase and Wirt:

> Chase: If I understand you correctly, you offer an argument to the . . . [trial] jury, to convince them that the . . . Sedition Law is contrary to the constitution of the United States and, therefore, void. Now I tell you that this is irregular and inadmissible, it is not competent for a jury to decide on this point. . . . we all know that juries have a right to decide the law, as well as the fact—and the constitution is the supreme law of the land, which controls all laws repugnant to it.

> Wirt: Since, then, the jury have a right to consider the law, and the constitution is a law, the conclusion is certainly . . . [logical], that the jury have a right to consider the constitution.

> Chase: A non sequitur, sir.[428]

That stopped Wirt from trying to convince the jury that the Sedition Act of 1798 was unconstitutional.[429] Chase went on to say: "the judicial power of the United States is the only proper and competent authority to decide whether any statute made by Congress is contrary to, or in violation of, the Federal Constitution."[430] In effect, Chase told the jury that it would be improper for it to exercise its right to determine the law even though the Sedition Act of 1798 explicitly gave juries the right to determine the law. Chase sentenced

Callender to nine months in prison and fined Callender. A "pro-Jefferson subscription drive" raised funds necessary to pay the fine and support Callender's children while he was in jail; Callender became a martyr in the Sedition Act controversy.[431] Chase's behavior in *Callender* was especially deplorable because, under the Judiciary Act of 1789, no criminal case could be appealed to the Supreme Court.

On one of the impeachment articles dealing with procedural mistakes in *Callender*, no votes were cast against Chase in the Senate; only four senators voted guilty on the other article relevant to procedural mistakes in *Callender*.[432] That was a clear repudiation of the prosecution's attempt to broaden impeachable offenses to include all misbehavior.[433]

The Senate acquitted Chase on March 1, 1805. Two days later, on the day before he was sworn in as vice-president of the United States, George Clinton wrote, relevant to the acquittal of Chase:

> "I will only observe that several of the members who voted for his acquittal had no doubt but the charges against him were substantiated and of course that his conduct was unproper and reprehensible, but considering that many parts of it were sanctioned by the practice of other Judges . . . [and] not prohibited by any express and positive law they could not consistently with their ideas of justice find him guilty of high crimes and misdemeanours. It was to such refined reasoning of some honest men that he owes his acquittal."[434]

Throughout Chase's impeachment trial, Chase made effective use of the fact that the House of Representatives had failed to impeach any of the district judges who had presided with Chase at the trials for which Chase's actions were impeached.[435] In all of the trials for which Chase's actions were impeached, *Callender* included, Chase was one of two judges. Apparently, the district court judges in those cases concurred with Chase's rulings. In deciding not to impeach the district court judges, the House probably considered: (1) that it was likely that the district court judges were reluctant to disagree with a member of the Supreme Court (especially in the middle of a high visibility trial in which the Supreme Court member was taking an unequivocal position); and (2) that the only common denominator in the cases involved in Chase's impeachment was Samuel Chase.

The partiality shown by Chase was obviously judicial misbehavior, but it was not *obviously* a high crime and misdemeanor. If all Republican senators had used the standard of "good Behaviour," Chase would have been removed from office. If no Republican senators had been alienated by Congressman John Randolph, the "refined reasoning" employed to acquit Chase may not have been employed. Randolph: (1) led the effort to impeach Chase in the House of Representatives; (2) was one of the prosecutors in Chase's trial in the Senate; and (3) had recently led a "revolt" in the Republican party relevant to the "Yazoo compromise" (The Yazoo struggle became intense after Chase was impeached but before Chase was tried.).[436]

There were 25 Republican senators and nine Federalist senators in the Senate during Chase's impeachment trial. To remove Chase, 23 guilty votes were needed on the same article.

This paragraph is a digression in that it discusses terminology used for early national political parties. From 1796 to 1824, members of the Democratic-Republican party were called Republicans by almost everybody. Most historians refer to members of the Democratic-Republican party as "Republicans." The Democratic-Republican party split into the Democratic party and the National Republican party. The National Republican party: (1) included most former members of the Federalist party; and (2) merged with the Anti-Masonic party to become the Whig party (Two Whigs were elected president; America has had four Whig presidents because two died in office.). Most Whigs, including Abraham Lincoln, joined the Republican party that was formed in 1854. Hence, modern Democrats *technically* trace more directly to "Jeffersonian Republicans" (members of the Democratic-Republican party) than do modern Republicans. Party lines are made even more fuzzy by the fact that some Democrats, including U.S. Supreme Court Justice McLean, switched to the Republican party shortly after it was formed in 1854.

Answers to the questions posed at the beginning of this subsection are as follows:

- It is constitutional to remove federal judges and justices from office other than by impeachment. Congress utilized the "good Behaviour" provision to enact the Act of 1790. That statute required federal judges to be removed from office if they were convicted of bribery in a court of law. To greatly reduce judicial misbehavior, Congress must enact a law which (1) requires federal judges to take lie detector tests, and (2) requires federal judges to be removed from office when tests indicate that they knowingly made rulings which were not impartial.

- It is misbehavior for judges to: (1) do anything related to their office that judges clearly should not do (such as making a ruling that they know is not impartial); (2) fail to do something that judges should clearly do (such as hold a trial in a reasonable amount of time); or (3) commit a felony.

- Judicial misbehavior which falls short of "high crimes and misdemeanors" is not impeachable. Why? The penalties for conviction of an impeachable offense are greater than "removal from Office" in that they include "disqualification to hold and enjoy any Office of honor, Trust or Profit under the United States." (After Senator William Blount was expelled from the U.S. Senate in 1797 by a vote of 25-1, as being "guilty of a high misdemeanor," he fought the authority of the U.S. Senate to try him on impeachment charges filed by the House.[437] The Senate voted 14-11 to dismiss impeachment charges against Blount. He wanted to remain eligible for federal office. Blount may have been on his way back to the U.S. Senate when he was elected to the Tennessee Senate in 1798 and chosen to preside by his fellow senators.[438] Blount, a framer of the Constitution, had a stroke and died in 1800.[439]) In the impeachment trial of Justice Samuel Chase, the Republican senators would have removed Chase if 23 of 25 of them thought all misbehavior was impeachable. At most, four senators thought so. It is possible that none of the senators thought all misbehavior was impeachable. (Some of Chase's misbehavior in *Callender* was very serious and could have honestly been considered a high crime and misdemeanor.) Although federal Judge John Pickering was impeached and convicted in 1804 for presiding while drunk—a questionable impeachable offense even though it was a misdemeanor—Pickering was also convicted of delivering opinions clearly contrary to a constitutional act of Congress.

• Federal judges can be constitutionally removed from office solely for being convicted of felonies unrelated to their office *if* the removal is accomplished under the "good Behaviour" provision. Although misbehavior in England usually involved behavior in "matters concerning office," it was well established (by noted common-law authority Lord Coke and others) that it was legal to remove from office officials with life tenure if those officials were convicted of an infamous crime (such as perjury or forgery) in a court of law. [440] It is unconstitutional to remove federal judges from office via the impeachment process solely because they were convicted of felonies unrelated to their office. All officials removed from office by Parliament via the impeachment process were removed for matters concerning office.[441] Even if it were constitutional for Congress to use the impeachment process to remove judges convicted of one or more felonies unrelated to their office, it would be far more sensible to simply pass a law to automatically remove such judges. However, Congress must do much more than that in order to facilitate the removal of unethical judges and mentally incompetent judges.

Inferior Courts

The Constitution authorizes Congress to establish "inferior Courts." The inferior courts established by the Judiciary Act of 1789 were probably different than most American voters anticipated in 1788.[442] Many Americans anticipated that Congress would authorize state supreme courts to try all federal cases except for maritime cases, military cases, and those cases for which the U.S. Supreme Court has original jurisdiction by virtue of the Constitution.[443] Trials were held in all state supreme courts in 1789.[444] Some members of the 1789 Congress favored a plan in which: (1) the only courts which would try only federal cases would be a few admiralty courts (to try cases of a maritime nature under maritime law), infrequently-held military courts, and the U.S. Supreme Court; and (2) the U.S. Supreme Court would serve as the *only* federal appellate court.[445]

Compensation Not Diminished

Why did the framers include a provision to prevent Congress from reducing the compensation of federal judges? The framers did not want Congress to use the power of the purse to pressure federal judges to comply with unconstitutional laws. Most framers and ratifiers understood that the federal courts would serve as a check on Congress and vice versa.

Although Congress has never reduced or withheld salaries to pressure judges, Congress has given the Court and its members several benefits which Congress can withdraw. This has put pressure on federal judges to comply with unconstitutional acts of Congress.

The framers intended, and ratifiers understood, that the Supreme Court would hear all cases which were properly appealed to it under its appellate jurisdiction. Congress eventually gave the Court the power to select the appeal cases it hears. That would have been regarded by most framers and ratifiers as an unconstitutional redelegation of power.

The Court did not have any control of the cases it heard until Congress enacted the Judiciary Act of 1891. Even then, the Court's control was quite limited. It was not until the Judiciary Act of 1925 was enacted that the Court gained substantial control of the cases it heard.[446] Chief Justice William Howard Taft "energetically lobbied" for the Judiciary Act of 1925 (popularly known as the "Judges Bill").[447] The 1988 Judicial Improvements and Access to Justice Act virtually eliminated the mandatory jurisdiction of the Court, giving the Court virtually total control of the cases it heard.[448]

Although Congress hasn't put it in writing, its lack of action against the Court or its members for clear unconstitutional rulings against states (requiring Miranda warnings, creating abortion rights, outlawing death sentences for murder, overturning convictions for pornography, etc.) indirectly says that Congress condones such rulings. There is effectively an unwritten understanding that Congress allows the Court to be the Supreme State Legislature in return for the Court condoning unconstitutional laws passed by Congress.

The framers did not intend, and the ratifiers did not understand, that Congress would have the power to grant pensions to members of Congress or the federal judiciary. Based on eighteenth-century statutes, pensions were envisioned to be awarded only to military officers and disabled war veterans. There was an interesting controversy in 1803 relevant to what to do about Justice Thomas Bradbury of the Massachusetts Supreme Court. Bradbury, who held his office "during good behaviour," had served well as a judge, suffered a stroke, "showed no signs of recovering," expressed his willingness to resign, but asked the legislature for a pension because he had no other source of income.[449] Federalist legislators proposed a bill to provide half pay for life for justices who retired from the Massachusetts Supreme Court. Republicans denounced the pension bill. On March 2, 1803, the *National Aegis*, a Worcester newspaper, stated:

> "Republican principles will suffer no man to feed upon the *public* bounty, without an equivalent service to the *Public*. . . . If a *Judge* accepts of an honorable office; which endangers neither his life nor his limbs, with an honorable and equivalent salary during his continuance in office, he has no claim upon his Country, because he may chance to grow old and become incapable any longer of earning his compensation. He knows the condition upon which he accepts. He knows the tenure by which he ought to hold his office; that he shall be able to perform its duties, and render to the public a service equivalent to his salary. No man ever accepted the appointment of a judge, unless he considered the honor and emoluments of his office, taken together, as a full satisfaction for the private business he might surrender, and the labor and fatigue of his official duty. He receives, then, his *quid pro quo*, while he is capable of rendering the services of a judge. When he is no longer capable he can no longer earn his salary and it is his duty to resign."[450]

The Jeffersonians maintained that "the people are not to suffer . . . to pay men for going out of office."[451] The pension bill was defeated, and the legislature voted to remove Justice Bradbury from office by address. A majority of the members of both parties voted to remove Justice Bradbury from office because he failed to resign when he was no longer capable of performing the duties of his office.[452]

No framer of the unamended Constitution intended, and no ratifier understood, that Congress would have the power to fund law clerks to help judges write opinions. Historian Wilfred Ritz wrote: "No state in 1789 had either judges who wrote opinions, or reporters who published opinions, or courts that could instruct other courts about what state law was."[453] At least one exception to that statement is that Connecticut supreme court judges and superior court judges wrote opinions after a 1784 statute required written opinions to be filed in order to establish "a more perfect and permanent system of common law in the state."[454] (Some Pennsylvania judges were probably also writing opinions in 1789, but none were published until 1790.) Ratifiers who knew about written court opinions were aware that judges wrote them by themselves.

Congress passed a law in 1922 which allowed each justice to employ one law clerk at an annual federal salary of up to $3,600.[455] Never before had Congress funded law clerks for justices. By the end of the twentieth century, each justice was allowed to have seven personal assistants whose salaries were paid by the federal government.[456] The seven assistants included four law clerks (Law clerks have a great deal of influence in the selection of cases that the Court hears.), two secretaries, and one messenger.[457] Retired "senior justices" came to be allowed to hire one law clerk and one secretary—to be paid by U.S. taxpayers.[458]

In 1889, with no help from law clerks, the Court produced 265 signed opinions.[459] In 1973, when the chief justice had four law clerks and each associate justice had three law clerks, the Court produced less than half the number of signed opinions it had produced in 1889.[460] It is not easy to legislate when you have to pretend that you are adjudicating. This was especially true in 1973 when the Court was perverting the Constitution to produce *Roe v. Wade*.

The 265 opinions written by the Court in 1889 is all the more noteworthy because: (1) Justice Stanley Matthews died on March 22, 1889, after being ill for some time, and, for the remainder of 1889, eight justices wrote all of the Court's opinions (Matthews' replacement was not sworn in until January 6, 1890.); and (2) members of the Court had circuit-court duties in 1889. Although the Judiciary Act of 1869 greatly reduced the circuit-court duties of justices, the justices continued to have circuit-court duties until the Judiciary Act of 1891 was passed.

There is far more of a conflict of interest between the Court and Congress than the framers intended, or the ratifiers understood, because Congress has empowered itself to: (1) give the Court the power to pick and choose the appeals it hears; (2) allow the Court to act as a Supreme State Legislature; (3) authorize federal pensions for members of the federal judiciary (and set the federal pension levels of members of the federal judiciary); and (4) authorize federally-paid personal staffs for justices and retired justices.

The concept that Congress and the Court serve as a check on the unconstitutional actions of each other must seem as hilarious as the flat-earth concept to the large majority of twenty-first century members of Congress and the Court.

Article III, Section 2, Paragraph 1

The judicial Power shall extend to all Cases, in Law and Equity, arising under this Constitution, the Laws of the United States, and Treaties made, or which shall be made, under their Authority;—to all Cases affecting Ambassadors, other public Ministers and Consuls;—to all Cases of admiralty and maritime Jurisdiction;—to Controversies to which the United States shall be a Party;—to Controversies between two or more States;—between a State and Citizens of another State;—between Citizens of different States;—between Citizens of the same State claiming Lands under Grants of different States, and between a State, or the Citizens thereof, and foreign States, Citizens or Subjects.

Original Meaning in 21st Century Plain English

Federal judicial power shall extend to:

- All criminal and civil cases which arise as a result of law included in the U.S. Constitution itself (However, Congress may empower state courts to serve as trial courts for cases involving the U.S. Constitution.)

- All *criminal* cases which involve the U.S. by virtue of the fact that they involve either statutes made by Congress under the authority of the U.S. Constitution or common laws of a kind which are used by sovereign entities and are accepted by states in the U.S. in 1787 (Constitutional acts of Congress shall prevail if there are any conflicts between such acts and the common law. Congress may empower state courts to serve as trial courts for criminal cases involving common-law crimes or federal-statute crimes.)

- All *civil* cases which involve the U.S. by virtue of the fact that they (1) involve statutes made by Congress under the authority of the U.S. Constitution, (2) involve 1787 common laws applicable to sovereign entities and accepted by states in the U.S., or (3) involve 1787 equity principles applicable to sovereign entities and accepted by states in the United States (Constitutional acts of Congress shall prevail unless superseded by *subsequent* constitutional treaties to which the U.S. is a party. Congress may empower state courts to serve as trial courts for civil cases involving acts of Congress, common laws applicable to the U.S., or equity principles applicable to the United States.)

- All criminal and civil cases in the U.S. which involve treaties agreed to by the U.S. under the Constitution and treaties agreed to by the United States before this Constitution was adopted (Congress may (1) enact laws which supersede treaties, and (2) empower state courts to serve as trial courts for cases involving treaties.)

- All criminal and civil cases in the United States involving officials of foreign countries (Congress may empower state courts to serve as trial courts for cases involving foreign officials who do not insist on having their cases tried in the U.S. Supreme Court.)

- All criminal and civil cases in the United States which can be tried under maritime law (Maritime law involves things that happen on or to commercial ships in ocean water. Congress may empower state courts to serve as trial courts for some cases of a maritime nature. However, no state court shall have the authority to determine whether captured ships or cargoes are legal captures.)

- Civil cases in which the federal government is a plaintiff and civil cases in which the federal government consents to be a defendant (Congress may empower state courts to serve as trial courts in cases in which the United States consents to be a party.)

- Civil cases between two or more states

- Civil cases between a state and citizens of another state (However, no state shall be forced to be a defendant in a lawsuit brought by a citizen of another state.)

- Civil cases between citizens of different states (Such cases are called diversity cases. Congress shall have the power to determine the amount of money required to be in dispute in diversity cases for such cases to be eligible to become federal cases.)

- Civil cases between citizens of the same state relevant to land granted by different states

- Civil cases between a state or citizens of a state on one side and, on the other side, foreign countries or citizens of foreign countries (Such cases are called alienage cases herein. No state shall be forced to be a defendant in a lawsuit brought by a citizen of a foreign country. Congress shall have the power to determine the amount of money required to be in dispute in alienage cases before such cases are eligible to become federal cases.)

Discussion of Article III, Section 2, Paragraph 1

During the period of ratification, considerable apprehension existed relevant to the words: "The judicial Power [of the United States] shall extend . . . to Controversies . . . between a State and Citizens of another State; . . . and between a State, or the Citizens thereof, and foreign States, Citizens or Subjects." Some Americans were deeply concerned that the federal judiciary might have the power to "summon a State as a defendant and to adjudicate" such cases.[461] At ratifying conventions, "Many delegates expressed the opinion that Article III, Section 2, Clause 1 of the Constitution did not authorize suits against a State by a private individual without the consent of the State."[462]

In *The Federalist*, No. 81, Alexander Hamilton wrote:

"I shall take occasion to mention here a supposition which has excited some alarm upon very mistaken grounds. It has been suggested that an assignment of the public securities of one State to the citizens of another would enable them to prosecute that State in the federal courts for the amount of those securities; a suggestion which the following considerations prove to be without foundation. It is inherent in the nature of sovereignty not to be amenable to the suit of an individual *without its consent.* This is the general sense and the general practice of mankind; and the exemption, as one of the attributes of sovereignty, is now enjoyed by the government of every State in the Union. Unless, therefore, there is a surrender of this immunity in the plan of the [Constitutional] convention, it will remain with the States and the danger intimated must be merely . . . [imaginary]. The circumstances which are necessary to produce an alienation of State sovereignty were discussed in considering the article of taxation and need not be repeated here. A recurrence to the principles there established will satisfy us that there is no color to pretend that the State governments would, by the adoption of that plan, be divested of the privilege of paying their own debts in their own way, free from every constraint but that which flows from the obligations of good faith."[463]

In response to objections to the Constitution raised by Patrick Henry and George Mason at the Virginia Ratifying Convention, James Madison said:

"[The Supreme Court's] jurisdiction in controversies between a State and citizens of another State is much objected to, and perhaps without reason. It is not in the power of individuals to call any State into court. The only operation it can have is that, if a State should wish to bring suit against a citizen [residing in another state], it must be brought before the federal court. This will give satisfaction to individuals, as it will prevent citizens on whom a State may have a claim being dissatisfied with the state courts. . . . It appears to me that this [provision] can have no operation but this—to give a citizen a right to be heard in the federal courts; and if a State should condescend to be a party, this court may take cognizance of it."[464]

In the 1793 case of *Chisholm v. Georgia*, the U.S. Supreme Court ruled that a citizen of state A had a right to sue state B "for breach of contract."[465] The Court's order of a judgment of default against Georgia in *Chisholm*—despite the fact that Georgia had presented a "remonstrance of protest" to the Court—"sent tremendous repercussions throughout the United States."[466] Because Georgia did not consent to the trial of *Chisholm v. Georgia*, Georgia was joined by several other states in maintaining that the Court had no jurisdiction in *Chisholm*. *Chisholm* led to the Eleventh Amendment which states: "The Judicial power of the United States shall not be construed to extend to any suit in law or equity, commenced or prosecuted against one of the United States by Citizens of another State, or by Citizens or Subjects of any Foreign State."

There was probably a genuine difference of opinion between the framers with regard to the right of citizens of state A to force state B to be a defendant in a lawsuit. Whatever a majority of the framers intended in this regard, the fact is that framers who supported the Constitution assured ratifiers that the Court did not have the power to force states to become defendants in lawsuits brought by individuals. Such assurances were essential to ratification. Hence, even though the words of Article III indicate that the Court had such power, it did not, and it should not have ruled in *Chisholm*. In Article III, Section 2, Paragraph 1, the word "all" is used for the various types of "Cases" (as "all Cases"), but the word "all" is not used before the various "Controversies." Since disputes between state A and citizens of state B fall under "Controversies," the intent of most framers with regard to such controversies was probably correctly asserted by Hamilton and Madison.

Alienage Cases and Diversity Cases

Article 4 of the Treaty of Paris (also called the Treaty of Peace because it officially ended the Revolutionary War) stated: "Creditors on either Side shall meet with no lawful Impediment to the Recovery of the full value in Sterling Money of all bona fide debts heretofore contracted."[467] Article 5 of the Treaty of Paris "required Congress to 'earnestly recommend' to the states that they restore the confiscated property of 'real British Subjects' and Loyalists (Tories) 'who have not borne Arms against' the United States, . . ."[468]

From 1783 to 1788, much discord existed in the United States relevant to alienage cases. In most alienage cases, British merchants sued Americans to collect debts (including interest) due as a result of contracts made before the Revolutionary War. At the beginning of the Revolutionary War, colonists owed British merchants at least five million pounds sterling.[469] Five million pounds sterling was worth more than sixteen million dollars by 1789 exchange rates. Considering inflation and interest due on debts, the money owed to British merchants by American citizens in 1783 was about double the cost of the Louisiana Purchase. In other alienage cases, "real British Subjects" sued purchasers of property confiscated by states during and after the war. Some state legislatures passed laws to prevent alienage cases from being heard in state courts.

In 1786, at the urging of John Adams (United States Minister to England) and Lord Carmarthen (British Foreign Secretary), John Jay (United States Secretary of Foreign Affairs) investigated the extent of compliance with the Treaty of Paris in the United States.[470] Jay found that violations of the treaty were widespread. He complained to Congress about the violations. As a result of Jay's complaint and Congress' findings, Congress, in the spring of 1787, requested all states to repeal all legislation contrary to the Treaty of Paris.[471]

Aliens and Tories were not the only people who suffered as the result of unfair state legislation and unfair decisions made in state courts. American creditors who were the inhabitants of state A often found it impossible to be treated fairly in the courts of state B.[472]

Congressman James Madison, in a letter to Virginia Governor Edmund Randolph on April 8, 1787, wrote: "an appeal should lie to some national tribunal in all cases which concern foreigners, or inhabitants of other states."[473] Large-scale refusal to pay debts to foreigners and out-of-state Americans threatened the security and prosperity of the United States. Ironically, total enforcement of debt contracts by the federal government would have been an even greater threat to the security and prosperity of the United States. In a July 24, 1788, letter to Thomas Jefferson (United States Minister to France), James Madison wrote that if the new federal courts provided "ill-timed or rigorous execution of the Treaty of Peace" against Americans who owed money to British citizens, it might be fatal to the Union.[474]

The framers of both the unamended Constitution and the Judiciary Act of 1789 were walking something of a tightrope on the question of debts due to British citizens. The Judiciary Act of 1789, a marvel of compromise with preservation of the Union being a key consideration:

• Gave federal circuit courts original jurisdiction for alienage cases and diversity cases in which the amount of money in controversy exceeded five hundred dollars but allowed state courts to hear such cases *if both the plaintiff and the defendant* preferred such cases to be resolved in state courts (This promised to (1) empower American and British merchants to have their high value lawsuits resolved in federal courts, (2) make British merchants more inclined to extend credit to American merchants, and (3) reduce complaints by the British government.)

• Gave the federal courts no jurisdiction for alienage and diversity cases where the amount of money in controversy was five hundred dollars or less[475] (This promised to prevent dissatisfaction with the federal courts from becoming widespread enough to tear the Union apart. The large majority of prewar debts of Americans to British merchants were less than one hundred pounds.[476] Five hundred dollars was worth one hundred fifty pounds in 1789. All alienage cases where the value in controversy was less than five hundred dollars would have to be heard in state courts or not heard in any court. Americans who were sued for amounts less than five hundred dollars would not be forced to either (1) incur travel costs greater than, or nearly as great as, the value in controversy to get themselves, their lawyers, and their witnesses to federal courts in other states, or (2) lose such cases by default.)

• Authorized appeals to the U.S. Supreme Court in alienage cases and diversity cases if (1) the suits had been tried in federal circuit courts, *and* (2) the amount of money in controversy exceeded two thousand dollars

Maritime Cases

In the eighteenth century, maritime cases involved things that happened on or to commercial vessels (ships) on the high seas or other bodies of ocean water. One type of maritime case involved the determination of whether captured commercial vessels were "prizes of war." This type of maritime case was of great interest to Congress during the Revolutionary War. About two thousand commercial vessels and their cargoes were captured by American privateers during the Revolutionary War.[477]

A privateer: (1) is an armed vessel owned by one or more private parties; *and* (2) has a commission (a letter of marque or a letter of marque and reprisal) from a government which authorizes the privateer to be used to capture vessels and cargoes of specified nations. Vessels and cargoes captured by privateers are called prizes. The owners and crew of privateers are awarded much of the value of the prizes which they capture *if* the prizes are determined to be prizes of war. Prizes of war were called "legal prizes" by some people.

When commercial vessels are captured by military vessels, determinations must be made as to whether the captured vessels or cargoes are prizes of war. General George Washington used some of his Continental army and militia resources to arm and crew a few vessels to capture British vessels and British cargoes.[478] The tiny Continental navy and American privateers—especially those from Massachusetts—captured British vessels beginning in 1775. Privateers were very successful, and their success greatly bolstered the spirits of Americans during the Revolutionary War.[479]

On November 8, 1775, General Washington sent a message to Congress in which he urged it to set up courts "for the decision of Property and the legality of Seizures: otherwise I may be involved in inextricable difficulties."[480] On November 11, 1775, Washington sent Congress a copy of a Massachusetts statute which, in the words of historian Henry Bourguignon, "provided for trial of ships captured by the vessels of that state."[481] That statute applied to ships and cargoes captured by privateers commissioned by Massachusetts. Since the Massachusetts statute did not apply to vessels fitted out at the expense of Congress, Washington stated:

> "Should not a Court be established by Authority of Congress, to take cognizance of the Prizes made by the Continental Vessels? Whatever the mode is which they are pleased to adopt, there is an absolute necessity of its being speedily determined on, for I cannot spare Time . . . to give proper attention to these matters.[482]

On November 25, 1775, Congress passed resolves which marked the origin of Congress' appellate jurisdiction in prize cases.[483] Among other things, Congress: (1) recommended that each colony establish a trial court to adjudicate prize cases; (2) recommended that all prize trial courts utilize juries (a recommendation which members of Congress would later regret); and (3) provided that "in all [prize] cases an appeal shall be allowed to the Congress, or such person or persons as they shall appoint for the trial of appeals, provided the appeal be demanded within five days after definitive sentence, and such appeals be lodged with the secretary of Congress within forty days afterwards, . . ."[484]

A January 1776 Continental marine recruiting poster enticed would-be marines with the prospect of "PAY and PRIZE MONEY" and other benefits.[485] The poster stated: "Daily Allowance of a Marine when embarked is—One Pound of BEEF or PORK.—One pound of BREAD . . . Raisins, Butter, Cheese . . . a Pint of the Best WINE or Half a Pint of the best RUM or BRANDY; together with a Pint of LEMONADE. . . ." Near the top of the recruiting poster was stated in large, bold-face print what may have been the Continental marine slogan: "The Continental Marines—When every Thing that swims the Seas must be a PRIZE!"

On March 23, 1776, Congress took "a long step closer to independence."[486] In a preamble to a resolve, Congress stated that Americans had a right by the law of nature to provide for their defense and security. Congress then resolved:

"That the inhabitants of these colonies be permitted to cruize on the enemies of these United Colonies. . . . That all ships and other vessels, their tackle, apparel, and furniture, and all other goods, wares, and merchandizes, belonging to any inhabitant or inhabitants of Great Britain, taken on the high seas, or between high and low water mark, by any armed vessel, fitted out by a private person or persons, and to whom commissions shall be granted, and being . . . prosecuted in any court erected for the trial of maritime affairs, in any of these colonies, shall be deemed and adjudged a lawful prize."[487]

On April 2, 1776, Congress completed detailed instructions for privateers based on instructions which the British admiralty employed during eighteenth-century wars. British admiralty instructions to privateers were modified by Congress only to incorporate provisions of congressional resolutions.[488] Among other things, Congress required all property seized by privateers be taken to a convenient American port for trial in a court which "may proceed, in due form, to condemn the said captures, if they be adjudged lawful prize."[489]

On July 4, 1776: (1) Congress issued its famous Declaration of Independence; and (2) "the first American federal court was born" (The first appeal was filed to Congress from a state court's sentence.).[490] That appeal was filed from the sentence of the admiralty court of Pennsylvania in the case of the schooner *Thistle*. The *Thistle* had been captured by a privateer commissioned by Congress. The jury concluded that the *Thistle* and its cargo were the property of enemies of the United Colonies.[491] Therefore, the trial judge condemned the schooner *Thistle* and its cargo as a lawful prize to be sold—with the proceeds going to the people connected with the privateer.[492] On September 9, 1776, Congress appointed a committee of five congressmen, including James Wilson, to hear lawyers for both parties relevant to the schooner *Thistle*. That committee heard the case on September 16, 1776, and, a few days later, issued a decree which reversed the sentence of the trial court.[493] Congress allowed the schooner *Thistle* to sail away with its crew, cargo, and a passport for safe conduct granted by Congress.

The second case appealed to Congress involved the brigantine *Elizabeth*. On September 30, 1776, Congress appointed a committee of five congressmen to hear the *Elizabeth* case. Three of the five had been *Thistle* committeemen. The *Elizabeth* committee filed a detailed report with Congress, and Congress voted to approve the report.[494] Congress concluded that the sentence of the New Hampshire maritime court ought to be reversed. Congress sent the case back to the New Hampshire maritime court to carry out Congress' determinations.[495]

The appellate prize court of Congress consisted of various congressional committees. It functioned from 1776 to 1780 and decided things such as: (1) whether commercial vessels and cargoes captured by American privateers were prizes of war (British vessels were prizes of war as were supplies going to the British army, even if the supplies were in non-British vessels); and (2) who would receive the proceeds of British vessels and cargoes which were captured. Committees of Congress heard and ruled on more than forty appeals.[496]

Congress established the first federal judicial court of appeals in 1780. The federal judicial Court of Appeals in Cases of Captures operated from 1780 to 1787. Of the approximately two thousand vessels captured by American privateers during the Revolutionary

War, less than one hundred resulted in prize cases appealed to the federal government.[497]

The Articles of Confederation took effect on March 1, 1781. Article IX of the Articles of Confederation stated:

> "The united states in congress assembled, shall have the sole and exclusive right and power . . . of establishing rules for deciding in all cases, what captures on land or water shall be legal, . . . and establishing courts for receiving and determining finally appeals in all cases of captures, provided that no member of congress shall be appointed a judge of any of the said courts. . . ."[498]

State courts and state legislatures sometimes frustrated the execution of decrees of federal appellate prize courts.[499] This upset national leaders for two reasons. First, it showed lack of respect for the federal government. Second, it could have led to serious problems with nations with which the United States was not at war. If a Spanish vessel was captured and declared a prize of war, Spain would be much more likely to capture American vessels and deny Congress' requests for loans.

The Virginia Plan at the Constitutional Convention stated:

> "Resolved that a National Judiciary be established to consist of one or more supreme tribunals, and of inferior tribunals to be chosen by the National Legislature, . . . that the jurisdiction of the inferior tribunals shall be to hear & determine in the first instance, and of the supreme tribunal to hear and determine in the . . . [last] resort, all piracies & felonies on the high seas, captures from an enemy; . . ."[500]

At the Constitutional Convention on June 5, 1787, John Rutledge moved that "the clause for establishing *inferior* tribunals under the national authority . . . should be expunged: . . . the State tribunals might and ought to be left in all cases to decide in the first instance. The right of appeal to the supreme national tribunal . . . [is] sufficient to secure the national rights & uniformity of Judgments: . . ."[501]

James Madison responded to Rutledge by saying: "unless inferior tribunals were dispersed throughout the Republic with *final* jurisdiction in *many* cases, appeals would be multiplied to a most oppressive degree; that besides, an appeal would not in many cases be a remedy. What was to be done after improper Verdicts in State tribunals obtained under the biased directions of a dependent Judge, or the local prejudices of an undirected jury? To remand the cause for a new trial would serve no purpose. To order a new trial at the Supreme bar would oblige the parties to bring up their witnesses, though ever so distant from the seat of the Court. . . ."[502]

James Wilson supported Madison by saying: "the admiralty jurisdiction ought to be given wholly to the national Government, as it related to cases not within the jurisdiction of particular states, & to a scene in which controversies with foreigners would be most likely to happen."[503]

Despite the logic of Madison and Wilson, Rutledge's motion to strike out "inferior tribunals" passed—five states to four, with two states divided.

Wilson and Madison then picked up on a statement made by John Dickinson, and moved "that the National Legislature be empowered to institute inferior tribunals." That motion passed—eight states to two with one state divided.[504]

Much later in the Constitutional Convention, Charles Pinckney moved to add the provision: "And a trial by jury shall be preserved as usual in civil cases."[505] Pinckney was supported by Elbridge Gerry. Few, if any, other delegates supported Pinckney's motion for jury trial in civil cases. It is interesting that Pinckney stated at the South Carolina Ratifying Convention that the Constitutional Convention delegates had wanted to make some declaration favoring jury trials in civil cases, but "when they reflected that all courts of admiralty and appeals (of admiralty cases), being governed by the civil law and the laws of nations, never had, or ought to have, juries, they found it impossible to make any precise declaration on the subject."[506]

It was understood during the ratification process in 1787–88 that, under the Constitution, all determinations of whether prizes were prizes of war would be made in federal judicial courts without juries.

Historian Henry Bourguignon stated that proponents of the Constitution at state ratifying conventions justified the creation of federal trial courts by citing "the need for a system of national courts at least in the area of admiralty jurisdiction, where the rights of foreign nations could be affected."[507]

In *The Federalist*, No. 83, Alexander Hamilton stated:

> "I feel a deep and deliberate conviction that there are many cases in which the trial by jury is an ineligible one. I think so particularly in cases which concern the public peace with foreign nations—that is, in most cases where the question turns wholly on the law of nations. Of this nature, among others, are all prize causes. Juries cannot be supposed competent to investigations that require a thorough knowledge of the laws and usages of nations; and they will sometimes be under influence of impressions which will not suffer them to pay sufficient regard to those considerations of public policy which ought to guide their inquiries. There would of course be always danger that the rights of other nations might be infringed by their decisions so as to afford occasions of reprisal and war. . . . in relation to prize causes, . . . they are determinable in Great Britain, in the last resort, before the king himself, in his privy council, where the fact, as well as the law, undergoes a re-examination. . . ."[508]

The Judiciary Act of 1789 gave federal courts "exclusive original cognizance of all civil cases of admiralty and maritime jurisdiction . . . saving to suitors, in all cases, the right of a common-law remedy (the right to resolve maritime disputes in state common-law courts), where the common law is competent to give it."[509] Therefore, any person who initiated a civil suit of a maritime nature for which state common law was "competent" had the choice of bringing it to: (1) a federal court where it would be tried under the rules of maritime law (no right to trial by jury); or (2) a state court where it would be tried under the rules of the common law (which included the right to trial by jury).

Most ratifiers of the Constitution and most framers of the Judiciary Act of 1789 almost certainly believed that no state court was "competent" to determine whether prizes were prizes of war. Competency of the common law in maritime cases probably varied from state to state. Jurisdiction of vice-admiralty courts in America from 1700 to 1760 "covered three categories of cases, instance (civil or commercial) suits, prize suits, and actions to enforce the acts of trade."[510] Instance cases included such things as seamen's wages, contracts for building and providing ships, salvage of wrecks, collision, ownership of ships, fishing rights, and whaling rights. In some colonies, many instance-type cases could also be heard in common-law courts.[511] Litigants in some colonies could get common-law courts to issue writs of prohibition to prevent vice-admiralty courts from exercising instance jurisdiction. It was not unusual for colonial common-law courts to have concurrent jurisdiction with vice-admiralty courts with respect to "suits for violations of the acts of trade."[512] However, it was unusual for colonial common-law courts to prevent colonial vice-admiralty courts from determining whether captured vessels or cargoes were prizes of war. During the eighteenth century, all prize cases in England were tried by the admiralty court—wherein there was no right to trial by jury.

"Federal Question" Suits

Many twenty-first century Americans would be surprised to learn that the Judiciary Act of 1789 gave to state courts the trial of suits involving the U.S. Constitution, federal statutes, and treaties.[513] Relevant to such "federal question" suits, only final decisions of state supreme courts could be appealed to the U.S. Supreme Court.[514]

Article III, Section 2, Paragraph 2

In all Cases affecting Ambassadors, other public Ministers and Consuls, and those in which a State shall be a Party, the supreme Court shall have original Jurisdiction. In all the other Cases before mentioned, the supreme

> Court shall have appellate Jurisdiction, both as to Law and Fact, with such Exceptions, and under such Regulations as the Congress shall make.

Original Meaning in 21st Century Plain English

Ambassadors of foreign governments, other foreign government officials who speak for foreign governments, and consuls (foreign government officials who look after commercial endeavors of citizens of their countries) have the right to have the U.S. Supreme Court be the trial court for all civil and criminal cases in the United States in which they are involved. Every state in the United States has the right to have the U.S. Supreme Court be the trial court in civil cases in which they are involved. Suits brought against states by individuals or private companies cannot be tried in any federal court unless the state involved consents. Congress may increase the U.S. Supreme Court's original jurisdiction. Relevant to types of cases for which the Constitution grants original jurisdiction to the Supreme Court, and cases for which Congress has the power to grant original jurisdiction, Congress may give concurrent original jurisdiction to various federal courts (including the Supreme Court) and state courts. In cases where the U.S. Supreme Court is the trial court, no court shall have appellate jurisdiction. In all other cases for which the federal government has the constitutional power to exercise jurisdiction, the U.S. Supreme Court shall have appellate jurisdiction, with the authority to determine both law and fact, unless:

- Congress enacts a law which limits the types of cases which may be appealed to the U.S. Supreme Court
- Congress, by law, reduces the U.S. Supreme Court's appellate fact-finding authority

Discussion of Article III, Section 2, Paragraph 2

The Judiciary Act of 1789 prohibited the U.S. Supreme Court from acting as an appellate court in diversity and alienage cases unless the amount of money in controversy was at least two thousand dollars, a large amount of money in 1789.[515] In many diversity cases and alienage cases over the years, "inferior courts" have had infinitely more authority than the U.S. Supreme Court. The Judiciary Act of 1789 made no provision for the U.S. Supreme Court to review criminal cases; during most of the next century, most federal criminal cases remained unreviewable by the Court.[516]

The U.S. Supreme Court has no appellate authority in cases heard in bankruptcy courts or military courts. The Seventh Amendment abolished the Court's appellate authority to find facts contrary to facts found by a jury. The Eleventh Amendment abolished the Court's power to hear (1) lawsuits brought against a state by citizens of another state, and (2) lawsuits brought against a state by citizens of foreign countries.

In 1868, Congress overrode a veto by President Andrew Johnson to enact a law which took away from the U.S. Supreme Court its appellate jurisdiction in a pending case. Why? Because most members of Congress did not want to be embarrassed by a lawful Court ruling which brought attention to the unconstitutional nature of federal "Reconstruction."[517] [518] The pending case taken away from the Court by Congress involved a newspaper editor in Mississippi named William H. McCardle. McCardle "was held in custody by military authority, for trial before a Military Commission, upon charges founded upon the publication of articles alleged to be incendiary and libelous, . . ."[519] Chief Justice Salmon P. Chase later said that had "the merits of the McCardle Case been decided the Court would doubtless have held that his imprisonment for trial before a military commission was illegal."[520]

The Supreme Court heard oral arguments before Congress passed the bill designed to take away jurisdiction. Because President Johnson was sure to delay his veto in order to give the Court a chance to render its decision, the Court had ample time to make a decision in *Ex Parte McCardle* before its jurisdiction disappeared.[521] Six of the eight justices decided not to make a decision because they were afraid that Congress would strip the Court of more power if it made a lawful decision.[522]

Congress can limit appellate jurisdiction in order to preclude the Court from ruling contrary to law. For instance, when the Court accepted *Roe v. Wade*, Congress could have passed a law denying the Court appellate jurisdiction in all "abortion rights" cases until such time as a constitutional amendment which addressed abortion rights was ratified.

The Judiciary Act of 1789 increased the original jurisdiction of the Court by giving the Court the power to issue writs of prohibition and writs of mandamus. There is no evidence that *anybody* questioned—during the eighteenth century—the constitutionality of the Court's original-jurisdiction power to issue writs of mandamus and writs of prohibition. Several cases involving such writs were litigated in the Court during the 1790s. It came as a shock when the Court ruled, in the 1803 case of *Marbury v. Madison*, that it was unconstitutional for Congress to increase the original jurisdiction of the Court. Appendix B of this book discusses, in some detail, events surrounding the fascinating case of *Marbury v. Madison*.

Cases Involving Foreign Officials

The Judiciary Act of 1789 eliminated the Court's original jurisdiction over consuls and vice-consuls despite the unambiguous constitutional requirement: "In all Cases affecting Ambassadors, other public Ministers and Consuls, . . . the supreme Court shall have original Jurisdiction. . . ."[523] "Consuls" refers to officials appointed by foreign governments to reside in the United States for the purpose of caring for the commercial interests of citizens of the governments that appointed the consuls.

Why were consuls denied the access to the U.S. Supreme Court which is required by the Constitution? Congress was (1) shielding many Americans who lived far away from the Supreme Court from being dragged into the Court as defendants, and (2) shielding the Court from the large majority of cases involving consuls. Only very high value alienage cases could be appealed to the Court under the Judiciary Act of 1789.

In denying consuls their constitutionally required access to the Court, the Judiciary Act of 1789 did not increase the power of the federal government or reduce the rights of U.S. citizens. Had the Judiciary Act of 1789 done either of these things, it would not have been enacted. The constitutional problem relevant to consuls could have been solved with a constitutional amendment with which few— if any—Americans would have objected. Senate Bill No. I in the first session of the first Congress under the Constitution, a bill now known as the Judiciary Act of 1789, was unconstitutional in at least one respect. That did not portend well for constitutional fidelity.

The Judiciary Act of 1789 (1) gave exclusive original jurisdiction to the Supreme Court in suits against ambassadors, other public ministers, and their domestics, and (2) gave concurrent original jurisdiction to the Supreme Court and other federal courts in suits brought by ambassadors, other public ministers, and their domestics. The provisions of the Judiciary Act of 1789 relevant to domestics were constitutional, even though they increased the Court's original jurisdiction, because of the flexibility given to Congress by the words: "In all other Cases before mentioned, the supreme Court shall have appellate Jurisdiction, . . . with such Exceptions, and under such Regulations as the Congress shall make." The concurrent original jurisdiction in suits brought by ambassadors and other public ministers was also constitutional.

Article III, Section 2, Paragraph 3

The Trial of all Crimes, except in Cases of Impeachment, shall be by Jury; and such Trial shall be held in the State where the said Crimes shall have been committed; but when not committed within any State, the Trial shall be at such Place or Places as the Congress may by Law have directed.

Original Meaning in 21st Century Plain English

Except in cases of impeachment and cases tried in military courts, trials of all persons accused of committing federal crimes shall be by a jury of twelve citizens whose qualifications may be specified by

Congress. Congress may specify that juror qualifications used in state courts in state A be used for trials in federal courts in state A. No person shall be convicted of a federal crime by a jury unless all twelve jurors vote to convict. All such trials shall be held in the state where the crimes were committed if the crimes were committed within a state. If federal crimes are not committed within a state, trials of persons accused of such crimes shall be held wherever Congress, by law, directs.

Article III, Section 3, Paragraph 1

Treason against the United States, shall consist only in levying War against them, or, in adhering to their Enemies, giving them Aid and Comfort. No Person shall be convicted of Treason unless on the Testimony of two Witnesses to the same overt Act, or on Confession in open Court.

Original Meaning in 21st Century Plain English

Treason against the United States is defined as (1) levying war against the United States, or (2) intentionally helping enemies of the United States. No person shall be convicted of treason against the United States unless:

- Two persons testify that they witnessed the same treasonous act (such as intentionally damaging a U.S. warship or voluntarily divulging secret U.S. military plans or codes to an enemy); or

- The accused traitor confesses, in a court that is open to the public, to levying war against the United States or intentionally helping an enemy of the United States.

Discussion of Article III, Section 3, Paragraph 1

During the seventeenth and eighteenth centuries, Parliament used the medieval treason statute 25 Edw. III to retroactively declare actions and inactions of high government officials to be treason.[524] *Severe* criminal penalties were usually imposed on officials who were found guilty of treason—even when treason was defined by what amounts to ex post facto laws.

At the Constitutional Convention, there was a debate on August 20 about what should be put in the Constitution relevant to treason. The draft constitution at that point contained a clause with a narrow definition of treason similar to that which appears in Article III of the Constitution. James Madison "thought the definition too narrow. It did not appear to go as far as the Stat. of Edw. III. . . . [Madison] did not see why more latitude might not be left to . . . [Congress]. . . ."[525] George Mason "was for pursuing the Stat. of Edw. III."[526]

How could the two men most associated with the Bill of Rights have tried to give Congress the power to retroactively define treason? Noted historian Raoul Berger provided an excellent clue. Berger wrote in 1973: "The heroic age in the struggle for parliamentary supremacy was the seventeenth century, . . . when Parliament claimed anew the power to declare ministerial acts treasonable retrospectively. Bloody as that power appears today, it played a mighty role in the achievement of English liberty. . . ."[527] Madison and Mason probably wanted to give Congress the power to retroactively enact laws which defined treason in order to insure legislative supremacy and liberty.

Raoul Berger referred to 25 Edw III as "the great treason statute."[528] It was enacted in 1351 or 1352. After it enumerated seven categories of treason (imagining the death of the King, violating the Queen, levying war against the King, being adherent to the King's enemies, counterfeiting the King's seal of money, bringing false money to the realm, and slaying the King's judges while performing their duties),[529] 25 Edw III stated:

> "And because that many other like cases of treason may happen in time to come, which a man cannot think nor declare at this present time, it is accorded, that if any other case, supposed treason, which is not above specified, doth happen before any Justices, the Justices shall tarry without any going

to judgment of the treason, till the cause be shewed and declared before the King and his Parliament, whether it ought to be judged treason or other felony."[530]

The Constitution's narrow definition of treason prevents some acts which many people would regard as treasonable from ever leading to treason convictions. It is amazing that the framers did not agree on a compromise between the *extremes* of 25 Edw III and the definition of treason which ended up in the Constitution.

The requirement for two witnesses to the same overt (open to view) treasonable act precludes the large majority of traitors from ever being convicted of treason. It would be easy to get a constitutional amendment passed to expand the definition of treason. This should be done. However, to solve the treason problem, a lie detector test will have to be developed which is both foolproof and practical. And a lie detector test will have to be given periodically to all people with knowledge of, or access to, information which could reduce the security of the United States and its citizens if that information were made available to a foreign government or nongovernmental terrorists.

If a foolproof and practical lie detector is developed, the large majority of lawyers will resist its use in courts. Famous lawyer F. Lee Bailey told the American Polygraph Association that courts were not interested in determining the truth.[531] Why might that be? There would be *much less* need for lawyers and judges if there was a way to readily ascertain the truth in legal proceedings. American lawyers are fighting the establishment of a good DNA data base in the United States. A good DNA data base would be quite beneficial in solving crimes. It would also be successful in reducing crimes, particularly rape and murder in conjunction with rape.

If the Fifth Amendment is modified to allow prosecutions for treason discovered with foolproof lie detectors, such lie detectors would become almost totally effective in preventing treason if the lie detectors were widely used. The Fifth Amendment: (1) should be modified to allow prosecution of treason detected by foolproof lie detectors; and (2) should be modified to allow prosecution of child molesters, murderers, rapists, corrupt judges, and terrorists (including those who are preparing for acts of terrorism even though they have not carried them out) found with foolproof lie detectors. Furthermore, anybody accused or convicted of crime should be allowed to attempt to prove their innocence via foolproof lie detectors.

If you think hard about the potential benefits of foolproof lie detectors in terms of *solving crimes, preventing crimes, and minimizing injustice*, you might conclude that one of the top priorities of the entire world should be the development of a lie detector which is foolproof and practical.

Article III, Section 3, Paragraph 2

> *The Congress shall have Power to declare the Punishment of Treason, but no Attainder of Treason shall work Corruption of Blood, or Forfeiture except during the Life of the Person attainted.*

Original Meaning in 21st Century Plain English

Congress shall have the power to declare the punishment for treason. However (1) the descendants of persons sentenced to death for treason shall not be prohibited from inheriting property from persons sentenced to death for treason, and (2) persons sentenced to death for treason shall not forfeit their property, except during the time they remain alive after being sentenced to death.

Discussion of Article III, Section 3, Paragraph 2

At common law, "Attainder of Treason" meant that all of the property of people sentenced to death for committing treason was forfeited to the government. "Corruption of blood" meant that descendants of persons convicted of treason could not inherit property from persons convicted of treason. Article III, Section 3, Paragraph 2 insures that the descendants of persons convicted of treason have the same right to inherit property as the descendants of law-abiding persons.

Article IV

CHAPTER 6

Article IV, Section 1

Full Faith and Credit shall be given in each State to the public Acts, Records, and judicial Proceedings of every other State. And the Congress may by general Laws prescribe the Manner in which such Acts, Records and Proceedings shall be proved, and the Effect thereof.

Original Meaning in 21st Century Plain English

All state courts shall allow to be admitted into evidence the acts of state legislatures, public records, and judicial proceedings of all other states. Congress may, by laws applicable to all states, specify the:

- Manner in which acts of legislatures, public records, and judicial proceedings shall be proven

- Effect which legislative acts, public records, and judicial proceedings in state A shall have in state B (However, Congress cannot make state A abide by judgments made in state B (1) in cases in which state B did not have jurisdiction, or (2) in cases in which due process of law was not complied with. Furthermore,

Congress may impose laws of state A on state B only for resolving disputes in the courts of state B relevant to things that happened in state A or contracts which specify that the laws of state A are to apply.)

Discussion of Article IV, Section 1

In the Constitutional Convention on August 29, the following draft article was discussed: "Full faith shall be given in each State to the acts of the Legislatures, and to the records and judicial proceedings of the Courts and magistrates of every other State." During the course of that discussion, James Madison said that he "wished the [federal] Legislature might be authorized to provide for the *execution* of Judgments in other States, under such regulations as might be expedient. . . . [Madison] thought that this might be safely done, and was justified by the nature of the Union."[532]

On September 1, a committee, "to whom were referred sundry propositions," suggested the following provision in its report to the Convention: "Full faith and credit ought to be given in each State to the public acts, records, and Judicial proceedings in every other State, and the [federal] Legislature shall by general laws prescribe the manner in which such acts, Records, & proceedings shall be proved, and the effect which Judgments obtained in one State, shall have in another."[533]

On September 3, Gouverneur Morris "moved to amend the Report concerning the respect to be paid to Acts Records & c of one State, in other States by striking out 'Judgments obtained in one State, shall have in another' and to insert the word 'thereof' after the word 'effect.'"[534] Morris' motion passed, six states to three. James Madison suggested two changes which were unanimously accepted; the words "ought to" were replaced by "shall," and "Legislature shall by general laws" was changed to "Legislature may by general laws."[535]

The Articles of Confederation stated: "Full faith and credit shall be given in each of these states to the records, acts and judicial proceedings of the courts and magistrates of every other state."[536] That statement must not have caused states to abide by the judgments of courts of other states. If the Articles of Confederation caused states to abide by the judgments of courts of other states, Madison would not have stated that he wished that Congress "might be authorized to provide for the *execution* of Judgments in other States." The "Full faith and credit" statement of the Articles of Confederation had the *effect* of merely requiring that public records, public acts, and judicial proceedings of state A be allowed into evidence in courts in state B. The ratifiers of the Constitution must have understood that "Full Faith and Credit" in the Constitution meant the same thing as "Full faith and credit" in the Articles of Confederation, especially since the Constitution immediately followed with the potent new provision: "Congress may by general Laws prescribe . . . the Effect thereof."

In 1790, Congress enacted a law which prescribed the manner in which to authenticate acts of state legislatures and records of judicial proceedings of state courts.[537] However, Congress did not prescribe the effect which the acts and records of state A would have in the courts of state B. In 1813 and 1818, the U.S. Supreme Court ruled that state A must abide by judgments made in the courts of state B if the courts of state B had jurisdiction and the judgments were consistent with due process of law.[538] In so doing, the Court assumed the power of Congress to "prescribe . . . the Effect thereof."

Article IV, Section 2, Paragraph 1

The Citizens of each State shall be entitled to all Privileges and Immunities of Citizens in the several States.

Original Meaning in 21st Century Plain English

Free, law-abiding citizens of all states shall be free to enter all other states, move about all other states, and leave all other states. While in state X, free citizens of state Y shall enjoy all of the trade privileges enjoyed by citizens of state X.

Discussion of Article IV, Section 2, Paragraph 1

The framers intended for the "Privileges and Immunities" clause of the Constitution to embody the principles contained in the "privileges and immunities" clause of the Articles of Confederation.[539] The Articles of Confederation said:

> "The better to secure and perpetuate mutual friendship and intercourse among the people of the different states in this union, the free inhabitants of each of these states, paupers, vagabonds and fugitives from Justice excepted, shall be entitled to all privileges and immunities of free citizens in the several states; and the people of each state shall have free ingress and regress to and from any other states, and enjoy therein all of the privileges of trade and commerce, subject to the same duties, impositions and restrictions as the inhabitants thereof respectively, provided that such restriction shall not extend so far as to prevent the removal of property imported into any state, to any other state of which the Owner is an inhabitant; . . . ."[540]

The phrase "all Privileges and Immunities" in the Constitution was not intended by the framers or understood by the ratifiers to mean what the words alone suggest.[541] Americans have never had the right to vote or run for office in states in which they were passing through or visiting.

Article IV, Section 2, Paragraph 2

A Person charged in any State with Treason, Felony, or other Crime, who shall flee from Justice, and be found in another State, shall on Demand of the executive Authority of the State from which he fled, be delivered up, to be removed to the State having Jurisdiction of the Crime.

Original Meaning in 21st Century Plain English

If a person who is charged with committing a crime in state A attempts to flee from justice in state A by going to state B, that person shall, upon the demand of the governor of state A, be turned over to agents of state A for the purpose of taking the accused back to state A to be tried for crimes for which state A has jurisdiction.

Discussion of Article IV, Section 2, Paragraph 2

Although there is no explicit grant of power to Congress to refine this provision, as there is in Article IV, Section 1, Congress constitutionally employed the necessary and proper clause to refine this provision in 1793. The Act of February 12, 1793, I Stat. 302, stated:

> "That whenever the executive authority of any state . . . shall demand any person as a fugitive from justice, of the executive authority of any state or territory *to which such person shall have fled* and shall moreover produce the copy of an indictment found, . . . it shall be the duty of the executive authority of the state or territory *to which such person shall have fled*, to cause him or her to be arrested and secured, and notice of the arrest to be given to the executive authority of the state making the demand, or to the agent of such authority appointed to receive the fugitive, . . . But if no such agent shall appear within six months from the time of the arrest, the prisoner may be discharged. And all costs or expenses incurred in the apprehending, securing, and transmitting such fugitive to the state or territory making such demand, shall be paid by such state or territory."[542]

Article IV, Section 2, Paragraph 3

No Person held to Service or Labour in one State, under the Laws thereof, escaping into another, shall, in Consequence of any Law or Regulation therein, be dis-

charged from such Service or Labour, but shall be delivered up on Claim of the Party to whom such Service or Labour may be due.

Original Meaning in 21st Century Plain English

No person who is a slave or indentured servant in state A, under the laws of state A, shall, upon escaping to state B, be discharged from their obligations as a slave or indentured servant in state A. Furthermore, state B shall turn over all persons who are legally slaves or indentured servants of citizens of state A upon claims of the citizens of state A to whom the labor of the slaves or indentured servants is due.

Discussion of Article IV, Section 2, Paragraph 3

This may be termed the "fugitive from labor" provision. Its focus is on fugitive slaves, but it also covers indentured servants. One consequence of the Thirteenth Amendment was that there could no longer be fugitive slaves. However, the "fugitive from labor" provision continued to apply to indentured servants where that practice was legal.

Article IV, Section 3, Paragraph 1

New States may be admitted by the Congress into this Union; but no new State shall be formed or erected within the Jurisdiction of any other State; nor any State be formed by the Junction of two or more States, or Parts of States, without the Consent of the Legislatures of the States concerned as well as of the Congress.

Original Meaning in 21st Century Plain English

Congress may admit new states into the United States. However;

- No state shall be split into two or more states without the consent of its state legislature and Congress.

- No state shall be created by combining two or more states without the consent of Congress and the legislatures of all of the states to be combined.

- No state shall be created by combining parts of two or more states without the consent of Congress and the legislatures of all states that would have their boundaries changed.

Discussion of Article IV, Section 3, Paragraph 1

In 1863, West Virginia became a state. A majority of Congress voted to split Virginia—as it stood in 1860—into West Virginia and Virginia—as it has stood since 1863. Was that constitutional? When a Virginia Constitutional Convention in 1861 voted to secede from the Union by a margin of eighty-eight to fifty-five, the delegates from the western part of Virginia voted against secession by a margin of thirty-two to eleven.[543] It would have been obviously unconstitutional to admit West Virginia at that time because there was one legislature in Virginia, and that legislature would not have consented. Congress waited for the Unionists in the western part of Virginia to form a government (which was called "the reorganized government of Virginia"), elect a legislature, and adopt a constitution.

When the legislature of "the reorganized government of Virginia" asked Congress to split Virginia into two states, it was *plausible* to admit West Virginia. However, it was unconstitutional to admit West Virginia because (1) the legislature of "the reorganized government of Virginia" was not representative of the Virginia electorate as a whole, and (2) the legislature of Virginia did not consent. The bill to admit West Virginia was highly controversial in Congress and the Cabinet despite the fact that the United States was in the middle of the Civil War.[544] President Abraham Lincoln was not totally happy when he signed the bill which allowed West Virginia to become a state in 1863. On December 31, 1862, Lincoln wrote:

"The consent of the Legislature of Virginia is constitutionally necessary to the Bill for the Admission of West Virginia becoming a law. A body claiming to be such Legislature has given its consent. . . . [The Union] can scarcely dispense with the aid of West Virginia in this struggle; much less can we afford to have her against us, in Congress and in the field. Her brave and good men regard her admission into the Union as a matter of life and death. They have been true to the Union under very severe trials. We have so acted as to justify their hopes, and we cannot fully retain their confidence and co-operation if we seem to break faith with them. In fact they could not do so much for us if they would. Again, the admission of the new State turns that much slave soil to free, and this is a certain and irrevocable encroachment upon the cause of the rebellion. The division of a State is dreaded as a precedent. But a measure made expedient by a war is no precedent for times of peace. It is said that the admission of West Virginia is secession, and tolerated only because it is our secession. Well, if we call it by that name, there is still difference enough between secession against the Constitution and secession in favor of the Constitution. I believe the admission into the Union of West Virginia is expedient."[545]

The law which allowed West Virginia to become a state was expedient—but it was not constitutional.

Article IV, Section 3, Paragraph 2

The Congress shall have Power to dispose of and make all needful Rules and Regulations respecting the Territory or other Property belonging to the United States; and nothing in this Constitution shall be so construed as to Prejudice any Claims of the United States, or of any particular State.

Original Meaning in 21st Century Plain English

Congress shall have the power to:

• Sell federal land to developers

• Give federal land to veterans of the Revolutionary War and who-ever else Congress deems worthy of it (For instance, Congress may give land to missionaries for their efforts to convert Indians to Christianity.)

• Make all laws it deems necessary in all territories and other prop-erty belonging to the United States (Other property includes (1) any district which may be ceded by one or more states and become the capital of the United States, (2) all United States military facilities which exist within the border of any state, and (3) all other land owned by the United States which is not part of a territory.)

Nothing in this Constitution shall be construed to impair any claim of land by the United States or any state.

Discussion of Article IV, Section 3, Paragraph 2

One purpose of this provision was to make it constitutional for Congress to enact laws like the Northwest Ordinance of 1787. The Northwest Ordinance of 1787 was made by Congress at the same time that the Constitutional Convention was going on. Congress, under the Articles of Confederation, had no authority to make such a law. The framers, quite aware of the Northwest Ordinance of 1787, clearly intended for Congress under the Constitution to have the authority to make such laws.

Article IV, Section 4

The United States shall guarantee to every State in this Union a Republican Form of Government, and shall protect each of them against Invasion; and on Application of the Legislature, or of the Executive (when the Legislature cannot be convened) against domestic Violence.

Original Meaning in 21st Century Plain English

The federal government:

- Guarantees a republican form of government to every state
- Shall protect each state against invasion
- Shall protect each state against insurrections within that state, such as rebellions by poor farmers or uprisings by slaves, if the state legislature requests such protection (If the state legislature cannot be convened, the request of the governor of the state will be sufficient to obtain federal protection against insurrections.)

Discussion of Article IV, Section 4

By "a Republican Form of Government," the framers meant;

- At least one chamber of the state legislature is composed of representatives elected directly by the electorate. In that chamber, each representative should represent *roughly* the same number of citizens.
- The directly elected chamber of the state legislature must concur on all statutes which are made by the state government. (The electorate may make laws via state constitutional amendments.)
- The state executive and judicial branches must abide by (1) the U.S. Constitution, (2) all provisions of their state constitution which are not in conflict with the U.S. Constitution, (3) all constitutional statutes made by their state legislature and Congress, and (4) all constitutional treaties made by the federal government unless they are overridden by subsequent constitutional federal laws (statutes, treaties, or amendments).

Article V

The Congress, whenever two thirds of both Houses shall deem it necessary, shall propose Amendments to this Constitution, or, on the Application of the Legislatures of two thirds of the several States, shall call a Convention for proposing Amendments, which, in either Case, shall be valid to all Intents and Purposes, as Part of this Constitution, when ratified by the Legislatures of three fourths of the several States, or by Conventions in three fourths thereof, as the one or the other Mode of Ratification may be proposed by the Congress; Provided that no Amendment which may be made prior to the Year One thousand eight hundred and eight shall in any Manner affect the first and fourth Clauses in the Ninth Section of the first Article; and that no State, without its Consent, shall be deprived of its equal Suffrage in the Senate.

Original Meaning in 21st Century Plain English

This Constitution can be amended if, and only if, one of the following four procedures is utilized:

- At least two-thirds of the House of Representatives and at least two-thirds of the Senate agree on an amendment to propose to the state legislatures, *and* at least three-fourths of the state legislatures ratify the amendment proposed by Congress.

- At least two-thirds of the House of Representatives and at least two-thirds of the Senate agree on an amendment to propose to state ratifying conventions, *and* ratifying conventions in at least three-fourths of the states ratify the amendment proposed by Congress.

- The legislatures of at least two-thirds of the states formally request Congress to call a national constitutional convention, Congress specifies ratification by state legislatures, a national constitutional convention proposes one or more amendments, *and* one or more of the proposed amendments are ratified by at least three-fourths of the state legislatures. Congress must call a national constitutional convention if at least two-thirds of the states request Congress to do so.

- The legislatures of at least two-thirds of the states formally request Congress to call a national constitutional convention, Congress specifies ratification by state ratifying conventions, a national constitutional convention proposes one or more amendments, *and* one or more proposed amendments are ratified by state ratifying conventions in at least three-fourths of the states.

No amendment shall deprive a state, without its consent, of equal representation in the Senate. Prior to 1808, no amendment shall in any manner affect the first or fourth paragraphs of Article I, Section 9.

Discussion of Article V

An important part of Article V is the fact that it virtually precludes an amendment to provide for representation in the Senate based on population. An amendment to change the structure of the Senate to representation based on population would have to be ratified by *all* states. The only realistic way for the United States to adopt a government approaching equal representation in Congress for Americans in all states is to drastically reduce the power of the Senate. Transforming the Senate into an advisory council would not only be in the interest of fairness—it would be an important step in leading to an efficient parliamentary system of government.

The framers devoted an entire article to the amendment process. The provisions of Article V could have easily been included with the provisions of Article VI. The framers obviously wanted to highlight the amendment process. They provided four lawful ways to amend the Constitution. The amending of the Constitution by the Court violates (1) the Constitution, (2) the rule of law, and (3) the principle of separation of powers.

All amendments but one have been ratified by state legislatures. The only amendment ratified by state ratifying conventions is the Twenty-first Amendment. (The Twenty-first Amendment repealed national prohibition which had been mandated by the Eighteenth Amendment.) All twenty-seven amendments have been proposed by Congress. The United States has not had a national constitutional convention since 1787.

Article VI

CHAPTER 8

Article VI, Paragraph 1

All Debts contracted and Engagements entered into, before the Adoption of this Constitution, shall be as valid against the United States under this Constitution, as under the Confederation.

Original Meaning in 21st Century Plain English

The United States under the Constitution shall assume all debts that the United States incurred under the Articles of Confederation. All contracts and treaties made by the United States under the Articles of Confederation shall remain in force under the Constitution.

Article VI, Paragraph 2

This Constitution, and the Laws of the United States which shall be made in Pursuance thereof; and all Treaties made, or which shall be made, under the Authority of the United States, shall be the supreme Law of the Land; and the Judges in every State shall be bound thereby, any

> *Thing in the Constitution or Laws of any State to the Contrary notwithstanding.*

Original Meaning in 21st Century Plain English

The supreme law of the United States shall consist of:

- This Constitution (including amendments which are made in accordance with this Constitution)

- All constitutional laws made by Congress under this Constitution

- All treaties agreed to by the United States prior to the adoption of this Constitution unless those treaties are repealed by Congress under the Constitution

- All constitutional treaties which shall be made by the United States under this Constitution (All treaties may subsequently be repealed by Congress via statutes.)

In all conflicts between the supreme law of the United States and a state law (state constitution, state statute, or any other state law), the supreme law of the United States shall prevail. No judge in any state shall rule contrary to the supreme law of the United States.

Discussion of Article VI, Paragraph 2

The ratifiers understood that Constitution would be the most supreme of the supreme laws of the land. Federal and state laws which violate the Constitution are invalid. Treaties made under the Constitution which violate the Constitution are invalid.

The Court has extended supremacy to "laws" made by federal entities other than Congress. In the arena of supreme law of the United States, the Court has unconstitutionally ruled that:

- Congress may delegate lawmaking power granted by the Constitution only to Congress.

- Congress may "delegate" lawmaking power not granted to the federal government by the Constitution. (An example of delegating an unconstitutional power is the delegation of the power to set the maximum gallons of water per flush for new toilets.)

- Once Congress has delegated lawmaking power in some area to a federal administrative agency, states cannot enact a law in that area even though the federal agency has not made a "law" in that area.[546]

Article VI, Paragraph 3

The Senators and Representatives before mentioned, and the Members of the several State Legislatures, and all executive and judicial Officers, both of the United States and of the several States, shall be bound by Oath or Affirmation, to support this Constitution; but no religious Test shall ever be required as a Qualification to any Office or public Trust under the United States.

Original Meaning in 21st Century Plain English

An oath or affirmation to support the United States Constitution shall be taken by:

- All members of Congress
- All members of every state legislature in the United States
- All executive and judicial officers of the United States
- All executive and judicial officers of every state in the United States

No religious test shall ever be required as a qualification for (1) any officer or employee of the federal government, or (2) any federal juror.

Discussion of Article VI, Paragraph 3

Dissenters from the Church of England were not allowed to hold office in England in 1787. In the United States, the large majority of state constitutions in 1787 required religious tests for officeholders.[547] To qualify for office in most states in 1787, an oath was required—by the state constitution—in which the oath-taker swore that they believed in (1) a Supreme Being, (2) the divine authenticity of the scriptures, and (3) a future state of rewards and punishments.[548] Hence, "no religious Test shall ever be required as a Qualification to any Office or public Trust under the United States" was not popular with many Americans.[549]

Strong arguments against the Article VI ban on religious tests were made in at least five states.[550] Article VI was "exhaustively discussed" at the first North Carolina Ratifying Convention.[551] Although Catholicism was probably the primary concern of North Carolinians who were opposed to Article VI, Jews and pagans (called "heathens" by some ratifiers) were also of concern.[552] The influential Reverend Caldwell, one of the leaders in the disestablishment of religion in North Carolina in 1776, said at the first North Carolina Ratifying Convention that Article VI was "an invitation for Jews and pagans of every kind to come among us."[553] During the framing of the Bill of Rights, at least one U.S. senator tried to add religious tests to the U.S. Constitution.[554]

Since oaths are associated with religion, the framers specified affirmation as a nonreligious alternative to an oath. An affirmation is as legally binding as an oath. Anyone who knowingly violates an oath or an affirmation has committed perjury.

Although the "Oath or Affirmation" provision of Article VI applies to federal and state officeholders, the "no religious Test" provision applies only to federal officeholders. The Constitution probably would not have been ratified by the requisite number of states if it required states to give up their religious tests. Nevertheless, the Court made the federal religious test ban applicable to the states in 1961 when it ruled unconstitutional a provision of the Maryland Constitution which required a religious test for people to be eligible for a state office in Maryland.[555] That Court action was unconstitutional.

Article VII

The Ratification of the Conventions of nine States, shall be sufficient for the Establishment of this Constitution between the States so ratifying the Same.

Original Meaning in 21st Century Plain English

States which approve this Constitution via ratifying conventions shall be permanently joined together under this Constitution if it is approved by the ratifying conventions of nine or more states.

Discussion of Article VII

Was it legitimate to establish the Constitution with the approval of the ratifying conventions of nine states, thus disestablishing the Articles of Confederation, when the approval of all thirteen state legislatures were required to change the Articles of Confederation? Yes! The Articles of Confederation *was ratified by state legislatures.* By 1787, it was considered improper for constitutions to have been ratified by legislative bodies. Constitutions established by legislative bodies were not totally legitimate. Proper constitutions were ratified either directly by the electorate or by conventions which had no authority to govern. Ratifying conventions were considered to be conventions of the electorate. The Constitution had the additional excellent quality of being created by a constitutional convention, a body with no governing authority, whereas the Articles of Confederation was created by Congress.

The first constitutional convention occurred in 1780 in Massachusetts. It is fortunate that the Articles of Confederation (proposed by Congress in 1777) was proposed by a governing body and approved by governing bodies. If the Articles of Confederation had been created by a constitutional convention and approved by ratifying conventions in all states, the Constitution would be unconstitutional.

When the Constitutional Convention presented the proposed Constitution to Congress—then operating under the Articles of Confederation—some members of Congress were opposed to it. Nevertheless, Congress *unanimously* voted that the proposed Constitution "be transmitted to the several [state] legislatures in order to be submitted to a convention of delegates chosen in each state by the people thereof."[556] Congress promptly transmitted the proposed Constitution to the states.[557] Furthermore, all state legislatures except Rhode Island complied with Congress' request for state ratifying conventions in a timely manner even though several state legislatures were opposed to the proposed Constitution.

There was another important reason for state conventions to ratify the Constitution. The Constitution would cause parts of state constitutions to be invalidated. At the Constitutional Convention, James Madison said: "These changes would make essential inroads on the State Constitutions, and it would be a novel & dangerous doctrine that a Legislature could change the Constitution under which it held its existence. . . ."[558]

Madison went on to say that he "considered the difference between a system founded on Legislatures only, and one founded on the people, to be the true difference between a *league* or *treaty*, and a *Constitution*."[559] Treaties can be superseded by statutes, and statutes can be superseded by constitutions. Under the Articles of Confederation, state legislatures often superseded actions of Congress which the Articles of Confederation authorized Congress to take. Madison was correct in implying that the Articles of Confederation was, in effect, a treaty. It was put into effect in a treaty-like manner, and, when in effect, it was no more powerful than a treaty.

The Bill of Rights

CHAPTER 10

Special Comments about the Bill of Rights

In 1833, the Supreme Court ruled that only the federal government must abide by the Bill of Rights. Was the Court right? This question is addressed in depth in the discussion of the Second Amendment in this chapter.

On September 25, 1789, Congress proposed twelve "amendments to the Constitution of the United States" to "the Legislatures of the several States." Those twelve proposed amendments are shown in Appendix C. Amendments one through ten (the Bill of Rights) are *Article the third* through *Article the twelfth* in Appendix C. All of the rights in the Second through Ninth Amendments are expressed in general terms except the last part of the Seventh Amendment. Rights which are expressed in general terms in amendments two through nine were almost certainly understood by most ratifiers of the Bill of Rights as limitations on all governments (federal, state, city, etc.) in the United States.

Congress took its first major step towards the Bill of Rights on June 8, 1789, when Representative James Madison suggested specific amendments in the House of Representatives. On that occasion, Madison said:

"There have been objections of various kinds made against the constitution: . . . I believe that the great mass of the people

who opposed it, disliked it because it did not contain effec-
tual provision against encroachments on particular rights,
and those safeguards which they have long been accustomed
to . . . nor ought we consider them safe, while a great number
of our fellow citizens think these securities necessary . . . it
will be practicable . . . to satisfy the public mind that their
liberties will be perpetual, and this without endangering any
part of the constitution which is considered as essential to
the existence of the government by those who promoted its
adoption. . . ."[560]

If you keep in the back of your mind Madison's words "provison
against encroachments on particular rights and those safeguards
which they have long been accustomed to," it will help you understand the original meaning of the Bill of Rights. The Bill of Rights
provides no rights that citizens of the United States did not have
prior to the adoption of the Constitution.

Congressman James Jackson said that Madison's proposed amendments were not worth "a pinch of snuff; they went to secure rights
never in danger."[561] Although the Bill of Rights secures rights which
were not in much danger at the time Congress proposed them, the
proposed Bill of Rights were worth much more than "a pinch of snuff."
The proposed Bill of Rights: (1) substantially increased support for
the Constitution among the electorate (That made it much less likely
that the state legislatures would demand a second federal constitutional convention. A federal convention in 1789 or 1790 may well
have led to one or more amendments which would have endangered
the existence of the United States.); (2) facilitated the reentry into
the Union of North Carolina and Rhode Island; and (3) helped some
members of Congress, including James Madison, get reelected.

The only reduction of federal constitutional power made by the
Bill of Rights is stated in the Seventh Amendment provision: "no
fact tried by a jury, shall be otherwise re-examined in any Court of
the United States, than according to the rules of the common law."
It nullified a portion of Article III.

First Amendment

Congress shall make no law respecting an establish-
ment of religion, or prohibiting the free exercise thereof; or
abridging the freedom of speech, or of the press; or the
right of the people peaceably to assemble, and to petition
the Government for a redress of grievances.

Original Meaning in 21st Century Plain English

Congress shall make no law which:

- Establishes a sect (Baptist, Catholic, Episcopal, Presbyterian, etc.)—(In other words, Congress shall make no law which gives legal superiority to any sect relative to any other sect.)

- Disestablishes a sect (Congress shall not disestablish any sect established by any state, territory, town, etc.)

- Establishes articles of faith

- Prohibits articles of faith (The words "no law . . . prohibiting the free exercise thereof" meant no law prohibiting religious beliefs.[562])

- Discourages religion (The Northwest Ordinance of 1787, reenacted in 1789, stated that religion was necessary to good government.)

Congress may continue to exercise its unwritten power to encourage religion by appropriating resources.

Congress shall make no law which restrains anybody from saying anything, writing anything, or using a printing press to publish anything. However, the federal government may prosecute, under the common law, those individuals whose speech, writing, or publishing is seditious relevant to the federal government. Sedition is committed by:

- Anyone who maliciously brings the federal government or its officers into disrepute or ridicule

- Anyone who incites others to violate one or more federal laws
- Anyone who promotes the cause of enemies of the United States in times of war
- Anyone who opposes the cause of the United States in times of war

Congress shall make no law which restrains citizens from assembling in a peaceful manner for the purpose of creating, printing, circulating, signing, or presenting petitions to the United States government.

Comments with Respect to the First Amendment's Provisions on Religion

What did the First Amendment phrase "establishment of religion" mean during the time that the First Amendment was framed and ratified? It is important to answer this question in some depth, especially in view of the fact that the Supreme Court has erroneously "interpreted" the meaning of "establishment of religion." In 1789, almost all of the American electorate agreed with future Chief Justice Oliver Ellsworth that "establishment of religion" meant legal supremacy of one sect relative to all other sects.[563] Nonestablishment of religion meant sect equality.[564]

Sir William Blackstone, in his *Commentaries on the Laws of England,* which were by far the most influential books on law in the United States from 1776 until at least 1800, said: "by establishment of religion is meant the setting up or recognition of a state church, or at least the conferring upon one church of special favors and advantages which are denied to others."[565]

By 1789, the large majority of Americans were hostile to the type of sect legal supremacy that had existed in most colonies. New Jersey, which never had an established sect, guarded against one in the future in its 1776 constitution which said: "[There] shall be no establishment of any one religious sect . . . in preference to another."[566] The Pennsylvania Constitution of 1776 (1) declared Pennsylvania to be a nonestablishment state, (2) authorized aid to religion, and

(3) stated: "Nor can any man, who acknowledges the being of God, be justly deprived of any civil right as a citizen." [567] The 1776 Delaware Constitution forbid the "establishment of any religious sect in preference to another."[568] The Delaware Assembly, under its nonestablishment constitution, aided and encouraged the Christian religion. For example, the Delaware Assembly took away the power of performing marriages from justices of the peace in 1790 and placed it exclusively in "ministers or preachers of the gospel."[569] A 1740 Delaware law was remodeled in 1795 to "more effectually prevent the profanation of the Lord's day, commonly called Sunday"; the 1795 law continued the prohibition of many worldly activities on Sundays.[570] Although Delaware never enacted a general tax assessment for "the maintenance of ministers of the gospel," such a tax was seriously considered there in 1786 despite the prohibition of religious establishments.[571]

The Anglican (Episcopal) Church had legal supremacy in the colonies of Georgia, Maryland, North Carolina, South Carolina, and Virginia. The 1776 North Carolina Constitution disestablished the Anglican Church by stating: "there shall be no Establishment of any religious Church or Denomination in this State in Preference to any other."[572] Nevertheless, in 1785, the North Carolina legislature provided public funding to rebuild a former Episcopal church, gave the church's title to a public institution, and ordered that the church "shall on every Sunday in every year be open to the ministers of every sect or persuasion, being Christians, there to inculcate the truths of their holy religion."[573] The governor of North Carolina, in his 1785 annual message to the legislature, urged it to support ministers of the gospel "without preference to denomination."[574] The Anglican Church legal supremacy ended in Maryland and North Carolina in 1776, in Georgia in 1777, in South Carolina in 1778, and in Virginia in 1786.[575] Virginia was the last state to disestablish its church. Although Virginia did not disestablish the Anglican Church until 1786, public support of religion via tax assessments ended in 1777.[576] New York disestablished the Anglican Church in its 1777 state constitution.[577] To encourage the founding of churches, four hundred acres of land in each frontier township was reserved for support of the gospel by the New York legislature in 1784.[578]

In the colonies of Connecticut, Massachusetts, and New Hampshire, Congregationalism was legally favored at the time the Revolutionary War began. By the end of 1784, no church was legally favored in any of these three New England states.

The 1780 Massachusetts Constitution forbid a religious establishment as follows: "no subordination of any one sect or denomination to another shall ever be established by law."[579] The 1780 Massachusetts Constitution required public worship, and irregular church attendance cost ten shillings.[580] Article III of the Massachusetts Declaration of Rights authorized the Massachusetts legislature to require towns to provide, at community expense, for "public worship" and "support and maintenance of Protestant teachers of piety, religion and morality."[581] A majority of the electorate in each town, parish, or society determined which sect(s) to settle therein and voted a tax on all inhabitants to raise money for church construction and payment for the services of a minister—two ministers if two sects were chosen.[582] People could avoid paying the local tax only by paying a similar tax to a church in another town and attending that church regularly. Connecticut, New Hampshire, and Vermont also empowered the local electorate to select a sect and determine the funding for a church building and a clergyman.

The 1784 New Hampshire Constitution stated:

> "As morality and piety, rightly grounded on evangelical principles, will give the best and greatest security to government . . . the people of this state . . . fully impower the legislature to authorize . . . the several towns, . . . within this state, to make adequate provision . . . for the support and maintenance of public protestant teachers of piety, religion and morality: . . . And no portion of any one particular religious sect or denomination, shall ever be compelled to pay towards the support of the teacher or teachers of another persuasion, sect, or denomination. And every denomination of christians demeaning themselves quietly, and as good subjects of the state,

shall be equally under the protection of the law: and *no subordination of any one sect or denomination to another, shall ever be established by law. . . .*"[583] (emphasis added)

On August 15, 1789, the U.S. House of Representatives reviewed the House Select Committee's recommended amendment: "No religion shall be established by [federal] law, nor shall the equal rights of conscience be infringed [by the federal government]."[584] Representative Elbridge Gerry said: "it would read better if it was, that no religious doctrine shall be established by law."[585] Representative Roger Sherman "Thought the amendment altogether unnecessary, inasmuch as congress had no authority whatever delegated to them by the constitution, to make religious establishments, . . ."[586] Representative Charles Carroll said: "as many sects have concurred in opinion that they are not well secured under the present constitution, . . . [I am] much in favor of adopting the words; . . . it would tend more toward conciliating the minds of the people to the [federal] government than almost any other amendment . . . proposed. . . ."[587] Carroll indicated that he would accept different "phraseology," as long as it satisfied "the wishes of the honest part of the community" that no sect would incur legal inferiority via federal law.[588]

Congressional records state that James Madison then:

"Said he apprehended the meaning of the words ['No religion shall be established by law, nor shall the equal rights of conscience be infringed.'] to be, that congress should not establish a religion, and enforce the legal observation of it by law, nor compel men to worship God in any manner contrary to their conscience; whether the words were necessary or not he did not mean to say, but they had been required by some of the state conventions, who seemed to entertain an opinion that under the clause of the constitution, which gave power to congress to make all laws necessary and proper to carry into execution the constitution, and the laws made under it, enabled . . . [Congress] to make laws of such a nature as might infringe the rights of conscience, or establish a national religion, to prevent these effects he presumed the amendment was intended, and he thought it as well expressed as the nature of the language would admit."[589]

A delegate to the 1788 North Carolina Ratifying Convention asked whether the national establishment would be Episcopal or Presbyterian.[590] In response, supporters of the Constitution asserted that national sect equality was assured by (1) the absence of an enumerated power for Congress to establish a religion, and (2) the multiplicity of sects in the United States.[591]

The First Amendment's provisions on religion were put there to reassure many people that: (1) Congress would not establish a national church (There would be no Church of the United States.); (2) no sect would enjoy legal superiority via an act of Congress; and (3) Congress would pass no law which imposed religious beliefs or restricted religious beliefs.

In 1789, the same Congress that proposed the Bill of Rights reenacted the Northwest Ordinance of 1787 "without a word of opposition."[592] Article III of the Northwest Ordinance of 1787 stated: "Religion, morality, and knowledge being necessary to good government and the happiness of mankind, schools and the means of education shall forever be encouraged. . . ."[593]

The New England colonies led the way in compulsory education and public schools.[594] A colonial schoolbook included illustrations to accompany biblical messages such as: (1) "In Adam's Fall We Sinned all."; (2) "Heaven to find, The Bible Mind."; and (3) "Christ crucify'd For Sinners dy'd."[595]

Public schools in the United States had a strong religious flavor from 1787 to 1791.[596] A 1789 Massachusetts act (1) required every town with at least fifty households to provide a schoolmaster to teach "reading, writing, . . . and the principles of piety . . .", and (2) authorized towns to vote on taxes to hire a schoolmaster.[597] Schoolmasters had to be certified by a learned minister in the vicinity. In 1789, the Boston School Committee: (1) specified the Bible and other texts for reading classes (In 1845, 258 out of 308 town committees in Massachusetts specified the Bible as a reading book in public schools.); and (2) determined that schoolmasters had the "indispensable duty

. . . daily to commence the duties of their office by prayer, and reading a portion of the sacred scriptures, at the hour assigned for opening the [public] School in the Morning; and close the same in the evening with a prayer."[598] The only constitutional justification for Congress to appropriate funds for education traces to the Northwest Ordinance of 1787. Such education was to involve religion and moral values in addition to subjects such as reading, writing, and arithmetic.

Article III of the Northwest Ordinance of 1787 was reenacted by Congress during the administrations of Presidents Washington, Adams (Indiana territory), Jefferson (Michigan Territory in 1805 and Illinois Territory in 1809), and Madison (Missouri Territory).[599] Each of the first four presidents signed into law the provision: "Religion, morality, and knowledge being necessary to good government and the happiness of mankind, schools and the means of education shall forever be encouraged."[600]

The First Congress under the Constitution did not intend to prevent succeeding Congresses from (1) approving grants of land in the territories to promote religion, (2) paying chaplains for services in Congress and among U.S. military personnel, and (3) encouraging religion in other ways, such as by paying missionaries to try to convert Indians to Christianity. For more than one hundred years, from 1785 to 1896, Congress appropriated money to pay missionaries of various Christian faiths to "propagate the Gospel" to Indians.[601] During the first decade after the First Amendment was ratified, "successive Congresses appropriated approximately 12,000 acres of land for one [religious] society, the United Brethren, for its efforts among the Indians in the Northwest Territories."[602] The United Brethren (1) disdained "points of difference among the various Protestant denominations," and (2) "espoused the 'great truths held in common'" by the various Protestant sects.[603]

Ratifiers of the First Amendment were aware that Congress, under the Articles of Confederation, had exercised its unwritten power to aid religion by expending precious funds for missionaries and by stipulating that land be used for religious purposes. In selling U.S. land to the Ohio Company in 1787, Congress stipulated that "lot No. 16" in every township be reserved for schools, and "lot No. 29" in each township "be given perpetually for the purposes of religion."[604]

Most, if not all, ratifiers of the First Amendment understood that Congress would have the unwritten power to expend United States resources on religion. The following statement was made by eight members of the fifteen-member Virginia Senate on October 18, 1789:

> "although it [*Article the third* which became the First Amendment] goes to restrain Congress from passing laws establishing any national religion, they might, notwithstanding, levy taxes to any amount, for the support of religion or its preachers; and any particular denomination of christians might be so favored and supported by the General Government, as to give it a decided advantage over others, and in process of time render it as powerful and dangerous as if it was established as the national religion of the country. . . ."[605]

Most framers intended that Congress could appropriate only modest resources for religion and education, and most ratifiers *probably* had a similar understanding.

Congress has funded clergymen of various faiths to provide prayers in Congress and to conduct religious services in the armed forces. Congress has passed income tax laws which: (1) allow taxpayers to deduct contributions they make to churches (so as not to discourage religion); and (2) exempt churches from paying taxes on the income they receive from church members and other people (to encourage religion). The framers and ratifiers would have undoubtedly approved.

A federal law even protects religious donations in bankruptcy proceedings.[606] It is doubtful that the framers intended for Congress to be able to pass such a law.

A ban on sect-neutral state support to religion was first proclaimed by the Supreme Court in 1947 when it ruled, in the case of *Everson v. Board of Education:* "The establishment of religion clause of the First Amendment, made equally applicable to the states by the Fourteenth Amendment, means that neither a state nor the Federal government can pass laws which . . . aid all religions, . . ."[607] It will probably always be uncertain as to whether the Fourteenth Amendment was understood by a majority of its ratifiers to make the Bill of Rights applicable to the states. What *is* certain is that the Fourteenth Amendment was framed and ratified in an extremely unconstitutional manner. The unconstitutional aspects of the framing and ratification of the Fourteenth Amendment are described in the following chapter in the discussion of the illegitimate "Fourteenth Amendment."

Even if we assume that the Fourteenth Amendment made the First Amendment applicable to the states, the states can constitutionally aid religion. The same Congress which proposed the Fourteenth Amendment funded missionaries (to "propagate the Gospel" to American Indians), and, after the Fourteenth Amendment was ratified, successive Congresses continued to fund missionaries.

Congress proposed the Fourteenth Amendment to the states in 1866. During a debate in the Senate in 1866, Senator Lyman Trumbull, chairman of the Senate Judiciary Committee and supporter of the Fourteenth Amendment, said: "the [federal] Government is to legislate in the interest of freedom. Now, our laws are to be enacted with a view to educate, improve, enlighten, and Christianize the negro; . . ."[608] If Trumbull believed that the Fourteenth Amendment incorporated the First Amendment, he did not intend for the Fourteenth Amendment to prevent the states from aiding religion.

Everson gave rise to many lawsuits and discouraged state legislators from providing nondenominational aid to schools which taught religion. When states did provide nondenominational aid to schools in which religion was taught, the courts often declared that aid unconstitutional. The antireligious attitude of the Court was intense in the 1970s. During that decade the Court ruled that states could not reimburse parochial schools for the costs of administering state-mandated tests.[609] In 1980, the Court reversed itself and voted 5 to 4 that it was constitutional for states to reimburse parochial schools for the costs of administering state-mandated tests.[610]

In 1971, the Court ruled unconstitutional a state law which provided for the payment of up to fifteen percent of teacher salaries in nonpublic schools.[611] In 1971 and 1977, the Court ruled that it was unconstitutional for states to provide nonpublic schools with: (1) secular instructional materials (maps, slide projectors, scientific gear, etc.); and (2) transportation for field trips similar to that provided to public schools.[612] *No provision of the Constitution was intended by its framers or understood by its ratifiers to prohibit state funds from going to parochial schools.*

When the Constitution and the Bill of Rights were being ratified, all thirteen of the original states aided and promoted religion.[613] However, only six states (Connecticut, Georgia, Maryland, Massachusetts, New Hampshire, and South Carolina) had laws which authorized taxes to be committed to support religion from the moment they were assessed.[614] In some states, taxes provided the primary financial support to churches.

In 1787–88, many Americans favored amendments to the proposed Constitution in the area of religion. The Virginia Ratifying Convention and the North Carolina Ratifying Convention both recommended:

> "That religion or the duty which we owe to our Creator, and the manner of discharging it, can be directed only by reason of conviction, not by force or violence, and therefore all men have an equal, natural and unalienable right to the free exercise of religion according to the dictates of conscience, and that no particular religious sect or society ought to be favoured or established by Law in preference to others."[615]

The New York Ratifying Convention recommended:

> "That the People have an equal, natural and unalienable right, freely and peaceably to Exercise their Religion according to the dictates of Conscience, and that no Religious Sect or Society ought to be favoured or established by Law in preference of others."[616]

The New Hampshire Ratifying Convention was the only convention to recommend a constitutional amendment which would have prohibited Congress from making any laws relevant to religion. In an effort to prevent Congress from intermeddling with New

Hampshire's nonsectarian support of religion, the New Hampshire Ratifying Convention recommended:

"Congress shall make no Laws touching Religion, or to infringe on the rights of Conscience."[617]

If the framers of the First Amendment intended to erect an impenetrable wall of separation between religion and the United States government, as the Court implied in *Everson*, the First Congress could have simply proposed the first part of New Hampshire's recommendation: "Congress shall make no Laws touching Religion." The House of Representatives at one point voted for the entire religious amendment recommended by the New Hampshire Ratifying Convention.[618] Upon re-examination, the House of Representatives rejected "Congress shall make no Laws touching Religion, . . ." Most members of the first House of Representatives wanted the United States government to at least gently touch religion.

Why did the framers in the House of Representatives want the federal government to touch religion? The Northwest Ordinance of 1787 and its offspring tell us that it was because the framers believed that religion and morality were "necessary to good government." The framers were committed to republican government and believed that a virtuous citizenry was one of the keys to the success of republican government. George Washington, in his famous farewell address, echoed the sentiments of most framers and ratifiers when he said:

"Of all the dispositions and habits which lead to political prosperity, Religion and Morality are indispensable supports, And let us with caution indulge the supposition, that morality can be maintained without Religion. . . . reason and experience both forbid us to expect that national morality can prevail in exclusion of religious principle."[619]

The Court implied in *Everson* that Thomas Jefferson was opposed to any touching of religion by government because Jefferson: (1) was the author of the "Bill for Establishing Religious Freedom" in Virginia; and (2) wrote, in an 1802 letter, "Believing with you that religion is a matter which lies between man and his God, . . . I contemplate with sovereign reverence that act of the whole American people which declared that their legislature should 'make no law respecting an establishment of religion, or prohibiting the free exercise thereof,' thus building a wall of separation between church and State."[620]

Compared to Jefferson's key reference points (Virginia during his youth and England in the seventeenth and eighteenth centuries), the First Amendment reinforced the wall of separation implied by the unamended Constitution. But it was not an impenetrable wall; it had windows through which government and religion could gently touch each other.

Although Jefferson was an Anglican vestryman (a person entrusted with the administration of secular affairs of a parish), he worked with George Wythe to challenge "a century and a half of the acquiescence of Virginia civil judges to the church law of England."[621] In 1771, Jefferson and Wythe received a favorable ruling in Virginia in a case notable because it was the first time that the Virginia General Court upheld the jurisdiction of Virginia courts over the Anglican Church.[622] That landmark ruling was appealed to England by the royal attorney general of Virginia, and the case was still pending several years later when the Virginia courts were closed as a result of the American Revolution.[623]

Jefferson wrote *Notes on the State of Virginia* between 1780 and 1784, and it was first published in 1785.[624] In that book, Jefferson discussed the enormous influence that the Church of England had on the colony of Virginia. Quakers, who were persecuted in England, were not welcomed in Virginia. Parents committed a crime in Virginia if they failed to baptize their children. Quakers did not believe in baptizing children. Virginia laws prohibited Quaker meetings and prohibited masters of vessels from bringing Quakers to Virginia.[625] To stay in Virginia, Quakers had to swear an oath to the colony of Virginia and the Crown; it was firmly against the Quaker belief to take an oath of any kind.[626] Quakers who were expelled from Virginia could be jailed on their first and second returns and executed on their third return.[627]

Anyone, Quaker or non-Quaker, accused of heresy against the Church of England could be burned at the stake in Virginia.[628] Heresy was not defined, but the Anglican Church would let you know if you committed it. Virginia enacted a less severe religious statute in 1705. That statute, still in effect in the early 1770s, provided that people could be jailed for three years and lose most of their civil rights (including custody of their children) if they denied the Scriptures to be of divine authority.[629] Thomas Jefferson, a person who had his doubts about some parts of the Bible, could not have been fond of the 1705 Virginia religious statute.

Powerful evidence that Jefferson's wall of separation was not impervious comes one year after his "wall of separation" letter. In 1803, President Jefferson asked the Senate to ratify a treaty with the Kaskaskia Indians which required the federal government to pay a Catholic priest $100 annually.[630] The document which the Senate ratified included the $100 per year salary plus $300 for the erection of a Catholic church.[631]

The United States purchased the vast Louisiana territory from France in 1803. The legislature of the territory of Orleans (now the state of Louisiana) sponsored the mingling of church and state in several laws which were not vetoed, or otherwise objected to, by President Jefferson.[632] (In 1811, President James Madison vetoed an act of the Mississippi territorial legislature which aided a church.[633]) In 1805, the Orleans territorial university was founded as a "supporter of rational religion."[634] An 1806 law incorporated an Episcopal church in New Orleans for which the territorial legislature required that a "faithful minister of Jesus Christ" be appointed.[635] In 1808, the Orleans territorial legislature appointed as superintendents of the New Orleans charity hospital (1) the "person exercising the function of chief of the Catholic church" in the territory, and (2) the governor of the territory.[636]

After Jefferson's second term as president, he returned to Virginia where he was the prime mover in the founding of the University of Virginia. Historian Garrett Ward Sheldon correctly stated: "Jefferson's solution to the problem of one dominant religious sect in the public university was not to exclude all religion from the institution, but to invite the free expression of all denominations within the university's walls."[637] Although Jefferson was opposed to a *single* Chair of Divinity because it would imply that only one denomination would be represented, he stated: "It was not, however, to be understood that instruction in religious opinion and duties was meant to be precluded by the public authorities, . . ."[638]

In an 1822 letter, Jefferson wrote:

> "In our village of Charlottesville there is a good deal of religion, with only a small spice of fanaticism. We have four sects, but without either church or meeting house. The [public] courthouse is the common temple, one Sunday in the month to each. Here Episcopalian and Presbyterian, Methodist and Baptist, meet together, join in hymning their Maker, listen with attention and devotion to each other's preachers and mix in society with perfect harmony."[639]

Although Thomas Jefferson and George Washington were not in total agreement about the desired relationship between religion and government, there was much common ground. Both men wanted religion to strengthen the United States by implanting moral values, especially moral values common to all Christian sects.[640] Both men knew that establishing one sect as the official religion of the United States or any state would be a major mistake because it would sharply increase divisiveness among the electorate. Both men wanted something of a wall of separation; Washington wanted large windows and Jefferson wanted small windows. Even if Jefferson wanted no windows, it would have had no bearing on the meaning of the First Amendment because a majority of its framers and ratifiers understood that it did not preclude windows.

On August 24, 1789, the House passed 17 amendments and sent them to the Senate. One of those amendments, "ARTICLE THE THIRD," stated:

> "Congress shall make no law establishing religion or prohibiting the free exercise thereof, nor shall the rights of Conscience be infringed."[641]

On September 2, 1789, the Senate began its deliberations on the Bill of Rights. At one point in their deliberations, the Senate changed the House amendment designated "ARTICLE THE

THIRD" to "Congress shall make no law establishing one religious sect or society in preference to others, nor shall the rights of Conscience be infringed."[642] On September 9, 1789, the Senate passed 12 recommended amendments. The only recommended amendment which addressed religion read:

> "Congress shall make no law establishing articles of faith, or a mode of worship, or prohibiting the free exercise of religion, or abridging the freedom of speech, or of the press, or the right of the people peaceably to assemble, and to petition the government for a redress of grievances."[643]

On June 8, 1789, James Madison got the Bill of Rights ball rolling in Congress by suggesting specific amendments to the Constitution. Relevant to what became the First Amendment, Madison suggested:

> "The civil rights of none shall be infringed [by Congress] on account of religious belief or worship, nor shall any national religion be established, nor shall the full and equal rights of conscience be in any manner, or on any pretext, infringed [by Congress]. The people shall not be deprived or abridged [by Congress] of their right to speak, to write, or to publish their sentiments; and the freedom of the press, as one of the great bulwarks of liberty, shall be inviolable. The people shall not be restrained [by Congress] from peaceably assembling and consulting for their common good; nor from applying to . . . [Congress] by petitions, or remonstrances, for redress of their grievances."[644]

Comments with Respect to Freedom of Speech and of the Press

Senator Ralph Izard wrote Thomas Jefferson to tell Jefferson that Madison's suggested amendments were a waste of time.[645] Senator Pierce Butler referred to the amendments suggested by Madison as a "few milk and water amendments."[646] Although Congress strengthened some of Madison's suggested amendments, Congress (1) did *not* strengthen Madison's suggested speech and press protections relevant to abridgements by the federal government, and (2) eliminated Madison's suggested amendment which would have prevented states from violating "the freedom of the press."[647]

Madison singled out freedom of the press for special praise ("one of the great bulwarks of liberty"). A printing press was brought to Massachusetts in 1639, but it was controlled by an official censor and used only to print religious works.[648] The first newspaper, named *Public Occurrences Both Foreign and Domestic*, appeared in 1679, but it was only published for a short time before Massachusetts suppressed it because it discussed a political question.[649] Publishing seemed so precarious that the second American newspaper, the *Boston News-Letter*, did not come into existence until 1704.[650] When James Franklin (Benjamin Franklin's brother) began to publish the *New England Courant* in 1720, some friends, trying to keep him out of trouble, said that one newspaper was enough for America.[651] Official censorship ended in England in 1695 when Parliament allowed the licensing act to expire; under the licensing act, it was illegal to publish anything without previous approval of an official censor.[652] Licenses were required for printing in the colonies well into the eighteenth century. Relevant to printing in the American colonies, historians Charles A. Beard and Mary R. Beard wrote: "The idea of printing, unlicensed by the government and uncontrolled by the church, was, however, slow in taking form."[653] By 1730, censorship of the press by licensing *effectively* ended in Massachusetts.[654] However, official licensing of presses lasted until 1755 in Massachusetts.[655] After censorship and licensing ended in the colonies, publishers in all colonies were "constantly liable to arrest for printing anything displeasing to colonial governments."[656]

Benjamin Franklin recorded that America had 25 newspapers in 1771, of which Boston led with five and Philadelphia had three.[657] Newspapers and pamphlets in the American colonies enlightened the electorate by an open discussion of political questions and played a major role in the evolution of American democracy into a government greatly influenced by public opinion.[658] Thomas Jefferson engaged in a bit of hyperbole when he said that if he was given a

choice between government without newspapers or newspapers without government, "I should not hesitate for a moment to prefer the
latter."[659]

The House Select Committee, of which Madison was a member:
(1) eliminated Madison's explicit mention of "write" and "publish"
(but implicitly included them in "the right of the people . . . to apply
to the government for redress of grievances" and the "freedom . . . of
the press"); and (2) expanded the freedom of petitioning so that
citizens could petition any part of the federal government. (Madison's
suggested amendments would have guaranteed freedom of petitioning only for petitions to Congress.) The House Select Committee
recommended:

> "The freedom of speech, and of the press, and the right of the
> people peaceably to assemble and consult for their common
> good, and to apply to the [federal] government for redress of
> grievances, shall not be infringed [by Congress]."[660]

The large majority of the framers and ratifiers of the Bill of Rights
would have been able to agree that, under the Constitution, before
and after the First Amendment became law:

- Congress had no authority to pass any law which required the
  approval of any person or entity to say, write, or publish anything.

- People could be prosecuted by the federal government, under
  the common law, if what they said, wrote, or published was seditious relevant to the federal government.

During the Revolutionary War, the states passed laws which imposed penalties ranging from heavy fines up to the death sentence
for people who said that the King was sovereign and states did not
have independent authority.[661] In 1780, Virginia passed a law which
authorized fines of up to 100,000 pounds of tobacco and five years
imprisonment for anyone who wished health to the King.[662] Despite
the fact that Pennsylvania made freedom of speech a constitutional
right in 1776, Pennsylvanians were persecuted if they "talked too

freely about the mistakes of Congress, or the virtues of the British government; . . ."[663]

During the six-year period between the end of the Revolutionary War in 1783 and congressional approval of the Bill of Rights in 1789, there were probably only a few prosecutions for sedition in the United States. In 1787, a man named Moses Harvey was convicted of using "seditious and inflammatory words" because he (1) implied that the legislators in the Massachusetts legislature were "thieves," and (2) advocated closing the courts.[664] He was fined 50 pounds and forced to undergo indignities.[665] In a more important case in Massachusetts, William Whiting was prosecuted. While he was chief justice of a county common pleas court in 1786, Whiting (using the pseudonym Gracchus) wrote an article which (1) severely criticized the Massachusetts legislature for making unjust laws, and (2) suggested that virtuous citizens who were denied redress of their grievances should "disturb the government."[666] In 1787, Whiting was dismissed from his judgeship, convicted of writing a seditious libel, fined 100 pounds, and sentenced to seven months in prison.[667] Obviously knowledgeable in the law, Whiting did not even claim that the free press clause of the 1780 Massachusetts Constitution precluded prosecution for seditious libel.[668]

In 1788, a Pennsylvania grand jury indicted newspaper editor Eleazor Oswald for gross libel against a private person. Before his trial, Oswald, in his newspaper: (1) alluded to "prejudices . . . against me on the bench," (2) requested a fair trial from his trial jury, and (3) anticipated that the trial jury would prevent a violation of freedom of the press "upon any refined pretense which oppressive ingenuity or courtly study can invent."[669] At that point, Pennsylvania Chief Justice Thomas McKean (signer of the Declaration of Independence, former president of the Continental Congress, former governor of Delaware, key supporter of ratification of the Constitution in Pennsylvania, Chief Justice of Pennsylvania for 22 years, and, as a member of Thomas Jefferson's political party, governor of Pennsylvania for eight years) had Oswald arrested, and, with no jury, convicted Oswald of seditious contempt of court.[670] Oswald was fined ten pounds and sentenced to one month in prison by McKean.[671] McKean ruled: "there is nothing in the constitution of this state, respecting the liberty of the press, that has not been authorized by the constitution of that kingdom [England] for nearly a century past."[672] Furthermore, McKean stated that the right to free press in the Pennsylvania Constitution protected people from being convicted of seditious libel only if their publications were made "with an eye solely to the public good, . . ."[673] Relevant to publications "intended to delude and defame, . . . it is impossible that any good government should afford protection and impunity."[674]

Despite occasional prosecutions for seditious libel, newspapers in America often published seditious material in the 1780s. For various reasons, the state governments rarely prosecuted. Benjamin Franklin wanted to see more action taken against libelers. Franklin wrote an essay in 1789 in which he said that if freedom of the press authorized people to falsely and maliciously accuse one another of crimes, the legislature should revise the law.[675] When people were libeled in the press, Franklin recommended that the offenders be given a good drubbing with a cudgel (a short heavy club).[676] Franklin declared that if freedom of the press meant "the Liberty of discussing the Propriety of Public Measures and Political opinions, let us have as much as you please."[677] As a punishment for members of the press who affronted the reputation of the government, Franklin suggested: "we should, in moderation, content ourselves with tarring and feathering and tossing them in a blanket."[678]

Sir William Blackstone, in his *Commentaries on the Laws of England*, said: "The *liberty of the press* . . . consists in laying no previous restraints upon publications, and not in freedom from censure for criminal matter when published."[679] Historian Leonard Levy found the common law definition of free press, as presented by Blackstone in his *Commentaries*, to have been universally accepted in the United States from 1787 to 1791.[680] For example, at the Virginia Ratifying Convention in 1788, George Nicholas maintained that freedom of the press was secure because the Constitution granted the federal government no power to license the press.[681]

Common-Law Crimes

The common-law crime of seditious libel is very important to understanding the First Amendment. Therefore, the relationship of the common law of crimes to the Constitution is discussed at some length in this subsection.

On October 14, 1774, the First Continental Congress resolved: "That the respective colonies are entitled to the common law of England, and more especially to the great and inestimable privilege of being tried by their peers of the vicinage, according to the course of that law."[682] When American colonists claimed they had a right to employ the common law of England, British authorities maintained that use of the common law in the colonies was not a right; it was a favor sometimes granted.[683] The Declaration of Independence addressed a violation of common law when it complained of "transporting us beyond Seas to be tried . . ."

Framer James Wilson indicated to ratifiers that federal courts would have jurisdiction in cases involving common-law crimes. (Wilson served as United States Supreme Court justice from 1789 to 1797.) After participating heavily in the Constitutional Convention, Wilson participated heavily in the Pennsylvania Ratifying Convention where he refuted charges to the effect that the United States government under the Constitution would be able to impair the freedom of the press.[684] Wilson said: "there is given to the general government no power whatsoever concerning it: and no law in pursuance of the Constitution can possibly be enacted, to destroy that liberty. . . . what is meant by liberty of the press is that there should be no antecedent restraint upon it; but that every author is responsible when he attacks the security or the welfare of the government, or the safety, character and property of the individual. With regard to attacks upon the public, the mode of proceeding is by prosecution. . . . if this libel is to be tried, it must be tried where the offence was committed; for under the Constitution, as declared in the second section of the Third Article, the trial must be held in the State; therefore on this occasion it must be tried where it was published, if the indictment is for publishing; and it must be tried likewise by a jury of that state."[685] Wilson's definition of freedom of the press and his assertion that the federal government would be able to prosecute seditious libel went unchallenged at the Pennsylvania Ratifying Convention.[686]

Before there were any federal statutes, and despite the fact that the Constitution did not authorize Congress to enact libel statutes or impair press freedom, Wilson was absolutely confident that federal courts could be used to prosecute writers and publishers of libels against the United States. Wilson obviously understood that federal courts would have jurisdiction in cases involving common-law crimes, including the common-law crime of seditious libel.[687] The other delegates at the Pennsylvania Ratifying Convention must have had the same understanding when they voted.

Why was Wilson so confident that the federal courts would have jurisdiction in cases involving common-law crimes? Article III includes the statement: "The judicial Power [of the U.S.] shall extend to all Cases, in Law and Equity, arising under this Constitution, the Laws of the United States, . . ." The word "Law," in "Law and Equity," must have been understood by Wilson to include that portion of the common law (civil and criminal) which was accepted in the United States in 1787.

During the 1790s, people were prosecuted in federal courts for the common-law crimes of counterfeiting, attempted extortion, attempted bribery, seditious libel, and assisting in the capture of a ship.[688] Three of the federal judges who accepted jurisdiction in those cases were influential framers (Justice Ellsworth, Justice Paterson, and Justice Wilson), and two other federal judges who accepted cases involving common-law crimes, Justice Iredell and Chief Justice Jay, had close ties to the framers.[689] It is extremely unlikely that all of those men would have accepted jurisdiction in cases involving only common-law crimes if they thought it was unconstitutional to do so. Consider the reaction of Court members to an act of Congress involved in *Hayburn's Case*[690] in 1792. At least five of the six justices (The Court had only six members during the 1790s.) refused to abide by the 1791 act of Congress involved in *Hayburn's Case* in their capacity as circuit-court judges because they believed that the act was unconstitutional.[691] [692]

The only place in the Constitution that uses the term "common law" is the Seventh Amendment, which uses the term twice. However, it is used in a way that strongly suggests that use of the common law by the federal courts was taken for granted.

When the federal courts first employed the common law of crimes, the practice seems to have been widely accepted. It is noteworthy that Thomas Jefferson, as Secretary of State in 1793, advocated the prosecution of a man in federal court for a common-law crime.[693] It was not until 1795, when a Jeffersonian (a person supporting Thomas Jefferson's political party) was indicted under the common law of criminal libel, that Jeffersonians maintained that it was unconstitutional for the federal government to prosecute common-law crimes. Nevertheless, a decade later, Jeffersonians obtained federal indictments for the common-law crime of seditious libel. In 1806, during Jefferson's second term as president, a federal grand jury indicted six men in the United States Circuit Court for the District of Connecticut for seditiously libeling President Jefferson.[694] [695]

For various reasons, including embarrassment to Jefferson, none of the six men indicted in federal court in 1806 for seditious libel were tried.[696] The case against one of the six men was not prosecuted. The federal government withdrew prosecutions against three of the other men in 1808.[697] The charges against two editors of the *Connecticut Courant* were not dropped. In 1806, the *Connecticut Courant* had charged President Jefferson and Congress "with having in secret voted two millions of dollars as a present to [Napoleon] Bonaparte for leave to make a treaty with Spain."[698] The editors, in their effort to get the United States Circuit Court for the District of Connecticut to dismiss the seditious libel charges, maintained that federal trial courts had no authority to try criminal cases involving only the common law.[699] The judges of the District of Connecticut Circuit Court were divided on the issue of jurisdiction, and this issue was taken to the Supreme Court for resolution. It was "resolved" in 1812 in the case of *U. S. v. Hudson and Goodwin*.[700] Hudson and Goodwin were the indicted editors of the *Connecticut Courant*. In *Hudson and Goodwin*, the Court:

- Ruled that federal courts can try crimes only if the crimes are defined in acts of Congress or the Constitution[701]

- Failed to mention any of the several relevant precedents set in United States circuit courts (All such precedents conflicted with the *Hudson and Goodwin* ruling, in that jurisdiction had always been granted in cases involving common-law crimes not defined by Congress or the Constitution.[702])

- Indicated that its opinion was a majority opinion, but failed to present any dissenting opinions or name the dissenters (Historian Leonard Levy indicated that three of the seven justices dissented, including Chief Justice John Marshall and Justice Joseph Story.[703])

- Indicated that its answer to the question of federal jurisdiction over common-law crimes was determined by "public opinion" and "the general acquiescence of legal men . . ."[704]

Although contempt was not involved in *Hudson and Goodwin*, it is a bit humorous that the Court made a special point of announcing that its ruling did not mean federal courts would lose their common-law power to penalize for contempt. The Court ruled: "The courts of the United States have no common law jurisdiction in cases of libel against the government of the United States. But they have the power to fine for contempts, to imprison for contumacy, . . ."[705] The federal courts obtained the power to fine for contempts and to imprison for contumacy (defiance of authority) from the same place they obtained the power to penalize for other common-law crimes.

The Sedition Act of 1798

The Sedition Act of 1798 made it illegal to say, write, or publish anything which was "false, scandalous, and malicious . . . against the government of the United States or either House of Congress, or the President of the United States, with the intent to defame said government . . . or to bring them or either of them into contempt or disrepute."[706] Relative to the common law of seditious libel, the Sedition Act of 1798 was libertarian because it explicitly stated the reforms of (1) allowing truth as a defense, (2) allowing the jury to decide both law and fact, and (3) requiring that criminal intent be present.[707] Those reforms reflected the longstanding practices of juries—going back to at least 1735 in the Zenger case. The Sedition Act of 1798 was unconstitutional because (1) the enumerated powers of Congress include no power to make such a law, and (2) the Tenth Amendment prohibits such a law. The Sedition Act of 1798 was also unnecessary, given that the common law of seditious libel was in place.[708] [709]

Why did the Federalist Party enact the Sedition Act of 1798? There were at least two reasons. A few months before the Sedition Act of 1798 was enacted, Justice Samuel Chase, one of two trial judges in a bribery case in the United States Circuit Court for the District of Pennsylvania, ruled that federal courts had no jurisdiction in cases involving common-law crimes.[710] Judge Richard Peters disagreed, and Chase reconsidered his ruling. Chase and Peters agreed to impose a sentence on the criminal defendant for the common-law crime of attempted bribery.[711] (The defendant was convicted of attempting to bribe the United States Commissioner of Revenue to award the defendant a government construction contract.[712]) Chase's blunder led a criminal defendant, who was accused of libeling President John Adams, to announce that he would rely on Chase's first opinion in the bribery case and contend that the federal government had no jurisdiction in cases involving common-law crimes.[713]

The primary reason for the enactment of the Sedition Act of 1798 was to silence newspapers which criticized the Federalist government—so that the Federalists would remain in power.[714] [715] Newspapers had been the primary vehicle for Republicans, led by Thomas Jefferson, to voice their criticisms of Federalist actions. Although Jefferson was very much opposed to the anti-U.S. things France did in 1798, he believed that President Adams and the Federalist-controlled Congress had overreacted.

The Sedition Act of 1798 did not protect Vice-President Thomas Jefferson. He was fair game for the Federalists and the Federalist press. Several Federalist newspapers printed a sermon delivered by

Yale University President Timothy Dwight, a Congregationalist theologian. Dwight said:

> "Can serious and reflecting men look about them and doubt that, if Jefferson is elected, . . . that those morals which protect our lives from the knife of the assassin, which guard the chastity of our wives and daughters from seduction and violence, defend our property from plunder and devastation . . . will not be trampled upon? For what end? . . . that we may see our wives and daughters the victims of legal prostitution? Shall our sons become the disciples of Voltaire and the dragoons of Marat?"[716]

The *Connecticut Courant* pulled out all stops when it warned that, if Jefferson was elected president: "Murder, robbery, rape, adultery, and incest will all be openly taught and practiced."[717] Writers and editors of Federalist newspapers could write and print defamatory material which was false and malicious with no fear of being prosecuted. However, writers (including Jefferson) and editors of Republican newspapers had to be very careful to avoid prosecution. Under the Sedition Act of 1798, the federal government prosecuted 25 writers, editors, and printers; ten were convicted and sentenced to prison.[718] Congressman Matthew Lyon was indicted and convicted in the United States Circuit Court for the District of Vermont for criticizing President Adams as a person who had a "continual grasp for power, in an unbounded thirst for ridiculous pomp, foolish adulation, and selfish avarice."[719] (That statement was much closer to the truth than were many statements published in Federalist newspapers.) Presiding Judge/Justice William Paterson (1) rejected Lyon's assertion that the Sedition Act of 1798 was unconstitutional, and (2) sentenced Lyon to four months in prison.[720] While in jail, Lyon was reelected to Congress.[721]

The common law of sedition—although popular with most judges and legislators—was unpopular with many citizens. The Federalists *may* have made sedition law more popular by putting it in statute form which explicitly incorporated libertarian reforms. However, the Sedition Act of 1798 proved to be a political blunder for the Federalists. The Republicans maintained that the act was unconstitutional, and the Federalists maintained that the act was constitutional.[722] The Republicans made major gains in the 1800 elections. Thomas Jefferson defeated President John Adams, and many Federalist members of Congress were defeated by Republicans.

The Sedition Act of 1798 expired in 1801 on the day before Jefferson was sworn in to serve his first term as president. The Supreme Court never ruled on the constitutionality of the act. The Judiciary Act of 1789 did not authorize the Court to review federal criminal cases.[723] However, if the constitutionality of the act could have been challenged in the Supreme Court, and it was challenged there, the Court would have ruled the act to be constitutional. In 1798 and 1799, all six members of the Court were Federalists, and all of them ruled that the Sedition Act of 1798 was constitutional in federal circuit courts.[724] (The Court had a maximum of six members until 1807.)

Free Speech Folly by the U.S. Supreme Court

The Court has ruled that many perfectly constitutional state laws were unconstitutional under the pretext that the laws "violated" the First Amendment right to free speech. The word "speech" in the First Amendment was almost certainly understood by the ratifiers to mean spoken words. Speech *may* have been understood to include written words, but speech was certainly not understood to go beyond *words*.

The framers of the First Amendment did not intend, and the ratifiers of the First Amendment did not understand, freedom of speech to create: (1) a right to burn anything (much less crosses and American flags in a manner to cause discord); (2) a right to public nudity; or (3) a right for people to profit from stories about their crimes.

Furthermore: (1) the Fourteenth Amendment (which, according to the Court, makes the First Amendment applicable to the states) was framed *and* ratified in a manner that was clearly unconstitutional; and (2) no framer or ratifier of the "Fourteenth Amendment" understood that freedom of speech created the right to do the things mentioned in the previous paragraph.

Unlawful Court rulings made under the pretext of being necessitated by the First Amendment right to free speech include:

- In the case of *Texas v. Johnson*,[725] the Court ruled in 1991 that states could not convict people for burning American flags in a manner that the burner knew would seriously offend one or more persons. Americans have been taught to revere their flag in many ways, including the Pledge of Allegiance ("I pledge allegiance to the flag of the United States of America . . ."), opening ceremonies of sporting events, and seeing American flags draped on the caskets of members of the armed forces and other national heroes. One can imagine the soul of Abraham Lincoln being very pleased to see Texas, a former Confederate state, voluntarily pass a tough law against desecration of an American flag, and see Lincoln's pleasure turn to dismay as the Court invoked the Fourteenth Amendment—which came about as a result of the Civil War and the Thirteenth Amendment—as part of its "justification" of its unconstitutional ruling in *Texas v. Johnson*. The 1971 book ". . . *So Gallantly Streaming*," states that in 1800 a man "was convicted by a military commission and hanged for tearing down a United States flag that flew over the Mint."[726] As of 1971, every state had a statute "forbidding defacing, desecration, or showing disrespect for the flag of the United States."[727] In 1968, a federal law was enacted which "declared that a person could be imprisoned for up to one year and/or fined up to $1,000 for intentionally casting contempt upon the United States Flag, a piece of one, a picture of one, or 'publicly mutilating, defacing, defiling, burning or trampling on it.'"[728] State laws have been used to prosecute people for flying a U.S. flag upside down, displaying U.S. flags with peace symbols on them, or wearing clothes patched with U.S. flags.[729]

- In the case of *R.A.V. v. City of St. Paul*,[730] the Court ruled in 1992 that states and cities could not enforce laws which made it illegal to burn crosses to alarm black people. A "skinhead" had burned a cross on the lawn of a black family which had moved into a white neighborhood in St. Paul, Minnesota.[731] The preposterous ruling in *R. A. V. v. City of St. Paul* was probably made in an effort to be consistent with the preposterous ruling in *Texas v. Johnson*.

- In the case of *Erznoznik v. City of Jacksonville*,[732] the Court ruled in 1975 that states and cities could not prohibit drive-in movie theaters from showing films containing nudity where the theater screens could be seen from public streets or other public places. A drive-in theater whose screens were visible from two streets and a church parking lot had, contrary to a Jacksonville law, shown a movie which showed "female buttocks and breasts." The law had the benefit of protecting minors from exposure to nudity, protecting adults from unwanted exposure to nudity, and increasing safety by reducing an obvious distraction. The Court ruled that the Jacksonville law violated "the First Amendment's guaranty of free speech . . ." That unlawful Court ruling reversed the lawful rulings of Florida courts. In *Erznoznik*, six of the nine members of the U.S. Supreme Court said they were unaware of any justification "for distinguishing movies containing nudity from all other movies in a regulation designed to protect traffic." Those six justices were either devoid of common sense or they were neutered at a very early age.

- In the case of *Simon & Schuster v. Crime Victims Bd.*,[733] the Court ruled in 1991 that states could not enforce laws which prohibited people from profiting from stories about their crimes. Such laws reduced the profit from criminal activities, reduced copycat crimes, and reduced the anguish of victims of crime and their families. Criminals were not being denied their right to free speech. Anything they said for money could have been said for free. That criminals cannot be restrained from talking and writing about their crimes is one of the prices we pay for the First Amendment. We do not have to pay the additional price of precluding state laws which prevent criminals from receiving anything of value in return for stories relating to their crimes. Within two weeks of the Court's ruling in *Simon & Schuster v. Crime Victims Bd.*, the murderer of musician John Lennon said he would take advantage of the ruling to get money back from the state of New York and use the money to pay legal fees.[734] That provides a good clue as to why many lawyers do not want to see criminals "deprived" of income from stories about their crimes. The late and great syndicated columnist Erma Bombeck wrote: "The problem is, crime pays. It is well rewarded with book contracts, miniseries, big lecture fees, and the covers of *Time* and *Newsweek*. . . . Television tends to glamorize criminals . . ."[735] Bombeck expressed concern for the difficult job parents have instilling in their children the correct perspective on success and the understanding that fame is not always synonymous with success.

On at least two occasions, the Court failed to protect the First Amendment right to free speech. The Hatch Act, passed by Congress in 1939 and amended in 1940, included a provision which provided for the firing of all but the very highest level federal employees if they made, on their own time, campaign speeches for or against any candidate for public office in any partisan election. Despite the fact that the Hatch Act clearly violated the First Amendment right to free speech, the Court ruled the Hatch Act constitutional in 1947[736] and 1973.[737]

Comments with Respect to the Right to Assemble and Petition

The right to petition dates back to at least 1215 when King John's charter recognized the right to petition the Crown.[738] In 1669, the House of Commons resolved: "That it is the inherent right of every commoner in England to prepare and present Petitions to the House of Commons in case of grievances, . . ."[739] Parliament often petitioned the Crown (king or queen) for a redress of grievances. If the Crown redressed Parliament's grievances, Parliament enacted laws to provide funds for the government.[740] Citizens frequently petitioned the Crown or Parliament. In an effort to eliminate "tumultuous petitioning," Parliament passed a law in 1661 to limit the number of people who could sign a petition to twenty and the number of people who could present a petition to ten.[741]

In a famous English trial in 1688, seven bishops were tried on a charge of seditious libel for their petitioning of King James II—even though the bishops submitted their petition in a respectful manner.[742] The jury found the bishops not guilty, a verdict that was quite popular. The *"Seven Bishops Case"* led to the fifth provision of the English Bill of Rights.

The English Bill of Rights, enacted in 1689, addresses redress of grievances in two of its thirteen provisions. The fifth provision states: "That it is the right of the subjects to petition the King, and all commitments and prosecutions for such petitioning are illegal."[743] The thirteenth provision of the English Bill of Rights states: "And that for redress of all grievances, and for the amending, strengthening, and preserving of the laws, parliaments ought to be held frequently."[744]

Even with the fifth and thirteenth provisions of the English Bill of Rights and the "inherent right" of commoners to present petitions, Englishmen who presented petitions to Parliament were prosecuted by Parliament if those petitions were deemed seditious by Parliament.[745] The Declaration of Independence complained: "Our repeated Petitions have been answered only by repeated injury. . . ." The framers of the First Amendment left the door open to prosecutions for seditious petitioning, under the common law of contempt or seditious libel, when they did not explicitly prohibit such prosecutions.

The right to assemble was regarded as an auxiliary right to the right to petition.[746] The word "peaceably" in the First Amendment was probably inspired by the memories of 1783 when mutinous soldiers gathered outside Congress—then meeting in Philadelphia—and demanded back pay. The soldiers did not harm any congressmen, but the congressmen were threatened. Congress fled from Philadelphia to the crowded, battle-scarred town of Princeton.[747] Congress soon moved on to Annapolis. General George Washington came to Annapolis on December 23, 1783, to resign his commission in an emotional speech to the members of Congress.[748]

The requirement that assemblies be peaceful was probably intended as an improvement to the 1661 English law against tumultuous petitioning. In 1781, Lord Chief Justice Mansfield ruled: "the [English] Bill of Rights does not mean to meddle with . . . [the 1661 law against tumultuous petitioning] at all . . . and consequently the attending a petition to the House of Commons by more than ten persons is criminal and illegal."[749] Any number of U.S. citizens can assemble to present a petition to the United States government as long as the assembly is peaceful.

Second Amendment

A well regulated Militia, being necessary to the security of a free State, the right of the people to keep and bear Arms, shall not be infringed.

Original Meaning in 21st Century Plain English

It is *necessary* to have a large majority of the free, able-bodied, white male citizens of the United States included in a well-regulated militia to:

- Help deter and repel invasions of military forces from foreign countries (Article I, Section 8, Paragraph 15 uses the words: "Militia to . . . repel Invasions.")
- Help deter and suppress insurrections such as rebellions by poor farmers and slave uprisings (Article I, Section 8, Paragraph 15 uses the words: "Militia to . . . suppress Insurrections.")
- Help enforce federal laws (Article I, Section 8, Paragraph 15 uses the words: "Militia to Execute the Laws of the Union.")
- Deter the United States government from using its military forces to establish a tyrannical government
- Defeat United States military forces which suppress, or attempt to suppress, United States citizens who oppose usurpation of power by the federal government (This point was powerfully made

by (1) James Madison in *The Federalist*, No. 46, and (2) Alexander Hamilton in *The Federalist*, No. 28.)

Militiamen must have arms and some proficiency in the use of those arms; therefore, the right of free, able-bodied, white male citizens to keep and bear arms shall not be infringed.

Comments with Respect to the Second Amendment

The American Revolution began in April of 1775 when British authorities attempted to violate the colonists' right to bear arms.[750] The best British troops in Massachusetts were deployed to seize fourteen cannons and "between ninety and a hundred barrels [of gunpowder] . . . at Concord."[751] The militia also had "20,000 pounds of musket balls and cartridges" and "50 reams of cartridge paper" at Concord.[752] The militia—mostly well-trained "minutemen"—suffered heavy losses, but they (1) inflicted heavier losses on British troops than the British troops inflicted on the militia, and (2) successfully protected almost all of the militia arms—thereby winning the "Battle of Lexington."

Also in April of 1775, the royal governor of Virginia seized Virginia's supply of gunpowder, but the imminent arrival of several thousand militiamen, led by Patrick Henry, caused the royal governor to restore the gunpowder.[753]

In June of 1775, various militia units from New England deployed to a hill just outside Boston. That deployment was triggered by knowledge that the British were planning an attack that was to include an attempt to capture militia ammunition and other supplies.[754] In what is known as the "Battle of Bunker Hill," the militia units near Boston were attacked by the British on June 17, 1775. The militia took heavy losses; but, as in the Battle of Lexington, the British forces suffered even heavier losses.[755]

Americans who lived through the Revolutionary War believed that the peak of patriotism occurred during the middle of 1775.[756] The large majority of the electorate were members of the militia. Most of the electorate felt quite involved and uplifted by the success of the militia.

George Washington had good reason to be frustrated with the militia. Nevertheless, militia units had a major impact at Bennington, Cowpens, King's Mountain, Oriskany, and Saratoga.[757] At Bennington and King's Mountain, the militia won battles with no help from the Continental army.[758] Responding to pleas of alarmed citizens, Colonel John Stark led 1,500 militiamen to Bennington. At Bennington, Stark reportedly shouted to his men: "We'll beat them before night or Molly Stark will be a widow."[759] Bennington cost British General John Burgoyne more than one thousand men.[760] Instead of helping American forces to "finish off the staggered foe," John Stark went home to Molly and the militiamen took their guns and unique American flag and went home.[761] (The "Bennington" flag had 13 stripes, a large "76" under an arch of 11 stars, and two stars in the top corners of the field.[762]) The militia, by itself, could *not* have won the Revolutionary War. That was understood by the framers and ratifiers of the unamended Constitution. Nevertheless, a large majority of the eighteenth-century ratifiers of the unamended Constitution and the Bill of Rights believed that a militia which included a majority of the electorate was a *necessary* cog in the engine called liberty.

Federal Government Only or All Governments?

Does the combination of the Second Amendment and the un-amended Constitution (A) prohibit only the federal government from infringing on the right of the people to keep and bear arms, or (B) prohibit all governments in the United States (federal, state, city, etc.) from infringing on the right of the people to keep and bear arms? This is a very interesting and important question. Rationale can be presented for answer A, but much stronger rationale can be presented for answer B. Although this subsection is focused on the right of the electorate to keep and bear arms, a good bit of the rationale in this subsection is applicable to rights expressed in general terms in the Third through Ninth Amendments. All rights guaranteed by the Second through Ninth Amendments are expressed in general terms except for the second part of the Seventh Amendment.

The rationale for the contention that only the federal government is prohibited from infringing on "the right of the people to
keep and bear Arms" is as follows:

- The amendments suggested in the state ratifying conventions in
  1787 and 1788 dealt with (1) limiting the power of the federal
  government, and (2) other aspects of the U.S. government.

- The Second Amendment does not explicitly prohibit states from
  infringing on the right of the people to keep and bear arms. The
  unamended Constitution explicitly prohibits states from doing
  many things in Article I, Section 10, and general language is
  used in Article I, Section 9 to prohibit only the federal government.

- The phrase "the right of the people to keep and bear arms shall
  not be infringed" was to be inserted in Article I, Section 9 (a
  section that restricts only the federal government) in the amendment proposals made by James Madison (the first step in a
  five-step process used to frame the Bill of Rights) and the amendments recommended by a select committee in the House of
  Representatives (the second of five milestones in the framing of
  the Bill of Rights in Congress).

- In 1833, the U.S. Supreme Court ruled, in the case of *Barron v.
  The Mayor and City Council of Baltimore*,[763] that only the federal
  government must abide by the Bill of Rights.

The following rationale suggests that *the combination of the Second Amendment and the unamended Constitution* prohibits federal, state,
and local governments from infringing on the right of the people to
keep and bear arms:

- The primary reason for forming the United States government,
  and for proposing various joint-colony governments from the New
  England Confederation (composed of four colonies, the "United
  Colonies of New England" was created in 1643 and terminated
  in 1684 when colonial charters were revoked) to the unratified
  Albany Plan of Union of 1754, was to provide for the common

defense. In *The Federalist*, No. 29, Alexander Hamilton said: "it would be natural and proper that the militia of a neighboring State should be marched into another, to resist a common enemy, . . . This was frequently the case . . . in the course of the late war; and this mutual . . . [assistance] is, indeed, a principal . . . [object] of our political association."[764] The militia were a "necessary" part of the common defense. The militia included the large majority of free, able-bodied, white men, and many militiamen supplied their own arms.[765] States provided arms to some men, but it was traditional for members of the militia to supply their own arms. In colonial times, there were often laws which made it mandatory for adult male citizens to supply their own arms. It was a "right and duty to be armed . . ."[766]

• Shays' Rebellion was a major factor leading to the Constitutional Convention. Historians Charles A. Beard and Mary R. Beard wrote: "Only by the most vigorous action was Governor Bowdoin able to quell . . . [Shays' Rebellion in Massachusetts]; . . . The need of national assistance for state governments in times of domestic violence was everywhere emphasized by men who were opposed to revolutionary acts."[767] In New Hampshire in 1786, it "was with difficulty that an armed rebellion [of poor farmers] was avoided."[768] Edmund Randolph "opened the main business" of the Constitutional Convention with a speech which enumerated the defects of the Articles of Confederation and presented the famous Virginia Plan. The second most important defect of the Articles of Confederation, based on Randolph's enumeration, was "that the foederal government could not check the quarrels between states, nor a rebellion in any, not having constitutional power nor means to interpose . . ."[769] The third most important defect had to do with "a productive impost" and "counteraction of the commercial regulations of other nations."[770] That Randolph, and probably the Virginia delegation as a whole (which included influential men such as George Washington, James Madison, George Mason, and George Wythe), considered checking rebellions to be so important is most significant. Shays'

Rebellion "created havoc [in the western part of Massachusetts] from late summer 1786 until early summer 1787, well after the beginning of the [Constitutional] Convention. Similar but shorter debt-based rural outbreaks in 1785, 1786, and 1787 temporarily closed local courts in South Carolina, Maryland, and Virginia [where a courthouse was razed], led to marches and tumults in New Jersey and Pennsylvania, and held the New Hampshire state legislature captive for five hours."[771] It was on February 21, 1787, that Congress, in New York City, "called for a convention to meet in Philadelphia 'on the second Monday in May next, for the sole and express purpose of revising the Articles of Confederation . . .'"[772] George Washington was concerned about "the combustibles in every state. I feel . . . infinitely more than I can express . . . for the disorders which have arisen, . . . Good God! Who besides a tory could have foreseen, or a Briton have predicted them!"[773] In a letter to Thomas Jefferson that was written on October 24, 1787, James Madison said: "the evils issuing from . . . [debtor pressure] contributed more to the uneasiness which produced the [Constitutional] convention [than the lack of power to tax and regulate trade]."[774] Although trade problems are often cited as triggering the Constitutional Convention, fear of insurrections may well have been the trigger. Many citizens in southern states were concerned about possible slave uprisings in addition to rebellions by poor farmers. Article I, Section 8, Paragraph 15 gives Congress the power to call "forth the Militia to execute the Laws of the Union, suppress Insurrections and repel Invasions." Article IV, Section 4 says that the United States will protect each state "against domestic Violence" if requested to do so by the state legislature of the state undergoing insurrection. When a state legislature cannot be convened, a request from the governor is constitutionally sufficient to obtain federal assistance. Article I indicates that such assistance would come from the militia. If states disarmed their citizens, there would have been no militia for the United States to call forth to honor its constitutional commitment to "suppress Insurrections." Except for small garrisons of federal troops on the Western frontier (to deter/

counter Indian raids), the electorate were generally very much opposed to having federal troops during peacetime. (The opposition to standing armies in America from 1787 to 1791 is indicated in the discussion of the Third Amendment in this chapter.) The militia were counted on to be ready to at least assist in quelling insurrections. Alexander Hamilton wrote in *The Federalist*, No. 29: "In times of insurrection, . . . it would be natural and proper that the militia of a neighboring State should be marched into another . . . to guard the republic against the violence of faction or sedition. . . ."[775]

- The Constitution takes it for granted that an armed militia exists in the states. To obtain "Armies," Congress has to "raise and support" them. To obtain "a Navy," Congress has to "provide and maintain" one. To obtain "the Militia," Congress merely has to call them forth. The only militia authority given to the states by the Constitution is "the Appointment of the Officers, and the Authority of training the Militia according to the discipline prescribed by Congress." Hence, the Constitution implicitly says that states cannot disarm able-bodied, law-abiding, white men.

- The Articles of Confederation stated: "every state shall always keep up a well regulated and disciplined militia, sufficiently armed and accoutred, and shall provide and constantly have ready for use, in public stores, a due number of field pieces and tents, . . ."[776] The purpose of the Constitution is stated as follows: "We the People of the United States, in Order to form a more perfect Union, . . . establish this Constitution for the United States of America."). The framers and ratifiers would have considered the Union to be much less perfect if the states were allowed to disarm able-bodied, law-abiding, white male citizens.

- About one year after the ratification of the Bill of Rights, Congress passed a law titled: "An Act more effectually to provide for the National Defence by establishing an Uniform Militia throughout the United States." It called for the "Uniform Militia" to be composed of all free, able-bodied, white male citizens between the ages of 18 and 45, and every such militiamen was required to provide himself with a musket or firelock, ammunition, and a bayonet.[777] That statute was passed under the authority granted to Congress by Article I, Section 8, Paragraph 16. *Congress cannot give up a constitutional power without a constitutional amendment to authorize it, and individual states cannot interfere with Congress' option to utilize the militia by disarming law-abiding citizens who could be part of the militia.* The militia statute enacted by Congress in the eighteenth century provided for a uniform militia in order to have a more effective defense. The militia would have been there without the act of Congress, but it would have been less organized and many militiamen would not have been armed as directed by the act of Congress.

- Article III specifies that the trial of all crimes in federal courts shall be by jury. When what is now the Sixth Amendment was read by its ratifiers and they saw that it provided the right to jury trial *in all criminal prosecutions*, it would have been reasonable for them to assume that the states would have to abide by this proposed amendment if it were ratified—and all other general provisions which were ratified. The right to jury trial in criminal cases in the Sixth Amendment would have been seen as redundant if it were meant to be applied only to the federal government. To avoid such a redundancy, Madison's suggested amendments stated: "That in article 3d, section 2, the third clause be struck out, . . ."[778] Congress did not propose to strike out anything.

- The Seventh Amendment guarantees the right to trial by jury in suits at common law "where the value in controversy shall exceed twenty dollars." Could a suit at common law be tried in a federal court in the eighteenth century if the value in controversy was fifty dollars? In answering that question, we will examine the Judiciary Act of 1789. It became law on September 24, 1789, and Congress proposed the Bill of Rights on September 25, 1789. The Judiciary Act of 1789 must have been considered to be consistent with the Bill of Rights by the ratifiers of the Bill of Rights. By virtue of the Judiciary Act of 1789, the value in controversy (1) had to exceed five hundred dollars for suits at common law between people in different states to be heard in federal courts,[779] (2) had to exceed five hundred dollars for suits at common law in which a citizen of a foreign country was a party to be heard in federal courts,[780] and (3) had to exceed one hundred dollars for suits at common law brought by the United States to be heard in federal court.[781] There was no right to sue the federal government. The United States did not have jurisdiction in suits at common law between citizens of the same state except "between Citizens of the same State claiming Lands under Grants of different States." There promised to be precious few suits at common law that could be tried in federal courts, or appealed to federal courts, if the value in controversy was fifty dollars. If the framers intended for the federal government to be the only government that must abide by the Bill of Rights, it would have been very misleading for the framers to propose: "In suits at common law, where the value in controversy shall exceed twenty dollars, the right of trial by jury shall be preserved, . . ." Hence, ratifiers of the Bill of Rights had good reason to understand that the Seventh Amendment's twenty-dollar threshold would have its primary effect in state courts. Furthermore, the twenty-dollar threshold did *not* became effective in federal courts upon ratification of the Seventh Amendment. I have seen no evidence that anybody said, during the eighteenth century, that the Seventh Amendment made the twenty-dollar threshold operative in federal courts. As indicated by the discussion of the Seventh Amendment in this chapter—and the subsection of Chapter 5 titled Alienage Cases and Diversity Cases—the framers and ratifiers of the Seventh Amendment had powerful reasons for not wanting the twenty-dollar threshold to apply in federal courts. The Seventh Amendment would *not* have been framed or ratified in the eighteenth century if it was understood that it would make the twenty-dollar threshold operative in alienage and diversity suits at common law in federal courts.

- Representative George Partridge, one of the framers of the Bill of Rights, made a motion in the House of Representatives on August 17, 1789, which shows that he believed that the general provisions of the Bill of Rights would pertain to the states and the federal government. The House was considering the provision: "No person shall be subject, except in case of impeachment, to more than one trial or one punishment for the same offence, . . ." Representatives Egbert Benson, Roger Sherman, and Theodore Sedgwick spoke in favor of Benson's motion to strike the words "one trial or," because they understood the provision to abridge the common-law right of defendants who were found guilty to try to arrest the judgment and obtain a second trial.[782] After Benson's motion was defeated, George Partridge made a motion to insert after "same offence" the words "by any law of the United States."[783] Partridge obviously wanted to salvage the right to try to obtain a retrial after being convicted in state courts. The members of the House pretty much knew on August 17 that all amendments would stand on their own because the amendments would be placed after the unamended Constitution. (Although the House did not get the two-thirds vote to place the amendments after the unamended Constitution—as opposed to inserting them here and there in the Constitution—until August 19,[784] it was obvious on August 13 that there was enough determined support for placing the amendments at the end of the unamended Constitution that two-thirds of the members of the House would not vote for any amendment which was not placed after the unamended Constitution.[785])

• Despite the fact that all of the amendments proposed by James Madison *and* the House Select Committee were unambiguous with regard to which governments the amendments applied, nine of the twelve amendments agreed to by Congress and proposed to the state legislatures on September 25, 1789, had provisions which were ambiguous with regard to which governments they applied. (The twelve amendments proposed to the state legislatures are shown in Appendix C. The ambiguous proposed amendments are *Article the second* and *Article the fourth* through *Article the eleventh.*) Congress made what is now the First Amendment (*"Article the third"* in Appendix C) crystal clear by using the simple phrase "Congress shall make no law." Congress knew how to make the rest of the proposed amendments unambiguous. Madison, if no one else, must have pointed out at least some of the ambiguities. The fact that Congress left most proposed amendments ambiguous suggests that Congress meant to imply that states would have to abide by them if they became amendments. Most state legislators who ratified the Bill of Rights probably understood that the Second Amendment and the general provisions in the Third through Ninth Amendments restricted state governments as well as the federal government.

- If the legislators of the states that ratified the Bill of Rights during the eighteenth century assumed that the general provisions in amendments two through nine restricted states, those legislators would have thought that existing laws in their states were in compliance except for a minor difference in the monetary amount in controversy required for trial by jury in suits at common law. (Most states were probably using the common-law monetary threshold of 40 shillings instead of the twenty-dollar threshold specified in the Seventh Amendment.) Assuming that the general provisions of amendments two through nine apply to the states, the states that ratified any of those amendments during the eighteenth century gave up little or nothing *other than the option of cutting back on individual liberties* in order to get something for which many people had been clamoring. The state legislators in those states would have found it very difficult to explain to their constituents why they did not vote to ratify the Bill of Rights if it was only because the state legislators wanted to retain the option of rescinding the individual liberties of their constituents.

- Based on a statement made by James Madison in the House of Representatives during the framing of the Bill of Rights, Madison was at least as concerned that state governments would violate individual rights as he was concerned that the federal government would violate individual rights. Madison considered the House Select Committee's proposed amendment: "No State shall infringe the equal rights of conscience, nor the freedom of speech, or of the press, nor the right of trial by jury in criminal cases" as "the most valuable amendment on the whole list; if there was any reason to restrain the government of the United States from infringing upon these essential rights, it was equally necessary that they should be secured against the state governments; . . ."[786] Madison's proposed amendments did not include freedom of speech. Madison had proposed: "No State shall violate the equal rights of conscience, or the freedom of the press, or the trial by jury in criminal cases." It is obvious that Madison was philosophically prepared to accept the Select Committee's push and accept even more restrictions on state action in the Bill of Rights.

- The House of Representatives voted that at least some restrictions on the states should be incorporated in the Bill of Rights. The seventeen amendments passed by the House on August 24, 1789, included one that stated: "No State shall infringe the right of trial by Jury in criminal cases, nor the rights of conscience, nor the freedom of speech, or of the press."[787] The House deemed it "necessary" that the substance of all amendments it passed "be proposed to the Legislatures of the several States, . . ."[788]

- Thomas Jefferson, a strong advocate of states' rights, approved of all of Madison's proposed amendments.[789] Hence, Jefferson supported at least some prohibitions against states being included in the Bill of Rights.

- President Washington, after having read Madison's proposed amendments before Madison offered them in Congress, wrote a note to Madison in which Washington said: "I see nothing . . . [objectionable] in the proposed amendments. . . . they have my wishes for a favorable reception in both houses."[790]

- On September 25, 1789, Congress proposed twelve amendments to the states. As shown in Appendix C of this book, those twelve proposed amendments were designated *Article the first* through *Article the twelfth*. On December 15, 1791, Virginia became the eleventh of the fourteen states in existence on that date to ratify *Article the third* through *Article the twelfth*— thereby making them Amendments I through X. When the Bill of Rights became law, only six states had ratified *Article the Second*.[791] [792] In 1873, Ohio became the seventh state to ratify *Article the Second*.[793] *Article the second* was rejected by the most states during the eighteenth century.[794] The probable reason that *Article the second* was the least popular during the eighteenth century is that some state legislators thought it would prohibit states from paying members of Congress as a means to reward them for acting in accordance with the policy of state legislatures. It is noteworthy that: (1) *Article the second* begins with the words "No law" rather than "Congress shall make no law" as *Article the third* begins; (2) the Constitution prohibits the president from receiving a salary or anything else of value from any state (Article II, Section 1, Paragraph 7); (3) the Constitution does not prohibit members of Congress from being paid by states; (4) under the Articles of Confederation, members of Congress were paid only by the states; and (5) in the Constitutional Convention, the delegates had a debate over a provision which stated: "that members [of Congress] be paid by their respective States." Delegate Roger Sherman moved that members of Congress be paid "5 dollars per day" by the federal government, "any further emoluments to be added by the States."[795] Daniel Carroll said that with the draft clause ("the members [of Congress] be paid by their respective States"): "The dependence of both Houses on the State Legislatures is compleat; . . . The States can now say: if you do not comply with our wishes, we will starve you: if you do we will reward you. . . ."[796] The unamended Constitution prevents states from starving members of Congress, but it does not prevent states from rewarding members of Congress.

- The Supreme Court's opinion in *Barron v. The Mayor and City Council of Baltimore* contains the absurd statement: "The unwieldy and cumbrous machinery of procuring a recommendation from two-thirds of Congress and the assent of three-fourths of their sister States, could never have occurred to any human being as a mode of doing that which might be effected by the State itself. . . ."[797] For Chief Justice John Marshall to feel the need to make such a statement weakens the Court's ruling. Marshall showed that he was not familiar with the legislative history of the Bill of Rights. Furthermore, he unwittingly cast as subhuman James Madison, Thomas Jefferson, George Washington, and a large majority of the members of the First U.S. House of Representatives. Marshall did not seem to understand that some major reforms might be implemented via the amendment process. Some states abolished slavery within their borders, but they could not by themselves abolish slavery in the United States. Some states granted women suffrage within their borders, but they could not by themselves grant women suffrage throughout the United States. In effect, Marshall said that human beings would not make amendments such as the Thirteenth and Nineteenth. Perhaps Marshall was trying to prevent such amendments.

• In 1833, before the Court's *Barron* ruling, it was probably rare to find an American who believed that states had the authority to prevent law-abiding, adult citizens from having arms. In 1825, William Rawle published the widely read *A View of the Constitution of the United States of America*. In it, Rawle maintained that the states were bound by a large majority of the general provisions in the Bill of Rights, including the Second Amendment.[798] In 1929, Rawle published his second edition. In it, in a discussion of the Second Amendment, Rawle said: "No clause in the Constitution could by any rule of construction be conceived to give congress a power to disarm the people. Such a flagitious attempt could only be made under some general pretence by a state legislature. But if . . . [Congress or a state legislature] should attempt it, this amendment may be appealed to as a restraint on both. . . ."[799] In 1832, Benjamin Oliver published *The Rights of an American Citizen*. In it, Oliver discussed the Second Amendment in a chapter titled: "Of the rights reserved to the people of the United States; not being granted either to the general government or to the state governments."[800]

• After *Barron*, many Americans continued to think that general provisions in the Bill of Rights restricted all governments in the United States. Deliberations in Congress during the framing of the Fourteenth Amendment in 1866 show that several members of Congress, unaware of *Barron* even though they were competent lawyers, thought that many provisions of the Bill of Rights were applicable to state governments as well as to the federal government.[801]

The Right to Keep and Bear Arms

Well known to most framers and ratifiers of the Bill of Rights was the essence of the following excerpt from Blackstone's *Commentaries on the Laws of England:*

> "The right of the subjects, . . . of having arms for their defence suitable to their condition and degree, and such as are allowed by law. . . . is indeed, a public allowance . . . of the natural right of resistance and self-preservation, when the sanctions of society and laws are found insufficient to restrain the violence of oppression. . . . So long as these [rights] remain inviolate, the subject is perfectly free; for every species of compulsive tyranny and oppression must act in opposition to one or other of these rights, . . . when actually violated or attacked, the subjects of England are entitled, . . . to the right of having and using arms for self-preservation and defence."[802]

When the Bill of Rights was framed and ratified, the electorate in the United States insisted on retaining their common-law rights—including the right to have and use arms for self-defense.[803] The right to have and use arms for self-defense was considered to be both a common-law right and a natural right. Most ratifiers of the Bill of Rights must have understood that the right to have and use arms for self-defense was (1) an unwritten part of the Constitution by virtue of being a common-law right and a natural right, and (2) further guaranteed by the Second Amendment or the Ninth Amendment.

The Second Amendment is focused on the right to have and use arms to maintain republican governments. Therefore, I prefer to locate the right to have and use arms for self-defense against private oppression in the Ninth Amendment. It includes common-law rights and natural rights. People who believe that the Second Amendment is the best place to locate the right to have and use arms for self-defense against private oppression might point to the words of a

Charleston, South Carolina, newspaper which observed that a well-regulated militia is "composed of the freeholders, citizen and husbandman, who take up arms to preserve their property as individuals, their rights as freemen."[804]

The right to have and use arms for self-defense against oppressive governmental forces is included in both the Second and Ninth Amendments. Alexander Hamilton wrote, in *The Federalist*, No. 28: "If the representatives of the people betray their constituents, there is then no resource left but in the exertion of that original right of self-defense which is paramount to all positive forms of government, . . ."[805]

James Madison, in *The Federalist*, No. 46, discussed the possibility that the federal government might encroach on the authority of state governments. In such a situation, Madison predicted that (1) the militia would side with the state governments, (2) the militia would be at least twenty times larger than any federal military force, and (3) the militia would defeat the federal troops.[806]

Federal Gun Control

Congress has: (1) enacted unconstitutional gun control laws (Some of those laws are mentioned later in this subsection.); and (2) seriously considered, but not enacted, additional unconstitutional gun control laws—laws which would have required almost all gun owners to obtain licenses and register their guns.

President Lyndon Johnson, in a special message to Congress in 1968, asked Congress to enact a law which would have required every gun owner to obtain a federal license and register their firearms with federal officials within 180 days.[807] After the 180 days, possession of an unregistered gun would have subjected the possessor to a $2,000 fine and two-years in jail.[808] President Johnson wanted to make it a felony to resist an absolutely unconstitutional law!

Constitutional laws can be enacted to greatly reduce the use of guns in crimes. Only criminals would oppose laws which *required* substantially increased penalties for people who use weapons while committing crimes. Experience has shown that such laws, if strictly enforced, are quite effective in reducing the use of guns in crimes.

Congress has no constitutional authority to prohibit interstate or intrastate commerce of arms. The power to regulate interstate commerce was intended to be used only to keep states from obstructing commerce between states; the Court ruled that way until 1903.[809] The framers did not intend, and the ratifiers did not understand, that the power to regulate interstate commerce included the power to prohibit the interstate commerce of anything. (The original intent and understanding of the power to regulate commerce "among the several States" is presented in Chapter 3 of this book, under Article I, Section 8, Paragraph 3.)

The Gun Control Act of 1968 unconstitutionally (1) required gun dealers and gun collectors to apply for and purchase federal licenses, (2) prohibited interstate shipment of firearms and ammunition to persons who were not federally licensed to receive them, (3) prohibited unlicensed persons from receiving firearms or ammunition from out of state, (4) prohibited some *intrastate* shipment of firearms, and (5) set minimum ages for Americans to purchase guns and ammunition.

A constitutional amendment to authorize Congress to pass laws to control machine guns would be easy to propose and ratify. Instead of behaving constitutionally, Congress passed a law in 1986 which prohibited anyone from possessing a machine gun without the consent of the Bureau of Alcohol, Tobacco and Firearms. Many law-abiding citizens who were upset that their constitutional rights were threatened by Congress were further exasperated by the Supreme Court's failure in 1991 to accept the case of *Farmer v. Higgins*. Mr. Farmer—a gun collector—had been denied permission to keep his machine gun.[810]

Advocates of ratification of the proposed Constitution insisted in 1787 and 1788 that United States citizens could not be disarmed under the proposed Constitution.[811] They were right. The unamended Constitution does not give the federal government the power to disarm its citizens. Hence, even before the Second and Ninth Amendments existed, it would have been unlawful for the federal government to disarm United States citizens.

The fact that Congress has taken an unconstitutional path to prohibit private citizens from owning machine guns—especially in view of the fact that a constitutional path was readily available— gives many law-abiding citizens good reason to fear that Congress will eventually pass a gun restriction law of a type for which it would be difficult or impossible to get an authorizing amendment proposed and ratified. The law banning machine guns is just one of many unconstitutional federal laws. If Congress were a person, it could be said that person was pathologically unconstitutional. When U.S. officials criticize foreign governments for not abiding by the rule of law, the U.S. officials imply that the rule of law prevails in the United States. This is hypocrisy even though the rule of law is abused more in many foreign countries than it is in the United States. It is only the ignorance of foreign officials that prevents them from pointing out the hypocritical rule-of-law statements made by U.S. officials.

The media does not seem to care that the needless notoriety it gives to the perpetrators of crimes—especially where guns are used by minors in schools—encourages more such crimes. Broadcasters of baseball games learned long ago to not televise people who run onto the field. Media attention obviously encourages people who do illegal things to attract attention to themselves. Except for efforts to capture criminals, media notoriety of criminals should be banned by an amendment.

Third Amendment

> *No Soldier shall, in time of peace be quartered in any house, without the consent of the Owner, nor in time of war, but in a manner to be prescribed by law.*

Original Meaning in 21st Century Plain English

No member of the armed forces shall, in time of peace, be quartered in any house without the consent of the owner. In time of war, military personnel may be quartered in houses, despite the objections of the owners of the houses, if, and only if, the quartering is done in a manner prescribed by law.

Background of the Third Amendment

The Third Amendment traces back to the Petition of Right which Parliament, at the insistence of the House of Commons, forced King Charles I to accept in 1628. In 1937, the Petition of Right was correctly called by noted historian William Holdsworth: "the first of those great constitutional documents since Magna Carta, which safeguard the liberties of the people by securing the supremacy of law."[812] One of the main grievances expressed in the Petition of Right was: "soldiers and . . . [sailors] have been dispersed into divers counties of the realm, and the inhabitants against their wills have been compelled to receive them into their houses, and there to suffer them to sojourn, against the laws and customs of this realm, and to the great grievance and vexation of the people."[813] When King Charles I assented to the Petition of Right, he agreed that all of his officers "shall serve . . . according to the laws and statutes of this realm, . . ."[814]

The English Bill of Rights of 1689 was almost certainly more familiar to the framers of the Third Amendment than was the Petition of Right. The preamble of the English Bill of Rights states: "King James the Second, by the assistance of divers evil counsellors, judges, and ministers employed by him, did endeavour to subvert . . . the laws and liberties of this kingdom. . . . By raising and keeping a standing army within this kingdom in time of peace, without consent of parliament, and quartering soldiers contrary to law. . . ."[815]

Parliament enacted the Quartering Act of 1765 which ordered the colonial governments to provide housing for British soldiers. The fact that many British soldiers were sent to enforce the Stamp Act of 1765 and the Sugar Act of 1764 made the Quartering Act even more unpleasant for the colonists. Despite the Petition of Right and the English Bill of Rights, the Quartering Act authorized British troops to commandeer private buildings if the colonists did not provide housing.[816] The Quartering Act of 1774, one of the five acts which were called the Intolerable Acts by American colonists, allowed British military officers to quarter their troops in Boston—and other towns in Massachusetts—despite the fact that the troops had barracks outside of Boston.[817] The First Continental Congress, in its Declarations and Resolves of 1774 (1) stated that it was illegal for Britain to maintain standing armies in the colonies without the consent of the colonial legislatures, and (2) cited the Quartering Act of 1774 as an infringement of colonial rights.[818] The Declaration of Independence complained that King George III had "quartered large bodies of armed troops among us: . . . ."

From 1770 to 1800, most Americans were opposed to "standing armies" (large bodies of troops in peacetime). At the Constitutional Convention, James Madison said: "armies in times of peace are allowed on all hands to be an evil, . . ."[819] Most framers (1) were opposed to standing armies, and (2) supported small garrisons of federal troops stationed near the frontier to deter and counter Indian raids. During the 1800 presidential campaign, Thomas Jefferson pledged to disband the "provisional army" created in 1798–99 and oppose a large army until the United States was invaded.[820] Patrick Henry took full advantage of the concerns of many Americans about standing armies when he said during a debate in the crucial Virginia Ratifying Convention:

> "the clause which gives Congress the power of raising armies . . . appears to be a very alarming power, when unlimited. . . . If Congress shall say that the general welfare requires it, they may keep armies continually on foot. There is no control on Congress in raising or stationing them. They may billet them on the people at pleasure . . . Here we may have troops in times of peace. They may be billeted in any manner—to tyrannize, oppress, and crush us."[821]

During wartime, states can have their own military forces without the consent of Congress. In time of peace, the consent of Congress is needed for states to "keep Troops, or Ships of War." The Third Amendment could easily have been understood by its ratifiers to apply to the federal government *and* the states.

Fourth Amendment

The right of the people to be secure in their persons, houses, papers, and effects, against unreasonable searches and seizures, shall not be violated, and no Warrants shall issue, but upon probable cause, supported by Oath or affirmation, and particularly describing the place to be searched, and the persons or things to be seized.

Original Meaning in 21st Century Plain English

No search warrant shall be issued unless:

- There is probable cause. (It is more likely than not that the place to be searched contains (1) evidence that a law has been violated, or (2) one or more people for whom an arrest warrant has been issued.)
- The probable cause is supported by oath or affirmation. (The person or persons who supply the information used to establish probable cause support that information by oath or affirmation.)
- The warrant describes the place to be searched and the persons or things to be seized.

No arrest warrant shall be issued unless:

- It is probable that the person to be arrested has violated the law.
- The person or persons who provide the information used to establish probability of guilt support that information by oath or affirmation.
- The warrant describes the persons to be arrested by name or physical characteristics.

A warrant is *not* needed for a search or an arrest. However, citizens have the right to be secure that they, their residences, their papers, and their effects will not be searched or seized unreasonably. Probable cause is required only for warranted searches. Unwarranted searches *may* be reasonable even though probable cause does not exist. Judges shall *not* refuse to admit any evidence found in searches. Any citizen who believes that they have been the victim of an un-constitutional warrant or an unreasonable search or seizure of themselves, their residence, their papers, or their effects should file a lawsuit against those responsible. Unless both parties in such a law-suit waive their right to a jury trial, juries shall determine whether Fourth Amendment rights have been violated. Juries can award citi-zens whose Fourth Amendment rights have been violated (1) actual damages, and (2) punitive damages in order to discourage future Fourth Amendment violations.

Discussion of the Fourth Amendment

The Fourth Amendment was designed primarily to prohibit the issuance of oppressive warrants.[822] The framers took it for granted that citizens could be arrested without arrest warrants and that searches of validly arrested people needed neither search warrants nor specific statutory authority.[823]

Although the Fourth Amendment requires probable cause for all searches with search warrants, probable cause is not required for searches without warrants. The only requirement for unwarranted searches is that the searches be reasonable if the searches are of a citizen, a citizen's residence, a citizen's papers, or a citizen's effects. Unwarranted searches of aliens, ships, wagons, warehouses, etc., are probably not required to be reasonable by the Fourth Amendment.

Let us assume that (1) a child is kidnapped by a person in a car, (2) witnesses identify the car by make and color, (3) no witness can describe the kidnapper, (4) there are no good clues except for the make and color of the car, and (5) there are one hundred cars in the vicinity that match the description. The police could not get a con-stitutional search warrant to search any of the cars because there would not be probable cause for searching any one car. However, it would not be unreasonable for the police to search all 100 cars with-out a warrant. (Although the searches would be reasonable, the Fourth Amendment may not require that searches of cars be reason-able. It is not clear that cars are included in "effects.") Let us assume that neither the child nor evidence of crime is found in any of the cars, and 97 of the car owners consent to have their residences searched. A constitutional search warrant could not be obtained to search the other three residences because there would not be probable cause for searching any one of the residences. However, it would not be unreasonable for the police to search those three residences.

Despite the Fourth Amendment and state laws to the same effect, judges probably did not exclude any search evidence from juries for at least ninety years after the Fourth Amendment became law in 1791. For about 85 years after the Fourth Amendment became law, exclusion of evidence gathered in searches was rarely even requested by criminal defendants.[824] The exclusionary rule relevant to evidence procured in unreasonable searches was first established in 1903 in Iowa.[825] In 1914, the Supreme Court first ruled that evidence procured in unreasonable searches was inadmissible in federal courts.[826] It was not until 1961 that the Court ruled that all states must abide by the exclusionary rule.[827]

Judge Harold J. Rothwax wrote, in his national bestselling, highly acclaimed 1996 book *Guilty: The Collapse of Criminal Justice:* "the hallmarks of the exclusionary rule are irrationality, arbitrariness, and a lack of proportion. Whenever it is applied, a criminal goes free— no matter how serious the crime or minor the police intrusion. The bald fact is that it is more lottery than law. . . ."[828] Rothwax points out, in a most compelling manner, that the exclusionary rule often works in opposition to truth, common sense, and justice. He also correctly points out that (1) judges have created the exclusionary rule, (2) the framers and ratifiers would have considered the exclusionary rule to be illogical, and (3) judges have interpreted the Fourth Amendment in a "convoluted" manner.[829] However, Rothwax does not explicitly state that the exclusionary rule is unconstitutional. It is hard for judges to acknowledge that it is unconstitutional for judge-made rules to override the intent of the framers and the understanding of the ratifiers.

Most framers of the Fourth Amendment undoubtedly intended, and most ratifiers undoubtedly understood, that juries would determine whether searches and seizures were reasonable or unreasonable.

Therefore, the exclusionary rule is unconstitutional. It deprives juries in criminal cases from seeing or hearing evidence gathered in what judges, often using no common sense, rule to be unreasonable searches. Every year since 1961, thousands of people who have committed crimes have not been convicted of committing those crimes because judges have ruled searches to be unreasonable. In addition, prosecutors have decided not to prosecute thousands of guilty people for the sole reason that prosecutors think judges will refuse to admit evidence gathered in searches.

The remedy for unreasonable searches or seizures was intended to be lawsuits by citizens. The framers did not intend for the Fourth Amendment to be invoked to suppress evidence, thereby setting criminals free. Citizens who thought that they had been the victim of an unreasonable search or seizure could sue the government officials or private citizens involved, and juries would decide whether unreasonable searches or seizures had been made. Juries could award actual damages and heavy punitive damages to strongly discourage future unreasonable searches and seizures. In 1765, Lord Mansfield ruled: "What is probable cause of suspicion, and what is a reasonable time of detainer, are matters of fact to be determined by a jury."[830] Mansfield was not establishing common law; he was merely upholding common law which was previously established in England and used in America.[831] That law was well known in the United States between 1776 and 1795.[832]

Most framers and ratifiers were familiar with at least some of the English cases of the 1760s which involved illegal searches and seizures. Many of those cases were related to John Wilkes. In 1763, Wilkes, a member of the House of Commons, anonymously published a pamphlet entitled *The North Briton*, No. 45. That pamphlet criticized a speech made by King George III. The Secretary of State, Lord Halifax, issued a warrant ordering "strict and diligent search for the authors, printers, and publishers of a seditious and treasonable paper, entitled, The North Briton, No. 45, . . . and them, or any of them, having found, to apprehend and seize, together with their papers."[833] That warrant would have been legal if it had been authorized by an act of Parliament in effect at the time the warrant was issued. Since no such statute was in effect at that time, the warrant was illegal because it contained things which were prohibited by the common law. The *North-Briton* warrant violated the common law because it (1) ordered arrests without describing the persons to be arrested, (2) ordered searches without describing the places to be searched, and (3) ordered papers to be seized without fully describing the papers to be seized.

Within three days of the issuance of the illegal *North-Briton* warrant, "no less than forty-nine persons" were arrested on suspicion.[834] One of the printers who was arrested disclosed that Wilkes was the author of *The North Briton*, No. 45. Wilkes was convicted of seditious libel by a jury, fined one thousand pounds, and jailed for twenty-two months.[835] Wilkes pointed out, although not at his criminal trial, the dangers of general warrants and seizures of private papers. However, I have heard of no evidence that Wilkes ever maintained that evidence gathered in illegal searches should be excluded from juries.

All of the printers who were arrested under Halifax's *North Briton* warrant brought suit against the people who had arrested them. The juries awarded 300 to 400 pounds—about fifteen to twenty times actual damages—to each of the printers whose cases went to trial.[836] The other printers agreed to settle for 200 pounds. (The government paid all judgments.)

Wilkes sued Lord Halifax. In a separate suit, Wilkes sued an assistant to Halifax named Robert Woods. Woods had supervised the execution of the *North-Briton* warrant. Wilkes won judgments totaling five thousand pounds (four thousand pounds against Halifax and one thousand pounds against Woods).[837] The verdicts in the civil cases related to Wilkes were quite popular in England and in the American colonies. Historian Nelson Lasson wrote: "'Wilkes and Liberty,' became the byword of the times, even in far away America."[838] In 1768 and later, Wilkes was repeatedly elected to the House of Commons and expelled by the House of Commons.[839] Many American leaders corresponded with Wilkes.[840] A formal honor to Wilkes was signed by John Adams, Samuel Adams, John Hancock, James Otis, and others.[841]

One of the things Wilkes attacked in *The North Briton*, No. 45, was the very unpopular cider tax which had been enacted in 1763 and supported by King George III. The King called for "a spirit of concord" to replace the discord over the cider tax. Wilkes wrote in No. 45: "Is . . . [a spirit of concord] to be expected between an insolent Exciseman, and a *peer, gentleman, free holder, or farmer*, whose private houses are now [due to enforcement provisions of the cider tax] made liable to be entered and searched at pleasure?"[842] During the seventeenth and eighteenth centuries, many Englishmen were opposed to laws which allowed tax enforcers to enter and search houses "at pleasure."

In 1762, Lord Halifax issued a warrant for the arrest of John Entick and the seizure of Entick's books and papers. Entick was arrested and his papers were seized. After his release from prison, Entick sued at least one of the men who had arrested him and seized his papers. The jury awarded Entick 300 pounds.[843] The 300 pound verdict was upheld in 1765 by Lord Camden and all of the judges in the Court of Common Pleas. The verdict was upheld primarily because the searchers/arrestors had not precisely complied with the warrant. Lord Camden ruled that the warrant was not valid, even though it had complied with the common law requirement of describing the persons to be arrested, because: (1) the act of Parliament which had previously authorized warrants to search for libelous papers had expired in 1696; (2) the warrant authorized the seizure of all papers (Even under the expired law, only libelous papers could be seized.); and (3) an oath of probable cause had not been given.[844]

The cases of Wilkes and Entick included the primary elements needed for the Fourth Amendment. Indeed, they were the only elements in the amendment recommended by the House Select Committee. It addressed only warranted searches and seizures of citizens and their residences, papers, and effects.

The House Select Committee's recommendation for what became the Fourth Amendment was:

"The right of the people to be secure in their person, houses, papers and effects, shall not be violated by warrants issuing, without probable cause supported by oath or affirmation, and not particularly describing the places to be searched, and the persons or things to be seized."[845]

The full House of Representatives beefed up the Select Committees' recommendation to come up with words almost identical to the Fourth Amendment. The full House recommended:

"The right of the People to be secure in their persons, houses, papers and effects, against unreasonable searches and seizures, shall not be violated, and no warrants shall issue, but upon probable cause supported by oath or affirmation, and particularly describing the place to be searched, and the persons or things to be seized."[846]

The framers intended for government officials who issued unconstitutional warrants to be sued by those whose rights were violated. Almost all warrants are issued by judges. The concept of judicial responsibility suffered a major setback when the Supreme Court ruled in 1869 that judges are immune from lawsuits for judicial acts "unless perhaps where the acts, in excess of jurisdiction, are done maliciously or corruptly."[847] When you get only a "perhaps" on "in excess of jurisdiction" *and* "maliciously or corruptly," judges are essentially immune from lawsuits for judicial acts. To prove that a judge acted contrary to law is doable—whether proving that a search warrant was issued contrary to the Fourth Amendment or any other judicial act was contrary to law. On the other hand, judges rarely act in excess of jurisdiction. There are probably thousands of corrupt decisions for every decision in excess of jurisdiction, and it is rare that corruption can be proven.

In a case in 1886 which involved neither search nor seizure, the U.S. Supreme Court first said that "mere evidence" cannot be the objective of a search warrant or seized during a warranted search because it would violate the Fourth Amendment.[848] In a 1921 case that involved search and seizure, the Court ruled unanimously that the Fourth Amendment was violated by a search warrant issued to obtain "mere evidence."[849] The Court said that search warrants must be confined to stolen property, illegal substances, and instruments of crime (such as a knife used to stab someone).[850] "Mere evidence" includes things such as bloody clothing, diaries, and other papers which contain evidence of crime but are not stolen, illegal, or instruments of crime. The Court extended the mere-evidence rule to warrantless searches in 1932.[851] After the Court-invented mere-evidence rule had proven to be a serious problem for many years, the Court finally abandoned (reversed) it in 1967, declaring that the distinction between different types of "property" was "wholly irrational."[852] The mere-evidence rule was illogical, but the framers and ratifiers may have considered it to be less illogical than the exclusionary rule.

What is meant by the word "effects" in the Fourth Amendment? It may or may not mean "other property." When James Madison proposed what eventually became the Fourth Amendment, he used the clear term "other property." However, the House Select Committee substituted the word "effects" for "other property."[853] Effects might be confined to things like handbags, saddle bags, and briefcases. After the House Select Committee substituted the word "effects," it remained undisturbed throughout the remainder of the framing of the Bill of Rights.

Why were the words "other property" rejected in favor of "effects"? Congress may have wanted to leave the door open to unwarranted, "at pleasure" searches of ships, wagons, and warehouses by customs agents as a means to prevent smuggling from flourishing. After all, the United States would be collecting taxes on imports— taxes which would be reasonable, perfectly constitutional, and very much needed. Smuggling flourished in the colonies because many colonists believed that smuggling merely avoided the payment of unreasonably high or unconstitutional taxes imposed by Parliament. The words "other property" may have been rejected simply because "effects" is shorter.

Was the Fourth Amendment originally understood to limit state governments as well as the federal government? The rationale presented under the Second Amendment discussion indicates that the Fourth Amendment was probably understood by most ratifiers to limit state governments and the United States government.

Fifth Amendment

No person shall be held to answer for a capital, or otherwise infamous crime, unless on a presentment or indictment of a Grand Jury, except in cases arising in the land or naval forces, or in the Militia, when in actual service in time of War or public danger; nor shall any person be subject for the same offence to be twice put in jeopardy of life or limb; nor shall be compelled in any criminal case to be a witness against himself, nor be deprived of life, liberty, or property, without due process of law; nor shall private property be taken for public use, without just compensation.

Original Meaning in 21st Century Plain English

No person shall be forced to undergo a trial for a crime for which the maximum penalty is death or imprisonment for more than one year unless (1) a majority of the members of a grand jury vote that the person has probably committed the crime, or (2) the person is in military service and a court-martial is held. No person who has been accused of committing crime A shall be held in jail on a charge of committing crime A after a majority of a grand jury has voted that the person probably did not commit crime A. However, if a subsequent grand jury votes that the person should stand trial for crime A, the person may then be held in jail awaiting trial. Grand juries shall be composed of at least 12 adult citizens—preferably 23 adult citizens. Grand juries are bodies of inquiry whose proceedings are secret. Grand juries cannot acquit or convict. Grand juries can:

- Function *independently* of prosecutors and judges to gather evidence and make presentments (Presentments are charges of (1) crimes committed by persons, or (2) problems with government. Presentments which charge crimes are instructions to judges to try cases and instructions to prosecutors to prosecute cases.)
- Work with judges to gather evidence

- Work with prosecutors to gather evidence

- Approve or reject written accusations of crime prepared by prosecutors or judges (An approval is an indictment.)

- Determine (1) the value of private property taken for public use, and (2) resolve special issues

Grand juries are authorized to: (1) issue their own subpoenas to compel the attendance of witnesses and the production of documents (Prosecutors cannot compel the attendance of witnesses or the production of documents.); (2) compel witnesses to answer all questions except those which might subject them to criminal penalties; (3) cite recalcitrant witnesses for contempt; and (4) bring perjury charges against witnesses who lie in grand jury proceedings.[854]

Grand jurors shall take an oath or affirmation to the effect that they will be honest and diligent in their grand jury duties.

No person who has been acquitted or convicted of a charge shall be tried again for the same offense if the maximum penalty for the offense is loss of life or loss of limb—unless a convicted person requests a retrial and a retrial is granted. If a trial jury cannot agree on a verdict, the accused may be tried again on the same charge.

No person shall be cited for contempt for refusing to answer questions which, if answered, admit something which subjects the answerer to a criminal penalty.

No person shall be executed, imprisoned, or compelled to give up property except in a manner consistent with law.

No private property shall be taken for public use without fair payment determined by a regular grand jury or a special-purpose grand jury.

Grand Juries

The grand jury system originated in England. In 1166, each grand jury was composed of twelve knights or twelve "good and lawful men" who presented to a judge sworn accusations against all persons that the grand jury believed had committed criminal offenses.[855] By 1700, grand juries, by refusing to approve unfounded accusations of crime laid before them, had become (1) highly prized as shields against royal persecution, and (2) defenders of the liberties of English citizens.[856] In the American Colonies, grand juries were often effective in helping colonists resist English laws which the colonists considered to be unfair or illegal.

Two grand juries refused to indict printer/publisher John Peter Zenger on a charge of seditious libel in 1734, despite being urged to do so by the chief justice of New York.[857] No grand jury indicted Zenger. After two grand juries refused to indict Zenger, he was arrested and held in jail for almost nine months until his trial on August 4, 1735.[858] The framers of the Fifth Amendment, aware of the abuses sustained by John Peter Zenger, intended to (1) prevent people from being tried without the approval of a grand jury, and (2) prevent people from being held in jail on a criminal charge after a grand jury had disapproved that charge—unless a subsequent grand jury approved that charge.

American colonists often used grand juries to protest against British colonial practices.[859] Grand juries were so effective in countering British policies in some colonies that Britain tried to prevent grand juries.[860] Lord North, the loyal prime minister of King George III before and during the Revolutionary War, got the House of Commons to revise the charter of Massachusetts to essentially eliminate town meetings; it was in town meetings that grand jurors were selected in Massachusetts.[861] Lord North also censured colonial grand juries.[862] In circular letters to other colonies, Massachusetts declared that its citizens were the victims of tyranny because grand jurors were being appointed by sheriffs.[863]

Grand juries became an indispensable part of government in each of the American colonies by the end of the Colonial period.[864] The grand jury system went into the Revolutionary War with great prestige and emerged from the war with even greater prestige. During the Revolutionary War, grand juries continued to play a major role in solving local problems. For example, grand juries inspected public records, audited the books of local governments, and complained when they discovered neglect of duty by public officials.[865]

In Virginia, the most populous state, grand juries performed the very important function of determining the value of tobacco. Public officials in Virginia, including members of the state legislature and the governor, "received their salaries in tobacco at the rate set by the grand jury of the General Court at Richmond."[866] The rate of exchange set by Virginia grand juries "also determined the value of tobacco in the purchase of military provisions and in loans made to the state."[867]

The first address by a federal judge to a grand jury—to inform/remind them of their duty—that was published was delivered by Judge Francis Hopkinson, who said to a federal grand jury in Philadelphia on November 10, 1789:

> "If any crimes or offences, cognizable by the jurisdiction of this Court have come to your knowledge, it is your duty to inquire concerning them, and present them for trial. Should you want any information respecting the law or instruction in points of form, the Court, or the Attorney for the United States, will be ready to give you all necessary assistance."[868]

In 1790, Chief Justice John Jay addressed four federal grand juries—in New York for the district of New York, in Hartford for the district of Connecticut, in Boston for the district of Massachusetts, and in Portsmouth for the district of New Hampshire. Chief Justice Jay used the following words in all four of his addresses to federal grand juries in 1790:

> "The objects of your enquiry are all offences committed against the laws of the united states in this district, or on the high seas by persons now in the district. . . . Direct your attention also to the conduct of the national officers—and let not any corruptions, frauds, extortions, or criminal negligence, with which you may find any of them justly chargeable, pass unnoticed. In a word, gentlemen, your province, and your duty, extend to the enquiry and presentment of all offences of every kind, committed against the united states, in this district, or on the high seas by person in . . . [the district]. . . ."[869]

The New York grand jury reported a mutiny. As a result, two men were convicted by a trial jury. Both mutineers were sentenced to stand in a pillory for one hour, be imprisoned for six months, *and* receive thirty-nine stripes (lashes with a whip) on their last day in prison.[870]

Well into the twentieth century, grand juries "frequently proved the only effective weapon against organized crime, malfeasance in office, and corruption in high places."[871] Grand juries were "the most potent weapon" in dealing with municipal corruption in many cit-ies—including New York City in 1871–1872, 1929, and 1935–1936, [872] Minneapolis in 1902,[873] and San Francisco in 1906–1907.[874] Despite the great success of grand juries in New York, the New York state legislature passed a bill in 1946 which would have prohibited grand juries from making presentments or otherwise censuring persons for misconduct which did not constitute a crime.[875] In vetoing the bill, Governor Thomas Dewey said that grand juries should remain "the bulwark of protection for the innocent and the sword of the commu-nity against wrongdoers."[876]

Dewey's veto was strongly encouraged and supported by newspa-pers, business groups, and civic groups which worked hard (1) to preserve the power of grand juries, and (2) to use grand juries to fight corruption and bureaucracies which did not serve the public interest.[877]

Until 1795, the grand jury system was held in high esteem in the United States and was viewed by most citizens as an important part of their heritage. Respect for the grand jury institution was reduced when grand juries, responding to pressure exerted by Federalist judges, particularly Justices James Iredell, Samuel Chase, and William Cushing, took several indiscriminate actions relevant to the crime of seditious libel.[878] In 1797, a grand jury in Virginia presented Con-gressman Samuel J. Cabell "for having 'disseminated unfounded calumnies' against the government of the United States in a letter he circulated to his constituents."[879] One of Cabell's constituents was Vice-President Thomas Jefferson. Jefferson "charged that Feder-alist judges had perverted grand juries 'from a legal to a political engine.'"[880] After the passage of the Sedition Act of 1798, federal judges (all Federalists) "became active prosecutors . . . urging [grand] juries to bring individuals to trial."[881] Grand juries, when packed with Federalist partisans, returned several questionable indictments for seditious libel under the Sedition Act of 1798. However, despite strenuous exhortations to indict by federal judges, federal grand juries in the 1790s often refused to indict.[882]

Supreme Court Justice James Wilson (one of the principal framers of the Constitution), in a law lecture he delivered in 1790, expressed the prevailing view of the electorate when he said that there was no limit on a grand jury's area of inquiry.[883] Wilson said:

> "The grand jury are a great channel of communication, between those who make and administer the laws, and those for whom the laws are made and administered. All the operations of government, and of its ministers and officers, are within the compass of their view and research. They may suggest publick improvements, and the modes of removing publick inconveniences: they may expose to publick inspection, or to publick punishment, publick bad men, and publick bad measures."[884]

In what may have been the first attack on the grand jury system, a Pennsylvania judge indicated in 1792 that it was dangerous to give a grand jury "too free a hand in their investigation."[885] That judge "was ahead of his time" in that he placed a grand jury "entirely under the control of the court."[886]

During the nineteenth and twentieth centuries, lawyers, judges, and "efficiency experts" worked diligently to overthrow the grand jury system.[887] Proponents of the grand jury system, including some lawyers and judges, fought a losing battle in some states even though they pointed out the democratic nature of the grand jury system, its unique effectiveness, its role as a focal point to express public needs, and the opportunity it provided citizens for direct participation in law enforcement.[888]

Opponents of the grand jury system leveled charges of tyranny against the citizen investigators and pictured them as expensive relics of the past.[889] Characterizations by lawyers of "Star Chamber" (very misleading) and "secret inquisition" (Grand juries inquire in secret, but that is one of the keys to their ability to ascertain the truth.) tended to discredit the grand jury system; the crusade to abolish the institution, under the guise of efficiency and reform, succeeded in many states.[890] In 1859, Michigan became the first state to abandon the grand jury system. Before 1859, judicial rulings substantially curtailed grand jury power in Tennessee in 1837 and Pennsylvania in 1844.[891]

The effort to curtail the power of grand juries did not have much momentum until after the Supreme Court ruled in 1833, in *Barron*, that the Bill of Rights did not restrict state governments. Justice Joseph Story displayed a prolawyer/anti-grand jury attitude in an article he wrote for the *Encyclopedia Americana* that was published in 1832. Story implied that a grand jury could not act independently to initiate investigations of their own.[892] Story's effort to reduce the power of grand juries may have been a hidden factor in the Court's unanimous ruling in *Barron*.

It was understood by the framers and ratifiers of the Fifth Amendment that grand juries guarded against:

- Overzealous judges and prosecutors who want to, for one reason or another, put people on trial even though there is not enough evidence to show that the people are probably guilty of the crime with which they are charged

- Prosecutors who, because of corruption or incompetence, fail to charge people with crimes even though there is evidence to show that the people probably committed crimes

- Oppressive laws by refusing to indict people who violated such laws (Grand juries in eighteenth-century America often refused to indict people on charges even though the accused were clearly guilty.)

- Government action and inaction that is not in the public interest

A federal judge who had studied law at Harvard under Joseph Story told a grand jury in 1842: "Your sole function is to pass upon indictments. The term presentment confers no separate authority. . . ."[893] Most ratifiers would have been astonished.

After the exclusionary rule was established by judges during the twentieth century, grand juries continued to have access to all evidence gathered in searches. That resulted in conflicts between grand juries and prosecutors in some cases where there was compelling evidence of guilt. When prosecutors thought that judges would exclude critical evidence from trial juries, some grand juries wanted a prosecution despite the fact that prosecutors did not want to prosecute.

Grand juries can be very effective in gathering evidence. So much so that criminals frequently waive their right to indictment by grand juries.[894] Most prosecutions in federal courts during the latter part of the twentieth century were accomplished without grand jury determination of probable guilt.[895] Suspects, on the advice of their lawyers, usually waived their right to grand jury review.

Many states have abolished grand juries. In 1884, the Supreme Court ruled, in *Hurtado v. California,* that states are not required to have grand juries.[896] In discussing *Hurtado,* noted historian Leonard W. Levy wrote that dissenting Justice John Marshall Harlan "had history on his side when he found grand jury proceedings to be an indispensable requisite of due process, . . ."[897]

It is incredible that the Court has invoked the due process clause of the Fourteenth Amendment to rule that: (1) states must do a myriad of things never historically associated with due process (such as allow abortions and abide by the First Amendment); and (2) states may abolish grand juries—long associated with due process of law.

Grand juries were explicitly associated with due process of law by Sir Edward Coke.[898] More than anyone else, Coke, as the "intellectual leader of the House of Commons" in 1628, was responsible for the Petition of Right.[899] The Petition of Right, agreed to by King Charles I on June 7, 1628, was, in the words of historians Richard Perry and John Cooper, "the first of those great constitutional documents since Magna Carta, which safeguard the liberties of the people by securing the supremacy of law."[900] Among other things, the Petition of Right "forbade the trial of civilians under the martial law."[901] That meant that civilians could not be tried without the approval of a grand jury. Coke was highly respected by most, if not all, framers. John Rutledge, a framer from South Carolina, Supreme Court justice from 1789 to 1791, and Supreme Court chief justice in 1795, wrote in 1779: "Coke's *Institutes* seems to be almost the foundation of our law. . . ."[902]

The *Five Knights' Case* of 1627 "presented the chief grievance, . . . before Parliament during its momentous session in 1628" which culminated in the Petition of Right.[903] In the *Five Knights' Case*, noted parliamentarian and lawyer John Seldon, in defense of the accused, equated "due process of law" and "law of the land," and included therein "either indictment or presentment."[904]

It is quite possible that the first provision of the Bill of Rights to be modified by a state was the right to a grand jury. The Connecticut Constitution of 1818 specified that "no person shall be holden to answer for any crime, the punishment of which may be death or imprisonment for life, unless on a presentment or an indictment of a grand jury. . . ."[905] Connecticut statutes in 1866 and 1875 authorized prosecutions without presentments or indictments for crimes for which the maximum imprisonment was less than life.[906] Such a practice *may* have been common law in Connecticut from 1789 to 1792.[907] *If so*, that might be one of the reasons Connecticut did not ratify the Bill of Rights during the eighteenth century. On April 19, 1939, Connecticut became the last of the original states to ratify the Bill of Rights.

A return to proactive, full-authority grand juries is probably the only effective way to deal with local government corruption and wasteful bureaucracy until such time as local officials are regularly given lie detector tests. Unfortunately, modern grand juries rarely make presentments or independently investigate governments.

Double Jeopardy

The double jeopardy concept traces to English common law, primarily through the efforts of Sir Edward Coke and Sir William Blackstone.[908] Blackstone wrote, in his famous *Commentaries on the Laws of England,* "no man is to be brought into jeopardy of his life more than once for the same offense."[909] The New Hampshire Constitution of 1784, the first to constitutionalize the main part of double jeopardy, stated: "No subject shall be liable to be tried, after an acquittal, for the same crime or offence."[910] American common law of this period did not require that the defendant's life or limbs be in jeopardy to invoke double jeopardy, as was required in England at the time.[911] The double jeopardy clause of the Fifth Amendment is closer to eighteenth-century common law in England than it is to eighteenth-century common law in the United States. Most states have copied the double jeopardy wording of the U.S. Constitution in their constitutions.

Although retrials after acquittals are prohibited by the Fifth Amendment and its state counterparts only for cases where the maximum penalty includes either death or loss of limb, American judges gradually expanded the constitutional coverage of double jeopardy to minor offenses.[912] Judges who did so were acting constitutionally, whether they realized it or not, because the Ninth Amendment encompasses the American common-law rights of 1789. In 1969, the Court first imposed double jeopardy on state criminal prosecutions.[913] Over the years, double jeopardy has become a complex and changeable concept in the United States as the Court often rewrites the rules.[914]

Despite the fact that the double jeopardy provision in the Fifth Amendment was intended to apply *only* when there was a prior acquittal or conviction for the same offense—except where those convicted were granted a retrial—the Court has ruled that double jeopardy applies when there was a previous start of a trial on the same offense.[915] (A trial is considered to have started when a jury is sworn in or after the first witness is sworn in for trials without juries.) It is not in the public interest to prevent new starts to partially completed criminal trials wherein prosecutors made technical mistakes.[916]

The wacky world of double jeopardy is further illustrated by Supreme Court cases in 1922 and 1958. In 1922, the Court ruled that both the federal government and a state government could prosecute people for the same crime.[917] Although this 1922 ruling is contrary to the original meaning of the Fifth Amendment, the Court has continued to rule that people can be prosecuted in both state and federal courts for the same conduct.[918]

Four members of the Court maintained in 1958 that when a person murders more than one person at about the same time, a state cannot prosecute each murder separately.[919] A man had murdered his wife and three children. All were shot in the head. Each murder was a separate offense. Knowing that some jurors are reluctant to impose the death penalty, the prosecutor prosecuted one murder at a time. At the first trial, for the murder of his wife, the jury convicted but only sentenced the murderer to 20 years in prison. At the second trial, for the murder of one of his children, the jury convicted and sentenced the murderer to 45 years in prison. At the third trial, for the murder of one of his children, the jury convicted and imposed the death sentence. Three justices stated in their dissent that the prosecution had harassed the accused with repeated trials and convictions. All four dissenting justices maintained that the prosecutor had violated the accused's double jeopardy rights. Fortunately, five members of the Court had a better understanding of the Constitution and justice. Unfortunately, the minority opinion seems to have had more influence on future policy. Multiple murder cases are now usually combined in one trial, and justice sometimes suffers.

The Right Against Self-Incrimination

The right to not "be compelled in any criminal case to be a witness against himself" traces to English common law that came into being during the seventeenth century, largely as the result of (1) creative opinions by Lord Coke—who claimed to infer the right against self-incrimination from Magna Carta, and (2) assertions of this right by defendants on trial for treason or seditious libel.[920] Juries often found such defendants not guilty, primarily because jurors thought that the laws were too broad in terms of restricting religious freedom and discussion of politics. The right against being compelled to be a witness against oneself in criminal cases was a fighting right; unless it was invoked, it provided no protection.[921] Even when invoked, the right probably did not help defendants charged with murder, rape, or robbery.

In 1641, Parliament prohibited church authorities from administering any oath which obliged anyone "to confess or to accuse himself or herself of any crime."[922] However, in common-law courts, people under oath continued to be asked incriminating questions for many years after 1641.[923] That practice was terminated by 1750. Criminal defendants were not permitted to testify on their own behalf in common-law courts from 1750 to 1800, although they were permitted to tell their story—unsworn.[924]

The Fifth Amendment does not require that suspects be warned that they have the right to remain silent. It is not clear that the framers intended for suspects to have the right to be silent when questioned by police.[925] The Fifth Amendment does not prevent police from questioning a suspect without the suspect's lawyer being present.[926] The Fifth Amendment does not prevent prosecutors from presenting to juries the responses of suspects to the questions of police, via police testimony, voice recording, or video tape. The Fifth Amendment does not prevent juries from taking into account the failure of suspects to answer questions.

During the eighteenth and nineteenth centuries, no police force had a policy of telling suspects that they had a right to remain silent during questioning by police. Such a policy appears to have been invented by the Federal Bureau of Investigation—the agents of which are lawyers—about midway through the twentieth century.[927]

The Constitution:

- Does not require police to inform suspects that they have the right to remain silent during police questioning

- Does not prevent prosecutors from presenting at trial the fact that the accused refused to answer one or more questions during police questioning

- Does not require police to allow a suspect to have his or her lawyer present during police questioning—even when both the suspect and their lawyer request such presence

- Does not require police to comply with a request by a suspect to confer with his or her lawyer before police questioning

- Does not require the appointment of a lawyer to represent any criminal suspect or any accused criminal during any phase of criminal proceedings—even at trial in capital cases when the accused requests the assistance of a lawyer and the accused is unable to pay for a lawyer

In the 1966 case of *Miranda v. Arizona*,[928] the Court ruled that the Fifth Amendment right of not being compelled to be a witness against oneself dictated that:

- "As a constitutional prerequisite to any questioning, an individual held for interrogation by a law enforcement officer must be warned, in clear and unequivocal terms, that any statement he does make may be used as evidence against him, and that he has a right to the presence of an attorney, either retained or appointed."

- "If an individual held for interrogation by police states that he wants an attorney, the interrogation must cease until an attorney is present; at that time, the individual must have an opportunity to confer with an attorney and to have him present during any subsequent questioning."

- "The prosecution may not use at trial the fact that an individual stood mute, or claimed his privilege against self-incrimination, in the face of an accusation made at a police custodial interrogation."

The only good purpose of "Miranda rights" is to prevent coerced confessions. To prevent coerced confessions *and* facilitate justice, "Miranda rights" should be terminated and video taping required during questioning of suspects. This could be done by statute.

In most criminal cases, defense lawyers (1) do not want the truth to come out, (2) advise their clients to provide no useful information to police, and (3) help their clients fabricate the best defense.[929] In the O. J. Simpson case, defense attorney Robert Shapiro actually stated in public: "We'll devise a defense once we know what the state has to offer."[930] By unconstitutionally limiting questioning of suspects by police: (1) the Court has made justice much more difficult to come by (In many cases, justice is made impossible.); and (2) the Court has substantially increased the amount of money going to members of the legal "profession." Most members of the legal "profession" believe that it is ethical and proper for defense lawyers to: (1) avoid the truth; (2) help their clients lie in a way to invent the best defense; (3) cross-examine prosecution witnesses that they know are telling the truth (in an effort to discredit their reliability and credibility); and (4) put witnesses on the stand who they know will commit perjury.[931] *Miranda* has put an enormous amount of money in the pockets of lawyers at the expense of justice and taxpayer dollars.

Due Process of Law

The Fifth Amendment states that no person shall "be deprived of life, liberty, or property, without due process of law." This means that no person may be executed, imprisoned, fined, or involuntarily forced to give up any of their property in a manner which violates the safeguards associated with law in America in 1789. Because most of the safeguards associated with due process of law—trial by jury, grand juries, etc.—are included elsewhere in the Fifth Amendment, the Bill of Rights, or the Constitution, the only unique aspect of the due process clause of the Fifth Amendment is that courts must honor traditional "procedural rights." "Procedural rights" include such things as making sure that people (1) are given fair notice of legal proceedings in which they are a party, and (2) have an opportunity to be heard in legal proceedings in which they are a party.

Government Taking Private Property

The Fifth Amendment provision "nor shall private property be taken for public use, without just compensation" means that if the government takes private property for public purposes—such as to build public roads or construct government buildings—the government shall provide fair compensation to the people from whom the government takes property.

How did the framers intend for just compensation to be determined? Congress passed a law in 1805 which empowered the part of the District of Columbia known as Georgetown "to open, extend, and regulate streets within the limits of said town; provided they make to the person or persons who may be injured by such opening, extension, or regulation, just and adequate compensation, to be ascertained by the verdict of an impartial jury to be summoned and swore by a justice of the peace of the county of Washington, and to be formed of twenty-three men, who shall proceed in like manner as has been usual in other cases where private property has been condemned for public use."[932] Thus, a special grand jury—created for the sole purpose of determining adequate compensation—or a regular grand jury determined just compensation.

Why did the framers place the takings provision, a purely civil matter, in the Fifth Amendment, in the middle of a bevy of provisions which deal with criminal matters? In addition to grand jury involvement in criminal matters, grand juries were involved in many noncriminal matters including the determination of fair compensation for people whose property was taken from them by government.

By the middle of the nineteenth century, juries were usually not involved in determining compensation in eminent domain proceedings. Compensation paid to persons whose land was taken was usually far below market value—especially when the land was used for railroads.[933] Constitutional historian Harry Scheiber stated: "eminent domain became an instrument for the subsidation, through cost reduction, of both governmental enterprises and favored private undertakings."[934] Because of the confiscatory nature of many eminent domain proceedings, the Ohio Constitution of 1851 provided the right to trial by jury when private property was taken for public use or condemned for use by a corporation.[935] The Ohio Constitutional Convention debates of 1850–51 show that the participants were concerned about commissions in eminent domain proceedings because of bribery and bias.[936]

Despite the fact that many farmers and other landowners have been cheated in eminent domain proceedings without juries, the Court ruled in 1970 that a judge may appoint a commission of three persons to determine compensation to the owner of property which is taken from them in eminent domain proceedings; and, if the owner does not agree, the owner has no right to get a jury to determine compensation.[937]

Although Congress has no constitutional authority to do so, it sometimes passes laws to protect wildlife which are endangered. This often amounts to the federal government converting private property into a wildlife preserve. The federal government has often tried to avoid compensating people whose land has been effectively taken from them in this way. Such laws have resulted in many Americans being oppressed. Some stories of this kind have been presented by *Reader's Digest*, including *Hounded by the Feds* in the July 1996 issue, and *This Land Was Your Land* in the October 1997 issue.

Sixth Amendment

In all criminal prosecutions, the accused shall enjoy the right to a speedy and public trial, by an impartial jury of the State and district wherein the crime shall have been committed, which district shall have been previously ascertained by law, and to be informed of the nature and cause of the accusation; to be confronted with the witnesses against him; to have compulsory process for obtaining witnesses in his favor, and to have the Assistance of Counsel for his defence.

Original Meaning in 21st Century Plain English

This amendment does not apply to impeachments, prosecutions in military courts, prosecutions for contempt of court, and prosecutions of petty crimes which statutes require be tried by one or more judges. In all other criminal prosecutions, the accused shall have the right to:

• A trial which is open to the public

- A trial which begins as soon as is practicable, although the accused shall have a reasonable amount of time to prepare his or her defense after being informed of the specific crimes with which they are charged

- A trial by an impartial jury of twelve adult citizens, all of whom must vote guilty to convict, all of whom have the right to vote not guilty despite the law and the facts if their conscience so dictates, and all of whom are residents of the state and district where the criminal activity took place, or is charged to have taken place, the district being the district established by law at the time the crime took place

- A trial in which the accused has the right to be confronted with, and cross-examine, prosecution witnesses (However, this amendment does *not* provide the accused with the right to know before the trial the identity of the prosecution's witnesses or any evidence the prosecution plans to present at trial.)

- A trial in which the accused has the right to compel the participation of witnesses whom the accused believes will be beneficial to his or her defense

- A trial in which the accused is allowed to have the assistance of a lawyer *if the accused can obtain such assistance*, and, if the accused arranges for a lawyer to assist, the accused and the lawyer can work together to prepare a defense to the criminal charges before the trial, and the lawyer is allowed to represent the accused at trial or to assist the accused represent himself or herself at the trial if both the accused and the lawyer agree (This amendment provides (1) no right for suspects to confer with lawyers before or during questioning by police or grand juries, and (2) no right to a court-appointed lawyer.)

Discussion of the Sixth Amendment

The Sixth Amendment will no doubt prove impossible for twenty-first century Americans to understand by its words alone.

Right to Trial by Jury

It would be logical for twenty-first century Americans to think that, because of the word "all" ("In all criminal prosecutions, . . ."), the Sixth Amendment provides the right to trial by jury for citizens charged with petty crimes and all other crimes. (A reasonable definition of a petty crime is a crime for which the maximum jail sentence is three months or less, the maximum fine is the equivalent of one hundred 1789 dollars or less, and the maximum corporal punishment is twenty lashes or less.) However, the Sixth Amendment provides no right to trial by jury for the common-law petty crime of contempt of court or petty crimes defined by statutes which require those petty crimes to be tried by one or more judges.

The eighth paragraph of the 1776 Virginia Bill of Rights states: "That in all capital or criminal prosecutions, a man hath a right . . . to a speedy trial by an impartial jury of his vicinage, without whose unanimous consent he cannot be found guilty, . . ."[938] In 1776, via Virginia statutes, "at least sixty-five offenses were entrusted to the summary power of magistrates without jury and without right of appeal."[939] Virginia statutes in effect in 1776 required bench trials for petty crimes involving liquor selling, peddling, hunting, and fishing. Virginia vagrancy statutes enacted in 1785 and 1787 increased the power of magistrates (usually justices of the peace) by enabling them to "inflict twenty lashes on 'disorderly persons,' to imprison them for three months or to bind them out to labor for that time."[940]

The Ninth Article of the 1776 Pennsylvania Declaration of Rights states: "That *in all prosecutions for criminal offenses, a man hath a right to* be heard by himself and his council, to demand the cause and nature of his accusation, to be confronted with witnesses, to call for evidence in his favour, and *a speedy public trial, by an impartial jury* of the country, without the unanimous consent of which jury he cannot be found guilty; nor can any man be justly deprived of his liberty except by the laws of the land, or the judgment of his peers."[941] (emphasis added) Two 1777 Pennsylvania statutes provided that the old laws of the colony should remain in force and that justices of the peace should exercise all powers that they exercised under the old laws.[942] From 1776 through at least 1791, citizens of Pennsylvania had no right to trial by jury for about thirty petty offenses—including drunkenness, vagrancy, swearing, sabbath-breaking, infractions of fish and game regulations, petty larceny, illicit sale of liquor, fraudulent weighing, and failure to observe standards fixed for beef, flour, and leather.[943] The penalties included (1) fines from five shillings to ten pounds, (2) imprisonment from one to three months, and (3) corporal punishment of from two hours in the pillory to twenty stripes.[944]

Legal proceedings with no right to trial by jury are called summary proceedings. According to Blackstone, the only common-law summary proceedings involved cases of contempt.[945] By 1776, Parliament had enacted statutes which provided for no right to trial by jury in England for at least one hundred petty offenses. All colonial legislatures enacted statutes which specified summary proceedings for some petty crimes. Massachusetts and some other New England states provided the right to trial by jury in appeals from summary judgments in petty-crime cases, but costs of appeals often worked to strongly discourage appeals from summary judgments in petty-crime cases. Ratifiers of the Sixth Amendment in New Hampshire and Rhode Island *may* have understood it to provide the right of trial by jury in appeals of convictions of petty crimes. (Massachusetts and Connecticut did not ratify the Bill of Rights until 1939.)

Right to "the Assistance of Counsel"

It is important to be aware that (1) prior to 1696, English law required self-representation by all defendants in felony cases, and (2) from 1696 to 1836, English law required self-representation by defendants being prosecuted for any felony except "treason." "Treason" usually involved sedition or maladministration of a nature which modern Americans would *not* think of as felonies, much less treason. By 1750, many, if not all, colonial judges allowed accused felons to have the advice of counsel if they could afford such services.[946] However, "even where counsel was permitted, the general practice continued to be self-representation. . . ."[947] By 1776, all accused felons in the colonies were probably allowed to pay a lawyer to represent them in court.[948] President Washington signed the Judiciary Act of

1789 into law on the day before Congress proposed the Bill of Rights to the states. The Judiciary Act of 1789 included the provision: "in all the courts of the United States, the parties may plead their own cases personally or by the assistance of . . . counsel."[949]

Under its authority to regulate the federal judiciary, Congress enacted 1 Stat 118 in 1790. It provided for the appointment of counsel in federal cases in which the death penalty could be imposed *if* the accused requested a judge to appoint a lawyer to represent them.[950]

Under a broad construction of the Sedition Act of 1798, a man named John Fries was charged with treason for obstructing the enforcement of an unpopular federal tax law.[951] Fries did not have a lawyer and was not offered a lawyer for his trial in a federal circuit court.[952] Fries was found guilty in 1800 and sentenced to death; only the intervention of President Adams—against the advice of his Cabinet—kept Fries from being hanged.[953]

If the members of the First Congress under the Constitution intended for the Sixth Amendment to mean that defendants in all felony cases, or all criminal cases, had the right to appointed counsel, they would have included something to that effect when they enacted 1 Stat 118 in 1790. It is almost always easier to enact a constitutional statute than it is to propose a constitutional amendment. This was especially true when George Washington was president. He rarely vetoed a piece of legislation because he was concerned that arbitrary use of the veto power would weaken the Union. The first veto made by President Washington occurred on April 5, 1792. That veto was made because a bill passed by Congress was clearly unconstitutional.[954]

Because the First Congress wanted to minimize differences between federal and state court rules for trials in state A, "the right . . . to have the Assistance of Counsel for his defence" is consistent with 1789 state laws.

- In Massachusetts, the accused had a right to be heard "by himself, or his counsel, at his election."
- In Pennsylvania, the accused had "a right to be heard by himself and his council. . . ."
- In New York, the accused "shall be allowed counsel."[955]

At the time the Sixth Amendment was framed, counsel were appointed for defendants accused of noncapital felonies in only one state (Connecticut). Only five states in 1789 had provisions for appointing counsel in all capital cases in which defendants requested such help.[956]

It was correctly understood that the Constitution provided no right to court-appointed lawyers until 1932 when the Court invented such a right in *Powell v. Alabama*. In *Powell*, the Court ruled that in capital cases, all inexperienced, illiterate citizens of the United States have the right to receive assignment of counsel because of the due process clause of the Fourteenth Amendment.

It was not until 1938 that the Court ruled that the Sixth Amendment provided a right to court-appointed lawyers. The Court invented a whopper when they ruled that:

- The assistance of counsel "is an essential jurisdictional prerequisite" to the power of a federal court to try and sentence criminal defendants.[957]

- The writ of habeas corpus can be used by federal prisoners to cancel their conviction if they did not waive their right to have counsel.

- Trial judges have the duty to make sure that criminal defendants understand their right to have counsel assigned if they are otherwise unable to obtain counsel. Allegations of waivers of the right to have counsel will be closely scrutinized by the higher courts.

In 1942, the Court ruled, in *Betts v. Brady/Maryland*,[958] that neither due process of law nor the Sixth Amendment requires state courts to provide counsel to indigent defendants who are charged with noncapital felonies—even when such defendants request appointment of counsel.

However, the Court overruled *Betts* in 1963 in the case of *Gideon v. Wainwright/Florida*. In *Gideon*, the Court ruled (1) the Fourteenth Amendment made the Sixth Amendment's "guaranty of counsel" obligatory on the states, and (2) "counsel must be provided for defendants unable to employ counsel unless the right is completely and intelligently waived."[959] Gideon had been sentenced to serve five years in state prison. Hence, it was not generally thought that the Court meant that states must provide counsel for indigent persons accused of petty crimes. However, the Court ruled in 1972: "Absent a knowing and intelligent waiver [of their right to a lawyer, court-appointed if they cannot afford a lawyer], no person may be imprisoned for any offense, whether classified as petty, misdemeanor, or felony unless he was represented by counsel at his trial."[960]

In 1964, the Court ruled in a 5-4 decision in *Escobedo v. Illinois,* that, because of the Sixth and Fourteenth Amendments, police officers must tell all felony suspects that they have a right to consult with their lawyer during initial questioning.[961] Escobedo (1) was a client of a lawyer at the time he was picked up for questioning, and (2) asked for his lawyer to be present during questioning by police. His lawyer was in the police station trying to get to speak to Escobedo, but the lawyer was denied permission to speak to his client until questioning was completed. In a dissenting opinion, three members of the Court said that law enforcement "will be crippled and its task made a great deal more difficult, . . . for unsound, unstated reasons, which can find no home in any of the provisions of the Constitution."[962] The other dissenting Justice said: "I think the rule announced today is most ill-conceived and that it seriously and unjustifiably fetters perfectly legitimate methods of criminal law enforcement."[963]

The Court's ruling in *Escobedo* overruled the 1958 case of *Crooker v. California* in which Crooker complained that his confession was obtained during a period of questioning by police in which he was prevented from communicating with his lawyer. Despite the fact that Crooker was sentenced to death, the Court ruled that it was appropriate for Crooker's confession to be presented as evidence against him at his trial.[964]

Although the rules invented by the Court in 1964 in *Escobedo* drew strong criticism from four members of the Court, the Escobedo rules were made almost insignificant by the Miranda rules invented by the Court in 1966. (The Miranda rules are discussed in this chapter under the Fifth Amendment.)

Jury Size in Criminal Trials

The framers of the Sixth Amendment intended, and the ratifiers understood, that all trial juries in felony cases would have twelve jurors, and that all twelve would have to vote guilty to convict. All trial juries in felony cases during the seventeenth and eighteenth centuries in the American colonies and the United States had twelve jurors. Nevertheless, in the case of *Williams v. Florida*, the Court ruled in 1970 that trials by a jury of six in noncapital felony cases in state courts do not violate the right of the accused to a trial by jury.[965] A jury of six will convict more often than a jury of twelve for the simple reason that there is less chance that a juror will vote not guilty.

The Court ruled in 1978 that trials with five-person juries in misdemeanor cases in state courts do not satisfy the right to trial by jury.[966] Since 1978, juries with six or more members have been "constitutional" in state courts in all criminal cases except capital cases.

In 1972, in the case of *Apodaca v. Oregon*,[967] the Court ruled that in noncapital criminal trials in state courts, convictions by a jury vote of 10-2 did not violate the Constitution. Also in 1972, in the case of *Johnson v. Louisiana*,[968] the Court ruled that in noncapital criminal trials in state courts, convictions resulting from 9-3 jury verdicts did not violate the Constitution. Convictions by 10-2 votes and 9-3 votes are unconstitutional because they deny criminal defendants due process of law.

After *Williams*, *Apodaca*, and *Johnson*, it became obvious to many people who were knowledgeable about those cases and *Escobedo* and *Miranda* that the Court's extreme activism in *Escobedo* and *Miranda* was motivated primarily by a desire to give lawyers more income and power.

In 1985, the Court continued its unconstitutional lawyer welfare program when it ruled that the Fourteenth Amendment guarantees convicted criminals the right to the effective assistance of a lawyer (appointed if they cannot afford to hire a lawyer) in making their first appeal of their convictions.[969] In their dissent, two members of the Court correctly stated: "In this case the Court cre-

ates virtually out of whole cloth a Fourteenth Amendment due process right to effective assistance of counsel on the appeal of a criminal
conviction. . . ."

Power of Jury to Acquit Despite the Law

The framers were well aware of the power of juries in criminal
cases to acquit despite the law and the facts. No case illustrates this
better than the 1735 trial of printer/publisher John Peter Zenger.
Zenger was charged with seditious libel. Zenger's lawyer, in a bit of
candor not often seen in modern courts, acknowledged that Zenger
had committed the offenses with which he was accused. Nobody
claimed that Zenger was insane. Zenger's lawyer declared that the
jury had "the right beyond all dispute to determine both the law and
the fact, . . ."[970] After being instructed by the chief justice that the
only possible verdict was guilty, it did not take the jury long to return a verdict of not guilty.[971] The Zenger trial jury said, in effect,
"we believe that the law of seditious libel is too harsh as applied to
the facts in this case." Two grand juries, in refusing to indict Zenger
for the same crimes in 1734—despite the strenuous efforts of the
judge—had come to a philosophical judgment similar to that of the
Zenger trial jury despite the fact that no lawyer was present to tell
them that they had the right to determine the law and the fact.
When a jury acquits, no court has the constitutional authority to
overrule the jury. Double jeopardy precludes the constitutional setting aside of any acquittal.

For almost a century after the acquittal of John Peter Zenger, it
was fairly well understood that trial juries had the power to acquit
defendants in criminal trials despite the law and the facts. That jury
power still exists and is referred to by various terms, including jury
nullification, jury veto, and jury power to determine both the law
and the facts. It is an unwritten part of the Constitution. It is written into the famous Sedition Act of 1798 which stated: "the jury
who shall try the cause shall have a right to determine the law and
the fact . . . *as in other cases.*"[972] (emphasis added) By the end of the
nineteenth century, many jurors did not realize that juries had the
power to acquit despite the law and the facts. In 1895, in the case of

Sparf v. United States, the Court ruled that juries were not to be given instructions which explained the right of the jury to acquit despite the law and the facts.[973]

In their powerful dissent in *Sparf*, Justice Horace Gray and Justice George Shiras pointed out that:

- In the 1800 treason trial of John Fries, Supreme Court Justice Samuel Chase said in his instructions to the jury: "It is the duty of the court in this case and in all criminal cases, to state to the jury their opinion of the *law* arising on the facts; but the jury are to decide on the present and in all *criminal* cases, *both the law and the facts*, on their consideration of the *whole* case."

- In the 1807 treason trial of Aaron Burr, Supreme Court Chief Justice John Marshall told the jury: "It was said that levying war is an act compounded of law and fact; of which the jury aided by the court must judge. To that declaration the court adheres. . . . [the jury] will find a verdict of guilty or not guilty as their own consciences may direct."

- In 1815, a defense lawyer told a federal jury: "The jury here are judges of law and fact, and are responsible only to God, to the prisoner, and to their own consciences"; after expressing his opinion upon the law in the case, Supreme Court Justice Gabriel Duvall said: "The jury are not bound to conform to this opinion, because they have the right in all criminal cases, to decide on the law and the facts."

- Supreme Court Justice Henry Baldwin told a jury in 1830, after stating the law applicable to the case: "you are judges both of the law and the fact in a criminal case, and are not bound by the opinion of the court; you may judge for yourselves, . . . if you are prepared to say the law is different from what you have heard from us [There were two judges in this case. Many early federal cases had more than one trial judge.], you are in the exercise of a constitutional right to do so. . . ."

- In many other criminal cases before 1835, juries were told by judges or defense lawyers that juries had the right to determine both law and fact.

- After Justice Joseph Story's instructions to the jury in the 1835 case of *United States v. Battiste*, the general tendency of judges was to maintain that juries had no right to determine law. (Story told the *Battiste* jury that the American Revolution was over, and Americans could trust their institutions, but he acknowledged that juries had the right to disregard the instructions of judges.[974])

- In Georgia and Louisiana, despite the fact that the state constitutions of those states declared: "in criminal cases the jury shall be judges of the law and the fact," judges eventually came to rule that those constitutional provisions did not authorize juries in criminal cases to decide the law against the instructions of the court.[975]

Some judges got so power crazy after Story's 1835 jury instructions that directed verdicts were ordered against criminal defendants. When the great reformer Susan B. Anthony was on trial in 1873 for voting in 1872 "for a representative in the Congress of the United States, without having a lawful right to vote," the judge ordered a directed verdict of guilty against her.[976] The judge knew that it was unlikely that the jury would unanimously vote guilty without being directed to do. When the judge ordered the directed verdict, Anthony's lawyer immediately insisted that it was the jury's responsibility to determine guilt or innocence.[977] The judge then ordered the court clerk to record a guilty verdict and discharged the jury even though they had not voted.[978] The judge fined Anthony one hundred dollars plus court costs.[979] Anthony told the judge: "I shall never pay a dollar of your unjust penalty."[980] The judge did not imprison Anthony, probably because he did not want the case ending up in the U.S. Supreme Court. Anthony hoped that the case could be taken to the Court in an attempt to get the Court to declare that women had the right to vote. It is extremely unlikely that the Court would have given women the right to vote. However, the Court would have almost certainly overturned the directed verdict. Anthony's trial received a great deal of press coverage. It was one of the finest hours in the life of Susan B. Anthony. The trial served to (1) strengthen the case for equality of women before the law, and (2) make an impact on the rights of criminal defendants and the rights of jurors in criminal cases.

During the twentieth century, judges rarely informed jurors that jurors have the right to determine the law in the cases before them.[981] In 1969, a judge indicated that to tell jurors they could use their conscience and common sense to determine the fairness of the law would invite anarchy.[982] One of the great American heritages has become virtually the unmentionable right. Would the jurors who convicted Dr. Kevorkian of murder in 1999 have done so if (1) the judge informed the jurors of their right to let their conscience be their guide and vote not guilty despite the law and the facts, and (2) the judge had allowed Kevorkian's primary defense witnesses to testify? Very unlikely. Why? Kevorkian's primary witnesses would have provided powerful evidence that the law was unfair as applied to that case.

Seventh Amendment

In Suits at common law, where the value in controversy shall exceed twenty dollars, the right of trial by jury shall be preserved, and no fact tried by a jury, shall be otherwise re-examined in any Court of the United States, than according to the rules of the common law.

Original Meaning in 21st Century Plain English

If the amount of money in controversy or the value of the things in controversy exceeds twenty dollars, the right to trial by jury shall be preserved for lawsuits of the kind triable under the common law in the United States in 1789. However, Congress shall have the power to change the value-in-controversy threshold from twenty dollars to whatever it deems appropriate for suits at common law of the following kind:

- Suits tried in federal courts between citizens of different states (Such suits are called diversity suits herein. Diversity suits are called diversity of citizenship suits by some people.)

- Suits tried in federal courts involving a citizen of a foreign country (Such suits are called alienage suits herein. Alienage suits are called diversity of citizenship suits by some people.)

- Suits tried in federal courts wherein the federal government is the plaintiff (The federal government cannot be a defendant unless it consents to be a defendant.)

In civil cases tried by juries, juries shall be composed of twelve adult citizens. All twelve jurors must agree on all verdicts. Trial judges may direct juries in civil cases to render a verdict for one party if the judges state that there are no issues of fact which are relevant to a lawful verdict. However, juries may render verdicts contrary to verdicts directed by trial judges. If a jury renders a verdict contrary to a verdict directed by a trial judge, the trial judge may order a new trial. However, no trial judge may reverse a jury verdict in a civil case without the unanimous concurrence of the jury.

No fact determined by a jury in a suit at common law shall be re-examined in any federal court other than according to the rules of the common law. (Were all parties in the case given sufficient notice of the trial? Did the trial judge make proper rulings? Did the trial judge provide the jury with correct and sufficient information about the law? Were there twelve jurors? Did all twelve jurors agree on the verdict? Was it appropriate to try the case under the rules of the common law?)

No federal appellate judge, or group of appellate judges, may reverse a jury verdict in a suit at common law without the unanimous consent of the jury. However, if federal appellate judges in suits at common law tried by a jury find that the rules of the common law were not complied with, the federal appellate judges may either (1) order the trial court to conduct a new trial, or (2) order a new trial at the federal appellate court over which they preside.

The common law cannot be used to determine whether prizes (captured ships and cargoes) brought to ports in the U.S. are lawful prizes. Federal judges shall employ maritime (admiralty) law to determine whether prizes brought to ports in the U.S. are legal prizes.

Discussion of the Seventh Amendment

What is now known as The Judiciary Act of 1789 became law on September 24, 1789, when President George Washington signed a bill titled: "An Act to establish the Judicial Courts of the United States."[983] [984] On September 25, 1789, Congress proposed twelve constitutional amendments to the state legislatures. Ten of those proposed amendments are now known as the Bill of Rights. The Judiciary Act of 1789 was considered to be consistent with the Bill of Rights by the framers and ratifiers of the Bill of Rights.

The lowest federal courts created by the Judiciary Act of 1789 were district courts, one in each state except for Virginia and Massachusetts which each got two district courts. The Kentucky district of Virginia got a district court, and the Maine portion of Massachusetts got a district court. Each district court was presided over by one judge. The district courts were not given jurisdiction to hear common-law diversity suits or common-law alienage suits.[985] Between the district courts and the Supreme Court were circuit courts. Each circuit court was presided over by two members of the Supreme Court and one federal district court judge. All three judges usually presided—with or without juries. Circuit courts were given concurrent jurisdiction with state courts over common-law diversity suits and common-law alienage suits where the value in controversy (amount of money in controversy or value of property in controversy) exceeded five hundred dollars. The Judiciary Act of 1789 stated:

> "That the circuit courts shall have original cognizance, concurrent with the courts of the several states, of all suits of a civil nature at common law or in equity, where the matter in dispute exceeds, exclusive of costs, the sum or value of five hundred dollars, and the United States are plaintiffs or petitioners; or an alien is a party, or the suit is between a citizen of the State where the suit is brought, and the citizen of another State."[986]

That left the state common-law courts as the only courts to hear common-law diversity suits and common-law alienage suits where the value in controversy was from $20.01 to $500.00. The first Congress under the Constitution:

- Chose to have no federal enforcement of low and moderate value debt contracts in order to preserve the Union (There was enormous resistance to enforcement of contracts made with British merchants before the Revolutionary War began.[987] Thousands of Americans owed from $20.01 to $500.00 to British merchants. Many of those Americans were poor, had suffered during the Revolution and the depression of the 1780s, hated the British, and were near to being forced into debtors' prison. Both nonviolent and violent means were used to prevent debt contracts from being enforced in state courts in the 1780s. Out-of-state American merchants also found it difficult to collect the full amount of debts in some state courts. There would have been little hope of preserving the Union if the federal courts had tried to totally enforce all debt contracts over twenty dollars. This point is made in more depth in Chapter 5 under the subsection titled Alienage Cases and Diversity Cases in the discussion of Article III, Section 2, Paragraph 1.)

- Did not want to antagonize citizens by dragging them to federal courts in distant states to do legal battle where the costs of travel for the citizens, witnesses, and lawyers would have been greater than, or nearly equal to, the amount of money in dispute (It would have put many defendants, especially the poor defendants, in a no-win situation in which they would have defaulted.[988])

The Judiciary Act of 1789 required the value in controversy to exceed one hundred dollars for lawsuits brought by the federal government to be heard in federal courts.[989] Because the United States was a sovereign nation, it was not considered possible to sue the United States without its consent.

The federal government has no jurisdiction in suits at common law between citizens of the same state except "between Citizens of the same State claiming Lands under Grants of different States." Between the Constitution and the Judiciary Act of 1789, there was very little in terms of suits at common law that could be tried in federal courts if the value in controversy was less than one hundred dollars. Hence, ratifiers of the Bill of Rights had good reason to think that the following Seventh Amendment provision would be applied primarily in state courts: "In Suits at common law, where the value in controversy shall exceed twenty dollars, the right of trial by jury shall be preserved, . . ."

On December 15, 1791, Virginia became the eleventh state to ratify the Bill of Rights. That made the Bill of Rights part of the Constitution. If ratifiers of the Seventh Amendment understood that Congress would be required—upon ratification of the Seventh Amendment—to give federal courts jurisdiction of diversity suits at common law and alienage suits at common law where the value in controversy exceeded twenty dollars, the ratifiers would have either:

- Not ratified the Seventh Amendment in order to avoid requiring Congress to give federal courts jurisdiction for the large majority of alienage cases and diversity cases; or

- Challenged the constitutionality of keeping the threshold at five hundred dollars for alienage and diversity suits after the Seventh Amendment became law in 1791 (The lack of challenges by ratifiers, framers, or creditors make it clear that it was widely understood that it was constitutional for Congress to keep the threshold at five hundred dollars after the Seventh Amendment was ratified.)

The Judiciary Act of 1789 required the value in controversy to exceed two thousand dollars for diversity cases and alienage cases to be appealed from a federal circuit court to the U.S. Supreme Court. Diversity cases and alienage cases could not be appealed to the U.S. Supreme Court if they had been adjudicated in a state court. It is interesting that the Judiciary Act of 1789 gave to state courts the trial of all lawsuits arising under the U.S. Constitution, treaties to which the United States had agreed, and laws of the United States.[990]

However, decisions in "federal question" cases (cases involving the U.S. Constitution, treaties, and federal statutes) could be appealed from the state supreme courts to the U.S. Supreme Court.

Major Controversies During Ratification of the Constitution

Two of the most controversial things about the proposed Constitution were (1) the lack of any statement about the right to trial by jury in civil cases, and (2) the provision which gave the Supreme Court appellate jurisdiction of both law and fact in civil cases. Some opponents of the proposed Constitution said that the provision to give the Court appellate jurisdiction in civil cases "both as to Law and Fact" worked to deprive citizens of their common-law right to trial by jury in civil cases.[991]

Alexander Hamilton struggled to defend the proposed Constitution in *The Federalist*, No. 83. Hamilton wrote:

"The objection to the plan of the convention, which has met with most success in . . . [New York], and perhaps in several of the other States, is *that relative to the want of a constitutional provision* for the trial by jury in civil cases. . . . The friends and adversaries of the plan of the convention, if they agree on nothing else, concur at least in the value they set upon the trial by jury; or if there is any difference between them it consists in this: the former regard it as a valuable safeguard to liberty; the latter represent it as the very palladium of free government. . . . The strongest argument in its favor is that it is a security against corruption. . . ."[992]

Palladium was probably not a common word in 1787–88. Where did the adversaries of the Constitution get it? They probably got it from the same place that a 1772 Boston town meeting got it. A 1772 Boston town meeting (1) framed "A List of Infringements and Violations of Rights," (2) hailed trial by jury as "the great bulwark and security of English property," and (3) praised Blackstone's remarks in his *Commentaries on the Laws of England* which characterized trial by jury as the "sacred palladium" of English liberties which might be undermined by different methods of trial.[993]

All states in 1787–88 had common-law courts, and the right to trial by jury existed in all common-law courts. During the Revolutionary War, each state had at least one "admiralty" court. However, the jurisdiction of these courts varied widely from state to state. In some states, the jurisdiction was limited to prize jurisdiction. (Massachusetts had three prize courts.) The right to trial by jury existed in "admiralty" courts in eleven states.[994] The function of juries in Revolutionary War prize courts was to determine whether vessels and cargoes captured by Americans were prizes of war. ("Prizes of war" is a synonym for "legal captures.") Ironically, in 1775 Congress made the novel suggestion that states use juries in prize courts.[995] That would prove to be a mistake. Congress ended up reversing many of the prize court decisions. By 1787, the prevalent view was that juries were inappropriate for prize determination. Alexander Hamilton, after acknowledging that trial by jury was "a valuable safeguard to liberty," stated in *The Federalist*, No. 83:

> "I feel a deep and deliberate conviction that there are many cases in which the trial by jury is an ineligible one. I think it so particularly in cases which concern the public peace with foreign nations—that is, in most cases where the question turns wholly on the laws of nations. Of this nature, among others, are all prize causes. Juries cannot be supposed competent to investigations that require a thorough knowledge of the laws and usages of nations; . . ."[996]

The Seventh Amendment was intended to preserve the right of trial by jury in common-law cases and cases of the same type, even where the common law was superseded by constitutional laws.[997] The Judiciary Act of 1789 gave federal courts "exclusive original cognizance of all civil causes of admiralty and maritime jurisdiction . . . saving to suitors, in all cases, the right of a common-law remedy, where the common law is competent to give it."[998] Thereafter, maritime law could only be applied in federal courts, but many lawsuits of a maritime nature could be resolved in state common-law courts. Plaintiffs in many disputes of a maritime nature—such as suits over seamen's wages and contracts to build ships—could either (1) have their suits heard in a federal court under the rules of maritime law in which there would be no right to trial by jury, or (2) have their suits heard in a state court under the rules of common law in which there would be a right to trial by jury.

It was understood by most of the ratifiers of the Seventh Amendment tht the common law was incompetent to determine whether prizes were lawful prizes.

Forms of Action in Civil Suits at Common Law in 1789

In 1789, civil suits at common law included various forms of action. These forms of action are important because they describe the types of cases protected by the Seventh Amendment. Most suits at common law in 1789 involved the following actions:

- Actions to obtain damages—compensation in the form of money—for injuries to a person's health, a person's reputation, or a person's property ("Trespass" was the name of such actions.)

- Actions to recover a specific amount of money owed ("Debt" was the name of such actions.)

- Actions to obtain damages for breach of a signed contract, under seal ("Covenant" was the name of such actions.)

- Actions to obtain damages for the nonperformance of an oral contract ("Assumpsit" was the name of such actions.)

- Actions to recover movable property wrongfully taken or detained ("Replevin" was the name of such actions.)

- Actions to obtain the monetary value of movable property wrongfully taken ("Trover" was the name of such actions.)

Expansion of Maritime Law

The framers intended that maritime law—no right to trial by jury— would extend only to things that happened on or to commercial ships on the high seas and other ocean water. The 1820 case of *The United States v. Wiltberger* and the 1825 case of *The Steamboat Thomas Jefferson* make it clear that disputes had to be relevant to ships in salt water in order to be tried under maritime law. However, the Court overruled itself in 1851 when it ruled that all disputes relevant to ships in "lakes and navigable waters connecting the same [within the United States]" could be tried under maritime law.[999] Later, the Court expanded maritime law to encompass all waters navigable in interstate or foreign commerce.[1000] The Court even expanded maritime law to encompass a bather injured by a surfboard.[1001]

Expansion of Bankruptcy Law

There were no statutes called bankruptcy statutes in the American colonies or in the United States prior to 1800.[1002] The framers and ratifiers of the unamended Constitution must have associated the word "Bankruptcies" in the Constitution with English bankruptcy statutes and bankruptcy proceedings in England. English bankruptcy statutes first came into existence during the first half of the sixteenth century—during the reign of Henry VIII. Bankruptcy statutes from Henry VIII to George III were: (1) both civil and criminal in nature—sometimes employing the death penalty; (2) applied only to traders (merchants); (3) allowed bankruptcy proceedings to be initiated only by creditors; and (4) required substantial creditor consent for the discharge of debts. All of those characteristics—except the death penalty—were included in the first U.S. bankruptcy statute in 1800.

Modern federal bankruptcy statutes are unconstitutional because (1) they allow debtors to initiate bankruptcy proceedings, (2) they allow various state laws to determine how much property debtors are allowed to retain after their debts are discharged, (3) judges can discharge debts without the consent of any creditors, and (4) once a bankruptcy suit is filed by a debtor, bankruptcy law prohibits creditors from exercising their right to trial by jury. The Court has ruled that modern bankruptcy laws are constitutional despite the fact that creditors are denied their constitutional right to a trial by jury.[1003]

The Court ruled, in the case of *Hanover National Bank v. Moyses*,[1004] that federal bankruptcy laws are constitutional even though: (1) they provide "that others than traders may be adjudged bankrupts"; and (2) bankruptcies can be initiated by debtors. Furthermore, the Court ruled: "The constitutional requirement that bankruptcy laws be uniform throughout the United States is not violated . . . because . . . bankrupts are allowed the exemptions prescribed by the state law in force at the time of the filing of the petition for bankruptcy."

The Court's ruling in *Hanover National Bank v. Moyses* relied heavily on remarks by "Mr. Justice Story, . . . that learned commentator . . ." Justice Joseph Story, as shown in the discussion of the Fifth Amendment (relevant to grand juries), Sixth Amendment (relevant to jury power in criminal cases), and the Seventh Amendment (relevant to the right to trial by jury in suits at common law) was an influential proponent of (1) increasing the power of judges and prosecutors, and (2) decreasing the power of juries.

Zenger Connection to Civil Cases

In the 1734–35 seditious libel case of John Peter Zenger—in which two grand juries refused to indict, no grand jury indicted, and the trial jury acquitted despite the law and the facts—one of the two issues of the *Weekly Journal* for which Zenger was prosecuted for printing/publishing featured an attack on the governor of New York for engaging in litigation tactics which sought to evade the right to trial by jury in civil cases. [1005]

Summary Judgments

In civil cases of the type where the right to trial by jury existed in 1792, the right has often been usurped by judges who have awarded summary judgments. When the Seventh Amendment was framed and ratified, there was no such thing as a summary judgment or summary civil procedure in the common law in civil cases. [1006] Blackstone made no reference to summary judgment or summary procedure in civil cases. [1007]

In 1792, the closest thing to summary procedure in civil cases in the United States was a 1769 South Carolina statute which made it lawful for judges "to determine, without a jury, in a summary way, on petition, all causes cognizable in the said courts, for any sum not exceeding 20 pounds sterling, except where the title of lands may come into question: . . ."[1008] There was a similar statute in Virginia for lawsuits where the value in controversy was between one pound and five pounds.[1009] When state courts employed the few summary procedure statutes in force in 1789, the courts were acting much like modern small claims courts.

In 1792, demurrers were used in the common law by defendants in civil suits to try to get cases dismissed by either (1) asserting that legal errors were made by plaintiffs, or (2) acknowledging the truth of matters about which plaintiffs complained—but asserting that there was no legal remedy for those matters. A small percentage of summary judgments are, in effect, constitutional because they are equivalent to granting a demurrer. However, most summary judgments are unconstitutional because material facts *are* in controversy.

Modern summary judgment law in the United States traces primarily to acts of Parliament in 1855 and 1873.[1010] In 1855, Parliament enacted the "Summary Procedure on Bills of Exchange Act." It was designed to speed up the process of getting judgments for plaintiffs who were owed money.[1011] It worked quite well and was perfectly lawful in England where all laws enacted by Parliament are constitutional. The English "Judicature Act of 1873" extended the summary procedure substantially.[1012]

When summary judgments were introduced in the United States, they were often restricted to such things as recovering debts. These judgments could only be awarded to plaintiffs. Even so, constitutionality was a problem.[1013] As time went by, summary judgments came to be used in more and more types of cases. By the end of the twentieth century, summary judgments could be used in all types of cases in which there were suits at common law in 1789. Summary judgments may now be granted (1) in both federal and state courts, and (2) to defendants as well as plaintiffs. In 1986, the Court substantially expanded the availability of summary judgments and encouraged judges to make more summary judgments.[1014] That was like firemen pouring gasoline on a fire that they are obligated to try to extinguish.

Summary judgments are unconstitutional when judges grant them when there are one or more material facts in dispute. Motions for summary judgment by lawyers being sued for malpractice have often been granted by their lawyer brethren in robes despite the fact that one or more material facts have been in dispute. Except for summary judgments which are effectively demurrers, summary judgments in federal courts are unconstitutional by virtue of the Seventh Amendment. The large majority of summary judgments in state courts are unconstitutional by virtue of state constitutions and, quite likely, the Seventh Amendment.

Demand for Trial by Jury

In order to obtain a trial by jury in a civil case in the United States, a party must demand a trial by jury early in the proceedings. A demand for a trial by jury in a civil case must take place long before a trial takes place. If a party fails to demand a trial by jury in writing—in an esoteric manner—the party is deemed to have waived their right to trial by jury. The explicit constitutional right to trial by jury, which is "waived" in an unknowing manner by many people (especially nonlawyers representing themselves), stands in *marked contrast* to the Court-invented "right" to appointed counsel for crime suspects and accused criminals—a "right" for which *knowing waivers* must be made.

Federal Rule 38 states: "The right of trial by jury as declared by the Seventh Amendment . . . shall be preserved to the parties inviolate. . . . Any party may demand a trial by jury of any issue triable of right by jury by (1) serving upon the other parties a demand therefor in writing at any time after the commencement of the action and not later than 10 days after the service of the last pleading directed to such issue, and (2) filing the demand as required by Rule 5(d). . . . The failure of a party to serve and file a demand as required by this rule constitutes a waiver by the party of trial by jury. . . ."[1015] State courts have similar rules.

Directed Verdicts and Judgments Notwithstanding the Verdict

Rule 50 of the modern Rules of Civil Procedure—for the federal government and most states—allows judges in civil cases to grant

(1) motions for directed verdicts, and (2) motions for judgments notwithstanding the verdict. The consent of the jury is *not* required for judges to grant Rule 50 motions. Is it constitutional for judges to grant motions for directed verdicts and make judgments notwithstanding the verdict? No! When many citizens in the United States were clamoring for the Seventh Amendment, they were not clamoring for the right to trial by jury in common-law cases where the unanimous verdicts of twelve jurors could be reversed by trial judges or any other judges without the unanimous consent of the jurors. Such a right would have been meaningless.

Legal scholar Wilfred Ritz wrote that state judges in the 1780s "were not empowered to make authoritarian common-law decisions because the jury had the final say, in both 'inferior' and 'superior' courts."[1016] Review of an inferior court by a superior court commonly involved a retrial with a new jury.[1017] State "superior" or "supreme" courts were all trial courts, usually with several judges sitting. Juries were often instructed that they "had the final say, not only as to facts, but also as to law."[1018]

According to noted historian Jack Rakove, Americans during the revolutionary period gave "preeminent importance" to two rights: (1) representation in the legislature; and (2) trial by jury.[1019] Citizens believed that almost all of their other rights would be sheltered if their two preeminent rights "were left to operate in full force."[1020]

A great deal of research on the legal system in Massachusetts from 1760 to 1830 was done by historian William Nelson in the early 1970s. The fruits of Nelson's research were published in a book in 1975. Nelson stated, relevant to the fifteen-year period prior to the Revolutionary War: "once a jury had incorporated its own view of the law into its verdict, judges had no power to set that verdict aside even if the jury had failed to follow their instructions. The fact that juries rather than judges regularly decided the law applicable to litigated cases tells us much about prerevolutionary law and society."[1021] It was not until the nineteenth century that laws were enacted which reduced the power of juries in Massachusetts.[1022]

John Adams became alarmed in 1771 when he heard of "Doctrines advanced for law, which if true, would render Juries a mere

Ostentation and Pageantry and the Court absolute judges of Law and Fact. . . . the common People should have as compleat a Controul, as decisive a Negative, in every Judgment in a Court of Judicature."[1023]

The *Independent Chronicle*, a Jeffersonian (Republican) newspaper published in Boston, printed an article in 1806 which opposed a bill sponsored by Federalists in the Massachusetts legislature. The bill declared juries incompetent in questions of law. In opposing the bill, the article in the *Independent Chronicle* stated on February 10, 1806:

> "The doctrine now attempted to be promulgated, to render the jury incompetent to law, is to depreciate the character of every man in society but practitioners of it. It is similar to the declaration that the people are their own 'worst enemies'— that they are ignorant as to every particular on which is founded either the political or legal principles of the constitution and the laws. Should this become the prevailing sentiment, in a few years no man would be considered any weight in society but those connected in the judiciary department."[1024]

The first case resembling the type now covered by Rule 50 occurred in England in 1758.[1025] Another such case occurred in 1759, followed by two such cases in 1762, one in 1763, and one in 1765.[1026] All of those cases occurred in England. It appears that in all of those cases the jury was told that their verdict might be reversed at a later time, thereby giving the juries something of a tacit approval of the process. Even if Rule 50 type common-law practices were firmly entrenched in England in 1789, they would have been rejected in America. In 1834, in the case of *Wheaton v. Peters*, the Court emphasized that only that portion of the common law of England which was suitable to conditions of the colonies was accepted by colonial governments.[1027]

I have seen no evidence that any "Rule 50" type rulings took place in the American colonies or the United States during the eighteenth century. The nearest thing to it is the part of the Constitution which says: "the supreme Court shall have appellate Jurisdiction, both as to Law and Fact, . . ." One month after the proposed Constitution was made public, "A Democratic Federalist" wrote: "The word *appeal*, if I understand it right, in its proper signification includes the *fact* as well as the law, and it precludes every idea of trial by jury."[1028]

The provision of the unamended Constitution which gave the Court appellate jurisdiction of fact and law in civil cases tried by juries caused such discontent that it is the only power granted to the federal government in the Constitution that is reduced by the Bill of Rights. Citizens were accustomed to juries which determined the facts and could, if they wanted, determine both the law and the facts. Supporters and opponents of the proposed Constitution agreed that the primary attribute of trial by jury in civil cases was that juries provide a valuable check on judicial corruption.[1029][1030] That check would vanish if judges, without obtaining the permission of juries, could reverse verdicts under the pretense of being necessitated by law.

Ratifiers of the Seventh Amendment thought that it would prevent judges from reversing jury verdicts in suits at common law without the consent of the juries that had provided the verdicts. Powerful critics of the Constitution would have probably been successful in obtaining a second national constitutional convention if most of the electorate thought that the Seventh Amendment would allow judges to reverse verdicts of juries without the unanimous consent of the jurors. From 1776 to 1791, juries in the U.S. were "collegially involved in the judicial search for 'the law.' Juries not only found the facts, but they also had the final word as to what the law was [for the purposes of the trial]. . . ."[1031]

The tradition of juries having the power to determine law in civil cases is indicated by jury instructions provided by Supreme Court Chief Justice John Jay in 1794 in the case of *The State of Georgia v. Brailsford, et. al.*, a very important case that was probably unique in that a jury was given the opportunity to determine the law in the United States Supreme Court *in a civil case in which no facts were in dispute, and all justices agreed on the law.* After hearing arguments in the Supreme Court for four days, Chief Justice John Jay "delivered the following charge [to the jury] on the 7th of February":

"This cause has been regarded as of great importance; and doubtless it is so. . . . The facts comprehended in the case, are agreed; the only point that remains, is to settle what is the law of the land arising from those facts; and on that point, it is proper, that the opinion of the court should be given. It is fortunate on the present, as it must be on every occasion, to find the opinion of the court unanimous: We entertain no diversity of sentiment; and we have experienced no difficulty in uniting in the charge, which it is my province to deliver. . . . We are also of the opinion, that the debts due to *Brailsford*, a *British* subject, residing in *Great Britain*, were by the statute of *Georgia* subjected, not to confiscation, but only to seques-tration; and, therefore, that his right to recover them, revived at the peace, both by the law of nations and the treaty of peace. . . . on the one hand, it is presumed, that juries are the best judges of facts; it is, on the other hand, presumable, that the court are the best judges of law. But still both objects are lawfully, within your power of decision. . . ."[1032]

In the 1780s and 1790s, it was unacceptable for trial judges to (1) reverse verdicts made by juries in common-law cases without the consent of all jurors, or (2) enter verdicts in common-law cases tried by juries without the consent of all jurors. The large majority of civil cases were common-law cases.

The American heritage of jury power was addressed by Thomas Jefferson in *Notes on the State of Virginia*, first published in 1785. Jefferson wrote: "magistrates have jurisdiction both criminal and civil. If the question before them be a question . . . of fact, or of fact and law combined, it must be referred to a jury. In the latter case, of a combination of law and fact, it is usual for the jurors to . . . refer the law arising on it to the decision of the judges. But this division of the subject lies with their discretion only. And if the question relate to any point of public liberty, or if it be one of those in which the judges may be suspected of bias, the jury undertake to decide both law and fact. . . . the common sense of twelve honest men gives still a better chance of just decision, . . ."[1033]

Jury Size and Unanimity

The framers and ratifiers of the Seventh Amendment understood that in all civil cases with juries (1) there would be twelve jurors, and (2) all verdicts would be unanimous.[1034] All trial juries in civil cases in the United States from 1776 to 1800+, and in England from 1376 to 1800+, were composed of twelve jurors who rendered unanimous verdicts or no verdicts. Until 1991, Federal Rule of Civil Procedure 48 specified twelve jurors per jury unless all parties agreed to less than twelve. Despite the federal rule and the Constitution, federal trial judges often imposed six-person juries prior to 1973.[1035] In 1973, the Court ruled that federal judges could impose six-person juries in civil cases.[1036]

In two 1897 cases, the Court upheld the longstanding requirement that jury verdicts must be unanimous. Both 1897 cases involved the federal territory of Utah. In *American Pub. Co. v. Fisher*,[1037] the Court ruled: "The Utah law of March 10, 1892, that a verdict in a civil case may be rendered on the concurrence therein of nine or more members of the [twelve member] jury, is invalid, . . . Unanimity is one of the . . . essential features of trial by jury . . ." In *Springville v. Thomas*,[1038] the Court ruled: "The 7th Amendment secured unanimity in finding a verdict as an essential feature of trial by jury in common-law cases; and [an] act of Congress could not impart the power to change the constitutional rule, . . ."

In state courts, civil cases during the twentieth century were sometimes decided by only 75 percent of the jurors despite the Seventh Amendment and state constitutional provisions similar to the Seventh Amendment. Juries in civil cases in state courts often consist of eight jurors, only six of which are required to agree on a verdict. Since the Court has never ruled that nonunanimous verdicts in state civil cases were unconstitutional, it is likely that the Court condones such verdicts.

Eighth Amendment

Excessive bail shall not be required, nor excessive fines imposed, nor cruel and unusual punishments inflicted.

Original Meaning in 21st Century Plain English

Except for persons charged with crimes for which the maximum penalty is death, no person shall be held in prison without having bail set by a judge. Furthermore, judges shall not set bail higher than that which is reasonably sufficient to prevent persons accused of crimes from fleeing or hiding to avoid trial. Fines imposed shall not be excessive. Cruel and unusual punishments, such as crucifixion and burning to death, shall not be inflicted.

Discussion of the Eighth Amendment

The Judiciary Act of 1789 and the Northwest Ordinance of 1787 (reenacted in 1789) both provided the right to bail for all persons charged with noncapital crimes. [1039] The "Excessive bail shall not be required" provision of the Eighth Amendment was almost certainly intended and understood to mean that (1) people who are indicted for noncapital offenses have the right to be released from prison on bail while awaiting trial *if* they post bail or if someone else posts bail for them, and (2) judges shall not set bail in amounts higher than what is required to make it likely that accused persons will voluntarily return to court for their trial—thereby avoiding forfeiture of their bail.

Cruel and Unusual Punishment

A man named Stanislaus Roberts was convicted of first-degree murder and sentenced to death for killing a gas station attendant by shooting him in the head during an armed robbery in Louisiana in 1973.[1040] The Court set aside the death sentence in 1976, thereby reversing the Supreme Court of Louisiana.[1041] In setting aside the death sentence, the Court made the following illogical and unconstitutional ruling in *Roberts v. Louisiana:*

> "The prohibition against the infliction of cruel and unusual punishment under the Eighth and Fourteenth Amendments is violated by the imposition of the death sentence for the crime of first-degree murder under a state's statutory scheme

whereby (1) the death sentence is mandatory whenever the jury finds the defendant guilty of first-degree murder, (2) first-degree murder is defined to include the killing of a human being when the offender has a specific intent to kill or inflict great bodily harm, and when the murder involves killing in connection with the commission of certain felonies, killing a fireman or a peace officer in the performance of his duties, killing for remuneration, killing with the intent to inflict harm on more than one person, or killing by a person with a prior murder conviction or under a current life sentence, and (3) the jury in every first-degree murder case must be instructed on the crimes of first-degree murder, second-degree murder, and manslaughter, whether or not raised by the evidence or requested by the defendant, and must be provided with verdicts of guilty, guilty of second-degree murder, guilty of manslaughter, and not guilty."[1042]

That ruling is clearly unconstitutional because (1) the same Congress that framed the Eighth Amendment made murder, robbery, rape, and forgery of United States securities punishable by death when it enacted the Act of April 30, 1790,[1043] and (2) from 1789 through 1791, all states followed the common-law practice of mandatory death sentences for murder.[1044]

In 1800, John Fries was sentenced to death in a federal circuit court because he obstructed the enforcement of a federal tax law.[1045] President John Adams pardoned Fries despite the opposition of his Cabinet and Alexander Hamilton.[1046]

The Eighth Amendment not only condones capital punishment, if done in a manner which is not cruel and unusual, it also condones some forms of corporal punishment. Whipping was, by an act of Congress (the Crimes Act of April 30, 1790), part of the punishment for stealing or falsifying records.[1047] The Judiciary Act of 1789 gave the federal district courts jurisdiction of crimes for which the punishment was limited to whipping not exceeding thirty stripes, a fine not exceeding one hundred dollars, and imprisonment not exceeding six months.[1048] Federal circuit courts were authorized to try *all* federal crimes including those for which the death penalty could be imposed.[1049]

The framers considered capital punishment as cruel and unusual for failure to pay taxes or debts. During the Constitutional Convention, George Mason said: "To punish the non-payment of taxes with death, was a severity not yet adopted by despotism itself: yet this unexampled cruelty . . ."[1050] In 1787, people in all states could be put into prison for failure to pay debts. Debtors in Virginia were quite fortunate that Virginia law allowed debtors to be released from prison if they made "faithful delivery of their whole effects, . . . but any property they may afterward acquire will be subject to their creditors."[1051]

At least two framers were jailed for debt during the late 1790s. Robert Morris, Superintendent of Continental Finance during the Revolutionary War and U.S. senator from Pennsylvania from 1789 to 1795, spent three and one-half years in debtors' prison and was fortunate to be released from prison as a result of the Bankruptcy Act of 1800.[1052] James Wilson, a principal framer, was jailed for debt while he was a United States Supreme Court justice.[1053]

Ninth Amendment

The enumeration in the Constitution, of certain rights, shall not be construed to deny or disparage others retained by the people.

Original Meaning in 21st Century Plain English

Although the Constitution explicitly guarantees only some rights to citizens, the Constitution shall not be construed to deny or disparage other rights generally accepted in the United States in 1789. Rights retained by the citizens by virtue of this amendment include both common-law rights and those natural rights which are inalienable.

Discussion of the Ninth Amendment

The unamended Constitution explicitly guaranties only a few individual rights, including:

- The right to trial by jury in federal criminal cases

- The right against bills of attainder (State legislatures and Congress are prohibited from passing bills of attainder. Bills of attainder were passed by legislatures in America during the Revolutionary War to: (1) name Tories (people in America who wanted Americans to submit to Great Britain) and confiscate their property without a trial; and (2) name bandits and condemn them to death without a trial.[1054])

- The right against ex post facto laws (State legislatures and Congress are prohibited from passing ex post facto laws. An ex post facto law directs that punishments be imposed on people who did X before it was a crime to do X.)

Conspicuous by their absence in the unamended Constitution were many individual rights to which the citizens were accustomed. If what is now the Ninth Amendment was the only amendment that was proposed or ratified, it would have guarantied (1) almost all of the rights identified in the Bill of Rights, (2) common-law rights of 1789 which are not explicitly identified in the Bill of Rights or by the unamended Constitution, and (3) some natural rights—the "unalienable Rights" mentioned in the Declaration of Independence. The fact that some common-law rights are identified in the Bill of Rights only emphasizes them more than does the mighty Ninth Amendment.

Representative Roger Sherman, an influential framer of the unamended Constitution, wrote in his proposed draft of a bill of rights: "The people have certain natural rights which are retained by them when they enter into Society."[1055] Similar sentiments were expressed by several state ratifying conventions.[1056] The *first* right in a national bill of rights proposed by the Virginia Ratifying Convention was: "That there are certain natural rights of which men, when they form a social compact cannot deprive or divest their posterity, among which are the enjoyment of life and liberty, with the means of acquiring, possessing and protecting property, and pursuing and obtaining happiness and safety."[1057]

James Wilson, one of the principal framers of the unamended Constitution, stated: "Enumerate all the rights of men! I am sure, sirs, that no gentleman in the late [Constitutional] Convention would have attempted such a thing."[1058] The Declaration of Independence asserts "certain unalienable Rights, that among these are Life, Liberty, and the pursuit of Happiness. That to secure these rights, Governments are instituted . . ."

What would a majority of the framers and ratifiers of the Bill of Rights have agreed were inalienable rights? They would have agreed that inalienable rights were that portion of natural rights which are retained by people when they agree to form a government, because those rights are so fundamental they can never be given up. The doctrine of natural rights was developed during the seventeenth century. Let us briefly review that doctrine before getting more specific about natural rights.

The primary developers of the doctrine of natural rights were Thomas Hobbes and John Locke. Hobbes' 1651 book *Leviathan* postulates that in a state of nature (before the existence of government), the desire for self-preservation justified "the war of all against all."[1059] In a state of nature, "life is solitary, poor, nasty, brutish, and short." The desire for a happier life led to a civil society with government. According to Locke's 1690 book *Two Treatises of Government*, the primary duty of government is the protection of rights to life, liberty, and property.[1060] All governmental actions must be for the public good. When people choose to leave a state of nature in order to obtain a happier existence in a civil society under a good government, the people must agree to respect the rights of other people. In other words, people living under a good government must forego some natural rights. For example, people must agree to forego killing people for the purpose of taking their property.

What specific natural rights do citizens retain under all governments because such rights are inalienable? A majority of the framers and ratifiers of the Ninth Amendment would have been able to agree that inalienable rights include:

- The right to defend oneself when the government fails to do so (Blackstone's *Commentaries on the Laws of England* stated: "The right of the subjects, . . . of having arms for their defence . . . is indeed a public allowance . . . of the natural right of resistance and self-preservation when the sanctions of society and laws are found insufficient to restrain the violence of oppression. . . ."[1061]

- The "natural and unalienable right to the free exercise of religion according to the dictates of conscience, . . ." (That phrase was used by both the Virginia Ratifying Convention and the North Carolina Ratifying Convention, and is almost identical to a phrase used by the New York Ratifying Convention.[1062])

- The right to acquire property by peaceful means

- The right to use one's property to farm, obtain firewood, obtain lumber, construct buildings, etc.

Those rights which the framers and ratifiers considered to be inalienable natural rights may not be constitutionally violated by the federal government, state governments, or local governments. Unalienable natural rights were (1) assumed to exist in all republican governments, (2) an unwritten part of the Constitution, and (3) reassured by the Ninth Amendment.

The Court has never used the Ninth Amendment as its primary justification for an unenumerated right.[1063] However, the Ninth Amendment was one of several amendments cited by the Court in its attempt to justify an unenumerated right in one case. The year was 1965. The case was *Griswold v. Connecticut*. The unenumerated right is the right to marital privacy.

A Connecticut law banned the use of contraceptives. In *Griswold*, the Court ruled that law unconstitutional. Seven justices concurred with the ruling and two justices dissented.

In the majority opinion in *Griswold*, five justices found a right to marital privacy in "penumbras, formed by emanations from those guarantees" in the First, Third, Fourth, Fifth, and Ninth Amendments.[1064] "Penumbras, formed by emanations . . ."? Perhaps a seance was held. Maybe some of the old boys got into something they should not have gotten into.

The Ninth Amendment probably includes the right to marital privacy, but it does not include the right to contraceptives. If the federal government or any state government made the use of contraceptives mandatory, that would violate the Ninth Amendment inalienable natural right to have children.

It is unlikely that the Court will rely on the Ninth Amendment to justify unenumerated rights in the future. Why? There are two reasons. First, the Court has illegitimately used "due process" so often in its attempts to justify unenumerated rights that it has ceased to shock. (The Court will almost certainly continue to fraudulently employ "due process.") Second, the more the Court brings up the Ninth Amendment the more likely it will be that Americans will realize that the Ninth Amendment protects their right to have and use arms for self-defense.

Tenth Amendment

> The powers not delegated to the United States by the Constitution, nor prohibited by it to the States, are reserved to the States respectively, or to the people.

Original Meaning in 21st Century Plain English

All power is reserved to state governments except: (1) the power delegated to the federal government by the Constitution; (2) the power prohibited to state governments by the Constitution; (3) the power retained by the electorate (election power, jury power, and the power to alter government constitutions); (4) the power to violate the inalienable rights of American citizens; and (5) the power to violate the constitutional rights of American citizens.

Discussion of the Tenth Amendment

Many of the delegates to the state conventions which ratified the Constitution, especially those delegates who were also state legislators, were concerned that, if the Constitution was ratified, the federal government might interfere with the internal affairs of the states. Delegates who were also framers assured other delegates that the framers had no intention of interfering with the internal affairs of the states. Internal affairs include such things as intrastate commerce, morality laws, health laws, criminal laws, education laws, and infrastructure laws (laws to build roads, courts, jails, etc.).

The unamended Constitution was ratified based on the understanding that the federal government would not interfere with the internal affairs of the states unless (1) one or more nonrepublican state governments came into existence, (2) one or more republican state governments approved of federal involvement in quelling insurrections or obtaining land therein, or (3) a state violated the Constitution. The Tenth Amendment serves as the second of two guarantees that states with republican governments would retain control of their internal affairs as long as they acted constitutionally.

The Tenth Amendment was also understood to embody the principle that the electorate have the power to alter the constitutions under which they live. The Declaration of Independence stated:

> "We hold these truths to be self-evident, that all men . . . are endowed by their Creator with certain unalienable Rights, . . . That to secure these rights, Governments are instituted among Men, deriving their just powers from the consent of the governed. That whenever any form of Government becomes destructive of these ends, it is the Right of the People to alter or to abolish it, and to institute new Government, . . ."

In *The Federalist*, No. 78, Alexander Hamilton stated: "I trust the friends of the proposed Constitution will never concur with its enemies in questioning that fundamental principle of republican government which admits the right of the people to alter or abolish the established Constitution . . ."[1065]

The Virginia Ratifying Convention recommended the following amendment:

"That all power is naturally vested in and consequently derived from the people; . . . Government ought to be instituted for the common benefit, protection and security of the People; and that the doctrine of non-resistance against arbitrary power and oppression is absurd slavish, and destructive of the good and happiness of mankind. . . ."[1066]

The New York Ratifying Convention recommended:

"That the Powers of Government may be reassumed by the People, whensoever it shall become necessary to their Happiness; that every Power, Jurisdiction and right, which is not by the said Constitution clearly delegated to the Congress of the United States, or the departments of the Government thereof, remains to the People of the several States, or to their respective State Governments to whom they may have granted the same; . . ."[1067]

In *The Federalist*, No. 17, Alexander Hamilton stated: "The administration of private justice between citizens of the same State, the supervision of agriculture and of other concerns of a similar nature, all those things, in short, which are proper to be provided for by local legislation, can never be desirable cares of a general jurisdiction. . . ."[1068] It was understood that the only involvement in agriculture by the federal government would be to prevent states from imposing duties or discriminatory sales taxes on the agricultural products of other states or foreign countries. Nevertheless, the Court ruled in 1942 that the federal government could regulate agricultural production, even that production which was "wholly for consumption on the farm."[1069] Federal regulation of agricultural production, without an amendment to authorize it, is unconstitutional.

The Court ignored the original meaning of the Tenth Amendment in 1985 when it ruled that the San Antonio Metropolitan Transit Authority, deep in the heart of Texas, must abide by federal minimum wage laws.[1070] That Court ruling reversed a 1976 Court ruling which said that the Tenth Amendment was violated by a federal law which set labor standards for state and local government employees.[1071]

The federal government should have more power than is granted to it by the Constitution. Most Americans would probably be happy to support a Food and Drug Administration with limited powers. However, it is doubtful that most Americans would agree to give such an agency the power to prohibit drugs which the agency has not approved. Many people would like to have the option of taking the risks associated with new drugs when the alternatives seem to be worse. Some drugs which have been approved by the Food and Drug Administration (FDA) have proven to be unsafe. Almost all Americans would willingly support giving the FDA constitutional power to:

- Require packaged food producers to put on the food packages the very useful information normally shown (ingredients, saturated fat, total fat, sodium, dietary fiber, calories, etc.), check the accuracy of that information with independent tests, *publish* those test results, and require packaged food producers to correct inaccurate information.

- Require drug manufacturers to provide doctors, pharmacists, and drug consumers with the FDA's opinion of the benefits and risks of all drugs and the uncertainty of the FDA on the benefits and risks of all drugs.

Another unconstitutional federal agency which often operates in a way the framers would find inconsistent with liberty is the Fish and Wildlife Service. The February 2000 issue of *Reader's Digest* pointed out the outrageous nature of federal actions relevant to the "Delhi Sands flower-loving fly." A hospital in California was forced to move a construction site 300 feet to protect the fly—at a cost of three million dollars. Two construction projects in San Bernardino County were halted until such time as the county obtains at least one hundred million dollars to protect the fly. Sewer and flood-control projects have also been held up because of the fly. Sterling Burnett of the National Center for Policy Analysis was quoted by *Reader's*

Digest as saying: "If one of these flies came into your house, you would probably swat it and not know the difference. If Fish and Wildlife caught you, they could fine you $75,000 and you might have to spend a year in jail." There is obviously a lack of common sense in this unconstitutional agency of the federal government. There are several other unconstitutional federal agencies whose actions often display an utter lack of common sense.

No corporation would put up with the massive inefficiency of having fifty of its branches doing the same thing. Yet, we have at least fifty state organizations doing the same thing in many areas (setting child support policy, setting state education policy for grade schools and high schools, making drunk driving laws, etc.) in which it would make more sense to set policy at the federal level. States have done a terrible job in the humane aspects of sporting events. Athletes involved in horse racing (humans and horses), football, basketball, and other sports should not be permitted to participate with pain-reducing drugs or other drugs which have a detrimental effect on their future health. As much as federal agencies are desirable from efficiency and humane standpoints, we should make it constitutional for such agencies to be created before they are created.

Eleventh Amendment through Twenty-seventh Amendment

CHAPTER 11

Eleventh Amendment

> *The Judicial power of the United States shall not be construed to extend to any suit in law or equity, commenced or prosecuted against one of the United States by Citizens of another State, or by Citizens or Subjects of any Foreign State.*

Original Meaning in 21st Century Plain English

Federal courts shall not have the power to hear any lawsuit brought against any state by (1) citizens of another state, or (2) citizens or subjects of any foreign country.

Discussion of the Eleventh Amendment

The Eleventh Amendment was precipitated primarily by the 1793 case of *Chisholm v. Georgia*. In *Chisholm*, a lawsuit was brought against

323

the state of Georgia by the executor of an estate. The executor, a citizen of South Carolina, was trying to recover money Georgia owed for the delivery of supplies.[1072][1073] Georgia did not deny the debt, but claimed sovereign immunity. The right of all states to sovereign immunity was assured in no uncertain terms by Alexander Hamilton in *The Federalist*, No. 81. James Madison assured the right of states to sovereign immunity at the Virginia Ratifying Convention. Important sovereign immunity statements made by Hamilton and Madison are quoted in this book in the discussion of Article III, Section 2, Paragraph 1. When the Supreme Court ruled against Georgia, despite the fact that Georgia strongly protested the Court's taking jurisdiction in *Chisholm*, several other state legislatures passed resolutions of protest based on state sovereignty. As a result of the "tremendous repercussions throughout the United States" caused by *Chisholm*, Congress proposed the Eleventh Amendment in 1794.[1074] It became law in 1795.

Article III of the Constitution implies that the Court had the power to rule in *Chisholm*. Most framers of Article III *may* have intended for the Court to have original jurisdiction in cases such as *Chisholm*. However, many delegates at the ratifying conventions "expressed the opinion that Article III . . . of the Constitution did not authorize suits against a State by a private individual without the consent of the State."[1075]

If all framers of the unamended Constitution intended for the Court to rule in cases such as *Chisholm*, the Court should not have ruled in *Chisholm* or any other such cases. Why? Because the Constitution would not have been ratified by the requisite number of states if the ratifiers understood that the Court would have the power to rule in cases such as *Chisholm*.

In response to the Court's ruling in *Chisholm*, the Georgia House of Representatives passed a bill which stated: "any Federal Marshal or other person who executed any process issued by the Court in their Case should be declared guilty of felony and shall suffer death, without benefit of clergy, by being hanged."[1076] Although the Georgia Senate did not pass the bill, Georgia was *not* about to comply with the Court ruling.[1077]

The Eleventh Amendment implies that the Court misconstrued Article III when it decided to rule in *Chisholm*. That implication is correct, given the assurances made by framers and the understanding of ratifiers. The only legitimate constitutional power taken from the Court by the Eleventh Amendment was the power to rule in suits brought by nongovernmental, out-of-state parties against states that were willing to be defendants.

The phrase "any suit in law or equity" is used in the Eleventh Amendment. The term "lawsuit" is used in the twenty-first century to mean a "suit in law" or a "suit in equity."

Twelfth Amendment

The Electors shall meet in their respective states and vote by ballot for President and Vice-President, one of whom, at least, shall not be an inhabitant of the same state with themselves; they shall name in their ballots the person voted for as President, and in distinct ballots the person voted for as Vice-President, and they shall make distinct lists of all persons voted for as President, and all persons voted for as Vice-President, and of the number of votes for each, which lists they shall sign and certify, and transmit sealed to the seat of the government of the United States, directed to the President of the Senate;—The President of the Senate shall, in the presence of the Senate and House of Representatives, open all the certificates and the votes shall then be counted;—The person having the greatest number of votes for President, shall be the President, if such number be a majority of the whole number of Electors appointed; and if no person have such majority, then from the persons having the highest numbers not exceeding three on the list of those voted for as President, the House of Representatives shall choose immediately, by ballot, the President. But in choosing the President, the votes shall be taken by states, the representation from each state having one vote; a quorum for this purpose shall consist of a member or members from two-thirds of the states, and a majority of all the states shall be necessary to a choice. And if the House of Representatives shall not choose a President whenever the right of choice shall devolve upon them, before the fourth day of March next following, then the Vice-President shall act as President, as in the case of the death or other constitutional disability of the President.—The person having the greatest number of votes as Vice-President, shall be the Vice-President, if such number be a majority of the whole number of Electors appointed, and if no person have a majority, then from the two highest numbers on the list, the Senate shall choose the Vice-President; a quorum for the purpose shall consist of two-thirds of the whole number of Senators, and a majority of the whole number shall be necessary to a choice. But no person constitutionally ineligible to the office of President shall be eligible to that of Vice-President of the United States.

Original Meaning in 21st Century Plain English

The electoral college is composed of electors appointed as specified in Article II, Section 1, Paragraph 2. The members of the electoral college shall meet in their respective states, and:

- Each member of the electoral college shall vote by ballot for one person to be president of the United States and another person to be vice-president of the United States. At least one of the two persons voted for by each member of the electoral college must have their legal residence in a state other than the state in which the elector resides.

- The members of the electoral college shall make a list of all persons who received votes to be president of the United States by members of the electoral college in their state, specify the number of electoral votes for president received by each person, and identify this list as the presidential electoral vote list of their state.

- The members of the electoral college shall make a list of all persons who received votes to be vice-president of the United States by members of the electoral college in their state, specify the number of electoral votes for vice-president received by each person, and identify this list as the vice-presidential electoral vote list of their state.

- Each member of the electoral college shall sign and certify the presidential and vice-presidential electoral vote lists of their state. Those lists shall then be sealed and transmitted to the president of the Senate of the United States.

The president of the Senate shall, in the presence of the members of Congress, unseal the certified lists transmitted by the members of the electoral college. The electoral votes shall then be counted. If more than half of the members of the electoral college have voted for the same person to be president of the United States, that person shall be president of the United States. If more than half of the members of the electoral college have not voted for the same person to be president of the U.S., the House of Representatives shall choose one of the three persons with the most electoral votes for president of the U.S. to be president of the U.S. unless:

- There is a tie for third (In that case, the House of Representatives shall choose one of the two persons with the most electoral votes for president of the United States to be president of the United States.)

- Three or more persons are tied for second (In that case, the person receiving the most electoral votes for president of the United States shall be president of the United States.)

When the House of Representatives chooses the president of the United States:

- At least one representative from two-thirds of the states must be present.

- Each state shall have one vote.

- A majority of *all* states must vote for the same person to be president of the United States before that person shall be chosen as president of the United States.

When the House of Representatives has the responsibility to choose a president of the United States and the House fails to do so before the fourth day of March, the new vice-president shall act as president until such time as the House of Representatives chooses a president or a new president is elected in the next presidential election cycle.

If more than half of the members of the electoral college have voted for the same person to be vice-president, that person shall be vice-president of the United States. If no person receives the votes of more than half of the members of the electoral college for vice-president, the Senate shall choose the vice-president from among the two persons receiving the most electoral votes for vice-president.

When the Senate chooses a vice-president of the United States:

- At least two-thirds of the members of the Senate must be present.

- More than half of the members of the Senate must vote for the same person to be vice-president before that person can become vice-president. (The Senate does not vote for vice-president by state.)

A person who is constitutionally ineligible to be president of the United States shall be ineligible to be vice-president of the United States.

Discussion of the Twelfth Amendment

The Twelfth Amendment was precipitated by the presidential election of 1800 in which Thomas Jefferson and his running mate, Aaron Burr, tied for the largest number of electoral votes. Even though it was well understood that Jefferson was the presidential candidate of the Democratic-Republican party, and Burr the vice-presidential candidate, the presidential electors (members of the electoral college) were required to vote for two persons without specifying which office each was to fill. The framers of the unamended Constitution did not anticipate national political parties or vice-presidential candidates.

Because Jefferson and Burr were tied for the lead in electoral votes, and both had the electoral votes of a majority of the members of the electoral college, the House of Representatives had the responsibility to "immediately chuse by Ballot one of them for President," with "the Representation from each State having one Vote." A majority of the members of the "lame-duck" House of Representatives were members of the Federalist party. Many Federalist representatives conspired with Burr's political allies in the House to vote for Burr for president.[1078] On the first thirty ballots, eight states voted for Jefferson, six states voted for Burr, and two states, being evenly divided, cast no vote; nine votes were needed to elect a president.[1079] It took seven days and thirty-six ballots in the House before the issue was decided in Jefferson's favor.[1080] Ironically, it was the "vigorous action" of Jefferson's longtime political opponent Alexander Hamilton, a member of the Federalist party, which kept Burr from winning.[1081]

The unamended Constitution does not explicitly state any qualifications for vice-presidents. The Twelfth Amendment explicitly states that vice-presidents must be constitutionally qualified to be president of the United States.

The provision of the Twelfth Amendment which specified "the fourth day of March" was superseded by the Twentieth Amendment which specifies "noon on the 20th day of January."

Thirteenth Amendment

Section 1. Neither slavery nor involuntary servitude, except as a punishment for a crime whereof the party shall

> *have been duly convicted, shall exist within the United States, or any place subject to their jurisdiction.*
>
> *Section 2. Congress shall have power to enforce this article by appropriate legislation.*

Original Meaning in 21st Century Plain English

Neither slavery nor involuntary servitude shall exist within the United States, or any place subject to the jurisdiction of the United States, except as a punishment for a crime for which a person has been lawfully convicted. Congress shall have the power to make laws to enforce this amendment.

Discussion of the Thirteenth Amendment

The Thirteenth Amendment led to questions. Was it constitutional? Does Congress' power to make laws to enforce the Thirteenth Amendment go beyond providing sanctions against the kind of slavery that existed in the United States prior to the Civil War?

Most framers of the Thirteenth Amendment probably intended for it to give Congress the power to enact civil rights laws. However, many ratifiers understood that Congress' power under the Thirteenth Amendment was limited to making laws which set penalties for people who kept slaves or governments that allowed "formal slavery." Secretary of State William Seward coaxed legislators in the former Confederate states to ratify the Thirteenth Amendment by assuring them that, under it, Congress would only be allowed to enforce a prohibition of formal slavery.[1082] The understanding of many ratifiers dictates that Congress' only legitimate power under the Thirteenth Amendment is to enforce a prohibition of formal slavery and involuntary servitude except as lawful punishment for a person convicted of a crime. The Thirteenth Amendment would not have been voluntarily ratified by a sufficient number of states if the ratifiers understood that it would enable civil rights laws.

The constitutionality of the Thirteenth Amendment has been brought into question because President Andrew Johnson threatened legislators in former Confederate states with continued military rule if they failed to ratify the Thirteenth Amendment. [1083] For the Thirteenth Amendment to become law in 1865, at least twenty-seven of the thirty-six states needed to ratify. Secretary of State William Seward declared the Thirteenth Amendment to be "part of the Constitution" on December 18, 1865. At that time, 28 of 36 states had ratified, including eight of the eleven states in the former Confederacy. (Georgia became the 27th state to ratify on December 6, 1865, and Oregon became the 28th state to ratify on December 8, 1865.)

The threats made by President Johnson cast enough doubt on the constitutionality of the Thirteenth Amendment that the Court could have legitimately ruled it unconstitutional. However, the Thirteenth Amendment would have probably been ratified without Johnson's threats. Three Confederate states ratified the Thirteenth Amendment before the Civil War was over. Arkansas ratified within a week after General Robert E. Lee surrendered the Confederate Army at Appomattox on April 9, 1865. The Thirteenth Amendment was (1) ratified by Virginia on February 9, 1865, (2) ratified by Louisiana on February 17, 1865, (3) ratified by Tennessee on April 7, 1865, and (4) ratified by Arkansas on April 14, 1865.[1084] Only two states, Kentucky and Mississippi, voted to reject the Thirteenth Amendment.

"Fourteenth Amendment"

(The "Fourteenth Amendment" is not quoted herein because it is unconstitutional beyond all doubt.)

Why is the "Fourteenth Amendment" Unconstitutional?

The "Fourteenth Amendment" was proposed by the Thirty-ninth Congress, a "Congress" that was unconstitutional because it refused to seat the senators and representatives from the eleven states that had been part of the Confederacy during the Civil War. Those eleven states adopted new state constitutions in 1865 which abolished slavery and were perfectly compatible with the U.S. Constitution.[1085]

The Thirty-ninth "Congress" met for the first time on December 4, 1865. On that day, Congress unconstitutionally refused to seat the senators and representatives from the eleven former Confederate states.[1086] Thaddeus Stevens, one of the leaders in the "House of Representatives," said in "Congress" that the former Confederate states "ought never to be recognized as valid States, until the Constitution shall be amended . . . as to give perpetual ascendancy" to the Republican party.[1087] (At least Stevens was honest.) The Joint Committee on Reconstruction, created by "Congress" in December of 1865, was chaired by Representative Thaddeus Stevens and Senator William Fessenden.[1088]

Had the senators and representatives from the eleven Southern states been admitted to Congress in December of 1865, as required by the Constitution, the "Fourteenth Amendment" (proposed to the states by "Congress" in June of 1866) would not have been approved by two-thirds of either the Senate or the House of Representatives.[1089] The unconstitutional exclusion from "Congress" of the Southern senators and representatives is just one of the reasons the "Fourteenth Amendment" is absolutely invalid.

When "Congress" proposed the "Fourteenth Amendment" to the states, Tennessee ratified it and was immediately rewarded by having its U.S. senators and representatives seated in "Congress"; however, the other ten Southern states rejected the proposed "Fourteenth Amendment."[1090] "Congress" then brought out more unconstitutional artillery—enacting "laws" which said that each of the ten Southern states that rejected the proposed "Fourteenth Amendment" would be under military rule and unrepresented in Congress until (1) they ratified the proposed "Fourteenth Amendment," AND (2) the proposed "Fourteenth Amendment" became part of the Constitution of the United States.[1091] Furthermore, West Virginia (1) ratified the "Fourteenth Amendment," and (2) participated in its framing. The admission of West Virginia as a state in 1863 was unconstitutional, as shown herein in the discussion of Article IV, Section 3, Paragraph 1.

"Congress" declared the "Fourteenth Amendment" to be ratified on July 21, 1868. At that point, several states which had remained in the Union during the Civil War had not ratified. Those states were California, Delaware, Kentucky, and Maryland.[1092] Two Northern states that had ratified, Ohio and New Jersey, formally retracted their ratifications before July 21, 1868.[1093] Oregon formally retracted its ratification in October of 1868.

A constitutional amendment (or at least a relatively constitutional amendment) *something* along the lines of the "Fourteenth Amendment" could have been proposed by the Thirty-eighth Congress. What might such a version of the "Fourteenth Amendment" have included? Might it have included the right to vote for black men? No. Only six states had granted black men the vote by 1865.[1094] In the same "Congress" that proposed the "Fourteenth Amendment," the following amendment was proposed in the Senate: "No state, in prescribing the qualifications requisite for electors therein, shall discriminate against any person on account of color or race."[1095] It lost by a vote of thirty-seven to ten at a time when all twenty-two senators from the former Confederate states were unconstitutionally excluded from the "Senate."[1096]

Might a constitutional proposed amendment by the Thirty-eighth Congress in 1865 have included integrated public schools? No. Five of the states that remained in the Union during the Civil War excluded black children from public schools in 1865, and eight other Union states had segregated public schools in 1865.[1097] Furthermore, "Congress" permitted and supported segregated public schools in the District of Columbia at the same time "Congress" proposed the "Fourteenth Amendment" in 1866.[1098]

Might a constitutional proposed amendment by the Thirty-eighth Congress have made the states abide by the Bill of Rights? Yes. However, it is not known whether the "Fourteenth Amendment" was intended by a majority of its framers, or understood by a majority of its ratifiers, to impose the Bill of Rights on the states. Rather than *straining your brain* trying to resolve the intent and understanding of the "Fourteenth Amendment" relevant to the Bill of Rights, it is suggested that you accept the reality that the "Fourteenth Amendment" is extremely unconstitutional.

A constitutional proposed amendment in 1865 might have included the features of the Civil Rights Act of 1866. It gave to the former slaves the same rights as white citizens in (1) making contracts, (2) giving testimony in courts, and (3) purchasing, selling, and leasing property.

Fifteenth Amendment

> **Section 1. The right of citizens of the United States to vote shall not be denied or abridged by the United States or by any State on account of race, color, or previous condition of servitude.**
>
> **Section 2. The Congress shall have power to enforce this article by appropriate legislation.**

Original Meaning in 21st Century Plain English

Citizens of the United States shall not be prevented from voting in any election in the United States because of their race, color, or the fact that they were formerly a slave. Congress shall have the power to make laws to enforce this amendment.

Discussion of the Fifteenth Amendment

As of January 1869, only nine of the twenty-six states which had not previously seceded from the Union allowed black men to vote.[1099] Many states which had not granted suffrage to black men before 1869 had recently rejected referendums which would have given adult black males the right to vote.[1100] The issue of black suffrage was so touchy in 1868 that the Republican party platform endorsed the mandatory right to vote for blacks only in states which had been part of the Confederacy during the Civil War.[1101] How could Congress get a two-thirds majority of both houses to approve the Fifteenth Amendment during the first quarter of 1869? How could three-fourths of the state legislatures ratify it by February 3, 1870? Was there a sudden moral turnabout? No. It was politics. After their narrow vic-

tory in the 1868 presidential race, the Republicans came to the conclusion that it was essential for the future of the Republican party to
make more adult black males eligible to vote in many states that had
never been Confederate states.[1102]

The Fifteenth Amendment was proposed by Congress after several important compromises. To obtain enough votes in Congress, a
provision was dropped which would have outlawed literacy tests and
property qualifications.[1103] When the Senate voted thirty-one to
twenty-seven for an amendment to prohibit tests on the grounds of
"race, color, nativity, property, education or creed," it "aroused a storm
of protest throughout the country, especially in regard to the prohibition of educational tests."[1104] The loopholes in the Fifteenth
Amendment were solidified when a provision was defeated which
would have given the federal government authority over voter qualifications.[1105] The conference committee which finalized the Fifteenth
Amendment's language dropped a provision which would have
banned racial discrimination in determining qualifications to hold
office.[1106][1107]

The primary objective of the Fifteenth Amendment, clearly understood by its framers and ratifiers, was to increase the number of
black voters in states that had never been part of the Confederacy—
in order to help the Republican party remain strong.[1108] Many
Americans realized in 1870 that it was probably just a matter of time
before states which had been part of the Confederacy would take
advantage of the substantial loopholes in the Fifteenth Amendment
to constitutionally prevent many blacks from voting. Fifteenth
Amendment historian John Mathews wrote: "The form in which
the [Fifteenth] Amendment was moulded gave rise to a widespread
belief that it would be in large measure evaded. . . ."[1109]

Many reformers who had worked for the abolition of slavery and
had supported the Thirteenth Amendment refused to support the
Fifteenth Amendment.[1110] Women reformers had joined forces with
black men reformers in demanding universal suffrage. Many of those
women, including Susan B. Anthony and Elizabeth Cady Stanton,
expected black men reformers, including Frederick Douglass, to join
them in an "all or nothing" approach. When black men reformers

supported amendments "fourteen" and fifteen, many women reformers regarded it as disloyal. A split occurred among the reformers. Some white suffragettes, including Lucy Stone, supported ratification of the Fifteenth Amendment. The struggle over ratification of the Fifteenth Amendment was difficult and uncertain until the day it was ratified.[1111] Ironically, the efforts of Anthony and Stanton to prevent the Fifteenth Amendment from being ratified may have helped it get ratified. At that time, women suffrage was seen as "freakish by the masses" and ridiculed in newspapers.[1112] An 1869 Currier and Ives print ridiculed male allies of woman suffrage.[1113]

On March 30, 1870, Secretary of State Hamilton Fish certified that the Fifteenth Amendment had become a part of the Constitution.[1114] Four of the States that ratified prior to March 30, 1870, were Virginia, Mississippi, Georgia, and Texas.[1115] All four of those states were required by "Congress" to ratify the Fifteenth Amendment as a prerequisite to having their senators and representatives seated in Congress.[1116] Although Georgia was one of seven Southern states "readmitted" to the United States by "Congress" in June of 1868, by the end of 1868 "Congress" placed Georgia under military rule because the Georgia legislature expelled many of its black legislators.[1117] It was necessary for twenty-eight states to ratify the Fifteenth Amendment for it to become part of the Constitution in 1870.[1118] As of March 30, 1870, thirty states had ratified, including the four states which had ratified under duress and New York. (New York, which had ratified in 1869, "withdrew" its consent on January 5, 1870. It is not constitutional for a state to withdraw its consent to an amendment. The "withdrawal" by New York indicates that the "Fifteenth Amendment" was quite controversial.)

The Fifteenth Amendment is illegitimate because the states of Georgia, Mississippi, Texas, and Virginia:

• Were unconstitutionally denied representation in Congress at the time that the Fifteenth Amendment was proposed by "Congress" (If all eight senators had voted against the Fifteenth Amendment, it would have been one vote short of getting a two-thirds majority in the Senate—unless another senator switched sides.)

- Were under unconstitutional duress to ratify the Fifteenth Amendment (If none of these four states ratified the Fifteenth Amendment, the requisite number of states would probably not have ratified during the nineteenth century.)

However, the Fifteenth Amendment is not illegitimate to the extent that the "Fourteenth Amendment" is illegitimate. The Fifteenth Amendment can be likened to driving 30 miles per hour in a 20 mile per hour school zone, and the "Fourteenth Amendment" as driving 90 miles per hour in a 20 mile per hour school zone.

At the time that the Fifteenth Amendment was framed and ratified, most senators and representatives from the two Pacific Coast states wanted to withhold suffrage from Chinese people. (Washington did not become a state until 1889.) The following resolution was made in the House of Representatives in 1869: "Resolved, that in passing the . . . Fifteenth Amendment . . . this House never intended that Chinese or Mongolians should become voters"; that resolution was defeated 106 to 42.[1119] California and Oregon rejected the Fifteenth Amendment by substantial majorities in both chambers of their state legislatures.[1120]

Sixteenth Amendment

The Congress shall have power to lay and collect taxes on incomes, from whatever source derived, without apportionment among the several States, and without regard to any census or enumeration.

Original Meaning in 21st Century Plain English

Congress shall have the power to impose and collect taxes on incomes of all entities (people, corporations, etc.) from all sources, and the total federal income tax receipts from all entities in state X do *not* have to be proportional to the population of state X.

Discussion of the Sixteenth Amendment

In one of the best examples of how constitutional problems have been resolved, the Sixteenth Amendment became law in 1913 after being proposed to the state legislatures by Congress in 1909.

In 1894, Congress for the first time enacted a federal income tax law during peacetime. It was not apportioned. An apportioned income tax could *not* have been enacted in 1894 because the per capita income in most states was significantly lower than the national average. (A person who lived in Mississippi would have had to pay a *much* higher tax than a person who had the same income and lived in New York.) In the extremely important 1895 case of *Pollock v. Farmers' Loan & Trust Co.*,[1121] the Court ruled that the 1894 federal income tax law was unconstitutional. Although the income tax imposed by Congress in 1894 was only two percent on all incomes larger than four thousand dollars, *Pollock* was understood to have great importance for the future. It received major newspaper coverage, and many Americans had intense feelings about it.[1122] Many Americans saw the peacetime income tax as the beginning of socialism or communism. Many Americans saw the tax as necessary to reduce the enormous disparities of wealth.

The Court's ruling in *Pollock* had three parts. In part one, the Court voted eight to zero: "A [federal] tax upon the income derived from municipal bonds is a tax on the power of the states and their instrumentalities to borrow money and is consequently repugnant to the U. S. Constitution." In part two, the Court voted six to two that a federal tax on the income from real estate is a direct tax within the meaning of the Constitution and is invalid unless it is apportioned. That ruling was partially correct. Framers and ratifiers of the unamended Constitution considered federal taxes on real estate (land and buildings) to be direct taxes which needed to be apportioned to be constitutional. Federal taxes on rental income from real estate are effectively real estate taxes. However, federal taxes on net income above fair rental value of real estate are not real estate taxes. If a store owned by its proprietor had a net income of $90,000 during a tax year and the fair rental value of that store was $20,000 for that tax year, a tax on $70,000 would not be a real estate tax.

The Court tied four to four on other issues, including the key issue of whether taxes on income from personal property (all property except real estate) was a direct tax. The Court heard those issues again and voted five to four that: (1) federal taxes on "the income from personal property (stocks, bonds, ships, etc.) are . . . direct taxes"; and (2) the federal income tax law of 1894 was invalid because key sections were unconstitutional and all sections were "mutually connected with and dependent on each other, as conditions, considerations for each other, . . ." The Court should not have ruled that taxes on income from personal property were direct taxes because nobody knows that the framers or ratifiers understood such a thing.

Pollock was a major victory for the wealthy at a time when trusts were stifling competition in the United States. The flames of Populist discontent in the U.S. were fanned by *Pollock*, especially in the "West and South."[1123]

Seventeenth Amendment

The Senate of the United States shall be composed of two Senators from each State, elected by the people thereof, for six years; and each Senator shall have one vote. The electors in each State shall have the qualifications requisite for electors of the most numerous branch of the State legislatures.

When vacancies happen in the representation of any State in the Senate, the executive authority of each State shall issue writs of election to fill such vacancies: Provided, That the legislature of any State may empower the executive thereof to make temporary appointments until the people fill the vacancies by election as the legislature may direct.

This amendment shall not be so construed as to affect the election or term of any Senator chosen before it becomes valid as part of the Constitution.

Original Meaning in 21st Century Plain English

All Americans who are eligible to vote for members of the most numerous branch of a state legislature shall have the opportunity to vote in elections of members of the United States Senate from their state.

When any state has less than two senators in the U.S. Senate, elections shall be held to fill the vacancy. However, the legislature of state X may empower the governor of state X to make temporary appointments to the U.S. Senate until such time as an election is held in compliance with state law.

This amendment shall not affect the election or term of any senator chosen before this amendment is ratified.

Discussion of the Seventeenth Amendment

Some provisions of the Seventeenth Amendment are redundant. The redundant provisions are (1) two senators from each state, (2) six-year terms for U.S. senators, and (3) one vote for each U.S. senator. The Constitution would have the same meaning if these provisions were not included in the Seventeenth Amendment. (They are included in Article I, Section 3.)

The Seventeenth Amendment was proposed in 1912 and ratified in 1913. Twenty-nine of the forty-eight states in existence in 1912 had given the electorate the power to elect U.S. senators before Congress proposed the Seventeenth Amendment.[1124] Why did so many state legislatures voluntarily give up the power to choose U.S. senators? One of the main reasons was that there were many scandals about the buying and selling of seats in the U.S. Senate.[1125]

Direct election of senators did not become a major political issue until late in the nineteenth century when newspaper articles pointed out that the undue influence of corporate monopolies and trusts prevented legislation in the public interest.[1126] Corporations gave money to political bosses who chose U.S. senators. Those senators almost always acted as corporations and wealthy Americans wanted them to act. Many reformers maintained that direct election of senators would eliminate the influence of special interests.[1127] A major factor in the movement to democratize the Senate was the difficulty of getting tax reforms, including income taxes, through the Senate.[1128]

In the House of Representatives in 1892 Representative Babbit said that the issue of direct election of senators was a war between "capital and the people."[1129] Representative Grantz spoke of the "corrupt use of money in politics."[1130] Representative Tucker said: "Combinations of wealth . . . when they . . . seek to control, against the interests of the people, the legislation of the country, . . . they will meet with the indignant protests of all true friends of the people."[1131]

Direct election of senators was a great victory for those who advocated public-interest legislation. It substantially reduced the undue influence of special interests. However, it certainly did not eliminate the undue influence of special interests. The problem may never be totally solved, but another major step would be made if the United States adopts campaign finance reform such as exists in the United Kingdom.

Eighteenth Amendment

Section 1. After one year from the ratification of this article the manufacture, sale, or transportation of intoxicating liquors within, the importation thereof into, or the exportation thereof from the United States and all territory subject to the jurisdiction thereof for beverage purposes is hereby prohibited.

Section 2. The Congress and the several States shall have concurrent power to enforce this article by appropriate legislation.

Section 3. This article shall be inoperative unless it shall have been ratified as an amendment to the Constitution by the legislatures of the several States, as provided in the Constitution, within seven years from the date of the submission hereof to the States by the Congress.

Original Meaning in 21st Century Plain English

This amendment:

- Prohibits the manufacture of alcoholic beverages in the United States and all other places (Alaska, etc.) subject to the jurisdiction of the United States

- Prohibits the importation of alcoholic beverages into the United States and all other places subject to the jurisdiction of the United States

- Prohibits the exportation of alcoholic beverages from the United States and all other places subject to the jurisdiction of the United States

- Prohibits the sale of alcoholic beverages within the United States and all other places subject to the jurisdiction of the United States

- Prohibits the transportation of all alcoholic beverages within the United States and all other places subject to the jurisdiction of the United States

- Shall take effect one year after it is ratified by the legislatures of three-fourths of the states *if* it is ratified by the legislatures of at least three-fourths of the states within seven years of the date it is proposed by Congress (If this proposed amendment is not ratified by the legislatures of at least three-fourths of the states within seven years of the date it is proposed by Congress, it shall not become law.)

- May be enforced by statutes enacted by Congress and by statutes enacted by state legislatures

Discussion of the Eighteenth Amendment

The proposal of the Eighteenth Amendment in 1917 was the climax of a movement which had begun more than half a century before.[1132] The "Daughters of Temperance" formed a secret society favoring prohibition of alcoholic beverages in 1846.[1133] In 1869, the National Prohibition Party was formed, and, in 1872, nominated its first presidential candidate.[1134] The National Prohibition Party did not become a major party. The majority of Americans who supported prohibition in the 1870s were women, and women could not vote in national elections during that decade. It was because of support for prohibition by many women that manufacturers of alcoholic beverages opposed giving women the right to vote.

Support for prohibition grew among men and women. Many states, by referendum, prohibited the buying, selling, and transportation of alcoholic beverages. At least thirty-two states out of forty-eight were "dry" in 1917 when Congress proposed the Eighteenth Amendment.[1135] It became law thirteen months later. It is ironic that the Eighteenth Amendment was proposed and ratified before women had the right to vote throughout the United States, and the Eighteenth Amendment was repealed after women gained the right to vote throughout the United States. The Eighteenth Amendment is the only amendment that has ever been *constitutionally* repealed. (The Second, Ninth, and Tenth Amendments have been unconstitutionally repealed.)

The Eighteenth Amendment is the first amendment with a deadline for its ratification. The ratification deadline was seven years after it was proposed to the state legislatures by Congress. Some subsequent proposed amendments included ratification deadlines and some did not. When ratification deadlines were used during the twentieth century, they were always seven years after Congress proposed the amendments.

Nineteenth Amendment

The right of citizens of the United States to vote shall not be denied or abridged by the United States or by any State on account of sex.

Congress shall have power to enforce this article by appropriate legislation.

Original Meaning in 21st Century Plain English

Citizens of the United States shall not be prevented from voting in any election because of their sex. Congress shall have the power to make laws to force all governments in the United States to abide by this amendment.

Discussion of the Nineteenth Amendment

Women could vote in the state of New Jersey from 1776 until they lost the right to vote in a state constitutional amendment in 1807.[1136] Between 1807 and 1890, no state allowed women to vote in all elections. In 1890, Wyoming joined the Union as a state which gave women the right to vote in all elections.[1137] The state of Colorado provided full voting equality in 1893, and the states of Utah and Idaho did so in 1896, making a total of four; the total remained at four for about fourteen years.[1138] Full voting equality for women was obtained in Washington in 1910, California in 1911, Arizona, Kansas, and Oregon in 1912, Montana and Nevada in 1914, New York in 1917, and Michigan, Oklahoma, and South Dakota in 1918.[1139]

By the time the Nineteenth Amendment became law in 1920, women were allowed to vote in at least some elections in most states.[1140] Ratification of the Nineteenth Amendment marked the climax of an enormous struggle led by women such as Susan B. Anthony and Elizabeth Cady Stanton. Millions of Americans, women and men, supported the struggle for women suffrage, and many of them were subjected to ridicule. The Nineteenth Amendment is a monument to proper way to amend the Constitution. It fully complies with Article V despite the enormous difficulties of getting it adopted.

Twentieth Amendment

Section 1. The terms of the President and Vice President shall end at noon on the 20th day of January, and the terms of Senators and Representatives at noon on the 3d day of January, of the years in which such terms would have ended if this article had not been ratified; and the terms of their successors shall then begin.

Section 2. The Congress shall assemble at least once every year, and such meeting shall begin at noon on the 3d day of January, unless they shall by law appoint a different day.

Section 3. If, at the time fixed for the beginning of the term of the President, the President elect shall have died, the Vice President elect shall become President. If a President shall not have been chosen before the time fixed for the beginning of his term, or if the President elect shall have failed to qualify, then the Vice President elect shall act as President until a new President shall have qualified; and the Congress may by law provide for the case wherein neither a President elect nor a Vice President elect shall have qualified, declaring who shall then act as President, or the manner in which one who is to act shall be selected, and such person shall act accordingly until a President or Vice President shall have qualified.

Section 4. The Congress may by law provide for the case of the death of any of the persons from whom the House of Representatives may choose a President whenever the right of choice shall have devolved upon them, and for the case of the death of any of the persons from whom the Senate may choose a Vice President whenever the right of choice shall have devolved upon them.

Section 5. Sections 1 and 2 shall take effect on the 15th day of October following the ratification of this article.

Section 6. This article shall be inoperative unless it shall have been ratified as an amendment to the Constitution by the legislatures of three-fourths of the several States within seven years from the date of its submission.

Original Meaning in 21st Century Plain English

The terms of the president and vice-president of the United States shall end at noon on the twentieth day of January of the years in which such terms would have ended if this amendment had not been ratified, and the terms of their successors shall then begin. The terms of the senators and representatives shall end at noon on the third day of January of the years in which such terms would have ended if this amendment had not been ratified, and the terms of their successors shall then begin. The dates specified in this paragraph become effective on the fifteenth day of October following the ratification of this proposed amendment by the legislatures of three-fourths of the states *if* this proposed amendment is ratified by the legislatures of three-fourths of the states within seven years of the time it is proposed.

Congress shall meet at noon on the third day of January of every year unless Congress passes a law to specify a different day or time for its mandatory annual assembly. The date specified in this paragraph shall become effective on the fifteenth day of October following the ratification of this proposed amendment by the legislatures of three-fourths of the states *if* this proposed amendment is ratified by the legislatures of three-fourth of the states within seven years of the time it is proposed.

If the president-elect of the United States dies before being sworn in as president, the vice-president-elect shall be sworn in as president at noon on the same day that the president-elect would have been sworn in. If a president is not chosen by the time fixed for the beginning of a new presidential term, or if the president-elect does not have the qualifications specified by the Constitution, the vice-president-elect shall act as president until either a president is chosen or the president-elect becomes constitutionally qualified. If neither the president-elect nor the vice-president-elect are constitutionally qualified for the office of president of the United States, Congress may enact a law to declare who should act as president, or specify a process to determine who should act as president until the president elect or vice-president-elect is constitutionally qualified to hold the office of president of the United States.

Congress has the power to enact laws which specify:

- How the House of Representatives is impacted in their choice of president by the death of any of the persons whom the House would have had the constitutional power to select as president
- How the Senate is impacted in their choice of vice-president by the death of any of the persons from whom the Senate would have had the constitutional power to choose as vice-president

This proposed amendment shall not take effect unless it is ratified by the legislatures of at least three-fourths of the states within seven years of the date it is proposed by Congress.

Discussion of the Twentieth Amendment

From 1790 to 1933, "lame-duck" sessions of Congress began on the first Monday in December of even-numbered years and ended about three months later, just prior to the expiration of the terms of members of the House of Representatives on March 4. Congress did not meet again until the first Monday in December unless a special session of Congress was called. Therefore, first-term members of Congress were usually not seated in Congress until about thirteen months after they were elected.

Congress, under the Articles of Confederation, chose the first Wednesday in March to begin government under the Constitution. The first Wednesday in March occurred on March 4 in 1789. The beginning and ending of all full terms of members of Congress and presidents took place on March 4 until the Twentieth Amendment took effect.

"Lame-duck" sessions of Congress were controversial as far back as 1801 when the "lame-duck" House of Representatives came close to selecting Aaron Burr to be president over Thomas Jefferson, even though Burr was Jefferson's vice-presidential running mate. Despite the large Republican victory in 1800, the "lame-duck," Federalist-controlled Congress of 1800–1801: (1) created 16 new federal judgeships, thereby nearly doubling the size of the federal judiciary (The lame-duck Senate confirmed Federalists for all 16 new judgeships in 1801.); and (2) created an unlimited number of justice of the peace positions for the District of Columbia. The lame-duck Senate confirmed 42 justices of the peace—the large majority of whom were Federalists. Four of the 42 were involved in *Marbury v. Madison*, an intriguing case discussed in Appendix B of this book.

To avoid legislation by "lame-duck" Congresses, filibustering was often employed by members of Congress who were members of the political party which would soon have increased strength in Congress.

The Twentieth Amendment eliminated "lame-duck" sessions of Congress unless special "lame-duck" sessions are called. It also reduced "lame-duck" presidential terms by 45 days. The ratification of the Twentieth Amendment was spurred by a desire to reduce the length of time a president serves after another president is elected. In the interval between the election of Franklin D. Roosevelt in 1932 and his inauguration on March 4, 1933, the American banking system essentially shut down.[1141]

Virginia became the first state to ratify the Twentieth Amendment when it did so on March 4, 1932. Alabama became the seventeenth state to ratify on September 13, 1932. No more states ratified until California did so on January 4, 1933. An extraordinary twenty-five states ratified in January of 1933. Utah provided the necessary thirty-sixth ratification on January 23, 1933. On that day, there were 42 days left in the term of President Herbert Hoover. Unfortunately, the Twentieth Amendment would not go into effect until October 15, 1933. By the time President Franklin Roosevelt was inaugurated on March 4, 1933, banks were shut down in thirty-two of the forty-eight states. Almost all banks in six other states were shut down. In the remaining states, banking was severely restricted. About five thousand banks had failed in the United States during the prior three years. America was, in the words of historian David Kennedy, "a wasteland of economic devastation."[1142]

Shortly after Roosevelt defeated President Hoover in 1932, Hoover took the unprecedented step of seeking the advice of the president-elect.[1143] President-elect Roosevelt refused to do anything to help reduce the severe economic problems. He would not even make a reassuring statement. Because the president-elect refused to cooperate or lead, the president could not lead.[1144]

On March 5, 1933, President Roosevelt; (1) called Congress into a special session to start on March 9, 1933, and (2) invoked the Trading with the Enemy Act to declare a four-day national banking holiday and stop all transactions in gold.[1145] Hoover had urged Roosevelt to endorse those actions in the preceding weeks.[1146] Roosevelt's men and Hoover's men joined forces in an intense effort to work out the details of an emergency banking bill. They worked night and day in a truly bipartisan manner to just barely get a bill (The Emergency Banking Act) to Congress by the time it convened at noon on March 9. The bill was approved by Congress on March 9, and President Roosevelt signed it into law on March 9. The American economy was saved, but Americans did not have to go through such an ordeal.

To his credit, Roosevelt made good use of the ideas of Hoover. One of Roosevelt's top men, Rexford G. Tugwell, despite his criticisms of Hoover's economic plan in the January 1932 issue of *Current History*, later said; "practically the whole New Deal was extrapolated from programs that Hoover started. . . ."[1147] Unfortunately, much of the New Deal was unconstitutional. If Roosevelt and Hoover had agreed on potential economic remedies one month before Roosevelt's inauguration, constitutional amendments to authorize Congress to enact those remedies would have probably been ratified by the time Roosevelt became president.

As good as the Twentieth Amendment is, it would probably be even better to supersede it with an amendment to seat members of Congress about one month after general elections. Such an amendment might provide that presidential terms begin on the second day of January.

Twenty-first Amendment

Section 1. The eighteenth article of amendment to the Constitution of the United States is hereby repealed.

Section 2. The transportation or importation into any State, Territory, or possession of the United States for delivery or use therein of intoxicating liquors, in violation of the laws thereof, is hereby prohibited.

Section 3. This article shall be inoperative unless it shall have been ratified as an amendment to the Constitution by conventions in the several States, as provided in the Constitution, within seven years from the date of the submission hereof to the States by the Congress.

Original Meaning in 21st Century Plain English

The Eighteenth Amendment of the United States Constitution is hereby repealed.

It shall be a violation of the United States Constitution for any person to either transport or import alcoholic beverages into state A for delivery or use in state A in violation of the laws of state A. Likewise, it shall be a violation of the U.S. Constitution for any person to transport or import alcoholic beverages into any U.S. territory or U.S. possession for delivery or use therein in violation of the laws thereof.

In order for this amendment proposal to become an amendment, it must be ratified by conventions of at least three-fourths of the states within seven years of the date it is proposed by Congress.

Discussion of the Twenty-first Amendment

The Twenty-first Amendment is the only one of the first twenty-seven amendments to involve state ratifying conventions. Thirty-eight states held elections in 1933 for delegates to the conventions, and a whopping seventy-three percent of the voters voted for candidates who favored ending national prohibition.[1148] The good that prohibition did was widely considered to be outweighed by the increase in criminal activity, disrespect for law, and loss of revenue. It made more sense to most voters to make alcoholic beverages legal, collect excise taxes, and decrease criminal activity.

During a debate in the U.S. House of Representatives on a U.S. Senate resolution that was to become the Twenty-first Amendment, Representative Emmanuel Celler said that repeal of the Eighteenth Amendment would "not mean the return of liquor, since liquor has always been with us; its flow has never been dammed. Prohibition simply opened the sluices. New York City had 26,000 saloons before prohibition; it now has over 32,000 speakeasies."[1149] About five times as many Americans under the age of twenty-one were arrested for drunkenness in the ten years after prohibition than in the ten years before prohibition.[1150] Representative Cellar had good reason to say: "Save the youth of the Nation by voting for this resolution."[1151]

The Twenty-first Amendment specifies that violations of certain kinds of state prohibition laws would also be a violation of the U.S. Constitution. Members of Congress in 1933 realized that the federal government would have no constitutional authority to help enforce state prohibition without Section 2 of the Twenty-first Amendment. The United States had no legitimate authority to limit interstate commerce of alcoholic beverages until one year after the Eighteenth Amendment was ratified, and the U.S. would have had no such authority after the Twenty-first Amendment was ratified if Section 2 had been omitted.

Twenty-second Amendment

Section 1. No person shall be elected to the office of the President more than twice, and no person who has held the office of President, or acted as President, for more than two years of a term to which some other person was elected President shall be elected to the office of President more than once. But this Article shall not apply to any person holding the office of President when this Article was proposed by the Congress, and shall not prevent any person who may be holding the office of President, or acting as President, during the term within which this Article becomes operative from holding the office of Presi-

> dent or acting as President during the remainder of such term.
>
> *Section 2. This article shall be inoperative unless it shall have been ratified as an amendment to the Constitution by the legislatures of three-fourths of the several States within seven years from the date of its submission to the States by the Congress.*

Original Meaning in 21st Century Plain English

No person shall be elected to the office of president of the United States more than twice. No person shall be elected to the office of president more than once if that person (1) held the office of president for more than two years of a presidential term to which someone else was elected, or (2) acted as president for more than two years of a presidential term to which someone else was elected. However, this amendment shall not apply to the person holding the office of president when this amendment was proposed by Congress. Furthermore, this amendment shall not prevent any person who is president or acting president from remaining in office during the term within which this amendment becomes law.

This amendment shall not take effect unless it is ratified by the legislatures of three-fourths of the states within seven years of the date it is proposed to the states by Congress.

Twenty-third Amendment

> *Section 1. The District constituting the seat of Government of the United States shall appoint in such manner as the Congress may direct:*
>
> *A number of electors of President and Vice president equal to the whole number of Senators and Representatives in Congress to which the District would be entitled if it were a State, but in no event more than the least populous State; they shall be in addition to those appointed by*

the States, but they shall be considered, for the purposes of the election of the President and Vice President, to be electors appointed by a State; and they shall meet in the District and perform such duties as provided by the twelfth article of amendment.

Section 2. The Congress shall have power to enforce this article by appropriate legislation.

Original Meaning in 21st Century Plain English

The District of Columbia, as long as it remains the seat of the United States government, shall appoint, in such manner as Congress may direct, the same number of electoral college members as if it were a state. However, in no event shall the District have more members of the electoral college than the least populous state. The members of the electoral college appointed by the District shall be in addition to those appointed by the states. Each member of the electoral college from the District shall have the same power as a member of the electoral college from a state. The members of the electoral college which are appointed by the District shall meet in the District and perform the duties specified by the Twelfth Amendment. If the seat of the United States government should be relocated to another district which is not part of a state, the new district shall appoint members of the electoral college as provided in this amendment. Congress shall have the power to enact laws to enforce this amendment

Discussion of the Twenty-third Amendment

The Twenty-third Amendment allows the District of Columbia to participate in the election of the president and vice-president of the United States. Even though this amendment effectively limits the District to three electoral votes in the electoral college, it guarantees the District three electoral votes. The District, like many of the less populated states, has disproportionate power in the election of the president and vice-president. However, the District has no power in Congress. The less populated states have disproportionate power in Congress. The Twenty-third Amendment was proposed by Congress in 1960 and ratified by a sufficient number of states in 1961.

Although the District of Columbia was initially a ten-mile square (100 square miles), it was reduced to 69 square miles in 1846 when the portion on the Virginia side of the Potomac River was returned to Virginia. Most counties in the United States are much larger than 69 square miles.

In 1978, Congress proposed an amendment which would have given the District of Columbia (1) representation in Congress as if it were a state, and (2) the power to ratify constitutional amendments as if it were a state.[1152] That proposed amendment was not ratified by three-fourths of the states within the seven-year deadline specified in the proposed amendment; it is one of only six amendments proposed to the states by Congress which has not been ratified by a sufficient number of states to become law.[1153]

Twenty-fourth Amendment

> **Section 1. The right of citizens of the United States to vote in any primary or other election for President or Vice President, for electors for President or Vice President, or for Senator or Representative in Congress, shall not be denied or abridged by the United States or any State by reason of failure to pay any poll tax or other tax.**
>
> **Section 2. The Congress shall have power to enforce this article by appropriate legislation.**

Original Meaning in 21st Century Plain English

Failure to pay a poll tax or any other tax shall not be used as a reason to deny any citizen of the United States their right to vote in any primary or other election for (1) president or vice-president of the United States, (2) electors for president or vice-president of the

United States, or (3) a member of the United States Congress. Congress shall have the power to make laws to enforce this amendment.

Discussion of the Twenty-fourth Amendment

Prior to 1964, several states, consistent with their constitutional power, established poll taxes for all elections. The Twenty-fourth Amendment, which became law in 1964, prohibited states from preventing people from voting in federal elections because of failure to pay poll taxes or any other taxes. A few states continued to employ poll taxes in state elections. In 1966, the Court unconstitutionally ruled, in *Harper v. Virginia Board of Elections*, that poll taxes in state elections violated the U.S. Constitution.

Twenty-fifth Amendment

Section 1. In case of the removal of the President from office or his death or resignation, the Vice President shall become President.

Section 2. Whenever there is a vacancy in the office of the Vice President, the President shall nominate a Vice President who shall take office upon confirmation by a majority vote of both Houses of Congress.

Section 3. Whenever the President transmits to the President pro tempore of the Senate and the Speaker of the House of Representatives his written declaration that he is unable to discharge the powers and duties of his office, and until he transmits to them a written declaration to the contrary, such powers and duties shall be discharged by the Vice President as Acting President.

Section 4. Whenever the Vice President and a majority of either the principal officers of the executive departments or of such other body as Congress may by law provide, transmit to the President pro tempore of the Senate and the Speaker of the House of Representatives their written declaration that the President is unable to discharge the powers and duties of his office, the Vice President shall immediately assume the powers and duties of the office as Acting President.

Thereafter, when the President transmits to the President pro tempore of the Senate and the Speaker of the House of Representatives his written declaration that no inability exists, he shall resume the powers and duties of his office unless the Vice President and a majority of either the principal officers of the executive department or of such other body as Congress may by law provide, transmit within four days to the President pro tempore of the Senate and the Speaker of the House of Representatives their written declaration that the President is unable to discharge the powers and duties of his office. Thereupon Congress shall decide the issue, assembling within forty-eight hours for that purpose if not in session. If the Congress, within twenty-one days after receipt of the latter written declaration, or, if Congress is not in session, within twenty-one days after Congress is required to assemble, determine by two-thirds vote of both Houses that the President is unable to discharge the powers and duties of his office, the Vice President shall continue to discharge the same as Acting President; otherwise, the President shall resume the powers and duties of his office.

Original Meaning in 21st Century Plain English

The vice-president shall become president of the United States whenever the president of the United States dies, resigns, or is removed from office because of being convicted by the Senate of an impeachment charge brought by the House of Representatives.

Whenever the vice-president dies, resigns, is removed from office, or becomes president of the U.S., the president of the U.S. shall nominate a vice-president. If the nominee is approved by a majority of both Houses of Congress, the nominee shall become vice-president.

Whenever the president of the United States transmits to the president pro tempore of the Senate and the speaker of the House of Representatives his written declaration that he is unable to discharge the powers and duties of his office, the vice-president shall be acting president of the United States until (1) the president of the United States transmits to the president pro tempore of the Senate and the speaker of the House of Representatives his written declaration that he is able to discharge the powers and duties of his office, or (2) the term of the president of the United States ends.

Whenever the vice-president and a majority of either the Cabinet (the principal officers of the executive departments) or another group that Congress, by law, designates to make recommendations as to whether or not the president of the United States is fit to perform all presidential duties, transmit to the president pro tempore of the Senate and the speaker of the House of Representatives their written declaration that the president of the United States is unable to perform all presidential duties, the vice-president shall immediately become acting president of the United States. Thereafter, when the president of the United States transmits to the president pro tempore of the Senate and the speaker of the House of Representatives a written declaration that he is able to discharge the powers and duties of his office, he shall resume the powers and duties of his office unless the vice-president and a majority of either the Cabinet or a group that Congress designates to make recommendations as to whether or not the president is fit to perform all presidential duties, transmits, within four days, to the president pro tempore of the Senate and the speaker of the House of Representatives, their written declaration that the president of the United States is unable to perform all presidential duties. If such a difference of opinion exists, Congress shall decide the issue. For that purpose, Congress shall meet within forty-eight hours even if Congress is not in session at the time the difference of opinion becomes known. If Congress, within twenty-one days after receipt of conflicting declarations—twenty-three days if Congress is not in session—determines by at least a two-thirds vote of both chambers that the president of the United States is unable to perform all presidential duties, the vice-president shall continue to be acting president; otherwise, the president of the United States shall resume the powers and duties of his office.

Discussion of the Twenty-fifth Amendment

Article II, Section 1, Paragraph 6 of the Constitution states: "In Case of the Removal of the President from Office, or of his Death, Resignation, or Inability to discharge the Powers and Duties of the said Office, the Same shall devolve on the Vice President, and the Congress may by Law provide for the Case of Removal, Death, Resignation or Inability, both of the President and Vice President, . . ." The unamended Constitution does not specify how to determine "Inability," but it implies (via the words quoted in this paragraph combined with the "necessary and proper" clause) that Congress has the power to pass a law that specifies how to determine "Inability." The "Inability" part of the Twenty-fifth Amendment—by far the most important part—could have been constitutionally enacted in statute form. However, Congress did not have the power to enact a law to specify how to fill a vacancy in the office of vice-president. That was not particularly important because it is not essential to have a vice-president. Since 1789, Congress has had the power to "by Law provide for the Case" that the offices of "both of the President and Vice President" are vacant.

Twenty-sixth Amendment

Section 1. The right of citizens of the United States, who are eighteen years of age or older, to vote shall not be denied or abridged by the United States or by any State on account of age.

Section 2. The Congress shall have power to enforce this article by appropriate legislation.

Original Meaning in 21st Century Plain English

United States citizens who are eighteen years of age or older shall not be prevented from voting in any election because of their age. Congress shall have the power to enact laws to enforce this amendment.

Discussion of the Twenty-sixth Amendment

In 1970, Congress passed a law which every member of Congress must have realized was absolutely unconstitutional. A provision of the Voting Rights Act of 1970 declared that United States citizens could not be prevented from voting because of age if they were eighteen years old or older. The Voting Rights Act of 1970 was challenged in the 1970 case of *Oregon v. Mitchell*, in which four members of the Court correctly held that Congress had no authority to set the voting age at eighteen in federal or state elections. Four members of the Court held that the Voting Rights Act of 1970 was constitutional because of the Fourteenth Amendment! The voting provisions of the "Fourteenth Amendment" apply only to male citizens who are at least twenty-one years of age. As unconstitutional as the "Fourteenth Amendment" is, it states: "when the right to vote . . . is denied to any of the male inhabitants of each State, being [at least] twenty-one years of age, and the citizens of the United States, or in any way abridged, except for participation in rebellion, or other crime, the . . . [number of representatives in the U.S. House of Representatives from that state] shall be reduced in proportion which the number of such male citizens shall bear to the whole number of male citizens twenty-one years of age in such State."

One member of the Court in *Oregon v. Mitchell* held that Congress could set the voting age in federal elections, but Congress could not set the voting age in nonfederal elections. That is the way the Court ruled. Only one member of the Court agreed with the Court's ruling!

The Court's ruling in *Oregon v. Mitchell* would have added complexity to elections because the voting age in federal elections would have been different than the voting age in nonfederal elections in most states.[1154] It would have doubled the types of ballots required. The desire to simplify the 1972 elections was probably the main reason that the Twenty-sixth Amendment was ratified by three-fourths of the state legislatures in record time, just 107 days after Congress proposed it on March 23, 1971.

Between 1942 and 1970, more than 150 proposals were introduced in Congress for an amendment to the Constitution to grant "suffrage to 18-year-olds."[1155] However, prior to 1971, Congress never proposed such an amendment to the states. Despite the fact that it was clear that a constitutional amendment was required to do such a thing (Witness the Fifteenth and Nineteenth Amendments and the 150+ attempts in Congress to get Congress to propose an amendment similar to the Twenty-Sixth Amendment.), in 1970 Senator Ted Kennedy "suggested that Congress might have the power to lower the voting age by statute, thus eliminating the need to amend the Constitution."[1156] Kennedy had been involved in an incident at Chappaquiddick Island in July of 1969, for which he received a two-month suspended sentence and was placed on probation for one year.[1157] Despite the Chappaquiddick incident and the obvious unconstitutional nature of the provision of the Voting Rights Act of 1970—which lowered the voting age as Kennedy suggested—the Senate adopted the provision. The vote in the Senate to adopt this provision was 64 to 17.[1158] The provision, co-sponsored by Kennedy, became Title III of the Voting Rights Act of 1970. On June 17, 1970, the Voting Rights Act of 1970 became law when it was signed by President Richard Nixon.[1159]

Twenty-seventh Amendment

No law, varying the compensation for the services of the Senators and Representatives, shall take effect, until an election of Representatives shall have intervened.

Original Meaning in 21st Century Plain English

No law that changes salaries or other compensation for the services of members of Congress shall take effect until an election is held for members of the United States House of Representatives.

Discussion of the Twenty-seventh Amendment

The Twenty-seventh Amendment took more than two centuries to be ratified by the legislatures of three-fourths of the states. It was the second of twelve amendments proposed by Congress on September 25, 1789. The third through the twelfth of those proposed amendments became law on December 15, 1791. The Twenty-seventh Amendment was not ratified by the legislatures of three-fourths of the states until May 7, 1992.

What was to become the Twenty-seventh Amendment had been ratified by only six of the fourteen states at the time the Bill of Rights became law on December 15, 1791, by virtue of having been ratified by eleven states.[1160] [1161] In 1873, Ohio became the seventh state to ratify, and, in 1978, Wyoming became the eighth state to ratify.[1162] At that rate, it was going to take a few millenniums to get the requisite number of states to ratify.

However, a momentous event took place in 1982. Gregory Watson, a twenty-year-old sophomore at the University of Texas, wrote a term paper for a government class he was taking![1163] [1164] Watson examined what was to become the Twenty-seventh Amendment and correctly concluded that it was viable. Watson's professor gave Watson a C on the paper—much to Watson's chagrin. The professor did not agree with Watson on viability, possibly because of the 1921 case of *Dillon v. Gloss*. In *Dillon*, the Court ruled that Article V implied that proposed amendments had to be ratified within a "reasonable" time after they were proposed.[1165] Watson intrepidly began a one-man crusade to get more state legislatures to ratify; he did it by writing letters to state legislators.[1166] Between 1983 and 1992, at least thirty states ratified.[1167]

On May 14, 1992, the Twenty-seventh Amendment was certified as part of the Constitution by the national archivist.[1168] Because of the contemporaneousness issue, some lawyers maintain that the Twenty-seventh Amendment is unconstitutional.[1169] They are wrong. Amendments proposed with no deadlines for ratification, including the one that is now the Twenty-seventh Amendment, have no ratification deadlines.

Out of the twelve amendments proposed to the states on September 25, 1791, *Article the second* (the Twenty-seventh Amendment) was ratified by the fewest number of states at the time the Bill of Rights became law. The relative unpopularity of *Article the Second* with eighteenth-century state legislators should be considered in determining the original meaning of most provisions of the Bill of Rights. This aspect of *Article the second* is addressed in this book in the discussion of the Second Amendment.

Debate:
Should Supreme Court
Rule by Law?

Moderator Comments

An unusual debate is about to take place. The debaters are knowledgeable advocates of their position, and they have agreed to debate in an absolutely honest manner. In order to protect their careers, the physical appearances and voices of both debaters have been disguised. Our debaters are a tall man wearing a stovepipe hat who we'll call Abe, and a man wearing a judicial robe who we'll call Earl. Earl will begin the debate.

Earl (United States Supreme Court Need Not Rule by Law): The shortcomings of the United States Constitution have made it almost necessary, if not absolutely necessary, for the Court to take on a legislative role. One of the main problems with the Constitution is that the federal government structure is largely incompatible with national political parties. The framers did not anticipate national political parties. With national political parties, the Constitution is usually impractical unless the president, a majority of the members of the House of Representatives, and a majority of the members of the Senate are members of the same political party. The checks on the lawmaking process required by the Constitution are so formidable that the federal government has usually been unable to deal with problems in a constitutional and timely manner. The Court may have always ruled by law if the Constitution had provided (1) a parliamentary system with a single national legislative chamber, and (2) an amendment process whereby constitutional amendments could be proposed by a majority of the members of the national legislature and become law *if* approved by three-quarters of the state legislatures.

In his book, *Constitutional Reform and Effective Government*, James Sundquist makes many interesting points, among which are:

- Policy conflict and legislative deadlock are usually "all but inevitable" because of divided control of the Senate, House, and presidency by the political parties. (Often the only way to get things done is with commissions such as military base closing commissions, extra-constitutional bodies such as the Federal Reserve Board, and constitutional bodies doing extra-constitutional things.)

- Members of Congress and presidents are preoccupied with the next national election which is never more than two years away.

- When the government is in gridlock and unable to deal with problems, there is no way to replace the government short of waiting for the next national election.

- It is more difficult to amend the U.S. Constitution than it is to amend the constitution of any other country or any state in the United States.

Preoccupation with national elections has resulted in (1) an enormous amount of time spent by politicians raising funds for election campaigns, and (2) political debts incurred by politicians as a result of their fund-raising activities. The framers would have regarded such fund-raising as corrupting, and it is corrupting in the sense that the public interest often takes a back seat to special interests. Election campaign laws in the United Kingdom are excellent. However, Congress will probably never pass such election campaign laws. Most members of Congress want to preserve their huge advantage relative to challengers for their offices. Members of Congress have huge tax-payer-paid staffs, substantial mailing privileges, and receive large campaign "contributions" in return for votes and other favors for wealthy people, corporations, or unions. Most staff members of senators and representatives are effectively campaign workers who do special favors for constituents and other things aimed primarily at getting their boss re-elected. (Each representative is allowed a full-time personal staff of eighteen at taxpayer expense. Each senator is allowed a personal staff of forty at taxpayer expense. In addition, there are about 3700 committee staffers in Congress.[1170])

Abe (United States Supreme Court Should Always Rule by Law): I agree with you that (1) good parliamentary systems of government are better than the federal government structure provided by the Constitution, and (2) the campaign length and spending limits in the United Kingdom are far superior to what we have in the United States. I would strongly support amendments to the Constitution designed to facilitate a more effective, public-interest-oriented federal government.

However, I do not believe that the lack of perfection of the Constitution and other constitutional laws justifies violating the rule of law. If all voters in America understood that U.S. Supreme Court justices often lie about the meaning of the Constitution in official actions, despite their oath to support the Constitution, I think the Court would come into disfavor.

Ulysses S. Grant wisely observed in his first inaugural address: "I know of no method to secure the repeal of bad or obnoxious laws so effective as their stringent execution."[1171] Juries, if properly informed of their power to determine law in individual cases, would not find people guilty of violating "bad or obnoxious laws." Legislators would get the message and revise "bad or obnoxious laws."

The focus of the Supreme Court on legislative activities has resulted in neglect of the Court's duty to rule by law. The Court's failure to consistently rule lawfully has encouraged lower courts to rule contrary to the law—often for corrupt reasons. This has resulted in an enormous uncertainty in the law which is *not* in the public interest.

It is, however, extremely beneficial to lawyers. The financial benefit to lawyers is behind many unconstitutional Court decisions.

Earl: Rulings of judges often benefit their fellow lawyers. In most occupations, there is a tendency to stick together. The tendency is particularly strong between lawyers and judges. Of much more concern is the fact that many lawyers and judges are corrupt. It is distressing that many honest lawyers are extremely reluctant to report judges they suspect of being corrupt because the lawyers are scared that their careers will be severely damaged.

I wish that members of the Court would acknowledge that they are amending the Constitution when they do so. It is unseemly for the justices to lie about it. However, members of the Court do not violate their oath for personal gain. If the justices acknowledged that they were legislating when they did so, it would be much more difficult for Congress to avoid impeaching them.

Judicial corruption and uncertainty in the law would be reduced by a Court which operated as it was intended to operate. However, the vast majority of judicial corruption is in state courts, and little of that corruption would be eliminated by a vigilant U.S. Supreme Court. Judicial corruption will remain a major problem until (1) lie detector tests are given regularly to judges, and (2) judges are removed from office if lie detector tests indicate that they made rulings in return for favors.

In the public interest, Congress and the Court have, in effect, eliminated some constitutional checks. Congress has given the Court and many federal agencies legislative power. The Court has given Congress extra-constitutional legislative powers. Congress, the Court, and most federal agencies have usually used their extra-constitutional powers wisely. Congress and the Court can always apply the brakes to these extra-constitutional powers.

If the Court was not allowed to amend the Constitution: (1) all U.S. money might still be gold, silver, or paper which is readily converted into gold or silver—if so, the supply of U.S. money would be drastically inadequate for a good economy; (2) we might not have a Federal Deposit Insurance Corporation (FDIC), an institution which restored public confidence in the banking system and prevented many Americans from losing their life savings; (3) there might not be any Social Security system; and (4) segregated schools and discriminatory voting restrictions might still exist in some states—if so, the resultant racial strife would probably be enormous.

Abe: I agree with you that judicial corruption will remain a major problem until such time as judges are tested regularly with lie detectors. The most effective way to put teeth into the "good Behaviour" provision of the Constitution—and related provisions of state constitutions—would be to remove from office judges that lie detector tests indicate were not impartial.

If Court amendments had not been used to solve national problems, I believe those problems would have been solved constitutionally. Although Congress and the Court *could* apply the brakes to eliminate extra-constitutional federal powers, Congress and the Court seem to have a very difficult time finding the brake pedal.

With respect to paper money (bills of credit), it was within the bounds of ratifier understanding for the federal government to issue paper money. A strong indication that Americans were satisfied with inconvertible paper money occurred in 1879 when people had an opportunity to redeem their "greenbacks" for gold coins, and relatively few greenbacks were redeemed.[1172] On the first day, $135,000 of greenbacks was presented for gold coin, and $400,000 of gold was presented for greenbacks.[1173]

An amendment to constitutionalize the FDIC and the Social Security system would have no trouble passing. One reason that we do not have amendments to constitutionalize the FDIC, Social Security, and inconvertible paper money is that politicians are afraid that such amendments would draw attention to the large number of unconstitutional laws which might not be accepted via the amendment process. Another reason is to foster the illusion that it is necessary to have judges legislate.

The strongest arguments for past Supreme Court amendments are in the area of ending racial discrimination by state and local governments. The protests of people such as Dr. Martin Luther King,

Jr., would have resulted in one or more legitimate constitutional amendments.

What do you say about Court amendments which (1) ruled that it was unconstitutional for state A to impose term limits on members of Congress from state A, (2) mandated busing to obtain racial balance, (3) created abortion rights, (4) prevented states from providing support to parochial schools, and (5) mandated "Miranda warnings."

Earl: Those are among the most questionable rulings the Court has made. It is obvious that they are arbitrary and not essential. Nevertheless, I support most of them.

Term limits on members of Congress from state A would prevent some of the wiser members of the Senate from remaining in the Senate unless they moved to state B. Of course, term limits would get rid of some poor members of Congress. Term limits would probably cause us to lose more wisdom than we gained.

Busing was a good thing in terms of speeding up integration in America. I think that the good that busing has done is largely unappreciated by most Americans.

The right to abortion has several advantages. It reduces unwanted children. It reduces the population explosion. It allows the earth's resources to last longer. It reduces the suffering of women. It increases the freedom of women. Abortions were legal in New York when the Court decided *Roe v. Wade*, and it was just a matter of time until most states legalized abortion.

The Court *may* have made a mistake in preventing tax money from helping to support parochial schools. If all public schools were as good as our better public schools, the Court's decision would have been wise. The idea was that students would obtain better educations if they studied only secular subjects, and the course material in secular subjects was unconstrained by religious beliefs. Unfortunately, the Court did not foresee the inefficiency that would creep into many public schools in large cities. It *may* have been better to have allowed more competition between public schools and parochial schools as a means to keep a stronger floor on the academic standards of public schools. Hindsight tells us that it *might* have been wiser for the Court to abide by the Constitution and let state legislatures retain the responsibility of deciding how much aid to provide to parochial schools.

It would have been wise to give public schools more authority to expel students if expelled students were given an opportunity to change their ways in special schools. Some alternative public schools have proven to be effective and desirable even though they are expensive.

We should devote much more effort to improving all public schools. The most important elements are *teacher effort* and knowledge of the subject matter they are teaching. In addition, teachers must know how to maintain order in the classroom. It is difficult to be an effective teacher. Teachers who are most effective, in terms of getting their students to learn, put much more effort into teaching than do teachers who are relatively ineffective. Substantial financial incentives should be used to keep the most effective teachers. Pay based on teaching effectiveness would also (1) encourage more of the best people to enter the teaching profession, and (2) encourage most teachers to try harder to get their students to learn.

The Miranda warnings were a gross overreaction to problems which could have been solved by simply requiring video taping of all questioning by police and making those tapes available to the prosecution and the defense. *Miranda* is probably the worst Court amendment ever made because of the injustice that has resulted from it. It has also substantially increased the cost of the criminal justice system.

We should be careful not to overreact to Court amendments which are bad—because the large majority of Court amendments are in the public interest.

Abe: Although term limits would result in Congress losing some wise members, the better members would still be able to serve outside of Congress if they chose not to run for Congress in another state. After eight years in the House and twelve years in the Senate, they could serve as administration officials, diplomats, presidential advisors, or members of commissions. There is no surplus of outstanding individuals. The nation would be fortunate if outstanding people were available to fill cabinet positions. We often get people filling cabinet posts who are not outstanding.

After John Quincy Adams served as president and U.S. senator, he served in the House of Representatives. Upon hearing a comment that it would be degrading for an ex-president to serve in the House of Representatives, Adams said that no person could be degraded by serving as a member of the House. Adams served in the House with great distinction.[1174] Adams opposed the expansion of slavery and heroically won a protracted struggle to repeal the House gag rule against discussion of slavery in the House.[1175] Another of Adams' "spectacular" contributions to the fight against slavery while he was a member of the House was his championing of the cause of mutineering Africans on the slave ship *Amistad*.[1176] The Africans mutinied near Cuba and brought the slave ship into United States waters.[1177] Against the efforts of President Martin Van Buren, who wanted the Africans returned to their masters, Adams won the freedom of the *Amistad* mutineers.[1178] Had those Africans been returned, they would have almost certainly been executed.

Busing was unnatural integration. Integration was coming naturally. It did not need busing. It would have been better to let integration happen more slowly with less resentment. Most students and parents, black and white, were unhappy with busing.

The large majority of Americans who are against legalization of abortion are honest law-abiding citizens who are very frustrated by their inability to deal with unlawful Court decisions. Law-abiding "right-to-lifers" have always held the moral and legal high ground, but they have been steamrolled much like many good citizens have been violated by corrupt lawyers and judges. If the people who advocated legalization of abortion had been able to keep abortion legal in New York, and influenced other state legislatures to legalize abortion—they would have won fair and square.

The difference between abortion and murder is tiny. Most of your arguments in support of abortion rights would also support the killing of newborn infants.

I support your ideas to improve the quality of teaching in public schools. I also agree with you about "Miranda warnings."

Earl: I agree that there is a small difference between abortion and murder. The abortion of healthy fetuses is certainly immoral. It is not pleasant for me to support, but it is for the good of society. The population explosion on our planet will lead to enormous human suffering.

You want to rely on constitutional changes in law to solve problems. That is too slow for me. Even if I believed that all Court rulings should be consistent with the Constitution, it would scare me to think of the enormous disruptions which could be caused in the United States if the Court were to suddenly change its ways and start ruling in a manner consistent with the Constitution. Can you imagine what would happen if the Court were to suddenly take actions such as ruling unconstitutional bills of credit, the Social Security system, the Federal Reserve Board, and the Federal Deposit Insurance Corporation?

Abe: There is a constitutional way to avoid severe problems with a Court constrained by the Constitution. Congress could pass a law to prevent the Court from hearing any appeals for a period of time—perhaps two years. That would provide time for constitutional amendments to be made. Congress can constitutionally impose a long Court recess. It was done in 1802. Amendments can be proposed by Congress or national constitutional conventions demanded by states. You can rest assured that bills of credit and Social Security would be made constitutional before they disappeared.

If we continue to allow judges to violate the rule of law, we can expect that the enormous corruption, injustice, and expense of the American legal system will continue until such time as lie detectors are used to determine whether or not to remove judges from office.

Marbury v. Madison

As Vice-President/President-elect Thomas Jefferson awoke in a boardinghouse in the District of Columbia on March 4, 1801, he knew the day would be eventful. Little did he know how eventful. He knew he would: (1) break tradition by wearing plain clothes and no sword, and walk to the Capital building to be sworn in as president of the United States (George Washington and John Adams had both dressed elegantly, worn swords, and rode in impressive carriages to their inaugurals.[1179]); (2) give his inaugural address in the Senate chamber where he would be sworn in by Chief Justice John Marshall; and (3) visit the Department of State after being sworn in. What Jefferson did not know was that a surprise with far-reaching consequences would await him as he entered the Department of State.

On that eventful day, key events of the past few years probably flashed through Jefferson's mind. Such events included:

- Jefferson's narrow defeat by Federalist John Adams in the 1796 presidential election (As a result of that election, Jefferson became vice-president in 1797.)

- Gains made by Jefferson's fellow Republicans in elections from 1796 through 1800 (Members of Jefferson's Democratic-Republican party were usually referred to as Republicans during Jefferson's time, and most historians refer to Democratic-Republicans as Republicans.)

- The pro-Federalist Sedition Act of 1798 which was enacted by the Federalists primarily to prevent newspapers from criticizing

President Adams or the Federalist Congress (The Sedition Act of 1798 caused Vice-President Jefferson to be careful to keep from being indicted or impeached. One Republican congressman was indicted, convicted, and jailed. The Sedition Act of 1798 is discussed in some detail in Chapter 10 of this book under the First Amendment.)

• The momentum for the pro-Federalist Judiciary Act of 1801 which built up in 1799 (Noted historian Kathryn Turner wrote: "Federalist leaders worriedly watched the growth of Republican strength, and in early 1799 began to turn their attention to the federal judiciary. Real momentum for strengthening the judiciary begins in that year ... [most elements of the] Judiciary Act of 1801, ... [were] introduced long before the [1800] election. Political defeat [of the Federalists in the 1800 election] then gave a driving urgency to fight for its passage."[1180])

• The national election of 1800 in which Jefferson defeated President Adams, and Jefferson's fellow Republicans defeated many Federalist members of Congress

• The lame-duck Senate's confirmation of John Marshall to be chief justice on January 27, 1801 (Marshall was secretary of state when he was confirmed as chief justice. He remained secretary of state until Adams' term as president expired. Lame-duck President Adams nominated Marshall to be chief justice on January 20, 1801, the same day that the lame-duck House passed the Judiciary Act of 1801. On February 7, 1801, the Senate passed the Judiciary Act of 1801. Among other things, the Judiciary Act of 1801 reduced the number of Supreme Court justices from six to five *upon the next vacancy*. If the Federalists were sincere about wanting a five-justice Court, they would have elevated one of the five justices to chief justice instead of adding Marshall to the Court on January 27, 1801. Adams nominated Marshall to be chief justice *on January 20* because Adams had received a note on January 19 about the proposed Judiciary Act of 1801. The note, written by the secretary of the navy at the request of some Federalist congressmen, said: "As the bill proposes a reduction of the Judges to five—and there are already five Judges in commission, it is suggested that there might be more difficulty in appointing a chief Justice without taking him from the present Judges, after the passage of this bill even by one Branch of the Legislature, than before."[1181])

- The attempt by most Federalists in the lame-duck House of Representatives to deny Jefferson the presidency (Jefferson and his vice-presidential running mate, Aaron Burr, tied with the most electoral votes. On February 11, 1801, the House of Representatives took its first vote to elect a president. It took seven days and thirty-six ballots before Jefferson was named president. If it had not been for Alexander Hamilton, a Federalist, Burr probably would have been elected president by the House. Hamilton disliked Burr more than he disliked Jefferson. The Burr–Hamilton animosity was mutual, as indicated by the fact that Vice-President Aaron Burr killed Hamilton in a pistol duel in 1804.)

- The Judiciary Act of 1801, which became law when signed by President Adams on February 13, 1801 (It increased the jurisdiction of federal courts, almost doubled the number of federal judgeships, and reduced the number of Supreme Court justices from six to five, upon the next vacancy. The Judiciary Act of 1801 promised: (1) to prevent Jefferson from appointing anyone to the Court upon the first vacancy; and (2) that Federalists would control the Court until four of the six members of the Court on February 13, 1801, vacated their office (As late as 1810, only two of the Federalists on the Court in 1801 had vacated their office.). On March 3, 1801, President Adams appointed Federalists to fill all sixteen federal circuit court judgeships created by the Judiciary Act of 1801. Federalist U.S. Senator Gouverneur Morris (one of the principal framers of the Constitution) wrote a letter on February 20, 1801, in which he "heartily" approved the Judiciary Act of 1801 and observed that the Federalists "are about to experience a heavy gale of adverse wind; can they be blamed for casting many anchors to hold their ship through the storm?"[1182 1183])

- A law enacted by Congress on February 27, 1801, that authorized the president of the United States to "from time to time" nominate justices of the peace "in and for" the District of Columbia[1184] (On March 2, 1801, President Adams nominated forty-two justices of the peace, the large majority of whom were Federalists, for the District of Columbia. That was probably an excessive number of justices of the peace for the district in 1801. The Senate confirmed all forty-two justices of the peace on March 3, 1801, the day before Jefferson was to be inaugurated. Adams appointed all forty-two by signing commissions. The commissions were completed in the office of Secretary of State John Marshall. The forty-two justice of the peace appointees, together with the sixteen new federal circuit court appointees, were commonly called "Mid-night Judges."[1185])

Chief Justice/Secretary of State John Marshall was *responsible* for seeing that all of the "Mid-night Judges" appointed by President Adams in 1801 received their commissions. Some of the justice of the peace commissions were not delivered. John Marshall arranged for his brother, James Marshall, to deliver at least some of the commissions.[1186][1187] An affidavit of James Marshall was read to the Court in *Marbury*. In the Court's ruling in *Marbury*, delivered in February of 1803, Chief Justice John Marshall wrote: "the affidavit of James Marshall, . . . stated that on the 4th of March, 1801, . . . [he went to] the office of the Secretary of State, for the commissions of the justices of the peace; that as many as 12, as he believed, commissions of justices . . . were delivered to him, for which he gave a receipt, which he left in the office. That finding he could not conveniently carry the whole, he returned several of them . . . Among the commissions so returned, according to the best of his knowledge, was one for Col. Hooe, and one for William Harper."[1188]

President Jefferson stated that he "found . . . [undelivered justice of the peace commissions] on the table of the department of State, on my entrance into office [on March 4, 1801], and I forbade their delivery."[1189] Did John Marshall really expect Jefferson, or soon-to-be Secretary of State James Madison, to order all of the undelivered justice of the peace commissions to be delivered?

William Marbury was one of the "Mid-night Judges" whose commissions were not delivered. Marbury and three other justices of the peace without commissions tried to get the Court to issue a writ of mandamus (a court order) commanding Secretary of State James Madison to "cause to be delivered to them respectively their several commissions as justices of the peace in the District of Columbia."[1190] The case of *Marbury v. Madison* began with a motion to the Court for a ruling to require James Madison to show cause why a writ of mandamus should not be issued against him.[1191] That motion was made on December 17, 1801, and, on the following day, the Court issued an order commanding Secretary of State James Madison to show cause why a writ of mandamus should not be issued against him.[1192] [1193]

Relevant to the show-cause order issued to Madison, historian Richard Ellis got it right when he stated: "This attempt to intimidate the Republicans failed; in fact, it had the opposite effect. Most Republicans, not only the militant ones but also the moderates, viewed it as a bold usurpation of power on the part of the Supreme Court and an attempt to embarrass the President. The Federalists' action went a long way toward uniting their opponents' disparate congressional majority."[1194]

On December 21, 1801, Senator Stevens Mason wrote a letter to James Monroe in which Mason stated:

> "The conduct of the Judges on this occasion has excited a very general indignation and will secure the repeal of the Judiciary Law of the last session about the propriety of which some of our Republican friends were hesitating."[1195]

On January 8, 1802, President Jefferson arranged to have a motion made in the Senate to repeal the Judiciary Act of 1801.[1196] The senators were equally divided, and Vice-President Aaron Burr voted against the motion. After a two-month struggle, the Judiciary Act of 1801 was repealed on March 8, 1802. The Senate voted 16 to 15 and the House voted 59 to 32. All votes were along party lines except for a few Republicans who voted against the repeal. The repeal was not at all appreciated by the members of the Court, all Federalists, because: (1) they would have to resume their circuit-court duties (and all of the travel that they hated); (2) all sixteen Federalist federal circuit court judges lost their judgeships; and (3) President Jefferson would be able to appoint a member of the Court upon the first vacancy.

During debates in Congress over the repeal of the Judiciary Act of 1801, Federalists frequently warned that the Supreme Court would declare any such repeal to be unconstitutional.[1197] *Marbury* was frequently mentioned in those debates.[1198] Republicans in Congress warned that if a repeal of the Judiciary Act of 1801 were declared unconstitutional by the Court, impeachment of the justices who made such a ruling "was sure to follow."[1199] (In 1802, Republicans had the votes to impeach but they did not have the votes to convict. However, it was fairly obvious that the Republicans would have the votes to convict in 1803.)

James Madison did not accept the jurisdiction of the Court in *Marbury* because the Court has no constitutional authority over the president for official acts. However, Madison did *not* contend that it was unconstitutional for the Court to issue any writs of mandamus. Nevertheless, the Court ruled in 1803 that it could not issue a writ of mandamus in *Marbury* because it was unconstitutional for the Judiciary Act of 1789 to give the Court original jurisdiction in any mandamus cases.

In 1789, it was so important for Congress to create a judicial system that it was the number one priority of the first U.S. Senate. The Judiciary Act of 1789 (Its actual title was "An Act to establish the Judicial Courts of the United States.") was Senate Bill No. I in the first session of the first Congress under the Constitution. The leading drafter of the Judiciary Act of 1789 was framer Oliver Ellsworth. Framers William Paterson and Caleb Strong also drafted some parts.

There were a few controversies relevant to the constitutionality of the Judiciary Act of 1789 during its enactment and the remainder of the eighteenth century. One such controversy occurred when some members of Congress "took the position that Congress had no power to withhold from the Federal Courts which it should establish any of the judicial power granted by the Constitution. . . ."[1200] Those members of Congress were not correct because it was understood by most framers and ratifiers that state courts could be empowered by Congress—and probably would be empowered by Congress—to exercise a great deal of the judicial power granted to the federal government by the Constitution.[1201] Noted historian Charles Warren correctly stated: "Congress withheld from the Federal Courts much of the jurisdiction which it might have bestowed under the Constitution. . . ."[1202]

The Judiciary Act of 1789 was clearly unconstitutional in that it eliminated the Supreme Court's original jurisdiction in cases involving consuls. Rationale as to why the Judiciary Act of 1789 was unconstitutional relevant to consuls is provided in this book in the discussion of Article III, Section 2, Paragraph 3. The constitutionality of the Judiciary Act of 1789 relevant to consuls was questioned during the eighteenth century in Congress and in a federal circuit court in the case of *United States v. Ravara*.[1203]

I have seen no evidence that the constitutionality of the part of the Judiciary Act of 1789 ruled unconstitutional in *Marbury* was questioned, in or out of Congress, during its enactment or during the remainder of the eighteenth century. The approach used by Abraham Lincoln to prove that Congress had the power to prohibit slavery in the territories, if applied to the power of the Supreme Court to issue writs of mandamus, would find the power of the Court to issue writs of mandamus to be constitutional because of its heavy framer involvement and lack of constitutional challenge during the eighteenth century. The Court's authority to issue writs of mandamus was: (1) drafted by a framer (Oliver Ellsworth); (2) approved by the first U.S. Senate at a time when half of its members were framers (Eleven of twenty-two senators were framers.) after *extensive vetting* outside of Congress; (3) approved by the first House of Representatives at a time when eight of its fifty-nine members were framers; (4) signed into law by framer George Washington; (5) unchallenged from the standpoint of constitutionality in the first Congress under the Constitution, many of whose members were not bashful about making constitutional challenges; and (6) unchallenged in any court during the eighteenth century despite the fact that the Court heard several such cases. The power of the Supreme Court to issue writs of prohibition and writs of mandamus was noncontroversial and quite natural. It was a power given only to a superior court. There was enormous newspaper coverage of the June 12, 1789, constitutional Senate judiciary bill that led to the Judiciary Act of 1789. For example, the *Boston Gazette*, on June 29, 1789, published a full copy of the Senate judiciary bill as it emerged from the "Special Judiciary Committee" on June 12, 1789, including the part that would authorize the Supreme Court to issue writs of prohibition and writs of mandamus. The *Gazette* stated: "The importance of the subject, and the anxiety of the public at large to know in what manner the Rulers of America proceed, induces us to embrace the earliest opportunity to publish the same. The Bill now under consideration will, it is likely, undergo some amendments; but perhaps will not vary, materially, from its present plan."[1204]

The Court's authority to issue writs of mandamus, included in section 13 of the Judiciary Act of 1789, was stated as follows: "the Supreme Court . . . shall have power to issue writs of prohibition to the district courts, . . . and writs of mandamus, in cases warranted by the principles and usages of law, to any courts appointed, or persons holding office, under the authority of the United States."[1205] Those words increased the Court's original jurisdiction. The Constitution can easily be interpreted to give Congress the power to increase the original jurisdiction of the Court. Article I, Section 2, Paragraph 2 states:

> "In all Cases affecting Ambassadors, other public Ministers and Consuls, and those in which a State shall be a Party, the supreme Court shall have original Jurisdiction. In all the other

Cases before mentioned, the supreme Court shall have appellate Jurisdiction, both as to Law and Fact, with such Exceptions, and under such Regulations as the Congress shall make."

The framers must have intended, and the ratifiers must have understood, that the word "Exceptions" would give Congress the power to increase the Court's original jurisdiction as well as decrease the Court's appellate jurisdiction. Why? Because the constitutionality of the Court's power to issue writs of mandamus—or writs of prohibition—was not questioned in Congress or in any court during the eighteenth century.

Section 13 was debated in the Senate on June 30 and July 1 of 1789. The debate did not include the provision involved in *Marbury*; the Senate was "concerned about which national court should exercise jurisdiction" in cases involving "Ambassadors, other public Ministers and Consuls."[1206] The bill was changed: (1) on June 30 to give concurrent original jurisdiction to the Supreme Court and lower federal courts in cases where ambassadors, other ministers, or consuls were plaintiffs, and (2) on July 1 to eliminate the Court's original jurisdiction in cases involving consuls.[1207] The July 1 change must have been contested—and reluctantly accepted by Oliver Ellsworth—because it was clearly unconstitutional.

In *Marbury*, the Court acknowledged that it had considered granting writs of mandamus several times during the 1790s in cases of original jurisdiction not mandated by the Constitution. In none of those cases did anyone suggest that a writ of mandamus issued by the Court would be unconstitutional. The requests for writs of mandamus were always refused for reasons other than constitutionality. After briefly reviewing the past mandamus cases, the Court in *Marbury* stated: "In none of these cases, nor in any other, was the power of this court to issue a mandamus ever denied. Hence it appears there has been a legislative construction of the constitution upon this point, and a judicial practice under it, for the whole time since the formation of the government [under the Constitution]."[1208]

The Supreme Court issued a writ of prohibition in 1795 in the case of *United States v. Judge Peters*.[1209] It was lawful for the Court to issue a writ of prohibition to Judge Peters. In *Marbury*, it would have been lawful for the Court to issue a writ of mandamus to Secretary of State Madison *if it did not interfere with the constitutional authority of the president*. The only constitutional remedies for noncriminal abuse of presidential power are removal of the president from office via either the impeachment process or the election process. The president cannot tell the Court what to do, and the Court cannot tell the president what to do.

Justice William Paterson was a member of the Court during (1) two mandamus cases heard by the Court in 1794, and (2) the prohibition case heard by the Court in 1795. As a U.S. senator in 1789, Paterson had participated heavily in the drafting of the Judiciary Act of 1789. He was familiar with it, and he voted for it. The fact that Justice Paterson did not assert that the Court lacked jurisdiction in the 1794 mandamus cases or the 1795 prohibition case is *most* significant—especially considering his 1795 jury instructions quoted in Chapter 1 of this book. Justice Paterson was still on the Court in 1803 when it unanimously ruled that the Judiciary Act of 1789 was unconstitutional because it authorized the Court to issue writs of mandamus!

The Court's show-cause order to James Madison in December of 1801 shows that the Court that ruled in *Marbury* either (1) thought in 1801 that it was constitutional for the Court to issue writs of mandamus, or (2) was simply harassing President Jefferson and Secretary of State Madison. A strong indication that it was understood by virtually everyone that it was constitutional for the Judiciary Act of 1789 to give the Supreme Court original jurisdiction to issue writs of mandamus is the fact that when the Court's ruling in *Marbury* came down in 1803, it astonished the press and the public.[1210]

It was expected that the Court would issue a writ of mandamus to Madison—a writ Madison was expected to defy.[1211] There was talk that Court members would be impeached if the Court issued a writ to Madison.[1212] In its day, *Marbury* "represented the determination of Marshall and his Associates to interfere with the authority of the Executive, and it derived its chief importance from that aspect."[1213] Marshall's inventive opinion in *Marbury*: (1) "aroused Jefferson's lifelong resentment"[1214] (Jefferson overcame his resentment of John Adams and Alexander Hamilton.); and (2) inspired Jefferson to write: "the judge, . . . has given us lessons of the plastic nature of law in his hands. . . ."[1215]

Wilfred J. Ritz, who has written extensively about the Judiciary Act of 1789, wrote: "Viewed from the 1789 standpoint, . . . the *Marbury v. Madison* interpretation of the Constitution . . . is untenable."[1216]

Although the Court's ruling in *Marbury* was astonishing, there was little criticism of the Court merely because it had declared an act of Congress to be unconstitutional.[1217] President Jefferson did *not* believe that *Marbury* established "the exclusive and superior power of judicial review."[1218] Chief Justice Marshall did not assert such a claim.[1219] Jefferson and most other Republicans maintained that the legislative, executive, and judicial branches had an equal right to determine constitutionality.[1220]

Chief Justice Marshall, who was himself in danger of being impeached, was so shaken by the impeachment of Justice Samuel Chase that Marshall wrote, in an 1804 letter to Chase: "I think the modern doctrine of impeachment should yield to an appellate jurisdiction in the legislature. A reversal of those legal opinions deemed unsound by the legislature would certainly better comport with the mildness of our character than a removal of the judge who has rendered them . . ."[1221]

In *Marbury*, the Court said: "A mandamus is the proper remedy to compel a Secretary of State to deliver a commission to which a party is entitled." According to the Court, Marbury and his fellow suitors had simply come to the wrong federal court. It would have been highly irregular for Marbury and his fellow mandamus seekers to have sought a writ of mandamus in an inferior federal court with no explicit authorization to issue writs of mandamus. (The Supreme Court had the only explicit authority to issue writs of mandamus.) It was *not* agreeable to the principles and usages of law for an inferior court to issue a writ of mandamus, much less to a high level executive branch official.

Despite the Court's ruling in *Marbury*, *none* of the mandamus seekers sought a writ of mandamus from an inferior federal court. *Why not?* In *Marbury*, a unanimous Supreme Court said, in effect, that Marbury and his fellow mandamus seekers could get a writ of mandamus issued to Secretary of State Madison in a federal circuit court. In every such court, one of the two judges was a U.S. Supreme Court justice. Had the mandamus seekers went to a federal circuit court, a writ of mandamus would have almost certainly been issued to Madison. That would *not* have been desirable for the judiciary because Madison would have probably defied the order, and some members of the judiciary would have been in very hot water. It is likely that, *before* the Court issued its ruling in *Marbury*, Marshall had assurances that all four mandamus seekers would cease their efforts to get a writ of mandamus issued to Madison after the Court issued its ruling in *Marbury*. The failure to deliver commissions prior to the time Jefferson was sworn in as president, and the opening moments of *Marbury*, were probably also orchestrated by Marshall. Chief Justice Marshall probably found it hard to conceal a mischievous smile as he swore in Jefferson on March 4, 1801.

The lawyer for Marbury and his fellow mandamus seekers was Charles Lee, United States attorney general from 1795 to 1801, and, at the time *Marbury* began, a circuit-court judge by virtue of his appointment as one of the "Mid-night Judges."[1222] Lee and John Marshall were friends as well as being fellow Federalists. In 1800, U.S. Attorney General Charles Lee "briefly acted as secretary of state and had the pleasure of forwarding a [secretary of state] commission to his friend John Marshall . . ."[1223] *Marbury* began as a case when federal Judge Charles Lee, in his capacity as a private lawyer, "moved the [Supreme] court" on December 17, 1801, on behalf of William Marbury, Dennis Ramsay, William Harper, and Robert Hooe.[1224] (*Marbury* could just as easily have been *Hooe*. *Hooe* would have been so much more appropriate.)

In *Marbury*, Chief Justice Marshall indirectly charged President Jefferson with an impeachable offense. Noted historian Richard Ellis was correct when he wrote that, in *Marbury*, Marshall characterized Jefferson "as a violator of the laws he was sworn to uphold."[1225] Secretary of State James Madison was also characterized in *Marbury* as being unfaithful to federal law. Although Marshall did not suggest that Jefferson or Madison had committed an indictable crime, Marshall did suggest, *at least subtly*, that Jefferson and Madison had both committed impeachable offenses.

In his 1987 book *The Supreme Court: How it Was, How it Is*, U.S. Supreme Court Chief Justice William Rehnquist tells us that "one must assuredly understand" *Marbury v. Madison* "in order to understand the Supreme Court's role in our nation's history."[1226] In a sixteen-page chapter on *Marbury*, Rehnquist describes *Marbury* in a way to make John Marshall appear angelic. Omitted by Rehnquist are all aspects of *Marbury* which indicate that Marshall acted like a general who foolishly took the offensive, was responsible for losing half of his troops, retreated while unfairly charging his opponent with unlawful behavior, and eventually got so scared that he suggested giving up much of his power in return for continuing to wear his uniform.

Rehnquist says that we must go back to *Marbury* to answer the question: "why . . . should . . . [the president] . . . be bound to take the word of the Supreme Court . . . as to whether or not his acts comply with the Constitution?"[1227] *Marbury* did not establish that the president is bound by the Supreme Court. President Jefferson was not bound by anything in *Marbury*. *Marbury* was decided the way it was because: (1) President Jefferson would *not* have complied with a Court order which he considered to be contrary to a constitutional law (Presidents have a constitutional duty to abide by constitutional laws when there is a conflict between constitutional laws and unconstitutional rulings made by the Court.); (2) the Court would have lost prestige (and, quite likely, some of its members) if President Jefferson and Secretary of State Madison decided to disobey a writ of mandamus because they believed that the writ was contrary to a constitutional law; (3) the Federalist Court could not resist an opportunity to attempt to stigmatize Jefferson and Madison as being guilty of impeachable offenses; and (4) the Court wanted to rule an act of Congress unconstitutional—thereby setting a precedent. That precedent was minor because in 1792 at least five of six Court members, in their capacity as circuit-court judges, had declared the act of Congress involved in *Hayburn's Case*[1228] unconstitutional. The Court could have quietly ended the *Marbury* case/crisis by simply refusing to grant a writ based on the separation of powers established by the Constitution.

Relevant to *Marbury*, historian Richard Ellis correctly wrote: "What . . . [Jefferson] would have objected to, and what Marshall did not assert, was a claim that the power of review was solely within the Supreme Court's province, or that the Court's judgment [of constitutionality] was superior to that of the other branches. . . ."[1229]

Although not for the reason Rehnquist suggests, *Marbury* must be understood. It must be understood because it *marks the beginning of the Court's role as a legislative body.*

Amendments Proposed to the State Legislatures by Congress on September 25, 1789

Article the first . . . After the first enumeration required by the first Article of the Constitution, there shall be one Representative for every thirty thousand, until the number shall amount to one hundred, after which, the proportion shall be so regulated by Congress, that there shall be not less than one hundred Representatives, nor less than one Representative for every forty thousand persons, until the number of Representatives shall amount to two hundred, after which the proportion shall be so regulated by Congress, that there shall not be less than two hundred Representatives, nor more than one Representative for every fifty thousand persons.

Article the second . . . No law, varying the compensation for the services of the Senators and Representatives, shall take effect, until an election of Representatives shall have intervened.

Article the third . . . Congress shall make no law respecting an establishment of religion, or prohibiting the free exercise thereof; or abridging the freedom of speech, or of the press, or the right of the people peaceably to assemble, and to petition the Government for a redress of grievances.

Article the fourth . . . A well regulated Militia, being necessary to the security of a free State, the right of the people to keep and bear Arms, shall not be infringed.

Article the fifth . . . No Soldier shall, in time of peace be quartered in any house, without the consent of the Owner, nor in time of war, but in a manner to be prescribed by law.

Article the sixth . . . The right of the people to be secure in their persons, houses, papers, and effects, against unreasonable searches and seizures, shall not be violated, and no Warrants shall issue, but upon probable cause, supported by Oath or affirmation, and particularly describing the place to be searched, and the persons or things to be seized.

Article the seventh . . . No person shall be held to answer for a capital, or otherwise infamous crime, unless on a presentment or indictment of a Grand Jury, except in cases arising in the land or naval forces, or in the Militia, when in actual service in time of War or public danger; nor shall any person be subject for the same offence to be twice put in jeopardy of life or limb, nor shall be compelled in any criminal case to be a witness against himself, nor be deprived of life, liberty, or property, without due process of law; nor shall private property be taken for public use without just compensation.

Article the eighth . . . In all criminal prosecutions, the accused shall enjoy the right to a speedy and public trial, by an impartial jury of the State and district wherein the crime shall have been committed, which district shall have been previously ascertained by law, and to be informed of the nature and cause of the accusation; to be confronted with witnesses against him; to have compulsory process for obtaining witnesses in his favor, and to have the Assistance of Counsel for his defence.

Article the Ninth . . . In suits at common law, where the value in controversy shall exceed twenty dollars, the right of trial by jury shall be preserved, and no fact tried by a jury shall be otherwise reexamined in any Court of the United States, than according to the rules of the common law.

Article the Tenth . . . Excessive bail shall not be required, nor excessive fines imposed, nor cruel and unusual punishments inflicted.

Article the eleventh . . . The enumeration in the Constitution, of certain rights, shall not be construed to deny or disparage others retained by the people.

Article the twelfth . . . The powers not delegated to the United States by the Constitution, nor prohibited by it to the States, are reserved to the States respectively, or to the people.[1230]

REFERENCES

Chapter 1

1. David Herbert Donald, *Lincoln*, 237–41, 250.
2. Roy P. Basler, *Abraham Lincoln: his speeches and writings*, 519–33.
3. Jack N. Rakove, *Original Meanings*, 9.
4. William Donohue Ellis, *The Ordinance of 1787*, 90–92.
5. Ibid.
6. Clinton Rossiter, *The Federalist Papers*, 239–240.
7. Roy P. Basler, *Abraham Lincoln: his speeches and writings*, 519.
8. David Herbert Donald, *Lincoln*, 263.
9. *Inaugural Addresses of the Presidents of the United States*, 124.
10. Ibid., 120.
11. Akhil Reed Amar, *The Bill of Rights*, 58.
12. Carl Sandberg, *Abraham Lincoln The War Years*, Volume One, 279–81.
13. *Inaugural Addresses of the Presidents of the United States*, 120.
14. Ibid., 112.
15. Mark Tushnet, *Taking the Constitution Away from the Courts*, 15.
16. Ibid.
17. Clinton Rossiter, *1787: The Grand Convention*, 105–06.
18. Akhil Reed Amar, *The Bill of Rights*, 99.
19. *Dred Scott v. Sandford*, 19 Howard 393.
20. Ronald A. Anderson, Ivan Fox, and David P. Twomey, *Business Law and the Legal Environment*, 50.
21. Ibid.

22. Ibid.

23. *Marbury v. Madison*, 1 Cranch 137.

24. Raoul Berger, *Impeachment: The Constitutional Problems*, 90.

25. Ibid.

26. Adrienne Koch, *Notes of Debates in the Federal Convention of 1787*, 341.

27. Raoul Berger, *Selected Writings on the Constitution*, 137–38.

28. Edward Dumbauld, *Thomas Jefferson and the Law*, 9–10.

29. Ibid., 9.

30. Arthur R. Hogue, *Origins of the Common Law*, 205.

31. A. V. Dicey, *Introduction to the Study of the Law of the Constitution*, 4, 36–37.

32. Richard L. Perry and John C. Cooper, *Sources of Our Liberties*, 276–77.

33. Ibid., 276.

34. Clinton Rossiter, *The Federalist Papers*, 484–85.

35. Raoul Berger, *Impeachment: The Constitutional Problems*; 90.

36. Richard L. Perry and John C. . Cooper, *Sources of Our Liberties*, 139.

37. Ibid., 245.

38. Edward Lazarus, *Closed Chambers*, 238, 243.

39. Ibid., 241, 532.

40. Ibid., 242.

41. Ibid., 243.

42. Ibid., 249.

43. Ibid., 245.

44. John R. Vile, *Encyclopedia of Constitutional Amendments*, 343.

45. 33 L Ed 2d, 349.

46. Edward Lazarus, *Closed Chambers*, 6.

47. Ibid.

48. 2 Dallas 409.

49. Leonard W. Levy, *Encyclopedia of the American Constitution*, First Edition, 908.

50. Ibid.

51. *Hayburn's Case*, 2 Dallas 409.

52. Ibid.

53. *Vanhorne's Lessee v. Dorance*, 2 Dallas 304.

54. Michael Kammen, *The Origins of the American Constitution*, xii.

55. Clinton Rossiter, *The Federalist Papers*, 466–68.

56. *Dred Scott v. Sandford*, 19 Howard 393.

57. Clinton Rossiter, *The Federalist Papers*, 465–66.

58. David Shrager and Elizabeth Frost, *The Quotable Lawyer*, 165.

59. Jack N. Rakove, *Original Meanings*, 218.

60. David Shrager and Elizabeth Frost, *The Quotable Lawyer*, 35.

61. Leonard W. Levy, *Legacy of Suppression*, 170–71.

62. *The New Encyclopedia Britannica*, 1998 Ed., Vol. 2, 109–10.

63. *The Encyclopedia Americana International Ed.*, 1996 Ed., Vol. 3, 559.

64. Paula Chin, Hayes Ferguson, and Margery Sellinger, "Little Uproar on the Prairie," *People* (November 1, 1999): 77.

65. William P. Linebury (editor), *Justice in America*, 190.

66. Ibid., 190–91.

67. Richard Neely, *Why Courts Don't Work*, 7.

68. Ibid.

69. "Recent HALT Accomplishments," *The Legal Reformer*, Fall 1999, 7.

70. Jack N. Rakove, *The Beginnings of National Politics*, 365.

71. Paul D. Carrington, *Encyclopedia of the American Constitution*, First Edition, 1913.)

72. Clinton Rossiter, *The Federalist Papers*, 322.

Chapter 2

73. William Peters, *A More Perfect Union*, 1.

74. Clinton Rossiter, *1787: The Grand Convention*, 49.

75. Charles A. Beard and Mary R, Beard, *History of the United States*, 140.

76. Ibid.

77. Clinton Rossiter, *1787: The Grand Convention*, 44.

78. Adrienne Koch, *Notes of Debates in the Federal Convention of 1787*, 15.

79. Ibid., 7.

80. William Peters, *A More Perfect Union*, 7.

81. Clinton Rossiter, *1787: The Grand Convention*, 56.

82. Ibid.

83. Jack N. Rakove, *The Beginnings of National Politics*, 175.

84. Ibid.

85. Wythe Holt, "'To Establish Justice': Politics, The Judiciary Act of 1789, and the Invention of the Federal Courts," *Duke Law Journal* (December 1989): 1427–30.

86. Clinton Rossiter, *The Federalist Papers*, 353.

87. *Inaugural Addresses of the Presidents of the United States*, 121–22.

88. Clinton Rossiter, *The Federalist Papers*, 41.

89. Adrienne Koch, *Notes of Debates in the Federal Convention of 1787*, 288.

90. Michael Kammen, *The Origins of the American Constitution*, 119.

91. Ibid.

92. Ibid.

93. Ibid., 120.

94. Ralph Ketcham, *James Madison: A Biography*, 270. Thomas Fleming, *Liberty! The American Revolution*, 379.

95. Adrienne Koch, *Notes of Debates in the Federal Convention of 1787*, 385.

96. Ibid., 396.

97. Jack N. Rakove, *The Beginnings of National Politics*, 207.

98. Michael Kammen, *The Origins of the American Constitution*, 10.

99. Wythe Holt, "'To Establish Justice': Politics, The Judiciary Act of 1789, and the Invention of the Federal Courts, *Duke Law Journal* (December 1989): 1466.

Chapter 3

100. Clinton Rossiter, *The Federalist Papers*, 202.

101. Leonard W. Levy, *Encyclopedia of the American Constitution*, First Edition, 113.

102. Richard L. Perry and John C. Cooper, *Sources of Our Liberties*, 1.

103. Clinton Rossiter, *The Federalist Papers*, 310, 322, 433.

104. Ibid., 322.

105. Adrienne Koch, *Notes of Debates in the Federal Convention of 1787*, 463.

106. Wilfred J. Ritz, *Rewriting the History of the Judiciary Act of 1789*, 141.

107. Ibid.

108. Ibid.

109. Ibid., 74.

110. James L. Sundquist, *Constitutional Reform and Effective Government*, 22.

111. Ibid.

112. Clinton Rossiter, *The Federalist Papers*, 378–79.

113. Jethro K. Lieberman, *The Evolving Constitution*, 152.

114. Ibid., 153.

115. Sotirios A. Barber, *Encyclopedia of the American Constitution*, First Edition, 552.

116. Ibid.

117. Ibid.

118. Joseph M. Lynch, *Negotiating the Constitution*, 102.

119. Ibid., 102–03.

120. Jethro K. Lieberman, *The Evolving Constitution*, 152.

121. *Congressional Quarterly Almanac, Vol. XLVI, 1990*, 59.

122. Louis H. Pollak, *Encyclopedia of the American Constitution*, First Edition, 1979–80.

123. Jethro K. Lieberman, *The Evolving Constitution*, 563.

124. Adrienne Koch, *Notes of Debates in the Federal Convention of 1787*, 401.

125. Ibid.

126. Ibid.

127. Ibid., 404.

128. Jethro K. Lieberman, *The Evolving Constitution*, 565.

129. Ibid., 566.

130. Ibid.

131. *Oregon v. Mitchell*, 27 L Ed 2d 272.

132. Michael Kammen, *The Origins of the American Constitution*, 11.

133. Jack N. Rakove, *The Beginnings of National Politics*, 218.

134. Ibid.

135. Adrienne Koch, *Notes of Debates in the Federal Convention of 1787*, 30–31.

136. Charles A. Beard and Mary R. Beard, *History of the United States*, 142.

137. *U. S. Term Limits, Inc. v. Thornton*, 131 L Ed 2d 881.

138. Clinton Rossiter, *The Federalist Papers*, 355.

139. Ibid., 349.

140. Adrienne Koch, *Notes of Debates in the Federal Convention of 1787*, 208.

141. *Lucas v. Forty Fourth General Assembly of Colorado*, 377 U. S. 713.

142. Clinton Rossiter, *1787 The Grand Convention*, 249.

143. Adrienne Koch, *Notes of Debates in the Federal Convention of 1787*, 494.

144. Ibid.

145. Ibid., 303.

146. Joseph M. Lynch, *Negotiating the Constitution*, 136.

147. Ibid.

148. Clinton Rossiter, *The Federalist Papers*, 142–43.

149. Ibid., 219.

150. 157 U. S. 429, 158 U. S. 601.

151. Adrienne Koch, *Notes of Debates in the Federal Convention of 1787*, 40.

152. Ibid.

153. Ibid., 39,41.

154. Clinton Rossiter, *1787 The Grand Convention*, 185.

155. Dennis J. Mahoney, *Encyclopedia of the American Constitution*, First Edition, 1665.

156. Gerald V. Bradley, *Church-State Relationships in America*, 74.

157. Ibid., 20–54, 75.

158. *U. S. Term Limits, Inc. v. Thornton*, 131 L Ed 2d 881.

159. Edward Dumbauld, *The Constitution of the United States*, 80.

160. Ibid.

161. Jethro K. Lieberman, *The Evolving Constitution*, 176.

162. Robert B. McKay, *Encyclopedia of the American Constitution*, First Edition, 1519.

163. Ibid.

164. Ibid.

165. Ibid., 1523.

166. Ralph Mitchell, *CQ's Guide to the U.S. Constitution*, 28–30.

167. Ralph Ketcham, *James Madison A Biography*, 279.

168. *Amendments to the Constitution: A Brief Legislative History*, 60.

169. Charles A. Beard and Mary R, Beard, *History of the United States*, 248.

170. *Amendments to the Constitution: A Brief Legislative History*, 62.

171. Adrienne Koch, *Notes of Debates in the Federal Convention of 1787*, 388.

172. Ibid., 457.

173. Dennis J. Mahoney, *Encyclopedia of the American Constitution*, First Edition, 351. Jethro K. Lieberman, *The Evolving Constitution*, 251.

174. Edward Dumbauld, *The Constitution of the United States*, 101.

175. 82 L. ed. 493.

176. Ibid.

177. Kermit L. Hall and Mitchell S. Ritchie, *The Oxford Companion to the Supreme Court of the United States*, 771.

178. Adrienne Koch, *Notes of Debates in the Federal Convention of 1787*, 460.

179. Jethro K. Lieberman, *The Evolving Constitution*, 152.

180. Sotirios A. Barber, *Encyclopedia of the American Constitution*, First Edition, 552.

181. Edward Dumbauld, *The Constitution of the United States*, 103.

182. Adrienne Koch, *Notes of Debates in the Federal Convention of 1787*, 32.

183. Ibid., 61.

184. Ibid.

185. Ibid., 462.

186. *Amendments to the Constitution: A Brief Legislative History*, 10.

187. Edward L. Barrett, Jr., *Encyclopedia of the American Constitution*, First Edition, 662.

188. William Peters, *A More Perfect Union*, 6.

189. Adrienne Koch, *Notes of Debates in the Federal Convention of 1787*, 7, 13.

190. Charles A. Beard and Mary R. Beard, *History of the United States*, 140.

191. Michael Kammen, *The Origins of the American Constitution*, 13.

192. Clinton Rossiter, *The Federalist Papers*, 262–64.

193. Robert J. Steamer, *The Oxford Companion to the Supreme Court of the United States*, 167.

194. Adrienne Koch, *Notes of Debates in the Federal Convention of 1787*, 7, 14.

195. Clinton Rossiter, *The Federalist Papers*, 143.

196. Ibid., 144.

197. Ibid., 145.

198. Ibid., 144–45.

199. Ibid., 292–93.

200. Adrienne Koch, *Notes of Debates in the Federal Convention of 1787*, 645.

201. Clinton Rossiter, *The Federalist Papers*, 89.

202. Robert J. Steamer, *The Oxford Companion to the Supreme Court of the United States*, 168.

203. Ibid.

204. *Champion v. Ames*, 188 U. S. 321.

205. Jethro K. Lieberman, *The Evolving Constitution*, 312.

206. 119 L Ed 2d 121.

207. 119 L Ed 2d 137–38.

208. Merrill D. Peterson, *Encyclopedia of the American Constitution*, First Edition, 1179.

209. Jack N. Rakove, *James Madison*, 137.

210. Adrienne Koch, *Notes of Debates in the Federal Convention of 1787*, 460.

211. Stephen E. Ambrose, *Undaunted Courage*, 78–79.

212. Ibid.

213. Ibid., 72.

214. Charles A. Beard and Mary R. Beard, *History of the United States*, 191.

215. Ibid.

216. Stephen E. Ambrose, *Undaunted Courage*, 101.

217. Ibid.

218. Edward Dumbauld, *The Bill of Rights*, 175.

219. *Hanover National Bank v. Moyses*, 186 U. S. 181.

220. Ibid.

221. Jethro K. Lieberman, *The Evolving Constitution*, 73.

222. Wythe Holt, *The Oxford Companion to the Supreme Court of the United States*, 473.

223. Bray Hammond, *Banks and Politics in America*, 103.

224. Adrienne Koch, *Notes of Debates in the Federal Convention of 1787*, 571.

225. Charles Warren, *Bankruptcy in United States History*, 52.

226. *Hanover National Bank v. Moyses*, 186 U. S. 181.

227. Mark S. Summers, *Bankruptcy Explained*, 2.

228. Barbara Ann Chernow, *Robert Morris: Land Speculator, 1790–1801*, 219.

229. 4 Wheaton 209.

230. *Ogden v. Saunders*, 12 Wheaton 213.

231. Robert Remini, *Daniel Webster, The Man and His Time*, 164.

232. Charles Warren, *Bankruptcy in United States History*, 26.

233. Ibid., 27.

234. Ibid., 100.

235. Ibid., 103.

236. Ibid., 110.

237. Theodore Eisenberg, *Encyclopedia of the American Constitution*, First Edition, 99.

238. *Hanover National Bank v. Moyses*, 186 U. S. 181.

239. William Peden (editor), *Notes on the State of Virginia*, 133.

240. Clinton Rossiter, *1787: The Grand Convention*, 247–48.

241. Ibid., 319.

242. Charles Warren, *Bankruptcy in United States History*, 13.

243. Jack N. Rakove, *The Beginnings of National Government*, 195.

244. Clinton Rossiter, *1787: The Grand Convention*, 321.

245. E. James Ferguson, *Encyclopedia Americana*, 1996 edition, Volume 19, 473–74.

246. Barbara Ann Chernow, *Robert Morris: Land Speculator, 1790–1801*, 216–222.

247. Ibid., 222.

248. Ibid., 217–18.

249. Ibid., 222.

250. Paul D. Carrington, *Encyclopedia of the American Constitution*, First Edition, 1920.

251. John Greenwald, "The Bankruptcy Game," *Time* (May 18, 1992): 60.

252. "Paralegals Behind Bars," *The Legal Reformer*, Volume XIII, Number 2 (April–June 1993): 5.

253. Charles W. McCurdy, *Encyclopedia of the American Constitution*, First Edition, 1270.

254. Adrienne Koch, *Notes of Debates in the Federal Convention of 1787*, 638.

255. Ibid.

256. Ibid.

257. Bray Hammond, *Banks and Politics in America*, 103–05.

258. Joseph M. Lynch, *Negotiating the Constitution*, 85, 86, 255.

259. Bray Hammond, *Banks and Politics in America*, 50.

260. Ibid., 48–49.

261. Ibid., 50.

262. Ibid., 50–51.

263. Ibid.

264. Ibid., 51.

265. Ibid., 52, 63.

266. Ibid., 103.

267. Ibid., 52–54.

268. Ibid., 54–62.

269. Ibid., 60–61.

270. Ibid., 114–15.

271. Ibid., 114–17.

272. Adrienne Koch, *Notes of Debates in the Federal Convention of 1787*, 389.

273. Ibid., 470.

274. Ibid.

275. Ibid.

276. Ibid.

277. Ibid.

278. Ibid., 471.

279. Ibid.

280. Charles W. McCurdy, *Encyclopedia of the American Constitution*, First Edition, 1271.

281. Adrienne Koch, *Notes of Debates in the Federal Convention of 1787*, 470.

282. Ibid., 471.

283. Charles W. McCurdy, *Encyclopedia of the American Constitution*, First Edition, 1272.

284. Ibid.

285. Ibid.

286. Ibid.

287. Ibid., 1272–73.

288. Jethro K. Lieberman, *The Evolving Constitution*, 390.

289. Joseph M. Lynch, *Negotiating the Constitution*, 103.

290. Clinton Rossiter, *The Federalist Papers*, 485 and 488.

291. Wythe Holt, *The Oxford Companion to the Supreme Court of the United States*, 472.

292. Ibid.

293. Ibid., 473–74.

294. *Black's Law Dictionary*, Abridged Fifth Edition, 501.

295. Ibid., 624.

296. Adrienne Koch, *Notes of Debates in the Federal Convention of 1787*, 639.

297. Noble E. Cunningham, Jr., *In Pursuit of Reason*, 223.

298. Roy G. Weatherup, *Gun Control and the Constitution*, 193.

299. Ibid., 197.

300. Ibid., 190.

301. Clinton Rossiter, *1787: The Grand Convention*, 56.

302. Ibid.

303. Ibid.

304. Wythe Holt, "'To Establish Justice': Politics, The Judiciary Act of 1789, and the Invention of the Federal Courts," *Duke Law Journal* (December 1989): 1454–55.

305. Ibid., 1453–54.

306. Clinton Rossiter, *The Federalist Papers*, 187.

307. Adrienne Koch, *Notes of Debates in the Federal Convention of 1787*, 512.

308. Ibid., 513.

309. Ibid.

310. Ibid.

311. Ibid., 581.

312. Edward Dumbauld, *The Constitution of the United States*, 182.

313. Clinton Rossiter, *The Federalist Papers*, 201.

314. Ibid., 202–03.

315. Ibid., 284.

316. Edward Dumbauld, *The Constitution of the United States*, 192.

317. Leonard W. Levy, *Origins of the Bill of Rights*, 68.

318. Ibid., 72, 77.

319. Ibid., 71.

320. Wythe Holt, "'To Establish Justice': Politics, The Judiciary Act of 1789, and the Invention of the Federal Courts," *Duke Law Journal* (December 1989): 1437.

321. Ibid.

322. Ibid.

323. Richard L. Perry and John C. Cooper, *Sources of Our Liberties*, 334–35.

324. Ibid., 336–37.

325. Ibid., 337.

326. Jethro K. Lieberman, *The Evolving Constitution*, 189.

327. Ibid., 155.

328. Ibid., 189.

329. Ibid.

330. Ibid.

331. Michael Kammen, *The Origins of the American Constitution*, 12.

Chapter 4

332. Joseph M. Lynch, *Negotiating the Constitution*, 54–55.

333. Ibid., 54.

334. Ibid., 60.

335. Ibid.

336. Clinton Rossiter, *The Federalist Papers*, 459.

337. Joseph M. Lynch, *Negotiating the Constitution*, 56.

338. Ibid., 55.

339. Ibid., 61–62.

340. Ibid., 62.

341. Clinton Rossiter, *1787 The Grand Convention*, 198.

342. Dennis J. Mahoney, *Encyclopedia of the American Constitution*, First Edition, 1927.

343. Ibid.

344. Charles A. Beard and Mary R. Beard, *History of the United States*, 183–84.

345. Ibid., 184.

346. Jethro K. Lieberman, *The Evolving Constitution*, 176–77.

347. Dennis J. Mahoney, *Encyclopedia of the American Constitution*, First Edition, 31.

348. Ibid.

349. Ibid.

350. Clinton Rossiter, *1787 The Grand Convention*, 301.

351. Jethro K. Lieberman, *The Evolving Constitution*, 544.

352. Ibid.

353. William C. Banks, *The Oxford Companion to the Supreme Court of the United States*, 878.

354. Jethro K. Lieberman, *The Evolving Constitution*, 544.

355. Ibid.

356. Raoul Berger, *Impeachment: The Constitutional Problems*, 54.

357. Ibid., 2.

358. Ibid., 55.

359. Ibid., 45.

360. Ibid., 59.

361. Ibid., 61.

362. Ibid.

363. Ibid., 67–69.

364. Ibid., 67.

365. Ibid.

366. Ibid.

367. Ibid., 67–68.

368. Ibid., 68.

369. Ibid.

370. Ibid.

371. Ibid., 69.

372. Ibid., 70, 90.

373. Ibid., 68.

374. Ibid., 69.

375. Ibid., 55–56.

376. Ibid., 55–56.

377. Ibid., 62.

378. Ibid., 2.

379. Ibid., 83.

380. Ibid., 83, 214.

381. Ibid., 214.

382. Clinton Rossiter, *The Federalist Papers*, 405–06.

383. Edward Dumbauld, *The Bill of Rights*, 188.

384. Ibid., 218.

Chapter 5

385. Raoul Berger, *Impeachment: The Constitutional Problems*, 125.

386. Ibid., 127–31, 151–52.

387. Jack N. Rakove, *Original Meanings*, 298–99.

388. Richard E. Ellis, *The Jeffersonian Crisis: Courts and Politics in the Young Republic*, 6.

389. Richard L. Perry and John C. Cooper, *Sources of Our Liberties*, 349.

390. Ibid., 385–86.

391. Raoul Berger, *Impeachment: The Constitutional Problems*, 145.

392. Ibid.

393. Ibid., 132–33.

394. Ibid., 150.

395. Adrienne Koch, *Notes of Debates in the Federal Convention of 1787*, 536.

396. Ibid., 537.

397. Raoul Berger, *Impeachment: The Constitutional Problems*, 311–12.

398. Richard E. Ellis, *The Jeffersonian Crisis: Courts and Politics in the Young Republic*, 15, 288.

399. Ibid., 20.

400. Ibid., 29.

401. Ibid., 30.

402. Ibid., 92–93, 157.

403. Ibid., 150.

404. Joseph M. Lynch, *Negotiating the Constitution*, 50–92.

405. Douglas Southhall Freeman, *George Washington, Volume Six, Patriot and President*, 346–47.

406. Raoul Berger, *Impeachment: The Constitutional Problems*, 126, 177.

407. Ibid., 126.

408. Ibid., 183–84.

409. Leon Friedman and Fred L. Israel (editors), *The Justices of the United States Supreme Court*, 196.

410. Ibid.

411. Ibid.

412. Ibid.

413. Raoul Berger, *Impeachment: The Constitutional Problems*, 228.

414. Ibid.

415. Ibid.

416. Raoul Berger, *Impeachment: The Constitutional Problems*, 226.

417. Noble E. Cunningham, Jr., *In Pursuit of Reason*, 272.

418. Willard Sterne Randall, *Thomas Jefferson: a life*, 540.

419. Ibid.

420. Raoul Berger, *Impeachment: The Constitutional Problems*, 236.

421. Ibid., 237.

422. Ibid., 237–38 and 318.

423. Ibid., 238.

424. Ibid.

425. Ibid.

426. Ibid.

427. Milton W. Hamilton, *Dictionary of American History*, Volume I, 132.

428. Akhil Reed Amar, *The Bill of Rights*, 99.

429. Ibid., 98–99.

430. Leon Friedman and Fred L. Israel, *The Justices of the United States Supreme Court*, 194.

431. Willard Sterne Randall, *Thomas Jefferson: a life*, 541.

432. Richard E. Ellis, *The Jeffersonian Crisis: Courts and Politics in the Young Republic*, 102.

433. Ibid.

434. Ibid.

435. Ibid., 97–98.

436. Ibid., 103.

437. Raoul Berger, *Impeachment: The Constitutional Problems*, 83, 214.

438. Clinton Rossiter, *1787: The Grand Convention*, 320.

439. Ibid.

440. Raoul Berger, *Impeachment: The Constitutional Problems*, 202–06.

441. Ibid., 70–71.

442. Wythe Holt, *The Oxford Companion to the Supreme Court of the United States*, 472.

443. Ibid.

444. Ibid.

445. Ibid.

446. John E. Semonche, *The Oxford Companion to the Supreme Court of the United States*, 476.

447. Peter G. Fish, *The Oxford Companion to the Supreme Court of the United States*, 476.

448. Ibid., 477.

449. Richard E. Ellis, *The Jeffersonian Crisis: Courts and Politics in the Young Republic*, 194.

450. Ibid., 195.

451. Ibid.

452. Ibid., 196.

453. Wilfred J. Ritz, *Rewriting the History of the Judiciary Act of 1789*, 51.

454. Richard E. Ellis, *The Jeffersonian Crisis*, 118.

455. Martha Swann, *The Oxford Companion to the Supreme Court of the United States*, 160.

456. Ibid.

457. Ibid.

458. Ibid.

459. Bryan A. Garner, *The Oxford Companion to the Supreme Court of the United States*, 610.

460. Ibid.

461. *Amendments to the Constitution: A Brief Legislative History*, 13.

462. Ibid.

463. Clinton Rossiter, *The Federalist Papers*, 487–88.

464. *Hans v. State of Louisiana*, 134 U. S., 847.

465. *Amendments to the Constitution: A Brief Legislative History*, 14.

466. Ibid.

467. Wythe Holt, "'To Establish Justice': Politics, The Judiciary Act of 1789, and the Invention of the Federal Courts," *Duke Law Journal* (December 1989): 1451.

468. Ibid., 1440.

469. Ibid., 1434.

470. Ibid., 1451.

471. Ibid.

472. Ibid., 1456–58.

473. Ibid., 1452.

474. Ibid., 1452–53.

475. Ibid., 1487–88.

476. Ibid., 1488.

477. Henry J. Bourguignon, *The First Federal Court: The Federal Appellate Prize Court of the American Revolution 1775–1787*, 77.

478. Ibid., 43.

479. Ibid., 76.

480. Ibid., 44.

481. Ibid.

482. Ibid.

483. Ibid., 45.

484. Ibid., 46–47.

485. Thomas Fleming, *Liberty! The American Revolution*, 197.

486. Henry J. Bourguignon, *The First Federal Court: The Federal Appellate Prize Court of the American Revolution*, 52.

487. Ibid., 53.

488. Ibid., 55.

489. Ibid.

490. Ibid., 78–81.

491. Ibid., 80.

492. Ibid., 80.

493. Ibid., 81.

494. Ibid., 84.

495. Ibid., 85.

496. Ibid., 90.

497. Ibid., 77.

498. Michael Kammen, *The Origins of the American Constitution*, 13–14.

499. Henry J. Bourguignon, *The First Federal Court: The Federal Appellate Prize Court of the American Revolution 1775–1787*, 297 and 318.

500. Adrienne Koch, *Notes of Debates in the Federal Convention of 1787*, 32.

501. Ibid., 71.

502. Ibid., 72.

503. Ibid.

504. Ibid., 73.

505. Ibid., 647.

506. Henry J. Bourguignon, *The First Federal Court: The Federal Appellate Prize Court of the American Revolution 1775–1787*, 335.

507. Ibid., 337.

508. Clinton Rossiter, *The Federalist Papers*, 504.

509. Stanley Morrison, "Workmen's Compensation and the Maritime Law," *Yale Law Journal*, Vol. 38, 473.

510. Henry J. Bourguignon, *The First Federal Court: The Federal Appellate Prize Court of the American Revolution 1775–1787*, 25.

511. Ibid.

512. Ibid., 26.

513. Wythe Holt, *The Oxford Companion to the Supreme Court of the United States*, 474.

514. Ibid.

515. Ibid., 473.

516. Paul M. Bator, *Encyclopedia of the American Constitution*, First Edition, 1076.

517. Edward Dumbauld, *The Constitution of the United States*, 160.

518. Bruce Ackerman, *We the People: Transformations*, 225–27.

519. *Ex Parte McCardle*, 74 U. S. (7 Wall) 506, 514.

520. Bruce Ackerman, *We the People: Transformations*, 225.

521. Ibid.

522. Ibid., 226.

523. Wilfred J. Ritz, *Rewriting the History of the Judiciary Act of 1789*, 179.

524. Raoul Berger, *Impeachment: The Constitutional Problems*, 7.

525. Adrienne Koch, *Notes of Debates in the Federal Convention of 1787*, 489.

526. Ibid.

527. Raoul Berger, *Impeachment: The Constitutional Problems*, 7.

528. Raoul Berger, *Impeachment: The Constitutional Problems*, 7.

529. Edward Dumbauld, *The Constitution of the United States*, 373–74.

530. Raoul Berger, *Impeachment: The Constitutional Problems*, 8.

531. William Lineberry, *Justice in America*, 191.

Chapter 6

532. Adrienne Koch, *Notes of Debates in the Federal Convention of 1787*, 546.

533. Ibid., 569.

534. Ibid., 570.

535. Ibid.

536. Michael Kammen, *The Origins of the American Constitution*, 11.

537. Thomas O. Sargentich, *The Oxford Companion to the Supreme Court of the United States*, 322.

538. Ibid.

539. Kenneth L. Karst, *The Encyclopedia of the American Constitution*, First Edition, 1458.

540. Michael Kammen, *The Origins of the American Constitution*, 11.

541. Kenneth L. Karst, *Encyclopedia of the American Constitution*, First Edition, 1458–59.

542. Edward Dumbauld, *The Constitution of the United States*, 417.

543. James Morton Callahan, *History of West Virginia*, 339.

544. Carl Sandburg, *Abraham Lincoln The War Years*, Volume One, 656.

545. James Morton Callahan, *History of West Virginia*, 365.

Chapter 8

546. Jethro K. Lieberman, *The Evolving Constitution*, 521.

547. Gerard V. Bradley, *Church-State Relationships in America*, 74.

548. Ibid.

549. Ibid.

550. Ibid.

551. Ibid., 74–75.

552. Ibid.

553. Ibid., 75.

554. Ibid., 94.

555. Edward Dumbauld, *The Constitution of the United States*, 451.

Chapter 9

556. Clinton Rossiter, *1787 The Grand Convention*, 275.

557. Ibid., 276.

558. Adrienne Koch, *Notes of Debates in the Federal Convention of 1787*, 352.

559. Ibid.

Chapter 10

560. Helen E. Veit, Kenneth R. Bowling, and Charlene Bangs Bickford, *Creating the Bill of Rights*, 79–80.

561. Gerald V. Bradley, *Church-State Relationships in America*, 88.

562. Ibid., 56.

563. Ibid., 19, 54–55.

564. Ibid., 19.

565. Ibid., 3, 16.

566. Ibid., 51.

567. Ibid., 47–48.

568. Ibid., 49.

569. Ibid., 49–50.

570. Ibid., 50.

571. Ibid.

572. Ibid., 33.

573. Ibid., 42.

574. Ibid.

575. Ibid., 30–31.

576. Ibid., 30–31, 40–41.

577. Ibid., 52.

578. Ibid., 53.

579. Ibid., 24.

580. Ibid., 21.

581. Ibid., 22.

582. Ibid., 23.

583. Richard L. Perry and John C. Cooper, *Sources of Our Liberties*, 382–83.

584. Helen E. Veit, Kenneth R. Bowling, and Charlene Bangs Bickford, *Creating the Bill of Rights*, 157.

585. Ibid.

586. Ibid.

587. Ibid.

588. Ibid.

589. Ibid., 157–58.

590. Gerald V. Bradley, *Church-State Relationships in America*, 79.

591. Ibid.

592. Roy P. Basler, *Abraham Lincoln: his speeches and writings*, 519.

593. *Baldwin's Ohio Revised Code*, Ohio Constitution Article IV to end, 634.

594. Charles A. Beard and Mary R. Beard, *History of the United States*, 44.

595. Ibid.

596. Gerard V. Bradley, *Church-State Relationships in America*, 125–131.

597. Ibid., 126–127.

598. Ibid. 127–28.

599. Ibid., 101.

600. Ibid.

601. Ibid., 99–100.

602. Ibid., 100.

603. Ibid.

604. Ibid., 99.

605. Leonard W. Levy, *The Establishment Clause*, 86, 207.

606. *Christian Century*, October 21, 1998, 962.

607. 91 L ed 712.

608. Horace White, *The Life of Lyman Trumbull*, 259.

609. *Levitt v. Committee for Public Education and Religious Liberty*, 413 U. S. 472. *New York v. Cathedral Academy*, 434 U. S. 125.

610. *Committee for Public Education and Religious Liberty v. Regan*, 444 U. S. 646.

611. Richard Morgan, *Encyclopedia of the American Constitution*, 1155.

612. Ibid.

613. Gerard V. Bradley, *Church-State Relationships in America*, 13.

614. Ibid.

615. Edward Dumbauld, *The Bill of Rights and What it Means Today*, 185 and 201.

616. Ibid., 189.

617. Gerald V. Bradley, *Church-State Relationships in America*, 76.

618. Edward Dumbauld, *The Bill of Rights*, 39.

619. Gerard V. Bradley, *Church-State Relationships in America*, 123.

620. Richard L. Perry and John C. Cooper, *Sources of Our Liberty*, 168.

621. Willard Sterne Randall, *Thomas Jefferson: a life*, 138–40.

622. Ibid., 139–40.

623. Ibid., 140.

624. Noble E. Cunningham, Jr., *In Pursuit of Reason*, 76–77.

625. Willard Sterne Randall, *Thomas Jefferson: a life*, 137.

626. Ibid.

627. Ibid., 137–38.

628. Ibid., 138.

629. Ibid.

630. Gerard V. Bradley, *Church-State Relationships in America*, 100.

631. Ibid.

632. Ibid., 101–02.

633. Ibid.

634. Ibid., 101.

635. Ibid.

636. Ibid., 102.

637. Garrett Ward Sheldon, *The Political Philosophy of Thomas Jefferson*, 109.

638. Ibid.

638. Ibid.

640. Ibid.

641. Edward Dumbauld, *The Bill of Rights and What it Means Today*, 213.

642. Ibid, 45.

643. Ibid., 217.

644. Ibid., 207.

645. Gerald V. Bradley, *Church-State Relationships in America*, 88.

646. Ibid.

647. Edward Dumbauld, *The Bill of Rights and What it Means Today*, 208.

648. Charles A. Beard and Mary R. Beard, *History of the United States*, 46.

649. Ibid.

650. Ibid.

651. Ibid.

652. Ibid. 47.

653. Ibid.

654. Leonard W. Levy, *Legacy of Suppression*, 36–37.

655. Charles A. Beard and Mary R. Beard, *History of the United States*, 47.

656. Ibid., 47–48.

657. Ibid., 47.

658. Ibid., 46.

659. Joel M. Gora, *The Rights of Reporters*, 25.

660. Edward Dumbauld, *The Bill of Rights and What It Means Today*, 210.

661. Leonard W. Levy, *Emergence of a Free Press*, 177.

662. Ibid., 178.

663. Ibid., 185.

664. Ibid., 214.

665. Ibid.

666. Ibid., 214–15.

667. Ibid., 215.

668. Ibid.

669. Ibid., 210–11.

670. Ibid., 207, 211.

671. Ibid., 211.

672. Ibid.

673. Ibid.

674. Ibid.

675. Ibid., 192.

676. Ibid.

677. Ibid.

678. Ibid.

679. Ibid., 12.

680. Leonard W. Levy, *Constitutional Opinions*, 164–65.

681. Ibid., 164.

682. Richard L. Perry and John C. Cooper, *Sources of Our Liberties*, 288.

683. L. Kinvin Wroth, *Encyclopedia of the American Constitution*, First Edition, 332.

684. Leonard W. Levy, *Emergence of a Free Press*, 204.

685. Ibid., 204–05.

686. Ibid., 205.

687. Ibid.

688. Ibid., 276–78.

689. Ibid., 279.

690. 2 Dallas 409.

691. Ibid.

692. Leonard W, Levy, *Encyclopedia of the American Constitution*, First Edition, 908.

693. Leonard W. Levy, *Emergence of a Free Press*, 276.

694. Leonard W. Levy, *Constitutional Opinions*, 167.

695. Leonard W. Levy, *Jefferson and Civil Liberties*, 61–65.

696. Ibid., 63.

697. Ibid., 66.

698. *U. S. v. Hudson and Goodwin*, 7 Cranch 32.

699. Ibid.

700. 7 Cranch 32.

701. Leonard W. Levy, *Jefferson and Civil Liberties*, 66.

702. Ibid.

703. Ibid., 66, 201.

704. *U. S. v. Hudson and Goodwin*, 7 Cranch 32.

705. Ibid.

706. Charles A. Beard and Mary R. Beard, *History of the United States*, 181.

707. Leonard W. Levy, *Emergence of a Free Press*, 297.

708. Leonard W. Levy, *Constitutional Opinions*, 166.

709. Leonard W. Levy, *Emergence of a Free Press*, 298.

710. Joseph M. Lynch, *Negotiating the Constitution*, 185.

711. Ibid.

712. Ibid.

713. Ibid.

714. Leonard W. Levy, *Emergence of a Free Press*, 297–98.

715. Willard Sterne Randall, *Thomas Jefferson: a life*, 528.

716. Ibid., 542.

717. Ibid., 543.

718. Ibid., 537.

719. Joseph M. Lynch, *Negotiating the Constitution*, 192.

720. Ibid.

721. Ibid.

722. Leonard W. Levy, *Emergence of a Free Press*, 280.

723. Paul M. Bator, *Encyclopedia of the American Constitution*, First Edition, 1076.

724. Leonard W. Levy, *Emergence of a Free Press*, 280.

725. 105 L Ed 2d 342.

726. M. R. Bennett, ". . . *So Gallantly Streaming*," 98.

727. Ibid.

728. Ibid., 98–99.

729. Ibid., 99.

730. 120 L Ed 2d 305.

731. Tony Mauro, *USA TODAY*, June 23, 1992, 1A.

732. 45 L Ed 2d 125.

733. 116 L Ed 2d 476.

734. "People Digest," *Dayton Daily News* (December 24, 1991): 2A.

735. Erma Bombeck, *Dayton Daily News* (August 18, 1992): 2C.

736. *United Public Workers of America v. Mitchell*, 91 L Ed 754.

737. *Civil Service Commission v. Letter Carriers*, 37 L Ed 2d 796..

738. Richard L. Perry and John C. Cooper, *Sources of Our Liberties*, 228.

739. Ibid., 229.

740. Charles E. Rice, *Encyclopedia of the American Constitution*, First Edition, 789.

741. Richard L. Perry and John C. Cooper, *Sources of Our Liberties*, 229.

742. Ibid., 228.

743. Edward Dumbauld, *The Constitution of the United States*, 12.

744. Ibid., 13.

745. Richard L. Perry and John C. Cooper, *Sources of Our Liberties*, 229.

746. Charles E. Rice, *Encyclopedia of the American Constitution*, First Edition, 789.

747. Willard Sterne Randall, *Thomas Jefferson: a life*, 355 and 357.

748. Thomas Fleming, *Liberty! The American Revolution*, 340.

749. Richard L. Perry and John C. Cooper, *Sources of Our Liberties*, 229.

750. Ibid., 231.

751. Thomas Fleming, *Liberty! The American Revolution*, 105–06.

752. Ibid., 114.

753. Ibid., 160.

754. Ibid., 134–35.

755. Ibid., 141–42.

756. Ibid., 151.

757. Ibid., 197, 246–47, 257–61.

758. Ibid., 197.

759. Ibid., 250.

760. Ibid., 249.

761. Ibid.

762. Ibid.

763. 7 Peters 243.

764. Clinton Rossiter, *The Federalist Papers*, 187.

765. Robert J. Cottrol, *Gun Control and the Constitution*, xvi.

766. Ibid., xv.

767. Charles A. Beard and Mary R. Beard, *History of the United States*, 142.

768. Ibid.

769. Adrienne Koch, *Notes of Debates in the Federal Convention of 1787*, 29.

770. Ibid.

771. Wythe Holt, "'To Establish Justice': Politics, The Judiciary Act of 1789, and the Invention of the Federal Courts," *Duke Law Journal* (December 1989): 1454–55.

772. Clinton Rossiter, *1787: The Grand Convention*, 55.

773. Ibid., 56.

774. Wythe Holt, "'To Establish Justice': Politics, The Judiciary Act of 1789, and the Invention of the Federal Courts," *Duke Law Journal* (December 1989): 1453–54.

775. Clinton Rossiter, *The Federalist Papers*, 187.

776. Michael Kammen, *The Origins of the American Constitution*, 12, 13.

777. Robert J. Cottrol, *Gun Control and the Constitution*, xviii.

778. Edward Dumbauld, *The Bill of Rights and What it Means Today*, 208.

779. Wythe Holt, *The Oxford Companion to the Supreme Court of the United States*, 473.

780. Ibid.

781. Wythe Holt, "'To Establish Justice': Politics, The Judiciary Act of 1789, and the Invention of the Federal Courts," *Duke Law Journal* (December 1989): 1486.

782. Helen E. Veit, Kenneth R. Bowling, and Charlene Bangs Bickford, *Creating the Bill of Rights*, 186–87.

783. Ibid., 187.

784. Ibid., 197–98.

785. Ibid., 117–28.

786. Ibid., 188–89.

787. Ibid., 41.

788. Ibid., 37.

789. Edward Dumbauld, *The Bill of Rights*, 34, 47.

790. Helen E. Veit, Kenneth R.Bowling, and Charlene Bangs Bickford, *Creating the Bill of Rights*, 242.

791. John R. Vile, *Encyclopedia of Constitutional Amendments*, 323.

792. Jethro K. Lieberman, *The Evolving Constitution*, 550.

793. Ibid.

794. *Amendments to the Constitution: A Brief Legislative History*, 11.

795. Adrienne Koch, *Notes of Debates in the Federal Convention of 1787*, 458.

796. Ibid.

797. 7 Peters 243.

798. Akhil Reed Amar, *The Bill of Rights*, 145, 148, 355.

799. Stephen P. Halbrook, *That Every Man Be Armed*, 90–91.

800. Ibid., 92.

801. Akhil Reed Amar, *The Bill of Rights*, 146–147, 182–183.

802. Stephen P. Holbrook, *That Every Man Be Armed*, 54.

803. Ibid., 51–55.

804. Leonard W. Levy, *Origins of the Bill of Rights*, 148.

805. Clinton Rossiter, *The Federalist Papers*, 180.

806. Ibid., 298–300.

807. *1968 CQ Almanac*, 553.

808. Ibid.

809. Robert J. Steamer, *The Oxford Companion to the Supreme Court of the United States*, 168.

810. James J. Kilpatrick, "What does the Second Amendment really mean?" *Xenia Gazette* (March 11, 1991): 4.

811. Leonard W. Levy, *Origins of the Bill of Rights*, 148.

812. Richard L. Perry and John C. Cooper, *Sources of Our Liberties*, 62.

813. Ibid., 65, 74.

814. Ibid., 75.

815. Ibid., 245.

816. Dennis J. Mahoney, *Encyclopedia of the American Constitution*, First Edition, 1890.

817. Richard L. Perry and John C. Cooper, *Sources of Our Liberties*, 278.

818. Ibid.

819. Adrienne Koch, *Notes of Debates in the Federal Convention*, 639.

820. Noble E. Cunningham Jr., *In Pursuit of Reason*, 223.

821. Akhil Reed Amar, *The Bill of Rights*, 60–61.

822. Telford Taylor, *Two Studies in Constitutional Interpretation*, 43.

823. Ibid., 43, 45.

824. Harold J. Rothwax, *Guilty: The Collapse of Criminal Justice*, 42.

825. Telford Taylor, *Two Studies in Constitutional Interpretation*, 45.

826. Ibid.

827. Harold J. Rothwax, *Guilty: The Collapse of Criminal Justice*, 42.

828. Ibid., 64.

829. Ibid., 40–42.

830. Akhil Reed Amar, *The Bill of Rights*, 71.

831. Ibid., 74.

832. Ibid., 74–75.

833. Nelson B. Lasson, *The History and Development of the Fourth Amendment to the United States Constitution*, 43.

834. Ibid.

835. Leonard W. Levy, *Emergence of a Free Press*, 145–46.

836. Nelson B. Lasson, *The History and Development of the Fourth Amendment to the United States Constitution*, 44–45.

837. Ibid., 45.

838. Ibid., 45–46.

839. Ibid., 46.

840. Ibid.

841. Ibid.

842. Ibid., 43.

843. Telford Taylor, *Two Studies in Constitutional Interpretation*, 32.

844. Ibid., 33–34.

845. Edward Dumbauld, *The Bill of Rights and What it Means Today*, 211.

846. Ibid, 214.

847. Theodore Eisenberg, *Encyclopedia of the American Constitution*, First Edition, 1039.

848. Telford Taylor, *Two Studies in Constitutional Interpretation*, 53–55.

849. Ibid., 55–56.

850. Jethro K. Lieberman, *The Evolving Constitution*, 328.

851. Ibid.

852. Ibid.

853. Edward Dumbauld, *The Bill of Rights and What It Means Today*, 207, 211.

854. Richard D. Younger, *The People's Panel: The Grand Jury in the United States, 1634–1941*, 4.

855. Ibid., 1.

856. Ibid., 2.

857. Jethro K. Lieberman, *Free Speech, Free Press, and the Law*, 15.

858. Ibid.

859. Leonard W. Levy, *Origins of the Bill of Rights*, 222.

860. Ibid.

861. Ibid.

862. Ibid.

863. Ibid., 222–23.

864. Richard D. Younger, *The People's Panel: The Grand Jury in the United States, 1634–1941*, 26.

865. Ibid., 36–40.

866. Ibid., 39.

867. Ibid.

868. Wilfred J. Ritz, *Rewriting the History of the Judiciary Act of 1789*, 118.

869. Ibid, 119.

870. Ibid.

871. Richard D. Younger, *The People's Panel: The Grand Jury in the United States, 1634–1941*, 3.

872. Ibid., 182–86, 233–35.

873. Ibid., 196–99.

874. Ibid., 204–08.

875. Ibid., 241.

876. Ibid.

877. Ibid.

878. Ibid., 49–51.

879. Ibid., 50.

880. Ibid.

881. Ibid., 51.

882. Ibid., 49.

883. Ibid., 60.

884. Akhil Reed Amar, *The Bill of Rights*, 85.

885. Richard D. Younger, *The People's Panel: The Grand Jury in the United States*, 59.

886. Ibid., 60.

887. Ibid., 3, 56–59, 143.

888. Ibid., 3.

889. Ibid.

890. Ibid., 3, 66.

891. Ibid., 62–64.

892. Ibid., 62.

893. Ibid., 63.

894. *The New Encyclopedia Britannica, Volume 5 Micropaedia*, 418.

895. Ibid.

896. Leonard W. Levy, *Encyclopedia of the American Constitution*, First Edition, 942.

897. Ibid.

898. Ibid.

899. Richard L. Perry and John C. Cooper, *Sources of Our Liberties*, 65–69.

900. Ibid., 62, 69.

901. Ibid., 62.

902. Jay A. Sigler, *Double Jeopardy*, 16–17.

903. Richard L. Perry and John C. Cooper, *Sources of Our Liberties*, 65.

904. Leonard W. Levy, *Encyclopedia of the American Constitution*, First Edition, 589.

905. Charles Fairman, *The Fourteenth Amendment and the Bill of Rights: The Incorporation Theory*, 164.

906. Ibid.

907. Ibid., 164–65.

908. Jay A. Sigler, *Double Jeopardy: The Development of a Legal and Social Policy*, 16.

909. Ibid., 17.

910. Ibid., 23.

911. Ibid., 23, 24.

912. Jay A. Sigler, *Encyclopedia of the American Constitution*, First Edition, 576.

913. Ibid.

914. Ibid., 576–78.

915. Ibid., 577.

916. Ibid., 576.

917. Jay A. Sigler, *Double Jeopardy: The Development of a Legal and Social Policy*, 56–57.

918. Ibid., 57–58.

919. *Ciucci v. Illinois*, 2 L ed 2d 983.

920. Leonard W. Levy, *Encyclopedia of the American Constitution*, First Edition, 1571.

921. Leonard W. Levy, *Origins of the Fifth Amendment: The Right Against Self-Incrimination*, xiii.

922. Leonard W. Levy, *Encyclopedia of the American Constitution*, First Edition, 1571.

923. Ibid.

924. Ibid., 1571–72.

925. Leonard W. Levy, *Origins of the Fifth Amendment: The Right Against Self-Incrimination*, xii.

926. Leonard W. Levy, *The Encyclopedia of the Constitution*, First Edition, 1576.

927. Leonard W. Levy, *Origins of the Fifth Amendment: The Right Against Self-Incrimination*, xi.

928. 16 L ed 2d 694.

929. Harold J. Rothwax, *Guilty: The Collapse of Criminal Justice*, 171–85.

930. Ibid., 172.

931. Ibid., 140–41.

932. *Bauman v. Ross*, 42 L Ed 280.

933. Harry N. Scheiber, *Encyclopedia of the American Constitution*, First Edition, 631.

934. Ibid.

935. *Page's Ohio Revised Code*, 1982 Edition, 217.

936. Ibid., 217–18.

937. 7th Amendment—Jury Trial, 40 L Ed 2d, 869.

938. Edward Dumbauld, *The Bill of Rights*, 171.

939. Felix Frankfurter and Thomas G. Corcoran, "Petty Federal Offenses and the Constitutional Guaranty of Trial by Jury," *Harvard Law Review*, Vol. 39, 963.

940. Ibid., 964.

941. Ibid., 955–56.

942. Ibid., 956.

943. Ibid., 955–56.

944. Ibid., 955.

945. *Schick v. United States*, 195 U. S. 81.

946. *Faretta v. California*, 45 L Ed 2d 577.

947. Ibid.

948. Francis A. Allen, *Encyclopedia of the Constitution*, First Edition, 1585.

949. *Faretta v. California*, 45 L Ed 2d 579.

950. Ibid., 580.

951. Joseph M. Lynch, *Negotiating the Constitution*, 200.

952. Leon Friedman and Fred L. Israel, *The Justices of the United States Supreme Court*, 194.

953. Ibid.

954. Douglas S. Freeman, *George Washington, Volume Six, Patriot and President*, 347.

955. *Faretta v. California*, 45 L Ed 2d, 578.

956. *Betts v. Brady/Maryland*, 86 L ed 1604.

957. Francis A. Allen, *Encyclopedia of the American Constitution*, First Edition, 1586.

958. 86 L Ed 1595.

959. *Gideon v. Wainwright/Florida*, 9 L ed 2d, 802.

960. *Argersinger v. Hamlin/Florida*, 32 L Ed 2d, 531.

961. *Escobedo v. Illinois*, 12 L ed 977.

962. Ibid., 991.

963. Ibid., 987.

964. Francis A. Allen, *Encyclopedia of the American Constitution*, First Edition, 1590.

965. Leonard W. Levy, *Encyclopedia of the American Constitution*, First Edition, 2065.

966. Norman Abrams, *Encyclopedia of the American Constitution*, First Edition, 97.

967. 32 L Ed 2d 184.

968. 32 L Ed 2d 152.

969. *Evitts v. Lucey*, 83 L Ed 821.

970. Jethro K. Lieberman, *Free Speech, Free Press, and the Law*, 17.

971. Ibid., 19.

972. *Sparf v. United States*, 156 U. S. 51.

973. Ibid.

974. William R. Pabst, *Jury Manual, A Guide for Prospective Jurors*, 76.

975. *Sparf v. United States*, 156 U. S. 51.

976. Barbara Weisberg, *Susan B. Anthony*, 13, 19.

977. Ibid., 19.

978. Ibid., 19, 20.

979. Ibid., 20.

980. Ibid.

981. William R. Pabst, *Jury Manual, A Guide for Prospective Jurors*, 76, 77.

982. Ibid., 77.

983. Wilfred J. Ritz, *Rewriting the History of the Judiciary Act of 1789*, 3.

984. Charles Warren, "New Light on the History of the Federal Judiciary Act of 1789," *Harvard Law Review 37* (November 1923): 131.

985. Wythe Holt, *The Oxford Companion to the Supreme Court of the United States*, 473.

986. Wilfred J. Ritz, *Rewriting the History of the Judiciary Act of 1789*, 57.

987. Wythe Holt, "'To Establish Justice': Politics, The Judiciary Act of 1789 and the Invention of the Federal Courts," *Duke Law Journal* (December 1989): 1438–55.

988. Wythe Holt, *The Oxford Companion to the Supreme Court of the United States*, 473.

989. Wythe Holt, "'To Establish Justice': Politics, The Judiciary Act of 1789, and the Invention of the Federal Courts," *Duke Law Journal* (December 1989): 1486.

990. Wythe Holt, *The Oxford Companion to the Supreme Court of the United States*, 473–74.

991. Dennis J. Mahoney, *Encyclopedia of the American Constitution*, First Edition, 1665.

992. Clinton Rossiter, *The Federalist Papers*, 495, 499–500.

993. Leonard W. Levy, *Origins of the Bill of Rights*, 226.

994. Wythe Holt, "'To Establish Justice': Politics, The Judiciary Act of 1789 and the Invention of the Federal Courts," *Duke Law Journal* (December 1989): 1427–28.

995. Ibid., 1427.

996. Clinton Rossiter, *The Federalist Papers*, 504.

997. Dennis J. Mahoney, *Encyclopedia of the Constitution*, First Edition, 1665.

998. Stanley Morrison, "Workmen's Compensation and the Maritime Law," *Yale Law Journal*, Vol. 38, 473.

999. *The Propeller Genesee Chief et. al. v. Fitzhugh*, 12 Howard.

1000. Charles L. Black, *Encyclopedia of the American Constitution*, First Edition, 30.

1001. Ibid.

1002. *Hanover National Bank v. Moyses*, 186 U. S. 181.

1003. Paul D. Carrington, *Encyclopedia of the American Constitution*, First Edition, 1920.

1004. 186 U. S. 181.

1005. Akhil Reed Amar, *The Bill of Rights*, 85.

1006. Robert W. Millar, "Three Ventures in Summary Civil Procedure," *Yale Law Journal*, Vol. 38, 194.

1007. Ibid.

1008. Ibid., 196.

1009. Ibid., 196–97.

1010. Charles E. Clark and Charles U. Samenow, "The Summary Judgment," *Yale Law Journal*, Vol. 38, 424.

1011. Ibid.

1012. Ibid.

1013. Ibid., 444.

1014. *Moore's Federal Rules Pamphlet*, 1998–99, 479.

1015. Ibid., 345.

1016. Wilfred J. Ritz, *Rewriting the History of the Judiciary Act of 1789*, 10.

1017. Ibid., 6.

1018. Ibid., 10.

1019. Jack N. Rakove, *Original Meanings*, 293.

1020. Ibid.

1021. William E. Nelson, *Americanization of the Common Law: The Impact of Legal Change on Massachusetts Society*, 3.

1022. Ibid., 166.

1023. Jack N. Rakove, *Original Meanings*, 301–02.

1024. Richard C. Ellis, *The Jeffersonian Crisis: Courts and Politics in the Young Republic*, 202.

1025. *Baltimore and C. Line v. Redman*, 79 L. ed. 1639.

1026. Ibid.

1027. Edward Dumbauld, *The Constitution of the United States*, 155–56.

1028. Jack N. Rakove, *Original Meanings*, 321.

1029. Ibid., 322–23.

1030. Clinton Rossiter, *The Federalist Papers*, 501.

1031. Wilfred J. Ritz, *Rewriting the History of the Judiciary Act of 1789*, 30.

1032. *The State of Georgia v. Brailsford, et. al.*, Dall. 3. 484.

1033. Adrienne Koch and William Peden (editors), *The Life and Selected Writings of Thomas Jefferson*, 248.

1034. Paul D. Carrington, *Encyclopedia of the American Constitution*, First Edition, 1916.

1035. Ibid.

1036. Ibid.

1037. 166 U.S. 464.

1038. 166 U.S. 707.

1039. Caleb Foote, *Encyclopedia of the American Constitution*, First Edition, 90.

1040. *Roberts v. Louisiana*, 49 L Ed 2d 976.

1041. Ibid., 983.

1042. Ibid., 976–77.

1043. Raoul Berger, *Death Penalties: The Supreme Court's Obstacle Course*, 47.

1044. Ibid., 142.

1045. Joseph M. Lynch, *Negotiating the Constitution*, 200.

1046. Ibid.

1047. Raoul Berger, *Death Penalties: The Supreme Court's Obstacle Course*, 113.

1048. Wilfred J. Ritz, *Rewriting the History of the Judiciary Act of 1789*, 114.

1049. Ibid.

1050. Adrienne Koch, *Notes of Debates in the Federal Convention of 1787*, 158.

1051. William Peden (editor), *Notes on the State of Virginia* (by Thomas Jefferson), 133.

1052. Clinton Rossiter, *1787 The Grand Convention*, 321.

1053. Ibid., 319.

1054. Richard L. Perry and John C. Cooper, *Sources of Our Liberties*, 345.

1055. Randy E. Barnett, *The Oxford Companion to the Supreme Court of the United States*, 590.

1056. Ibid.

1057. Edward Dumbauld, *The Bill of Rights and What it Means Today*, 182.

1058. Randy E. Barnett, *The Oxford Companion to the Supreme Court of the United States*, 590.

1059. Christopher Wolfe, *The Oxford Companion to the Supreme Court of the United States*, 581.

1060. Ibid.

1061. Stephen P. Holbrook, *That Every Man Be Armed*, 54.

1062. Edward Dumbauld, *The Bill of Rights*, 185, 189, 201.

1063. Jethro K. Lieberman, *The Evolving Constitution*, 346.

1064. *Griswold v. Connecticut*, 14 L ed 2d 510.

1065. Clinton Rossiter, *The Federalist Papers*, 469.

1066. Edward Dumbauld, *The Bill of Rights and What it Means Today*, 182–83.

1067. Ibid., 189.

1068. Clinton Rossiter, *The Federalist Papers*, 118.

1069. *Wickard v. Filburn*, 87 L ed 122.

1070. *Garcia v. San Antonio Metropolitan Transit Authority*, 83 L Ed 2d 1016.

1071. *National League of Cities v. Usery*, 426 U. S. 833.

Chapter 11

1072. Jethro K. Lieberman, *The Evolving Constitution*, 177.

1073. *Amendments to the Constitution: A Brief Legislative History*, 13.

1074. Ibid., 14.

1075. Ibid.

1076. Ibid., 14.

1077. Leonard W. Levy, *Encyclopedia of the American Constitution*, First Edition, 251.

1078. Charles A. Beard and Mary R. Beard, *History of the United States*, 184.

1079. Alan P. Grimes, *Democracy and Amendments to the Constitution*, 21.

1080. *Amendments to the Constitution: A Brief Legislative History*, 19.

1081. Charles A. Beard and Mary R. Beard, *History of the United States*, 184.

1082. Harold M. Hyman, *Encyclopedia of the American Constitution*, First Edition, 1891.

1083. Ibid.

1084. *Amendments to the Constitution: A Brief Legislative History*, 27.

1085. Bruce Ackerman, *We the People: Transformations*, 105.

1086. Ibid., 101.

1087. Raoul Berger, *Government by Judiciary*, 15–16.

1088. John R. Vile, *Encyclopedia of Constitutional Amendments*, 139.

1089. Bruce Ackerman, *We the People: Transformations*, 102.

1090. Ibid., 110.

1091. Ibid., 110–11.

1092. *Amendments to the Constitution: A Brief Legislative History*, 32–33.

1093. Ibid., 32.

1094. Ibid., 106.

1095. John M. Mathews, *Legislative and Judicial History of the Fifteenth Amendment*, 12.

1096. Ibid.

1097. Raoul Berger, *Government by Judiciary*, 137.

1098. Ibid., 137–38.

1099. William Gillette, *The Encyclopedia of the American Constitution*, First Edition, 725.

1100. Ibid.

1101. Ibid.

1102. Ibid., 725–26.

1103. Ibid., 726.

1104. John M. Mathews, *Legislative and Judicial History of the Fifteenth Amendment*, 33–34.

1105. Ibid.

1106. Ibid.

1107. John R. Vile, *Encyclopedia of Constitutional Amendments*, 128.

1108. William Gillette, *The Encyclopedia of the American Constitution*, First Edition, 726.

1109. John M. Mathews, *Legislative and Judicial History of the Fifteenth Amendment*, 44.

1110. Barbara Weisberg, *Susan B. Anthony*, 74–75, 83.

1111. William Gillette, *The Encyclopedia of the American Constitution*, First Edition, 726.

1112. Charles A. Beard and Mary R. Beard, *History of the United States*, 565.

1113. Barbara Weisberg, *Susan B. Anthony*, 20–21.

1114. *Amendments to the Constitution: A Brief Legislative History*, 38.

1115. Ibid.

1116. John R. Vile, *Encyclopedia of Constitutional Amendments*, 129.

1117. Alan P. Grimes, *Democracy and the Amendments to the Constitution*, 51, 55.

1118. *Amendments to the Constitution: A Brief Legislative History*, 37.

1119. John M. Mathews, *Legislative and Judicial History of the Fifteenth Amendment*, 42–43.

1120. Ibid., 71–72.

1121. 158 U. S. 429 and 158 U. S. 601.

1122. Loren P. Beth, *The Oxford Guide to United States Supreme Court Decisions*, 241.

1123. Charles A. Beard and Mary R. Beard, *History of the United States*, 466.

1124. Jethro K. Lieberman, *The Evolving Constitution*, 488.

1125. Ibid.

1126. Alan P. Grimes, *Democracy and Amendments to the Constitution*, 75.

1127. Ibid.

1128. Ibid., 82.

1129. Ibid., 75.

1130. Ibid.

1131. Ibid.

1132. Charles A. Beard and Mary R. Beard, *History of the United States*, 591.

1133. Ibid., 557.

1134. Ibid., 591.

1135. Ibid., 592.

1136. Jethro K. Lieberman, *The Evolving Constitution*, 563.

1137. Ibid

1138. Charles A. Beard and Mary R. Beard, *History of the United States*, 565.

1139. Ibid., 566, 568.

1140. Deborah L. Rhode, *Encyclopedia of the American Constitution*, First Edition, 1316.

1141. David M. Kennedy, *Freedom from Fear*, 104.

1142. Ibid., 133.

1143. Ibid., 105.

1144. Ibid., 110.

1145. Ibid., 135.

1146. Ibid.

1147. Ibid., 85.

1148. David E. Kyvig, *The Oxford Companion to the Supreme Court of the United States*, 883.

1149. Alan P. Grimes, *Democracy and the Amendments to the Constitution*, 113.

1150. Ibid.

1151. Ibid.

1152. John R. Vile, *Encyclopedia of Constitutional Amendments*, 125.

1153. Ibid.

1154. Dennis J. Mahoney, *Encyclopedia of the American Constitution*, First Edition, 1929.

1155. *Amendments to the Constitution: A Brief Legislative History*, 89.

1156. Ibid.

1157. Ronald Kessler, *The Sins of the Father*, 419.

1158. *Amendments to the Constitution: A Brief Legislative History*, 89.

1159. Ibid.

1160. John R. Vile, *Encyclopedia of Constitutional Amendments*, 323.

1161. Jethro K. Lieberman, *The Evolving Constitution*, 550.

1162. Ibid.

1163. John R. Vile, *Encyclopedia of Constitutional Amendments*, 343.

1164. "The Man Who Would Not Quit," *People*, (June 1, 1992): 72.

1165. *Amendments to the Constitution: A Brief Legislative History*, 94.

1166. "The Man Who Would Not Quit," *People*, (June 1, 1992): 72.

1167. John R. Vile, *Encyclopedia of Constitutional Amendments*, 324 and 343.

1168. Ibid., 324.

1169. Ibid.

Appendix A

1170. Martin L. Gross, *The Government Racket*, 46.

1171. *The Inaugural Addresses of the Presidents of the United States*, 129.

1172. Charles A. Beard and Mary R, Beard, *History of the United States*, 454.

1173. Ibid.

1174. *The New Encyclopedia Britannica*, Volume 1, 86.

1175. Ibid.

1176. Ibid.

1177. Ibid.

1178. Ibid.

Appendix B

1179. Noble E. Cunningham, Jr., *In Pursuit of Reason*, 238.

1180. Kathryn Turner, "Federalist Policy and the Judiciary Act of 1801," *William and Mary Quarterly* 22 (January 1965): 8, 32.

1181. Ibid., 18–19.

1182. Ibid., 20.

1183. Richard E. Ellis, *The Jeffersonian Crisis: Courts and Politics in the Young Republic*, 15, 288.

1184. *Marbury v. Madison*, 1 Cranch 137.

1185. Leon Friedman and Fred L. Israel, *The Justices of the United States Supreme Court*, 291.

1186. Duane Lockard and Walter F. Murphy, *Basic Cases in Constitutional Law*, Third Edition, 11.

1187. *Marbury v. Madison*, 1 Cranch 137.

1188. Ibid.

1189. Jethro K. Lieberman, *The Evolving Constitution*, 320.

1190. *Marbury v. Madison*, 1 Cranch 137.

1191. Richard E. Ellis, *The Jeffersonian Crisis: Courts and Politics in the Young Republic*, 43.

1192. Ibid., 43–44.

1193. Leonard W. Levy, *Encyclopedia of the American Constitution*, First Edition, 1200.

1194. Richard E. Ellis, *The Jeffersonian Crisis: Courts and Politics in the Young Republic*, 44.

1195. Ibid., 44, 294.

1196. Willard Sterne Randall, *Thomas Jefferson: a life*, 551.

1197. Richard E. Ellis, *The Jeffersonian Crisis: Courts and Politics in the Young Republic*, 58.

1198. Ibid.

1199. Ibid.

1200. Charles Warren, "New Light on the History of the Federal Judiciary Act of 1789," *Harvard Law Review* 37 (November 1923): 67.

1201. Wythe Holt, *The Oxford Companion to the Supreme Court of the United States*, 472.

1202. Charles Warren, "New Light on the History of the Federal Judiciary Act of 1789," *Harvard Law Review* 37 (November 1923): 67.

1203. 2 Dallas 297.

1204. Charles Warren, "New Light on the History of the Federal Judiciary Act of 1789," *Harvard Law Review* 37 (November 1923): 63, 64.

1205. *Marbury v. Madison*, 1 Cranch 137.

1206. Wilfred J. Ritz, *Rewriting the History of the Judiciary Act of 1789*, 178–79.

1207. Ibid., 179.

1208. *Marbury v. Madison*, 1 Cranch 137.

1209. 3 Dallas 121.

1210. Jethro K. Lieberman, *The Evolving Constitution*, 321.

1211. Leonard W. Levy, *Encyclopedia of the American Constitution*, First Edition, 1200.

1212. Ibid.

1213. Edward Dumbauld, *Thomas Jefferson and the Law*, 40.

1214. Ibid.

1215. Ibid., 42.

1216. Wilfred J. Ritz, *Rewriting the History of the Judiciary Act of 1789*, 179.

1217. Noble E. Cunningham, Jr., *In Pursuit of Reason*, 249.

1218. Ibid.

1219. Ibid.

1220. Ibid.

1221. Leonard W. Levy, *Encyclopedia of the American Constitution*, First Edition, 1202.

1222. E. Lee Shepard, *American National Biography*, Volume 13, 364.

1223. Ibid.

1224. *Marbury v. Madison*, 1 Cranch 137

1225. Richard E. Ellis, *The Jeffersonian Crisis: Courts and Politics in the Young Republic*, 66.

1226. William H. Rehnquist, *The Supreme Court: How it Was, How it Is*, 99.

1227. Ibid.

1228. 2 Dallas 409.

1229. Richard E. Ellis, *The Jeffersonian Crisis: Courts and Politics in the Young Republic*, 66.

Appendix C

1230. Edward Dumbauld, *The Bill of Rights and What it Means Today*, 220–22.